In the Catskills

In the Catskills

A Century of the Jewish Experience in "The Mountains"

Edited by
PHIL BROWN

Columbia University Press ⚜ New York

"The Catskills at the End of World War II" is from *Woodridge, 1946* by
Martin Boris, copyright © 1979 by Ghame Writing Corp. Reprinted by
permission of Crown Publishers, a division of Random House, Inc.

"The Pool" is from *Paradise, NY* by Eileen Pollack. Published by
Temple University Press, 1999. Copyright © 1999 by Eileen Pollack.

"The Social Director in the Adult Summer Camp" is from *Act One* by
Moss Hart, copyright © 1959 by Catherine Carlisle Hart & Joseph M. Hyman,
Trustees. Used by permission of Random House, Inc.

"Bungalow Summer" is from *Boychiks in the Hood* by Robert
Eisenberg, pp. 181–205. Copyright © 1995 by Robert Eisenberg. Reprinted by
permission of HarperCollins Publishers, Inc.

"The Shul in Kaaterskill Falls" is from *Kaaterskill Falls* by Allegra
Goodman, copyright © 1998 by Allegra Goodman. Used by permission of The
Dial Press/Dell Publishing, a division of Random House, Inc.

Additional permissions information appears in the acknowledgments section.

COLUMBIA UNIVERSITY PRESS
PUBLISHERS SINCE 1893
NEW YORK   CHICHESTER, WEST SUSSEX

Copyright © 2002 Phil Brown
All rights reserved
Library of Congress Cataloging-in-Publication Data
In the Catskills : a century of Jewish experience in the mountains / Phil Brown,
editor.
     p. cm.
     Includes bibliographical references (p.).
     ISBN 0–231–12360–4
     1. Jews—New York (State)—Catskill Mountains Region—Social life
and
customs. 2. Jews—Recreation—New York (State)—Catskill Mountains Region.
3. Catskill Mountains Region (N.Y.)—Social life and customs. I. Brown, Phil.
     F127.C3 I5 2002
     974.7'38004924—dc21
             2001042319

Columbia University Press books are printed on permanent and durable
acid-free paper.

Designed by Brady McNamara
Printed in the United States of America
c 10 9 8 7 6 5 4 3 2

This book is dedicated to my wife, Ronnie Littenberg;
my daughter, Liza Littenberg-Brown;
and my son, Michael Littenberg-Brown.

CONTENTS

Writing *Catskill Culture: A Mountain Rat's Memories of the Great Jewish Resort Area* was the most meaningful piece of writing work I have ever done. I poured my heart into reliving my Catskills memories, getting in touch with my parents' lives, and retracing my own personal history. Somewhere in the process of writing that book, I knew I wanted to do another, complementary volume that would put together fiction, nonfiction, and music from many sources. That desire has only grown since *Catskill Culture* was published. I realized that an untold number of people shared similar desires to recapture the Catskills memories. I have been gratified by the reception from readers and from audiences at the many shuls, colleges, Jewish organizations, and bookstores where I speak. Many people at these events ask if I am writing another book. I am pleased to finally be able to say, "Yes, I am." Of course, I am not writing it from scratch, but am including new material of my own with a collection of articles and excerpts that speak from my voice, in tandem with others' voices.

These were the ideal pieces with which to capture the feeling of the Catskills legacy. When I have wanted to learn more about this rich heritage, sought to suggest readings to others, considered who were the people who really understood this culture, and needed to create a syllabus for my Brown University seminar, "A Summer Eden: The Jewish Experience in the Catskills," I've thought of these writers. A good number of them informed my original work, *Catskill Culture*, and are quoted there. In the course of running the annual History of the Catskills Conference since 1995, I have met many of these writers and scholars when I've brought them up to speak. Some were people whom my Catskills Institute colleagues and I encouraged to write about the Catskills. Others were friends and colleagues in and outside the Institute who were active in recounting and preserving the Catskills history.

I feel bonds with the people whose words appear in this anthology. Irwin Richman has been a consistently creative explorer of Catskills life, and his charm and humor have graced the stage at many History of the Catskills Conferences. Eileen Pollack, whose upbringing in the hotel business was the grist for her novel, was a sparkling reader at two of our events. Sidney Offit charmed our audience when he shared his selections from his novel, and in the short time that the Catskills Institute has been around, enough interest has been generated that his 1959 book was reissued in 1999. Terry Kay captured a different slice of Catskills life in his novel and stole the hearts of conference listeners. His elegant prose and his delight in joining the conference participants were testimony to the impact the Jewish Catskills could have on a non-Jew. Martin Boris spoke twice at our conferences and was encouraged by our activities to do the research on Grine Felder that appears here. Sadly, he died while this book was in preparation. Arthur Tanney garnered an audience of bungalow colony lovers through his online postings and brought those essays to the podium of our Catskills Institute, making people laugh and cry with his tender recollections. Reuben Wallenrod died some years ago, but I met his daughter, Naima Prevots, and it was a delight to witness her pleasure at seeing her father's little-known novel included. Herman Wouk couldn't accept the invitation to speak at our very first conference, but he sent a letter with warm greetings to "all the tummlers" that we proudly read aloud. Abraham Lavender and Clarence Steinberg are fellow excavators of Catskills history, and Clarence has frequented and spoken at the conferences. Eugene Calden came up to me once and thrust into my hands his marvelous kuchalayn memoirs. Tania Grossinger and Henry Foner have shared with me not only the stage at conferences but also the microphones on radio appearances. Thane Rosenbaum and Vivian Gornick shared their fiction and essays with us as well. Joyce Wadler came to one conference. Jerry Jacobs, one of the few sociologists to join me in writing about the Catskills, was a long-time supporter of this collection and of *Catskill Culture* before it. So this book has an intimate feel to it, from my experience of knowing most of the contributors. I thank them so much for their deep conviction that the Catskills are worth writing about.

Terry Kay, when he spoke at the History of the Catskills Conference, mused on the wealth of material that the Catskills provided for his novel *Shadow Song*, and wisely remarked that "Some places are just natural repositories of stories." Clearly the Mountains have been that kind of place for many other writers, as this collection shows. I hope you will appreciate the breadth of writing that has framed the Catskills experience.

My editor at Columbia University Press, John Michel, was intrigued by this project from the very first, and I appreciate his enthusiastic collaboration. Jerry Jacobs gave very helpful suggestions concerning the selections and format. Berit Kosterlitz worked hard to line up the reprint permissions, looked up original versions of some selections, and helped in preparing the manuscript. My colleagues on the Executive Committee and Advisory Board of the Catskills Institute have lent their energy to this book through their long-standing commitment to keeping alive the Catskills memory. Alan Barrish, one of the Executive Committee members, is my frequent partner in long car cruises to locate hotel remnants, an important task that helps generate excitement about this kind of project and that nourishes my research and writing. I am also grateful to Alan for his comments on the annotated bibliography, and to two other Executive Committee members for their input—Deborah Dash

Moore for her comments on my introductory essay and Irwin Richman for comments on that essay and the bibliography. I must also thank the countless people who write, e-mail, and speak to me every day about how much they love to remember this great culture. Their feedback has energized my project.

ACKNOWLEDGMENTS

"Jewish Farmers of the Catskills" by Abraham Lavender and Clarence Steinberg is reprinted with the permission of the University Press of Florida.

"Hotels and the Holocaust" is from *Dusk in the Catskills* by Reuben Wallenrod, published by the Reconstructionist Press, © 1957. Reprinted with permission.

"The Yearning Heifer" is from *The Collected Stories* by Isaac Bashevis Singer. Copyright © 1982 by Isaac Bashevis Singer. Reprinted by permission of Farrar, Straus and Giroux, LLC.

"Grine Felder—A Place in the Country" by Martin Boris first appeared in the Sept./Oct. 1998 issue of *B'nai B'rith International Jewish Monthly*.

"Bingo by the Bungalow" is from *Elijah Visible* by Thane Rosenbaum. Copyright © 1996 by Thane Rosenbaum. Reprinted by permission of St. Martin's Press, LLC.

"Bungalow Colony Life" is excerpted and reprinted from the chapters entitled "Daily Life: Mostly Adults" and "The Quest for Entertainment," included in *Borscht Belt Bungalows: Memories of Catskill Summers* by Irwin Richman, by permission of Temple University Press. © 1998 by Temple University. All Rights Reserved.

"Bungalow Stories" by Arthur Tanney is first printed here, with permission of Arthur Tanney.

"Old Stock" by Hortense Calisher is reprinted by permission of Donadio and Olson, Inc. Copyright 1975 by Hortense Calisher.

"Young Workers in the Hotels" is from *Catskill Culture: A Mountain Rat's Memories of the Great Jewish Resort Area* by Phil Brown. Reprinted by permission of Temple University Press. © 1998 by Temple University. All Rights Reserved.

"Growing Up at Grossinger's" is reprinted with permission of Tania Grossinger.

"Five and Three House" by Sidney Offit is excerpted from *He Had It Made* (1959). Reprinted by permission from Beckham Publications, Inc.

"Reflections on the Delmar Hotel and the Demise of the Catskills" is first printed here, with permission from Jerry Jacobs.

"The Casino" by Harvey Jacobs is reprinted by permission of Harvey Jacobs.

"The Fine Art of Mountain *Tummling*" by Joyce Wadler was first published in *Esquire* magazine, June 1985. Reprinted courtesy of *Esquire* and the Hearst Corporation.

"Shoot the Shtrudel to Me, Yudel!" music and lyrics, reprinted with the permission of Henry Foner.

"Forbidden Fruit" by Harvey Jacobs is reprinted with the permission of Harvey Jacobs.

"Marjorie at South Wind" is excerpted from *Marjorie Morningstar* by Herman Wouk. Copyright © 1955 by Herman Wouk. Reprinted by permission from Doubleday, a division of Random House, Inc.

"Amy Lourie" is excerpted from *Shadow Song* by Terry Kay. © 1994 by Terry Kay. Reprinted with permission of Pocket Books, a division of Simon & Schuster.

"Eating at the Hotel" copyright © 1964 by Sarah Sandberg. Reprinted by permission of McIntosh & Otis, Inc.

"The Catskills Remembered" is excerpted from *Approaching Eye Level* by Vivian Gornick. Copyright © 1996 by Vivian Gornick. Reprinted by permission of Beacon Press, Boston.

"Bungalow" is excerpted from *Miriam's Kitchen* by Elizabeth Ehrlich, copyright © 1997 by Elizabeth Ehrlich. Used by permission of Viking Penguin, a division of Penguin Putnam Inc.

In the Catskills

Part 1

HISTORY

O. & W. R. R. Station, Liberty, N. Y.

Ontario and Western Railroad Station in Liberty, 1920s. The O&W, nicknamed the "Old and Weary," was the primary mode of transportation for much of the first half of the century. It ceased operating in 1956. Its annual publication, "Summer Homes Among the Mountains," was a major source of advertising for the hotels and boarding houses. Resort owners would send wagons, and later autos, to pick up guests. Some large hotels even sent bands to play for the arrival of the trains. The Friday evening train, bringing up husbands for the weekends, was termed the "bull train." CATSKILLS INSTITUTE

Abandoned chicken farm, Glen Wild, 1998. Farming provided the basis for the first Jewish settlement in the Catskills. Dairy farming was not very successful, but farmers raising poultry and eggs fared better. In the 1950s and 1960s, Sullivan County produced more eggs than any other county in the state. Farmers began taking in boarders very early on, often continuing to operate their farms while the guests enjoyed the country. Many hotels and bungalow colonies grew from such humble origins.   PHIL BROWN

Hotel and bungalow colony signs. Roads and highways were full of individual bill-boards, but large signboards like this were also common, since there were so many hotels and bungalow colonies.
EILEEN KALTER

BROWN'S HOTEL ROYAL, White Lake, N. Y. — Telephone White Lake 120

Brown's Hotel Royal, White Lake. William and Sylvia Brown owned this hotel from 1946 to 1952. Phil Brown has been in touch with the family of the man who sold it to them as well as two subsequent owners, including the present owners of the Royal's current incarnation, the Bradstan Country Inn. This card is by Alfred Landis, the most artistic of all postcard printers.   PHIL BROWN

The Main House at the Seven Gables Hotel, Greenfield Park, 1952. Sylvia Brown was chef at the Seven Gables from 1955 to 1960, and it is the hotel that was the most formative in Phil Brown's life in the Catskills.   FRANK DAPSKI

William Brown in front of the casino at the Seven Gables. For a couple of years he ran the concession, located in the casino, and Phil Brown helped out, young as he was.   PHIL BROWN

From ruin to renewal. The pool at the Grand Mountain Hotel, Greenfield Park, went from a weed-overgrown wreck in 1999 to a beautiful, appealing pool in 2000. There have been a few revivals of small and medium-size hotels. The Grand Mountain probably held 250 guests, and in the 1960s was famous for its late-show strippers.
PHIL BROWN

The history of the Jewish Catskills really starts on the farms. Baron de Hirsch, a major Jewish philanthropist, funded many agricultural projects that put Jews onto farms in places such as Argentina, South Dakota, Saskatchewan, New Jersey, and the Catskills. From the first years of the twentieth century, the farms of Ulster and Sullivan counties were a major part of the early Jewish settlement there, providing a year-round Jewish population base and the building and support of synagogues. These were primarily dairy and chicken farms, since not much else grew well in the region. In the middle of the twentieth century, Sullivan County led the state in egg production. The long-term impact of the farms was their taking in boarders to supplement their meager income. Some farmers decided to make the boarding business their main enterprise. Once the boarding house was established, it might develop along one of two routes. Some became kuchalayns (boarding houses where renters shared kitchen facilities), which frequently transformed into bungalow colonies. Others became hotels (as did some kuchalayns later). These transformations will be the subject of the following two sections. Here, we focus on the origins of the farms and offer some glimpses of the impact of World War II and the Holocaust on local life and on resorts.

Phil Brown's opening essay, "Sleeping in My Parents' Hotel," sets the stage for this collection. Through his account of sleeping in the current incarnation of what had been his parents' hotel in the 1940s and 1950s, he notes the themes that shape the book.

Abraham Lavender and Clarence Steinberg's selection, "Jewish Farmers of the Catskills," comes from their book of that title, a masterful study from documents, interviews, and personal experience. They offer a slice of farm life, the challenges farmers faced, the support they got from the Jewish Agricultural Society, and their importance in the local Jewish community. Clarence Steinberg grew up on a farm in Ellenville and later worked for the U.S. Department of Agriculture, so he well understands the legacy of the Jewish farmers.

Reuben Wallenrod's "Hotels and the Holocaust" comes from *Dusk in the Catskills*, his novel tracing the seasonal life of a small hotel modeled on Rosenblatt's Hotel in Glen Wild, where Wallenrod often stayed. This excerpt illustrates the conflict between having a good time on vacation and the reality of the massacre of Jews in Nazi Europe.

Martin Boris, in "The Catskills at the End of World War II," also addresses this era, but right after the war and with reference to local residents. This is an excerpt from his *Woodridge 1946*, which centers on Our Place, a Woodridge restaurant, and its owners, workers, and customers. Among other things, Boris deals with conflicts between traditional religious traditions and leftist politics. Indeed, this book is one of the few writings we have about communist and socialist activities in the Catskills.

Sleeping in My Parents' Hotel:
The End of a Century of the Jewish Catskills

Phil Brown

On beautiful August 3, 1998, I was sleeping in my parents' old hotel in the Catskills. A half century ago, that would have been pretty unremarkable, but William and Sylvia Brown owned Brown's Hotel Royal on White Lake only from 1946 to 1952. It's a miracle the place still stands, recycled as the Bradstan Country Hotel and beautifully detailed with luxurious antiques and appointments far exceeding an old Catskills hotel. Most small hotels—the Royal would be stuffed at 60 guests—long ago collapsed, burned, or simply were reclaimed by the land. For my book, *Catskill Culture*, I compiled a list of 926 hotels (subsequently expanded to 1,094 on the Catskills Institute Web site) that graced the Jewish summer paradise of Sullivan and Ulster counties over the last century. Less than two handfuls remain, none of them as small as the Royal, and they close at an alarming rate.

That's why the Royal's survival is so spectacular. I "found" it in 1993, on my first field trip to the Catskills, after having stayed away since 1979. Like many others who worked hard in the Catskills or who tired of the culture, I fled after finishing college. It took many years to integrate into my adult life the ambivalence that I had always experienced there. I had been uprooted every year in May from school and friends to go there and live with my parents in cramped rooms. I watched my parents work extremely hard each summer, three months' labor with not a single day off. We never had our own summer vacation, but only served

other people on theirs. Also, like many others, I fled from the strong Jewish culture of the area, not knowing until recently how to make sense of it.

I say that I "found" the Royal because my parents, until they died—my father
in 1972, my mother in 1991—hid from me their failed venture into the hotel business. Certainly, they had told me that they once had a hotel, when I was born.
They even showed me some photos of us there. But they said the hotel was
"gone." Surely they knew it still stood, in various reincarnations, including a seedy
rooming house, since they worked the Catskills their whole lives and knew an
enormous number of people and places there. My father died working in his coffee shop concession at Chaits Hotel in Accord, and my mother remained cooking
there till 1979. For many of their years working in Swan Lake, they drove right past
White Lake en route to Monticello. My father often worked for Dependable Employment Agency, driving new hires all over the Mountains, so he would un-
doubtedly have passed it many times. And nowhere was that far that they couldn't
have shown me their old hotel, especially since I often asked. All I ever got was,
"It's gone," even when we spent several weeks in May on the Kauneonga side of
White Lake at our friends George and Miriam Shapiro's bungalow colony while
my parents looked for work.

When my mother died, I found among her few papers a postcard of the hotel,
the only memento apart from a few photos. I knew that somehow I would discover what I expected to be the remnants of Brown's Hotel Royal. The postcard
would be my magic key and treasure map, even if I only located foundation
stones. But I was shocked to see an operating hotel, the Bradstan, that was so
clearly the Royal. It lacked the symmetrical side rooms that had once framed the
front porch, a common Catskills architectural detail (they had been torn down
due to deterioration). And its white clapboards were not the old stucco facade.
But the whole shape was there, comfortably nestled on Route 17-B across from
the most beautiful lake in the Mountains.

Each year since 1993 I have visited the hotel for one reason or another. One
year I brought a *New York Times* reporter who wrote a story on me and the History of the Catskills Conference. Another year I came to collect an old menu, hand-
written by my mother in 1950, that owners Ed Samuelson and Scott Dudek had
turned up. Once I brought my wife and children to see the place where I lived as
a baby and toddler. A year after that I went to pick up a box of old dishes from the
hotel's past. I kept thinking, "I should stay here as a guest once." So I did!

Who slept in this room fifty years ago? Actually, the question is who slept in
each half of this room, for two small rooms had since been made into a single

larger one. Was it one of my aunts, uncles, cousins—the many family members who often stayed and/or worked here? Max, Laura, Gloria, Bess, Nat, Gene, Eugene, Sylvia, Sylvia, and Sylvia (so common a name then)—did you fall asleep here, across from White Lake shimmering in the August moonlight? Did you enjoy summer here in the Catskills, swim in the lake, play poker at night, hear my cousin Gene play violin, drink schnapps?

I would have been conceived here at the Royal if my parents were already up here April 1, getting ready for Passover. But they did not open for Passover, the place being so small.

The one story I remember my parents telling many times concerned me as a toddler, roaming through the dining room. Fearful I'd crack my head on a table corner, my father ran in front of me, covering the corners with his hand. It's a simple tale of a protective father, but it happened here, downstairs in our family's hotel.

What a strange idea, my parents amid these many hundreds of very ordinary people thinking they could run simple hotels in the Catskills. Not much business experience, precious little capital, and a reliance on relatives, friends, and *landsmen* (coresidents of one's European hometown) who would accept shared baths and cramped rooms. But despite the precarious finances and difficult labor, these New York Jews had a tender feeling that they could come up here and make a summer celebration of their interconnected lives in the fresh Catskills air. That was it—same story everywhere—lots of Morrises, Sylvias, Abes, and Mollies. They weren't the fancy dressers of The Nevele or Grossinger's, just plain Jewish folk who had great fun and a good time on the cheap.

Now I come back to roam country roads in search of abandoned hotels to film as a record for people, both veterans of the Catskills and many younger people who will never quite understand how a million vacationers each summer came to relax in hotels and bungalow colonies, or how their present doctors and professors worked each summer to be their culture's first generation of college students.

My camera records dybbuks grazing in the fallen timbers of old kitchens, hotel spirits lurking in the half-moon facades of "Catskills mission" architecture. My tape recorder picks up from overgrown weeds the murmurs of requests for pickled lox, embraces in the staff quarters, cha-chas from champagne night in the casino. My heart logs a million desires, hopes, and dramas of every sort of East Coast Jew looking for people and a place to make a life with.

My hope is that within the next ten years, every Jewish fiction writer worth his or her kosher salt will have written, or will be in the process of writing, a book, novella, or story based on the Catskills. A previous generation of these Litvak literati and Galitzianer storytellers found the Lower East Side to be central to Jewish storytelling, much as the English romantic poets feasted on swans and vales. But that was the generation leaving the East Side. The current generation just left the Catskills and can't find the Mountains anymore. If more writers can capture this summer Eden in literature, it won't be only about sleeping in my parents' old hotel, but about a whole culture of greenhorns and "all-rightniks" who learned to play and enjoy life in White Lake, Monticello, Loch Sheldrake, Woodridge, Fallsburg, Woodbourne, and Greenfield Park.

To situate the sociology and history of the Jewish experience in the Catskills, I want to highlight some of the themes that run through this book: the adaptation to American culture while preserving Jewishness,the sense of community in the hotels and bungalow colonies, and the significance of the Catskills legacy for current culture.

In the Catskills, Jews could become Americanized while preserving much of their Jewishness. The resort area was the vacationland and workplace of Jews, mostly from Eastern Europe, starting at the turn of the twentieth century and continuing through the turn of the twenty-first, though it is now only a shell of its onetime glory. Jews could have a proper vacation like regular Americans, but they could do it in Yiddish if they wished, and with kosher food, varying degrees of religious observance, and a vibrant Jewish culture of humor, theater, and song. Jewish-American humor grew up in the Catskills, where any Jewish comedian worth a laugh got his or her start. While Jewish music largely originated in Eastern Europe, its new variants were very much a Catskills product. The Jewish popular entertainment of New York, a Yiddish vaudeville style, shaped the night life of the Catskills and entered the mainstream rather than remaining isolated in the Lower East Side Jewish theaters.

Farms, boarding houses, kuchalayns, bungalow colonies, hotels, adult "camps," and children's camps housed people of all classes and occupations. While there was class stratification due to the range of costs in different resorts, even some of the more expensive places were nevertheless accessible, if only for a weekend. People in their teens and twenties came to work their way through college and professional or graduate school, making the Catskills a core element of Jewish upward mobility. From John Gerson's first Jewish boarding house in the late 1890s, the Catskills beckoned people to come up for fresh air, recovery from illness, a place in the country, a *haimishe* vacation. The modest farmhouses and boarding houses eventually gave way to bungalow colonies ranging from five to more than 100 bungalows each, and to hotels holding from 20 to 2,000 people. There was always someplace for everyone, inexpensive or luxurious.

A sense of community pervaded the Catskills. The very vastness of the resort culture made this possible—people were involved in an individual community and were also part of a gigantic Catskillswide community. Like the *landsmanshaftn* that Jews created to provide friendship and security for their friends and kin from European *shtetls* and towns, these resorts were full of people sharing a common background. Smaller hotels frequently employed "solicitors" to recruit guests from their neighborhoods, and hotels acquired that local culture, which continued into the rest of the year. Guests returned year after year, and often generation after generation—a child in the day camp might later be a junior counselor, when older work as a busboy or waiter in the dining room, and in the near future return with a spouse and children. Guests developed loyalty to the hotel and its owners, based on family, friendship, and participation in a miniature society where relationships were amplified by proximity. Even in many of the larger hotels, owners reported knowing and greeting the majority of their guests prior to the expansion of the 1960s. But even without that personal connection to owners, the larger hotels had a small-town feeling. Many of the workers were closely bonded with each other, with the owners, and with long-standing guests. Staff shared that community for the whole summer, frequently working for years in the same resort, and many friendships lasted past the summer. Staff-guest romances also contributed to the continuing connections.

These hotels, colonies, and kuchalayns were not merely resorts but miniature societies, where people knew lots about each other and created intricate relationships in a neighborhood and family milieu. Further, the accumulation of these many small communities built a giant community extending through Ulster, Sullivan, very southern Greene, and the tiniest sliver of southeastern Delaware counties, a phenomenon unlike any other resort culture then or since. Much like in their home towns and neighborhoods, people would experience this larger community through frequent visits to delis and shops in nearby towns, constant walking down the road past numerous other resorts, and visiting friends and relatives in other hotels and bungalow colonies. Bungalow dwellers were always sneaking into hotel casinos for the shows, guest at small hotels were doing the same in larger hotels, and staff were perpetually visiting other hotels for romance. Through the small and large communities they built, the Jews created in the Catskills a cultural location that symbolized their transformation into Americans: their growth into the middle class, their ability to replace some anxiety with relaxation, their particular way of secularizing their religion while still preserving some religious attachments and ethnic identification.

At present, the Catskills appear quite different from even two or three decades ago. Literally hundreds of hotels have ceased to exist since the 1960s. Driving there today, Catskills veterans will find that Kutsher's Country Club and The Raleigh look, feel, and taste familiar. So too do the Homowack and Aladdin, though both are now ultraorthodox, and the Aladdin no longer runs as a hotel. Smaller places like the South Wind in Woodbourne and the Rainbow Hotel in Ulster Heights will captivate you with their original look, untouched by even the renovations craze of the 1950s. Also bearing a faithful old-time look is the Grand Mountain in Greenfield Park, only recently refurbished after a long closure. The Nevele and Fallsview, now combined as the Nevele Grande, resemble the past less. The Hudson Valley Resort in Kerhonkson (formerly The Granit) and the Swan Lake Resort in Swan Lake (formerly Stevensville Lake Hotel) are far less familiar under their new owners. A tremendous number of bungalow colonies remain, many orthodox and Hasidic, though there are more secular ones than popular lore leads you to expect. Yoga ashrams, Zen meditation centers, drug rehab programs, and mental health and developmental disabilities facilities have taken over the shells of many old hotels. But the town streets, once crowded with guests, workers, and locals who serviced the resorts, are subdued, lined with many vacant storefronts. Recent hotel closings of the large Pines and the largest ever, The Concord, resonate widely. The small hotel Sunny Oaks, run by four generations of women in the Arenson family and home of the first five History of the Catskills Conferences, stopped operating in 2000, causing less dramatic but still noticeable changes in the landscape.

The promise of a renaissance of sorts looms—The Concord and Grossinger's, both owned by the same developer, are scheduled to reopen in stages over the next five years. Kutsher's has entered an arrangement with an Indian gambling casino that will greatly expand the hotel while the casino will open next door. No one, of course, expects a resurgence of resort building that would ever approximate the past, but the Catskills do remain a powerful memory and a draw. Many people have bought summer homes, including condos or co-ops developed out of old bungalow colonies and even out of the old Brown's Hotel (now Grandview Palace). Orthodox Jews of many types continue to make the Catskills a distinctively Jewish location through their widespread network of bungalow colonies, camps, and yeshivas.

These changes prompt some questions: Why are such past forms of adaptation and community meaningful to people in the present? Why is it now important to revisit the Catskills legacy? Jews today have a deep longing to understand and re-live their history in this country. This is much more than nostalgia, for it involves an attempt to grasp their place in American society, to figure out how far they have come, and to reaffirm the importance of family circles, friendship groups, neigh-borhood life, and organizational connections. In the last two decades, Jewish life has been reinvigorated with increasing religious and cultural expressions: Jewish studies grows as an academic enterprise; klezmer music enjoys tremendous popu-larity; Jewish genealogical interest thrives. In this current milieu, the past Catskills setting is central, since this is where Jews learned to vacation and enjoy themselves, found a source of mobility, nourished their culinary and comic culture, took small farms with few resources and built a complex civilization hosting a million people each summer by the 1950s and 1960s.

Whenever I speak about the Catskills, I am struck by the strength of people's de-sire to relive their experiences in the Mountains. Let me recount one such occa-sion. I could tell that the audience of forty people at my Borders bookstore read-ing in Newton, Massachusetts in 1998 was going to be a hot one. People crowded to say hello before I started, including the mother of an emcee from Brickman's whom I had interviewed. During question time after the talk, the emcee's mother said, "I have to tell a story," and took the podium away from me. She recounted how her son told her to say hello to Milton Berle at the hotel, and she comically went up to owner Murray Posner, who was sitting with Berle, and said, "Excuse me, are you Henny Youngman?" Following her, a woman in the audience who had been a Catskills comic ran down a whole comedy routine. It was such a Catskills atmosphere, with everyone playing together and having a good time. I only wish I had had a tape recorder on which to catch it. A younger woman who collects postcards donated twenty-five cards to the Catskills Insti-tute. Many other people commented on their treasured memories; some prom-ised to send photos and interviews. Several people struck up conversations with each other while waiting for me to sign books. They discovered a warm, shared nostalgia; were grateful to have the occasion to talk with other people; and left with each others' names and numbers written down. They commented to me that it was just like I was talking about in the reading and the book: the Catskills was a magical place to form communities and friendships.

This nostalgia is invigorating. People remember the Catskills with a feeling of longing and memory, paired with a broad consciousness of the historical, cultural, and religious influence of the Jewish Catskills century. It is a desire to reaffirm the communal consciousness that was so much a part of the Jewish experience.

In the midst of this kind of activity, I feel like I have an extended Catskills family. Returning years later, I meet up with people old enough to be my grandparents, people I knew forty and fifty years ago. In 1998 I sat with Irene Asman in her Monticello home, talking about the years she grew up in and then owned the Esther Manor. She welcomed me into her home like a long-lost friend of the family, though I had not seen her in more than forty years. But I belonged there, like I belong in any number of other Catskills locales. Irene, her sister Esther Strasberg, and her brother Carl Goldstein (who died in early 2001) were old friends of the family. Later that year, I chatted with Esther in her New York apartment. My parents would always point out the Esther Manor as we drove past, mentioning that it belonged to their old friends. Both Esther and Irene recalled me as a baby at my family's Brown's Hotel Royal. Irene is just one of the old hotel owners and hotel workers I now chat with, people in their eighties and nineties with whom I have a long history. Sol and Dorothy Eagle, 87 and 91 when I saw them in 1997, are other such friends. They lived in our house in Florida in the off season. Sol used his saladman's skills to do beautiful gargimiere work for my bar mitzvah (the saladman handled all cold food, including fruits and juices that started the meal, all salads, endless varieties of lox and herring, bowls of cole slaw and pickles, cold main dishes, and the famous "livestock," such as butter and milk). When I visited with him in 1997, he was playing tennis and gardening like a young person. Besides these people who know me from my childhood, I meet new people who have such long roots in the Mountains, like Carrie Komito, running her Aladdin hotel for six decades until she sold it in 1999. It's almost like having grandparents strung through the Catskills. It's just another way that my life is connected with these hills.

Sometimes I think the whole Catskills experience is a kind of collective unconscious. Hundreds of thousands of us, maybe millions, sharing in a world of our own, where we were all plugged into a joint reality. Here is a recent example. In 1997 I wrote a short story, "The Make-Believe Hotel" about a girl wandering in the ruins of the River Walk Hotel (a name I made up, though it sounds like several other real names) in South Fallsburg. In her imagination she revives the hotel, including its famous River Walk, lined with Japanese lanterns. She rebuilds the dancing platform at the Neversink River where people can have refreshments and enjoy the band. I had never seen such a riverside arrangement—I must have just assumed there would have been such a place. There had to be!

Well, in October 2000, Julius Merl called me up. His parents owned the Ambassador Hotel on Route 42, a hotel they built up from its 1910 origins as the Gamble Farm, then the Cedar Inn, and in 1921 renamed the Ambassador. That year they built the Japanese Gardens, lined with kerosene-burning Japanese lanterns that cast their spell on the guests as they walked across a bridge to a small island in the Neversink where they were entertained. I was struck by the *déjà vu* of this experience, though it was perhaps not so unique. I feel sure, though, that I can conjure up anything about the Catskills legacy and then find out it really was that way.

The hotels are magical to me. For me, the classic look of a Catskills hotel is the small-sized main house with a stucco finish, windowed gables on the top, a side room on either side of the porch, a canopy over the central entrance, and a broad staircase descending to a walkway. Take a casual glance at the many buildings, including my parents' hotel, that fit this description, and there is no doubt about it—the hotels are smiling. Stone gateposts frequently stood by the roadside, making up part of the decorative fencing and framing the walkway up to the main house. You can see this today at the still-operating Rainbow Hotel—the walkway is lined with benches that held a multitude of conversations as you strolled up to the central entrance of your personal summer Eden. This was the Yiddish promenade, the boulevard of the Jews, along which you approached the main house, whose unique Catskills design smiled and beckoned you into an oversized home full of warmth and activity. The hotels stood upright and secure, offering the haven of their lobbies for shmoozing, the endless food of their dining rooms for nourishment.

There is no end to what we can find as we search through the generations. Having discovered my parents' hotel, I continue to encounter people who played a role in its history before and after my parents owned it. In November 1998, Esther Strassberg, co-owner of the Esther Manor Hotel in Monticello, told me that she was a real estate broker in the off season and had brokered the sale of the Royal to my family. Around the same time, I got an e-mail from Phil Neiss in New York, who wrote: "Recently, I was visiting a friend's house who happened to show me your book, *Catskill Culture*. I was thumbing through it and noticed a recent picture of what was Brown's Royal Hotel. I was quite surprised, and impressed with the job that the present owners had done to the place. You see, I owned the property for a brief period from 1982 to 1985. I had purchased the facility from the Pasternack family, whom I believed had bought it from your parents in the early 1950s." He was hoping to have a family getaway, but it fell through. We met and talked about this amazing piece of shared memory.

When I gave a talk at the Monticello Library in August 1999, a man told me afterward that he had stayed at my parents' hotel when he was six, in 1946. While he didn't remember details, he promised to call his mother to get some. She reported that their family got a recommendation from a friend in the Bronx who had a Chrysler dealership. What was his name? Moise Lipsit. I said, "That's my cousin."

Then in December 2000 I was contacted by Joel Waldman, whose grandfather Max Waldman had sold my parents the Royal. I had already found in county archives the papers showing that Max Waldman sold the hotel in 1946 to my parents, who took out a $16,500 first mortgage and a $4,500 second mortgage. Like me, Joel Waldman used to sleep in one of the porch rooms. I also have in my possession a copy of the August 4, 1952 deed that Joseph Jacobs obtained when he bought the hotel as a mortgage foreclosure for $15,325. Even though the place was crawling with *mishpocheh*, some working and some staying as guests—who could tell the difference?—they were not enough to make it operate.

I have also located relatives in this process. A number of people have asked for help in finding relatives and friends who owned hotels or had other Catskills connections. It has been gratifying to link some people up with family members, but in June 1999 something special happened along this line. A woman e-mailed me, saying that the announcement for our August conference was interesting, though she couldn't make it. Perhaps, however, I could help her with a family tree problem. It seemed that one of her Snyder family married a Brown who owned a Catskills hotel. I wrote back saying that it sounded like my mother marrying my father, and indeed it was. This woman is my mother's first cousin, and I never knew she existed. Through her I have located a bunch of other relatives as well, one of whom is even a graduate student at Brown University, where I teach. And we have had a couple of family reunions. Such is the miracle of the Catskills.

What memories we have of the golden years of the Catskills, from the end of World War II into the early 1970s. In Pamela Gray's unique film, *A Walk on the Moon*, depicting life in a bungalow colony, the loudspeaker blares out, "The knishman is here," though it doesn't mention Ruby the Knishman by name. But we know who he is—a vendor renowned throughout the Catskills bungalow colonies. What can it mean that Ruby the Knishman is such an amazing person to remember? *A toizint taamen fun di peddlers* (a thousand tastes from the peddlers), each and every one bringing something special to eat, but none so delicious as the fresh knish from Ruby.

And of all the memories of Ruby that are now circulating, none is so delicious as this e-mail I got in December 1998 from Dara Oshinsky-Deitz:

> Your Catskills Institute webpage is only the latest of amazing sources of fondness that I have recently uncovered on my father, Ruby the Knishman. It started last summer when my husband was looking for a gift for my aunt and came across *Borsch Belt Bungalows* by Irwin Richman at Amazon.com. Then, a few months later, he was reading his Penn State Alumni Magazine and found a review of the book, and the reviewer mentioned Ruby the Knishman. No sooner than a few days later, my neighbor, who grew up in the same neighborhood of Canarsie, Brooklyn that I did, told me that my father has his own Webpage in the "Official Canarsie" Webpage, where the author has asked people to send him stories of their memories of my dad. Now, I discover when doing a Net search for "Ruby the Knishman" on America Online, that Arthur Tanney's memoirs [found in this collection] come up, and he dedicates almost his entire Chapter 8 to his memories of my dad. It is now clear to me and my family that my father touched the lives of thousands of people. His family misses him terribly. I appreciate your response and your devotion to the memories we all cherish.

What a *mechiah*. These are the little miracles of Catskills culture—a woman discovering the importance her father played in the everyday lives of so many ordinary people.

There's a special miracle in all this for me. I find it striking that virtually all the hotels my parents and I worked in are still standing and being used. Given the number of burned, decayed, fallen in, and demolished hotels, this is beyond the realm of statistical probability. Sometimes I feel I have been called back to these places to document their history and the history of their inhabitants. In 1993, when I started my research, I made a field trip to visit nearly all the resorts at which my parents or I had worked, and in subsequent years located those that I couldn't find on the first attempt. Of course, the most spectacular for me is my parents' hotel, Brown's Royal in White Lake, now the Bradstan. In Accord, Chait's was Su Casa, since taken over by Elat Chayim, a Jewish Renewal center. The Karmel in Loch Sheldrake is Stage Door Manor, a renowned children's theater camp. In Swan Lake, the Fieldston Hotel is now Camp B'Nai Yaakov. Also in Swan Lake, Paul's Hotel is Daytop Village, a drug treatment center, and the Stevensville has reopened as the Swan Lake

Resort. In Parkville, the Grand Hotel is another Daytop Village facility. In Kiamesha Lake, the Evans Kiamesha is a housing development and Jewish day school.

In 1999 I found The Cherry Hill in Greenfield Park, which I couldn't locate originally because the road from Route 52 was closed years ago due to a bridge collapse. I located the road at the Briggs Highway end and found the old place. This hotel, where I first bused tables in 1962, the year of my bar mitzvah, is now Or Shraga, an orthodox camp. It is in incredibly great shape, as if it were still back in the early 1960s. Unlike the typical ultraorthodox places that are so run down, Or Shraga is clean and well maintained. Unlike at the many orthodox places where I have been chased away as I took photos, the campers and staff of Or Shraga were incredibly welcoming. Boys gathered around me, eager to hear my story about the history of their place. As a knot of eight or so boys would drift away, more would join me, escorting me proudly all around the grounds as I repeated my story. "Was the gazebo here then?" they asked. It certainly was, and how amazing that this little thing still stood. "Was it kosher? Did they have a *mashgiach* [resident kosher inspector] in the hotel?" Virtually every hotel was kosher, I told them, but probably not up the standards they were used to, and few had a *mashgiach*, certainly not The Cherry Hill. We walked to the building that held the casino, some staff rooms, and some cheaper guest rooms. The casino itself had been turned into a *shul* (synagogue), though recently replaced by a newer building. The boys had trouble understanding what I meant by a casino, and were most curious about the kinds of shows they had there. The room where my parents and I slept the year my mother was chef was a small study lined with books, and I told the boys and the rabbi who was sitting there that I had lived in that very room. The room in back of ours was the girl counselors' bunk, and my recollection of this really made the boys jump, surprised to imagine me living all summer next to such a room, full of young women. The boys eagerly prodded me, "Come see the new *shul*," and they showed me this brand-new, modern building. Quite a difference from the usual house of prayer in the typical orthodox camp up here!

These old hotels, continuing into new lives, are living reminders of the way the area used to look, when you could drive forever and see nothing but hotel after hotel, punctuated by bungalow colony after bungalow colony.

Miracles! The Catskills are full of miracles. Turning little boarding houses into hotels and bungalow colonies is a miracle. Making a place for the Jewish working class to get some fresh air is a miracle. Building a summer Eden that stretched for two counties' worth of eternity is a miracle. Think of the pleasure experienced by any one of New York's millions who first stepped onto the grounds of the kuchalayn, bungalow colony, or hotel and saw the cannas in the garden, smelled the fresh-mown grass, heard the gurgle of the stream, smelled the brisket in the oven and the rugelach on the table. Think of the pride of ownership among hotel and bungalow colony proprietors who tended their family-style summer havens. Think of the waiters, busboys, counselors, and musicians who were so pleased to support themselves through college, and the fun they had while doing it.

It is a world mostly lost to us physically, yet so powerful in our memories and emotions. I hope this collection of writings will return you to the places and times where this all happened. Welcome back to the Mountains.

Jewish Farmers of the Catskills

Abraham Lavender and Clarence Steinberg

It was not until the late 1800s and early 1900s, when Sullivan County in the lower Catskills developed an important summer resort trade, that it was accepted as part of the legendary resort Catskills, and it was in the mountains of Sullivan County and the southern part of Ulster County that the largest and most successful Jewish farm settlements developed. The lower Catskills were relatively close to New York City, an important factor in the survival of the Jewish farmers. Orange County to the south, Greene County to the north, and Delaware County to the west also had a smaller number of Jewish farmers. But Sullivan and Ulster counties comprised the area that later would be referred to by some as "the Jewish Catskills." In fact by the 1920s Jewish resort owners in Green County were accusing Sullivan County of having stolen "the Catskill Mountains" trademark.[1] It was mostly in southern Ulster and Sullivan counties that "Jewish shop workers and small store keepers from the city wended their way for a whiff of fresh air, and in the meantime began transforming a poor, run-down agricultural area into flourishing, prosperous Jewish resort and farming communities."[2]

When they started coming, the Catskill area already had many Christian farmers, and the upper Catskills had a number of resorts. Farming had been a major activity from the earliest days of settlement by the Dutch, expanding on a base developed by local Native Americans. Christian summer resorts in the upper Catskills had begun in the early 1800s, when the first major resort hotel was built in 1823 in Haines Falls.[3] Greene County, the northern part of Ulster County, and a northeastern tip of Delaware County had developed fame as the Catskill resort area by the 1840s. These resorts served New York City Christians who came up by boat to Kingston and then went by stagecoach to their destinations, mostly in Ulster County. The more prestigious older resorts in Greene and northern Ulster counties catered primarily to the Protestant aristocracy, and immigrants—mostly German or Irish in the earlier years—were unwelcome.

Both farming and operating resorts profited from and expanded with the building of railroads in the upper and lower Catskills in the robber baron era.[4] In the lower Catskills, the railroad began as the Midland, planned five years after the Civil War to compete with the New York Central's New York to Chicago line. By 1870, the Midland ran its track from downtown New York City to the Catskill foothills, in Summitville, near a juncture of Sullivan and Ulster counties. It then branched into two lines, one from Summitville to Ellenville, paralleling the old and then-functioning Delaware and Hudson Canal. The other line, opening a little later, snaked through Sullivan County's high passes and ravines—what really amounted to a wilderness, a kind of frontier—breaking out into New York's central plateau and the Finger Lakes. This line was planned by its promoters to terminate in Chicago.[5]

Although the Midland never got out of New York State and never rivaled the New York Central, it was significant both as the world's first milk line and as a developer and mainstay of summer resorts. It opened a frontier that, after less than a quarter of a century of development, would become the most populous and the most successful of the Jewish farming efforts in the country. With an eye on the benefits to its future fares and freight revenues, the Midland offered almost from its beginning free freight for building materials from the city to any station on its line where one wished to build a summer resort or a farm.[6] The Ellenville branch went through an area long built up because of its proximity to the old colonial highway (now U.S. Highway 209) and the canal and thus had less need for promotional offers.[7] Some resorts, several quite posh and frequented by New York society, had operated in the Ellenville area before the railroad, but none served Jews. Wood was the predominant building material, and nearly all at one time or another were damaged by fire before being rebuilt and later bought by Jews.

The branch of the train route through Sullivan County led through rural areas that until then had been populated thinly by tanners who were stripping hemlock for the only known source of tannin and were building a leather trade connected by stagecoach and a turnpike to the outer world.[8] Centreville (later renamed Woodridge), Sandburg (later renamed Mountaindale), Liberty, Liberty Falls (later renamed Ferndale), Luzon Station (later renamed Hurleyville), Pleasant Lake (later renamed Kiamesha Lake), Loch Sheldrake, Livingston Manor, and Parksville were the Midland Railroad's principal Sullivan County stops, and near them the presence of the railroad led to growth in these locations.

Those farmhouses benefited that offered summer board for New York City guests arriving and departing by Midland (and subsequently by Midland's successor, the Ontario and Western). The development of the summer boarding business on a large scale would not have been possible without the railroad. Farmers and boardinghouse keepers encouraged the railroad to provide even more transportation. Speaking of Woodridge, for example, Erna Elliott noted that "the railroad was cooperative. It offered weekend round-trip specials. Often the service was inadequate and the village board repeatedly petitioned for additional trains."[9]

The fully fledged resort hotel, offering board and some entertainment, also benefited. Fishing and hunting were major features at the farmhouses, and parasoled lawn parties were held at the best of the hotels. Wakefield's old photographs tell their stories in the splendid ladies and gentlemen pictured on a Centreville train platform. Those catered to at these resort hotels were largely Wall Street's and Tammany Hall's most powerful men, and at the farmhouses those operatives' subordinates.[10] The latter must have fished for pleasure, because the period's boardinghouse advertisements feature fishing for recreation. As early as the 1830s, Sullivan County was famous for the fishing in its streams and lakes, and fishing would remain its major attraction for decades.[11]

New York's Christian (primarily Protestant) semiaristocracy, which had vacationed in the Catskills for decades before the advent of railroads, engaged in recreations other than fishing. They watered at the great resorts of the period such as Lackawack House, Yama Farms Inn, and Mt. Meenahga, all near Ellenville, and all of which could be traced to the stagecoach and Delaware and Hudson Canal eras. These remained Christian resorts well into the twentieth century but, like Bloomingburg's Sha-Wanga Lodge which came with the Midland, they were sold to Jews and became Jewish resorts in the 1920s. It was poetic justice that the Dan family, Jewish purchasers of the Sha-Wanga, had brochures printed that were identical to those their Christian predecessors had used except that they replaced "No Hebrews Accommodated" with "Kosher Cuisine Featured."[12] Victorian elegance characterized hotel pleasures: cigars, bustles, parasols, oysters, and, of course, the ubiquitous local staples feeding both social classes: dairy products, produce, and, in some cases, game. In addition to fishing, hayrides entertained the boarders. And, to the extent that the Midland's and the Ontario and Western's "Summer Homes" listings of churches actually represent that their boarders participated in religious events, some went by buggy to Sunday church services in a nearby town.[13] Midland's publication, "Summer Homes," appeared first in 1878 as part of its effort to promote the resort business it subsidized through free transport of building material and free stocking of trout streams. Photos and snippets from local newspapers, added to extracts from "Summer Homes," chronicle customs and dimensions of that Catskill resort business.

Jews entered this Christian world of farms and summer resorts as early as 1892 in the person of Yana "John" Gerson, recognized by the society as the first Jewish farmer in the area.[14] He was born in a village near Vilna, Lithuania (then Russia), in 1854. In 1873, he married Annie Griff. He migrated to the United States in 1888 when he was thirty-four years old, leaving behind his wife, their two sons, Elias, about thirteen, and Benjamin, nine, and their two daughters, Esther, four, and Rebecca, one. Two years later, in 1890, the two sons joined their father. Annie and the two daughters migrated a year later. According to the family's oral history, the Gerson family lived on Ludlow Street on the Lower East Side and for a while had a farm on Pitkin Avenue in Brooklyn. In the United States, Yana became "John" and Elias became "Alex."[15]

By 1892, the Gerson family was in Glen Wild, near Woodridge, in Sullivan County. They began with an abandoned farm and built a boardinghouse and a successful dairying operation. Abe Jaffe, with his father and later with his brother, farmed property across the road from what he describes as the old Gerson place. According to Jaffe, the Gerson boardinghouse of tiny rooms and two porches burned in 1925. Today, a small section of a dam walling and a few concrete steps remain, next to a small stream. Like their Christian neighbors, the Gersons produced the area's specialty, iced fresh milk for New York City. The Midland was the first railroad to move bulk milk, drawing it initially from old, established farms along its Bloomingburg to Middletown run, where a farmer in 1871 put ice in a can of milk, shipping it on a passenger train. Shortly thereafter the Midland built a business of shipping iced milk, moving 900 cans (presumably of 20 gallons each) a day from Liberty to Middletown and then to New York City. Soon afterwards, the Midland built creameries to buy, pasteurize, and separate milk at most stations along its main tracks on both the Ellenville and Oswego branches. Gerson probably dealt with the Liberty creamery on the Oswego branch. Bankrupted by the Panic of 1873, the Midland curtailed the milk operation, but the dairy farms and their Catskill towns were so dependent upon the milk operation that one town, Ellenville, in 1877 raised a significant tax of $1,000 to give to the railroad in an effort to restore their service and hence their milk deliveries. The milk operation resumed and was flourishing by 1892.[16]

Not only was Gerson considered the first Jewish farmer in the area, but in 1899 he published one of the first advertisements for a "Jewish Boarding House." His advertisement, which appeared in "Summer Homes" in 1899, said: "J. GERSON— Rock Hill Jewish Boarding House. 5 miles; accommodate 40; adults $6, children $3; transients $1; discount to season guests; transportation free; new house, newly furnished; prepare our own meats; raise our own vegetables; scenery unsurpassed. Jewish faith and customs throughout; ¼ mile from Post Office; good road to station; fine shade; good airy rooms."[17]

The Gerson household history illustrates a typical Jewish Catskill family combining farming and boarding. When the 1900 census was taken, John was forty-six years old; his wife, Annie, was forty-five; their two sons, Alex and Benjamin, were twenty-three and twenty-one, respectively; and their two daughters, Esther and Rebecca, were sixteen and thirteen, respectively. Alex was listed as having been married three years. Also in the household was Emma Gerson, aged twenty-eight, listed as John's sister-in-law. John's four nieces—Ettie, eight, Celia, six, Sarah, three, and Fannie, one—and a nephew, Nathan, three, also were in the household, although the census indicated that no more than three of the five children were children of Emma the younger. Bringing the household to a total of fourteen were Ida and Abram Block, listed as "servants." Emma the younger and the Blocks were born in Russia, and the five children were born in New York. Emma came to the United States in 1892, and the Blocks had come only the year before, in 1899. With fourteen people in the household, at least John and Annie Gerson had help on the farm and in the boardinghouse. John Gerson later moved to Fallsburg, and in partnership with family members operated a boardinghouse, the "New Prospect." John later lost his fortune when he signed a note for a bakery that went bankrupt. He died in 1935 at age eighty-one, leaving a legacy of having been a very religious person.[18]

Contemporary with Gerson, immigrant Jews by the hundreds yearly had bought or built boardinghouses and farmhouses in "the mountains" (as the clientele of their Christian predecessors in the resort business had spoken of the area), settling independently of the Hirsch philanthropies. Legal records, local newspaper accounts of property sales to "Hebrews," and the increase of listings of "Strictly Kosher" and "Hebrews Only" in the Ontario and Western's "Summer

Homes" boarding advertisements show the transfers of Catskills farms and board-inghouses from Christians to Jews around the turn of the century.[19]

Many of these new residents had come to the mountains first as summer guests and returned later to settle.[20] Unlike the New Jersey settlements, the Catskill Jewish farm settlement was unplanned. Paradoxically, the Catskill settlements were on rocky land harder to till and less fertile than that of the New Jersey colonies or of the settlements in Connecticut, Ohio, and the western states. Some of the Catskill land had been cleared, farmed, and then partly abandoned to reforestation in the course of the nineteenth century before Jews bought it. Jews bought some of the farms at exorbitant prices, setting themselves up for failure. As Herman Levine stated, "They started out behind the eight ball. They started out with a neglected farm, overpriced and on terms that doomed them."[21] "Let us bear in mind," he wrote, "that even most of the natives, with no mortgages to worry them, hardened by the rugged lives they led, and with generations of farm experience behind them, also found it difficult to eke out a living from farming alone. They, too, kept boarders and worked off the farm to earn a livelihood. The climate and soil were unfavorable to agriculture; poor transportation and marketing facilities made farming very unprofitable."[22]

When German-speaking visitors had begun going to the upper Catskills in the 1870s when the railroad had expanded in that area, religion generally was not important to them. Most were Protestants, many were Catholics, and some were Jews, but all stayed in the same boardinghouses. By the end of the 1880s, however, successful Eastern European Jews were frequent guests in the upper Catskills, and boardinghouses began to be segregated into Christian or Jewish houses. Some of the segregation was voluntary, as many visitors preferred to stay with others of similar backgrounds. This seemed to be particularly true of less-educated visitors.[23] The visitors separated not only by religion but also within religious groups by national origins. Russian Jewish, Polish Jewish, and Hungarian Jewish boardinghouses developed.[24] Even some Jews—especially German Jews—criticized the behavior and lack of sophistication of some of the Eastern European Jews.

In the late 1880s many boardinghouses began to post signs and print advertisements saying that they did not accommodate Jews, regardless of their values or economic or social status. The exclusion was mainly due to prejudice against Jews, and in 1889 the *New York Times* referred to "the anti-Hebrew crusade" in the Catskills.[25] The *Times* concluded that most newspapers in the Catskills spoke out against discrimination and that the discrimination was not as extensive as reported. By 1889, the anti-Hebrew crusade had failed for economic reasons, but most small boardinghouses remained segregated by religion.[26]

As the Jewish farms and boardinghouses increased in Sullivan County and in southern Ulster County around Ellenville, the northern Catskill boardinghouses became less attractive to Jews. The southern Ulster-Sullivan area was closer to New York City, was blessed with the O&W railroad, and offered largely Jewish resort areas in which prejudice was less likely to be encountered on a daily basis. The mountains in Sullivan County and southern Ulster County were not as high as those in the upper Catskills, but to Jews who knew no mountains in Russia or Poland, they were high enough to have scenic beauty and cool breezes. There were also more lakes and streams, and less pollution from tanning, in the lower Catskills.

One Jewish writer described the beauty of the lower Catskills area: "Embraced between the Shawangunk and the Catskill Mountain ranges is a sketch of land which nature in her pleasant moments graced and beautified—an area that is a succession of sunkissed hills and verdant dales. Here countless streams rush from the hillsides and ripple along through vale and meadow. Here are lakes of entracing beauty dotting the landscape like jewels in a golden setting. Here, indeed, is a countryside, the charm and beauty of which have inspired the brush of an Inness and the pen of a Burroughs. And, adding bounty to bounty, nature has also blessed this region with an air that is invigorating and a climate that is healthgiving. It was natural for such richly endowed regions to become attractive spots for the seeker after health and recreation."[27]

For the Jewish visitors, compared to the Christian visitors, socialization was more important and communing with nature less important, a fact that also decreased the appeal of high mountains. Esterita Blumberg's descriptions, although written of a later time, also apply to this time period. She acknowledged that they used "high flown" names for their hotel accommodations, that "our 'Pine Lodge' was formerly a chicken coop, 'Deluxe' described nothing at our hotel, and we called any two spaces 'A Suite.' " She noted that they countered these conditions with the sales spiel that little time was spent in the rooms anyway because of all the activities offered the guests. Blumberg concluded that "the funny thing was that we were right. We were giving wonderful value at affordable prices—the rooms were the least of it. Summer in the Catskills became a way of life, with a population that returned year after year."[28]

Around the turn of the century, sizeable numbers of Jews began to farm in the Catskills. Some farmed for only a short time, then gave it up for other callings. Others farmed for decades, frequently combining it with summer boarding. Most were born in Eastern Europe and spent some years in New York City before going to the Catskills, but patterns varied. The Weinberger brothers and their father, for example, arrived in Leurenkill in 1900 and began to farm. They were all shoemakers by trade, however, and one year of farming persuaded them to switch back to their first vocation. Samuel H. Berger settled in Ellenville in 1900, later moved to a farm in Kerhonkson, and during World War I moved back to Ellenville to operate the Fountain Hill House. Samuel Jacobwitz went to the Catskills in 1901 and became a farmer. He then turned to peddling meat and in 1907 opened a butcher shop in Ellenville.

Kalman Goldman became a farmer in Greenfield in 1902, after immigrating to the United States from Russia when he was sixteen and living in New York City for fourteen years. He spent two years in Greenfield, building and operating the Grand Hotel as well as farming, and in 1904 moved to Ellenville. Max Rosenberg came from New York City in 1903, and became a farmer and owner-operator of the West Orchard House. He continued a combination of farming and hotel-keeping at the West Orchard House and at the Echo House for many years, finally switching to hotel operating only. Benjamin Cherney began work as a farm laborer in Pataukunk in 1903. His European fiancée soon joined him and they married, but she was "unprepared to meet the hardships or manage the chores of a farm-hand's wife," and they moved to Ellenville where he became a grocer.

Hyman Levine had a peddler's route between Ellenville and Kingston from 1880 to 1895, lived in Ellenville from 1895 to 1903, and in 1903 purchased a farm on Cape Avenue. The Morris Kinberg family bought a dairy farm and boarding-house in Leurenkill in 1905, raised ten children there, and moved to Ellenville in 1920. Israel Rosen farmed in Mountaindale and Spring Glen before settling on a farm near Ellenville in 1905, but later he became a builder of bakers' ovens. Jacob Benenson was a bookkeeper, but, after arriving from the Ukraine in 1906, he spent only one month in New York City before deciding that he wanted a farm. He was the first Jewish settler in Honk Hill, and for years he operated a farm with summer boarders there. In addition to these examples, there were numerous other Catskill Jewish farmers too numerous to discuss. As these examples show, some gave up farming and moved into towns, but many others stayed on the farm.[29]

By 1907, when the founding of the Ellenville Hebrew Aid Society marked a milestone in Catskill Jewish settlements, the increase in the number of Jewish farmers and nonfarmers was "shifting into high gear." The Jewish Agricultural and

Industrial Aid Society found that by 1908 there were 684 Jewish farms in New York state, 500 of them in Sullivan and Ulster counties.[30] That count was based on second mortgages the society issued. Not all Jews on farms in New York state took those mortgages, however. Financing was in most cases arranged privately, usually through a personal lender, and not recorded. Another estimate was higher. A triangular area with sides of about twenty miles each, with route 209's Wurtsboro through Ellenville and Kerhonkson on the east and Woodbourne through Woodridge (Centreville) and Mountaindale on the west, was said to have supported one thousand Jewish farm households. With easily five hundred more to the northwest, around Monticello, Liberty, Hurleyville, Loch Sheldrake, and Parksville, on the O&W main line, Sullivan and Ulster counties had three tenths or more of all the Jewish farmer households in the United States around 1911.[31]

They inherited from Christian predecessors the general farm, with some field crops and some poultry raised for meat and eggs. The major farm income for these Jewish farmers came from dairying, selling to outlets serving the New York City milk market, and shipping on the O&W. If they did not buy such a farm, they built one like it simply because there was a ready milk market in New York City, because crops and poultry could be sold locally to the summer trade, and because the farmer could (at least in theory) eat off his own land.

Nearly all of the Jews who moved into the area were part of the largest migration in U.S. history, which began in the early 1880s and basically ended with the advent of World War I. As noted, the majority of these immigrants settled in New York City.[32] A small percentage of these Eastern European Jews, but a large number, as well as many Eastern European Christians and Italian Catholics, went up the Hudson River and fanned out into surrounding areas. In Ulster County in 1900, 10.5 percent of the people were foreign born, increasing to 15.5 percent in 1910. In Sullivan County, the figures were 9.4 percent in 1900 and 13.3 percent in 1910.[33] Based on an analysis of given names and surnames, it appears that most of the residents born in Russia or Poland were Jewish and that nearly all of the Jewish immigrants were from Russia or Poland.[34] But most of the 1900 foreign-born in Ulster and Sullivan were not from Russia or Poland and were not Jewish.

The years 1900–1910 were the first period of great growth in numbers of Jewish immigrants. For example, in the Ellenville area (Wawarsing township) in 1900 there were only three heads-of-household born in Russia with apparently Jewish names. One reported that he was a farmer, another that he had a boardinghouse on a farm, and the third that he had a store and tin shop. By 1910, this same area had 166 apparently Jewish families of Russian or Polish background (plus a small number from other areas of Eastern Europe). Of the heads-of-house-hold, 110 were famers and 56 were not. The farmers averaged 4.9 people to the family, the nonfarmers 4.8. The Jewish immigrant heads-of-household overall were young or middle-aged, most still in the years for having children: two were under twenty; nineteen were in their twenties; seventy-five in their thirties; forty-eight in their forties; seventeen in their fifties; three in their sixties; and two in their seventies. Of the 153 who indicated when they came to the United States, seventy-three had come since the beginning of 1900, fifty-six had come in the 1890s, twenty-one in the 1880s, and three in the 1870s. The farmers did tend to have been in the United States fewer years. Whereas 40 percent of the nonfarmers had come since 1900, 51 percent of the farmers had come in that pe-riod. Of the nonfarmers, 25 percent had been in the United States for at least twenty years, but only 11 percent of the farmers had been.[35]

Few of these Jews came with the skills needed to farm successfully. In the cen-tury before the mass migration began, there was great movement in Eastern Europe from villages to towns to cities, in a desperate and unsuccessful attempt to escape persecution and poverty. In 1793, for example, Lodz had 11 Jews; it had 98,677 in 1897 and 166,628 in 1910. Warsaw had 3,532 Jews in 1781 and 219,141 in 1891. Many Jews changed their occupations in an attempt to survive. Fewer than 5 per-cent of Eastern European Jews were farmers, although, for those who remained in villages or small towns, agriculture frequently was a supplementary source of in-come. One writer noted that "in the villages almost every Jewish family owned a cow or goat, often the sole dependable source of income, as well as some fowl. Jews cultivated their own gardens; they raised the 'Jewish fruits'—beets, carrots, cabbage, onions, cucumbers, garlic, and horseradish; and, despite restrictions, many rented orchards on a seasonal basis from neighboring peasants and gentry."[36]

Some of the new Jewish Catskill farmers probably could harness a horse and milk a cow, but those skills alone were no guarantee of profitable farming. The society noted in this time period that one of its problems was that the vast ma-jority of Jewish immigrants, who comprised nearly all of the Jewish farming community, had little or no farming experience. A random survey of Jewish farmers in the United States taken years later indicated that 63 percent had cho-sen farming because they liked it, 20 percent because they were dissatisfied with city life, 7 percent because they had to for health reasons, and only 10 percent because they had previous experience as farmers in Europe.[37] Noting that these new farmers came from a great variety of occupational backgrounds, having been "tailors, merchants, carpenters, butchers, vegetable and fruit store operators, workers in shops and factories, peddlers, and odd-job laborers,"[38] the society concluded that "most of our applicants, therefore, are of necessity obliged to establish themselves upon their farms first and acquire their agricultural experience afterwards—a process not only tedious and expensive, but involving considerable risk."[39]

As U.S. census entries for 1910 indicate, many of the Catskill Jewish farmers spoke and read only Yiddish and so could not read English-language books about farming techniques and New York State Experiment Station bulletins or, a decade later, gain instruction from English-speaking county agricultural extension agents. Catskill Jewish settlers who knew how to read English, however, could gain such technical knowledge from encyclopedias and handbooks on farming.

The society's Long Island Test Farm, the 500-acre King's Point training school operating from 1904 through 1911, placed its first group of immigrants on the farm in the spring of 1905. But by the fall of 1908 the society had decided that the results did not justify the expense and discontinued the experiment. Under private management, test farmers were placed on the farm for several more years. Of the total of fifty-eight potential farmers placed on farms by the test farm, twenty-nine were graduated and provided with farms. Of these twenty-nine, nine gave up after "a more or less protracted struggle." Even in the cases in which it was successful, however, the test farm focused on preparing young urban Jews for work and subsequent settlement on the New Jersey colonies or Long Island, not on training those who had already settled and certainly not on training the Catskill Jewish farmers who could easily slip from a farmhouse to a boarding economy.[40] The society was interested in proving that Jews could farm, not run resorts. It realized, however, that in order to survive many Jewish farmers also had to have summer boarders.

While the process of converting a farm into a boardinghouse sometimes was necessary for survival, it was not easy. As Jonas Nass remembered, "We had to build a mile of our own utility poles for electric light and power, and install plumbing to make it habitable for city folk."[41] But, once converted, the rural setting of the boardinghouse seduced the city people. A typical advertisement for a hotel, which, although not a farm boardinghouse, gave city visitors a taste of their farm, read: "The proprietor keeps a dairy of Guernsey cows, noted for rich milk, butter, eggs, poultry, maple sugar and vegetables."[42]

Some of the farmers who started boardinghouses in this period were to become famous success stories. The immigrant Kutsher brothers came to Sullivan County from New York City in 1907 and purchased a farm because one of the brothers was frail and thought country living would be healthy.[43] Like many other Jewish farmers, they took in summer boarders in order to help meet their expenses. Kutsher's Country Club would later become one of the Catskills' major resorts. Selig and Malke Grossinger were restauranteurs in New York City but, encouraged by the society, moved to a farm in Ferndale in 1913. The Grossinger farmhouse, opened in 1914, would grow into the famous Grossinger's Hotel and Country Club.[44]

Charles Slutsky bought a farm in Leurenkill in 1901. His wife and three sons were still in Europe, and for two years Charles tended the farm without any family help. His daughters and another son worked "in New York City to supplement the farm income and make possible the immigration of the other members of the family in 1903." Morris Slutsky, brother of Charles, settled in the area in 1904, and other relatives followed. The Slutsky family in Ellenville would see their Nevele Falls Farm House grow into the Nevele Hotel and Country Club.[45] Other hotels associated with the Slutsky family included the Fallsview, Arrowhead Lodge, Evergreen Manor, and Breeze Lawn.

Max Levinson came to the United States in 1891, and bought his farm, later the Tamarack Lodge, in 1903. Mrs. Ben Miller and Daniel Roher described its beginnings: "Today's well-known summer resort was then only a small, down-at-the-heels farm, stocked with a small herd of cows and a horse past retirement age. Mr. Levinson played the plural role of farmer, hotelman, and tailor to his children in those early days, and like many other farmers of the period, left for New York City each fall, after the departure of the last guest, to help meet the mortgage payments and taxes, while Mrs. Levinson and the family remained to carry on the farm chores through the Winter months."[46]

And so a kind of spontaneous colonizing developed in the Catskills, aided but not initiated by the society. The rural colonies were like a series of shells around small established operating towns whose economies included Jewish artisans, craftsmen, merchants, food vendors, farm suppliers, farm produce buyers, barbers, tailors, glazers, mechanics, and physicians. Jews lived with their rural Christian counterparts as in the Russo-Polish shtetls. In 1908, the society stated that "some of the bustling villages, such as Centreville and Parksville, have an almost exclusively Jewish population. Nearly every one of them has its physician, dentist, druggist, and all that goes to make up a typical Jewish rural settlement in the Old Country, but so unlike the native American village."[47]

The Catskill settlements differed from the beginnings of the planned Jersey and midwestern colonies and from self-segregated religious communities like the

Amish, Mennonites, or Shakers. The little Catskill towns possessed the social amenities such as synagogues and Jewish businesses that the society found it had to bring to the New Jersey colonies to keep people there. For example, in Ellenville, in addition to the Hebrew Aid Society, which had been founded in 1907, a synagogue was dedicated in 1910, and a Workmen's Circle was founded in 1911.[48] Comparing the New York settlements to other areas, as early as 1906 the society could state that "in New York, however, there is a large number of Jewish farmers of whom we never hear except by chance as our investigators run across them. They do not need our aid and do not ask for it."[49]

By 1906 there were forty-five Jewish farmers' associations in the United States, eleven of them in the lower Catskills. The Livingston Manor Jewish Farmers' Association had sixteen members, the Parksville Jewish Farmers Association sixty-six, the Hebrew Farmers' Association of Ferndale and Stevensville seventy-eight, the Hebrew Farmers' Association of Fallsburg and Hurleyville one-hundred-forty, the Monticello Jewish Farmers' Association fifty-seven, the Jewish Farmers' Association of Centreville Station ninety-nine, the Jewish Farmers' Association of Mountaindale eighty-six, the Hebrew Farmers' Association of Ellenville ninety, the Hebrew Aid Society of Briggs Street sixty-eight, the Hebrew Farmers' Association of Kerhonkson and Accord fifty-seven, and the Spring Glen Hebrew Aid Society eighteen.[50]

Moreover ten Jewish farmers in Leurenkill established a Hebrew school for their children in 1913. The children could not walk to the Hebrew school in Ellenville, and so their farmer parents put an advertisement for a Hebrew teacher in a New York City newspaper. Ephraim Yaffe, who had arrived in the United States from Europe only a few days earlier, saw the advertisement and immediately traveled to Leurenkill to apply for the position. Yaffe fell in love with the area, was hired, and first lived in the Slutsky family's Nevele Falls Farm House. Yaffe noted that "the farmers had no automobiles, their horses were needed on the farms, the roads were muddy after a rain, covered with snow during the winter, and it was impossible for the children to walk after school hours to the Ellenville Hebrew school and back home, in the dark, a distance of three miles or more."[51] Several years later Yaffe became a farmer, but he also taught two classes at the Ellenville Hebrew school "from 4 to 6 P.M., five days a week for $10 per week. This was much more than I could make per hour on the farm in those 'good old days.'"[52]

By the eve of World War I, there was a Jewish village network in southern Ulster County, Sullivan County, and, to a lesser extent, in Orange County (around

Port Jervis). Nearly all of these inhabitants were Eastern European immigrants speaking Yiddish and heavily accented English; nearly all were transplanted there after some years in New York City and were living in a kind of uneasy symbiosis with indigenous Christians. They did not have anywhere near the capital and experience to begin such businesses as banks, insurance agencies, creameries, lumber yards, blacksmith and harnessmaking establishments, hardware stores, plumbing supply stores, and machinery dealerships, businesses that remained out of their reach for several decades.

Notes

1. Evers, *The Catskills*, 659, 690.
2. "Jewish Agricultural Unit Shows Sanitation Exhibit," *Kingston Daily Freeman*.
3. Evers, *The Catskills*, 456.
4. Wakefield, *To the Mountains by Rail*.
5. Helmer, *O.&W.: The Long Life and Slow Death of the New York, Ontario & Western Ry*, 1–29; Wakefield, *To the Mountains*, 8.
6. Helmer, *O.&W.*, 51, 67.
7. Wakefield, *Coal Boats to Tidewater*; Shaughnessy, *Delaware and Hudson*, 1–29; Sanderson, *The Delaware and Hudson Canalway*.
8. Wakefield, *To the Mountains*, 5–6; Levenson, "No Hebrews Taken," 14.
9. Elliott, *Centreville to Woodridge*, 39.
10. Wakefield, *To the Mountains*, 68, 71.
11. Evers, *The Catskills*, 25.
12. Blumberg, "Those Were the Days," September 1993, 18; Webster, reproduction of the log of the canal boat *Iowa* on the Delaware and Hudson Canal, Sept. 7 to 23, 1891; Wakefield, *To the Mountains*, 35.
13. Wakefield, *To the Mountains*, 17, 181, 182–84; DeLisser, *Picturesque Catskills—Greene County*.
14. Goodwin and Levine, "A Historical Review," 12.
15. Interviews with Bruce W. Gerson, June 18, 1992, with Frances S. Gerson, June 21, 1992, and with David Gerson, June 22, 1992; U.S. Bureau of the Census, *1900 Census of Sullivan County*, 293b.
16. Abraham Jaffe, interviewed by Clarence Steinberg, May 4, 1987: Wakefield, *To the Mountains*, 167–70; Helmer, *O.&W.*, 62, 67, 42; DeLisser, *Picturesque Catskills—Greene County*.
17. Quoted in Wakefield, *To the Mountains*, 80.
18. U.S. Bureau of the Census, *1990 Census of Sullivan County*, 293b; interviews with Bruce W. Gerson, June 18, 1992, with Frances S. Gerson, June 21, 1992, and with David Gerson, June 22, 1992.
19. Miller and Roher, *50 Golden Years*; Gold, "Jewish Agriculture in the Catskills, 1900–1920," 31–49.
20. Gold, "Jewish Agriculture in the Catskills, 1900–1920," 35.

21. Herman J. Levine, interview with Abraham D. Lavender, July 22, 1982.
22. H.J. Levine, "The Jewish Farmers' Contributions to Ellenville's Growth," 52.
23. Rhine, "Race Prejudice at Summer Resorts," 527.
24. Evers, *The Catskills*, 691.
25. "The Anti-Hebrew Crusade," *New York Times*, 1.
26. Evers, *The Catskills*, 467, 476–79, 516–19.
27. Davidson, "A Glimpse at Jewish Life in the Mountains."
28. Evers, *The Catskills*, 663, 695; Blumberg, "Those Were the Days," December 1992, 21.
29. Miller and Roher, *50 Golden Years*, 27–30.
30. Jewish Agricultural and Industrial Aid Society, *Annual Report for the Year 1908*, 17–18.
31. Goodwin and H.J. Levine, "A Historical Review"; Robinson, "Agricultural Activities of the Jews in America."
32. Fishman, *The Jews of the United States*, 38.
33. U.S. Bureau of the Census, 1990 and 1910 censuses of Sullivan and Ulster counties.
34. See Lavender, "United States Ethnic Groups in 1790: Given Names as Suggestions of Ethnic Identity," 36–66, and Lavender, "Hispanic Given Names in Five United States Cities: Onomastics as a Research Tool in Ethnic Identity," 105–25.
35. U.S. Bureau of the Census, 1900 and 1910 censuses of Ulster County.
36. Rischin, *The Promised City*, 29.
37. Davidson, "Jewish Farm Movement," 2.
38. Goodwin and Levine, "A Historical Review," 14.
39. Jewish Agricultural and Industrial Aid Society, *Annual Report for the Year 1910*, 29.
40. Ibid., 30–31.
41. Nass, "I Remember," 73.
42. Strauss, "When the All-Inclusive Weekly Rate Was $9," xx–3.
43. Foster, "The Magic Words in the Catskills: 'More, More, More,' " xx–33.
44. Kanfer, *A Summer World*, 75.
45. Miller and Roher, *50 Golden Years*, 28.
46. Ibid., 29.
47. Jewish Agricultural and Industrial Aid Society, *Annual Report for the Year 1908*, 19.
48. "Notable Event in Ellenville," *Ellenville Journal*; "New Synagogue Dedicated," *Ellenville Journal*, 45; Miller and Roher, *50 Golden Years*, 76.
49. Jewish Agricultural and Industrial Aid Society, *Annual Report for the Year 1906*, 8.
50. Ibid., *1911*, 29.
51. Yaffe, "The Leurenkill Farmers Start a Hebrew School," 59.
52. Ibid.

Bibliography

"The Anti-Hebrew Crusade: Not So Extensive in the Catskills as Reported." *New York Times*, May 7, 1889, 1.
Atkinson, Oriana. *Big Eyes: A Story of the Catskill Mountains*. Cornwallville, N.Y.: Hope Farm Press, 1980.

Blumberg, Esterita R. "Those Were the Days." *Jewish Star*, December 1992, 20–21.

——. "Those Were the Days." *Jewish Star*, September 1993, 18–19.

"Creditable Enterprise: Jewish Farmers' Creamery Association Ready for Business." *Ellenville Journal*, May 25, 1916.

Davidson, Gabriel. "A Glimpse at Jewish Life in the Mountains." *Mountain Hotelman*, April 1933.

——. "Jewish Farm Movement." *Ellenville Journal*, August 2, 1923.

DeLisser, R. Lionel. *Picturesque Catskills: Greene County*. Cornwallville. N.Y.: Hope Farms Press, 1983.

Elliott, Erna W. *Centreville to Woodridge: The Story of a Small Community*. Woodridge, N.Y., 1976.

Evers, Alf. *The Catskills: From Wilderness to Woodstock*. Woodstock, N.Y.: The Overlook Press, 1982.

Fishman, Priscilla, ed. *The Jews of the United States*. New York: Quadrangle, 1973.

Foster, Lee. "The Magic Words in the Catskills: 'More, More, More.'" *New York Times*, March 5, 1972, xx–1, 33, 34.

Gold, David. "Jewish Agriculture in the Catskills, 1900–1920." *Agricultural History* 55, no. 1 (January 1981): 31–49.

Goodwin, Edward A., and Herman J. Levine. "A Historical Review of Farming by Jews in New York." In *Report of the General Manager 1956*, edited by the Jewish Agricultural Society, 10–31. New York: Jewish Agricultural Society, 1957.

Helmer, William F. *O.&W.: The Long Life and Slow Death of the New York Ontario & Western Ry.* Berkeley: Howell-North, 1959.

Jewish Agricultural and Industrial Aid Society. *Annual Report of the General Manager*. New York: Jewish Agricultural and Industrial Aid Society, 1906–21.

Jewish Agricultural Society. *Annual Report of the General Manager*. New York: Jewish Agricultural Society, 1922–58.

"Jewish Agricultural Unit Shows Sanitation Exhibit." *Kingston Daily Freeman*, September 10, 1940.

Kanfer, Stefan. *A Summer World: The Attempt to Build a Jewish Eden in the Catskills*. New York: Farrar Straus Giroux, 1989.

Lavender, Abraham D. "Hispanic Given Names in Five United States Cities: Onomastics as a Research Tool in Ethnic Identity." *Hispanic Journal of Behavioral Sciences* 10, no. 2 (June 1988): 105–25.

——. "United States Ethnic Groups in 1790: Given Names as Suggestions of Ethnic Identity." *Journal of American Ethnic History* 9, no. 1 (Fall 1989): 36–66.

Levenson, Gabe. "Catskill Resorts Still the Place to Relax." *Miami Jewish Tribune*, April 26–May 2, 1991, 10B.

——. "No Hebrews Taken." *Jewish Week and The American Examiner*, December 23, 1983.

Levine, Herman J. "The Jewish Farmers' Contributions to Ellenville's Growth." In *50 Golden Years: The Ellenville Hebrew Aid Society 1907–1957*, edited by Mrs. Ben Miller and Daniel S. Roher, 52–53. Ellenville, N.Y.: Ellenville Hebrew Aid Society, 1959.

Miller, Mrs. Ben, and Daniel S. Roher, eds. *50 Golden Years: The Ellenville Hebrew Aid Society 1907–1957*. Ellenville, N.Y.: Ellenville Hebrew Aid Society, 1959.

38

Nass, Jonas. "I Remember." In *Fifty Years Working Together*, edited by Esterita R. Blumberg, 73. Fallsburg, N.Y.: Fallsburg Printing Company, 1963.

"Notable Event in Ellenville." *Ellenville Journal*, April 29, 1909.

Rhine, Alice Hyneman. "Race Prejudice at Summer Resorts." *Forum* 3 (1887): 527.

Robinson, Leonard. "Agricultural Activities of the Jews in America." In *The American Jewish Year Book*, edited by Herbert Friedenwald, 3–89. Philadelphia: Jewish Publication Society of America, 1910.

Sanderson, Dorothy Hurlbut. *The Delaware & Hudson Canalway*. Ellenville, N.Y.: Rondout Valley Publishing Company, 1974.

Shaughnessy, Jim. *Delaware & Hudson*. Berkeley: Howell-North, 1967.

Sandman, Abraham. *The New Country: Jewish Immigrants in America*. New York: Charles Scribner's Sons, 1976.

Simons, Howard. *Jewish Times: Voices of the American Jewish Experience*. Boston: Houghton Mifflin Company, 1988.

Strauss, Michael. "When the All-Inclusive Weekly Rate Was $9." *New York Times*, June 12, 1966, xx-3.

U.S. Bureau of the Census. *1840 Census of Ulster County, New York, Wawarsing Township*. Washington, D.C., 1840.

——. *1900 Census of Sullivan County, New York, Thompson Township*. Washington, D.C., 1900.

——. *1900 Census of Ulster County, New York, Wawarsing Township*. Washington, D.C., 1900.

——. *1910 Census of Ulster County, New York, Wawarsing Township*. Washington, D.C., 1910.

——. *Rural and Rural Farm Population: 1990*. Washington, D.C.: Government Printing Office.

——. *Sullivan County, Ulster County, Delaware County, Greene County, Orange County Censuses*. 1940–1990.

Wakefield, Manville. *To the Mountains by Rail*. Grahamsville, N.Y.: Wakefair Press, 1970.

Webster, Albert L. Reproduction of the log of the canal boat *Iowa* on the Delaware and Hudson Canal, September 7 to 23, 1891 in Webster, *Then and Now*. High Falls, N.Y.: D & H Canal Historical Society, December 4, 1971.

Yaffe, Ephraim. "The Leurenkill Farmers Start a Hebrew School." In *50 Golden Years: The Ellenville Hebrew Aid Society 1907–1957*, edited by Mrs. Ben Miller and Daniel S. Roher, 59. Ellenville, N.Y.: Ellenville Hebrew Aid Society, 1959.

Hotels and the Holocaust

Reuben Wallenrod

In the evening the casino becomes the center of Leo Halper's hotel in Brookville. The band plays, the young people dance, and the joyous sounds fill the grounds and the road. The casino hall is flooded with light and men and women seek one another, draw close to one another. The drum beats out the rhythm definitely, urgently; the violin doubts and prays, the saxophone sounds pour forth with vehemence and joy; and the piano sounds run beside them like little animals down the hill. . . . Men and women dance, separate for a short while and come close again; men and women are dancing in narrow circles: you and I; he and she; let us rush down together; what else is there besides our narrow circles? All these two or three hundred people, men and women dancing in one of the casinos in the Catskill mountains, these two or three hundred lives are nothing but little narrow circles, dancing their own dance, desiring only their own little desires, living their own little lives.

The heart knows well that there is another great wide, threatening world outside you, but you are afraid to stop your dancing and think of that world. Such knowledge may well break up the charm of the circle, it may well break up your very being, all of you. Outside there are lakes and woods and the moon is pouring soft light on the frightful distances, but your heart is afraid to look at all that.

Tomorrow you will go out of your circle and buy your newspaper, and you will read in it before eating your roast chicken about one hundred Jews that have died a frightful death. You will read about thirty girls who have been thrown into whorehouses, about towns full of memories that have been erased and are no more. If you let this news enter you, become a part of you, you will become insane. You will be no more, you will become one of them. Don't! For your own sake. Don't! Don't go out of your little circle. While in New York you keep away those terrible sounds and visions. You keep them away with the sounds of your machines, of your typewriters, with your bargaining, your laughter, your quarrelling. Now you have escaped to the Catskill mountains, try to keep those sounds away, through your rush for enjoyment, an excited nervous enjoyment. Close yourself up in your narrow circle, listen to the sounds of the band, to the sounds of the dancing people. Let all those terrible sounds and visions become just numbers; let the one hundred, the thirty become a mere statistical, visionless number, and you will not see the contorted faces of your tortured brethren, of the women dragged into whorehouses, of their strangled children.

They come, however, those people and stand before you. You see among them men and women you actually knew. You have known them with your eyes and you have known them in your imagination. And then they come separately, and distinctly, and at times they rush towards you as one terrible face, a frightened face.

Chase away all these visions and repeat to yourself that hundreds, that *thousands* of men and women were killed and are dead. Numbers will dispel your fear. Death also dispels fear.

The finality of death and the indifference of numbers will relieve you. Your calculation will reassure you and cheer you. The calculation is simple: so many Nazis in the world, so many people who are against the Nazis, and of course, "those bastards, those gangsters will be exterminated." Even your curses reassure you somewhat. That is, you feel now that you have done your part, you have cursed them. And now you may again return to your circle and follow the music. Again you hear the wild pommeling of the big drum and little drums, the triumphant tones and sudden passionate impatient ecstasy of the saxophone, the heavy self-satisfaction of the bass, and the little rushing broken sounds of the piano. But you can't run away. The visions and sounds blended into one terrible contorted face will beckon to you and admonish you.

The youngsters dance their new steps like young heifers with joyous jumping and animal enthusiasm, but fear is creeping into the hearts of their elders.

Leo Halper stands near the entrance to the casino. He comes from time to time to check up on the cleanliness of the hall, on the playing of the band, and to show the guests and the musicians that there is an eye that sees them. Besides, it is also necessary to keep an eye from time to time on the conduct of the various men and women who come to the hotel. Not that he wants to be a watch dog for their morals. He knows that people come to have a good time in the Catskills, otherwise they would not come here. Still, let them know that Halper sees. He knows what is going on in other hotels, and he will not allow that in Brookville. Not while he is here.

And while he is standing and watching, various thoughts come crowding each other. Here they are, Jewish boys and girls, dancing and enjoying themselves. And he is angry at his previous anger and resentment at them. Aren't the youngsters entitled to a little happiness? Are there many places left in the world where a Jewish boy and girl could have a bit of joy? Let them dance! Who knows what the morrow will bring?

Halper stands at the entrance to his casino and mumbles within himself: "Dance, youngsters, dance," but he knows that someone within him is protesting, and a sharp pain is awakened. It seems that every passing moment is strained and tense like those strings of the violin, that another moment and it may tear apart, and then all these boys and girls will suddenly stop their dancing, and their faces will blend in that terrible face of those that are far away.

Halper leaves the entrance to his casino and the sounds follow him into the summer night.

The Catskills at the End of World War II

Martin Boris

Douglas soaked, scrubbed, then polished the glasses until they shone brilliantly when stacked against the ceiling-to-floor window. The clear glasses caught the sun. He smiled at the sparkle and shine.

Andy had come in before him. In his favorite spot opposite the register, at his favorite angle, hovering over a cup of coffee the way Douglas was told he did over bourbon and soda at the Red Cat in Monticello before the war. A sip, a look out the window, up the street toward the bank and down where the sidewalk ended at the City Hall, then a puzzled stare into the cup, as if searching for something he might have dropped. Followed by the ritual of smoking. First a fresh pack of Luckies, square and white, with a red circle in the center. He tore a thin ribbon of cellophane around the top, ripped the corner off the roof, then coaxed out a cigarette by hammering the pack against his hand. He removed the cylinder, and tapped the loose cuts of tobacco into place against the tabletop. Next the magic of transferring the dormant fire in the match to a smoldering in the cigarette tip. He inhaled deeply while the smoke infused his blood, his lungs, his brain, then exhaled through funneled lips. Douglas wondered how much of a man's life was surrendered to the near-religious act of lighting a cigarette, start to finish, without even assessing the years stolen because of the poisons it contained. If George Seldes's newsletter *In Fact* were fact about the link between smoking and cancer.

Douglas remembered that the pre–Pearl Harbor Andy was a study in restless energy failing to be confined within the boundaries of a chicken farm. Despite a mother and a father to whom work was a religion Andy had spent endless hours foraging the countryside for attractive, easy women. Douglas admired that wild free look in Andy's eyes, that Lord Byron look, as he sped by in his Ford pick-up truck going to or coming from some fabulous adventure. Andy was small and stringy, with a curly head a little too large for his bantam-rooster body. When he stood straight his legs bowed as if bent by the weight of that oversized head.

Harry, never one to judge a man out in the open, said to Douglas at the time that he thought Andy had gone over the edge with Jed Parker's wife. Amelia Dooley, twenty-one, had married Jed, twice her age. Fear was the matchmaker. She wasn't pretty, she had no prospects and Jed worried himself into an ulcer about leaving the farm to the county, there being no more Parkers left. After a week of courtship he had married Amelia. During the next five childless years they had increasingly little to say to each other. Then one day Amelia moved into Monticello, leaving Jed a short businesslike note devoid of feeling or re-crimination. She took a job in Warren Senstacker's hardware store where Andy found her, ripe for picking. Some said she knew Andy before that, but Harry wasn't sure.

Douglas heard that Andy and Amelia entertained each other at her place, sometimes until four in the morning. Since no law was broken, neighbors in town could only express concern and indignation. Another time that would have been enough to send her scurrying back to the farm, but small-town censure had lost its bite by then and they were merely a gossip item for three months. Then Amelia upped and moved east someplace. Harry liked Jed Parker and blamed Andy for not returning her to the farm when the flame died.

Andy finally stirred his coffee. Without lifting his head he knew that he was being observed, scrutinized, judged by Douglas. The Strong kid with his distant yet worshipful eyes was waiting for him to do something spectacular. Andy felt the burden of being someone's idol. War had taught him that there were no idols, both captains and corporals had run like hell when the shrapnel exploded. He had once seen a major general vomit all over himself after a particularly bloody battle. He'd like to tell that to Douglas and sink his obvious case of hero worship. Dumb kid.

Andy looked at Douglas, who was freshening up the chicken salad with may-onnaise. He suddenly felt the need to say something to the boy.

"Do you remember how my grandfather used to walk, Douglas? Those short baby steps? As if each one was a small miracle?"

Douglas nodded.

"You know, sometimes a week goes by and it's like he never was, then sometimes he's so real that I could swear he's in the next room."

There were moments, too, when Douglas's memories of Zaida captured his present. Andy's summoning up of the old man stirred as well the sweet heavy scent of apple blossoms. In the air-conditioned luncheonette Douglas could swear he smelled apple blossoms. It was happening all over again and he could not believe how vivid the memories were.

A warm April afternoon long ago that hinted of abundant life and growth. All the trees sprouted green tips that became, on close examination, tight little fists of leaves. Douglas remembered wondering then why the dead couldn't also return to life every year, for a little while. His mother's death still cut like a thin knife when he thought of it. He remembered that times were bad and they couldn't even *give* the eggs away, then.

He recalled firing strikes at the apple trees with pebbles when Harry had come to tell him that it was time that he became a Jew.

"What do you mean become a Jew? I already am a Jew."

"You still have to become one."

"Even if I am one?"

"Even if."

"Would you explain that?"

"No. Nothing to explain."

"But I have baseball practice. The team needs me. It's an obligation."

Douglas had him there. As he learned both new words and Harry, he tried mixing intelligences. Harry was big on duty, morality, obligation.

"No," his father said.

Harry was short on explanation. The shorter the explanation the shorter the next argument.

"That's not right, Harry. I went to *shul* with you last Yom Kippur. Doesn't that make me a Jew?"

Harry walked toward him with one of his here-we-go-again looks.

"Yom Kippur wasn't for you. It was for me. My sins. You haven't been around long enough to have your own. Except for when you play these . . . games, but that's small potatoes."

"C'mon, Harry, what kind of sins could you have?"

But it wasn't all sham. It had never occurred to him that his father was composed of the same inferior material as the rest of mankind. Douglas continued to stare at his father, surprised at his own surprise. Thomas Jefferson owned slaves;

Babe Ruth could be traded to Boston when the Yankees decided that he was of no further use. It was that level of disenchantment.

"Do I have to become an American, too?"

"Not the same thing."

"Why? Tell me why."

"I got something else to do."

"Isn't this important, too? Just because you don't make any money from it . . ."

"You know, you're giving me a headache with this damn rube routine of yours. I'm too busy for games. Case closed. Personally it doesn't matter to me one way or the other, but I promised Stella, I promised your mother to have you bar mitzvahed. That should be enough. For both of us. You're going and you're going to do it with the least amount of noise. With *no* noise. From now on no discussion and no having fun at my expense. You want to resist, do it passively, like Mahatma Gandhi."

"Do I go there or does he come here?"

"You'll go there."

"Where is there?" Douglas asked. Now it was about ninety percent question and ten percent mosquito biting.

"Starting Monday and every day until it's over, except Saturday, you'll go up the road to the Foremans.' Go into the kitchen and ask for Ben's father-in-law. His name is Mr. Baum. Ask civilly, now, none of your intellectual card tricks. You'll also make sure you've washed up. I don't want you touching the books with dirty hands. You'll sit down with Zaida, that's what everyone calls him, and you do what he tells you. Simple. No fuss, no noise. Easy as cracking an egg. You do it until August and I won't bother you. About that."

"What about my chores?"

"You idiot, if I take you away from your chores then I *intend* to have them done for you. Give me credit for some intelligence."

Harry had an immobile gray face with gray eyes that could convince you that you just didn't exist and jet-black hair combed straight back in a no-nonsense fashion. A policeman's face or a bill collector's. When provoked it rubberized and became animated, unused blood vessels suddenly swelled and ran red. Douglas knew how to bring life to Harry's face but only at the risk of triggering his tongue. He hated his father the most when that happened.

Times like those he felt defeated, alone, worthless. It made him wonder if the sharp edges they faced each other with would have been rubbed smooth by now if his mother were the buffer between. They needed a translator and Stella spoke both their languages. Harry had been changed by her death. Douglas did not remember if Stella could move Harry. Maybe she might have convinced him that their son wasn't just another day laborer on the farm.

Genuinely surprised, he remembered saying to Harry, "I didn't know the old man was a rabbi."

"He's not."

"He's not? Then I guess he's a teacher of bar mitzvahs, if there's such a thing."

"No, he's not a teacher of anything. Just an old man, a very religious old man who happens to be handy. That's credentials enough for me."

Harry walked Douglas up the steep hill to the Foreman place. It was raining that day. Douglas was not prepared to begin. He needed sunshine to start new things. Harry wouldn't listen.

"So you're finally joining the flock," Ben said with a broad peasant grin that always infuriated Andy. "*Mazel tov.*"

Douglas looked at him vacantly.

"The Jewish people, the Jewish people, *boychik*," Ben added.

He's been with his chickens too long, Douglas thought, talking about flocks. And he wasn't joining anything, just submitting to Fascist pressure like the Czechs.

The house was old, older than anyone who was living in it, and like the elderly it had begun to bend into itself. The porch sagged in the middle and little puddles of water had formed there. The roof had buckled, too. In the rear, behind the parlor, was a large old-fashioned kitchen with the highest ceiling Douglas had ever seen. An enormous woodburning stove, like a metal dragon, covered the back wall. It breathed fire and belched smoke intermittently. He heard hissing and crackling noises escape from its bowels. Something strange and delicious was cooking on it.

The long wooden table and six chairs near the stove were simple and rough. Hanging from a fuzzy white cord, thumbtacked into a ceiling beam, was a circular staircase of flypaper. It, too, was in poor condition due to exposure to light, heat and the rigors of the previous winter.

Old Mr. Baum sat in the far corner of the room on a small bench that was bleached of all color. He was slumped over a nondescript table, his head supported by an arm, reading the Torah, his lips moving with an uneven regularity. The presence of visitors meant little to Zaida. Douglas looked out the window at the steady, perpendicular rain and knew that there would be difficulties.

"Zaida," his son-in-law called, the way you do to someone you wish to awaken without frightening. The old man turned up his hand like a traffic cop to silence yet hold Ben while he finished the page. Then he closed the book and looked at them. Douglas swore that the old man actually looked through, and past them as if they were clear glass statues of no particular merit.

He was short and shaped like a barrel. Possibly if he arched his back he could manage five feet. A yellowish shredded-wheat beard hung from his face like a shade on a window. Above it was a pair of eyes unlike anyone's he had ever seen before. Maybe once. His mother had taken him, long ago, to the Bronx Zoo, where he had watched a sick old elephant who had great difficulty in rising. An attendant told them that the animal was to be destroyed soon. She told Douglas that someday he might meet people who had eyes like the elephant and carried the pain of the world in them. He now looked into Zaida's eyes and knew what she meant.

Zaida finally stood up and seemed no taller. He and Ben spoke in a strange language Douglas thought was Yiddish.

"He says he'll be ready in a few minutes, he's got to take a leak," Ben said. "You should be so kind and wait."

"Would you ask him please if he might speak English," Douglas said when Zaida had managed a slow, laborious exit.

Ben shrugged. "Zaida speaks some nine languages. Can you imagine that, nine languages? Hebrew and Yiddish and Polish and Russian and German. A little Hungarian, too. I forget the rest, but English ain't one of them. I figured you knew."

Douglas thought he caught Harry looking a little puzzled for a second, the way the first American Indian might have looked when he felt the first Caucasian's bullet. No matter, Harry had quickly readjusted.

"No big deal," he said. "You're not here for polite conversation. Just get started and stick with it. That's how things get done."

Without looking, Zaida motioned him to sit down next to him with a short, flyswatting slap. Douglas complied cautiously, uncomfortably. The old man smelled of musty wood and mildewed rooms, of dried tobacco and deeply ingrained sweat. His beard had indistinct particles trapped in its mesh. Under a maroon sweater that had begun unraveling a long time ago at the cuffs he wore suspenders. Douglas saw the outline of the buckles on each side like tiny square breasts.

Shifting his weight to one side Zaida dug an amputated stub of a pencil from his pocket. It was pointless and withered with age—like the crap he's going to make me learn, Douglas thought. As if unused to writing, Zaida smothered the pencil with stumpy, nicotined fingers. He turned to the end of the book which was its beginning and fell on a small group of mysterious symbols that bore no relationship to any of the twenty-six letters in Douglas's alphabet.

"*Baruch,*" Zaida growled, and it could have come from some wounded animal deep within its lair.

"Pardon me?"

The old man repeated the growl and tapped impatiently waiting for its echo.

"*Baruch?*" Douglas replied, disoriented. He couldn't see how the old man could get *that* sound from *those* symbols.

Zaida advanced to the next cluster, showing neither satisfaction nor disappointment in his pupil. Showing nothing.

"*Attoy.*"

"*Attoy,*" Douglas repeated shakily. He lifted his head when something flew across the corner of his eye.

Andy strode into the kitchen without the basic salutations and sat in a rocking chair next to the stove. He opened a book of crossword puzzles, then got up to fill his Parker pen from a hexagonal bottle of ink in the cupboard. After finding the right puzzle he settled back comfortably in the rocker and threw a nod in Douglas's direction, which Douglas quickly snapped up and returned.

"*Baruch,*" Zaida grunted when those symbols reappeared again, which Douglas failed to recognize and felt stupid about.

"*Baruch*—that's a six-letter word meaning blessing, which the next few months ain't going to be," Andy volunteered from his place by the fire. He chuckled and reburied himself in the puzzle.

The old man ignored the chuckler. He continued to point and growl—sometimes waiting a second for Douglas to return the growl, sometimes not. But the pattern was clearly established that first day. Either Douglas would follow closely or he would fall hopelessly behind.

The first session depressed Douglas. His eyes thumped and he had a nauseous headache. It was education by echo, religion by rote. It was neither education nor religion, but it elated him, too, because Andy was there to witness the stupidity of it all even though he expressed his opinions to no particular audience. They were brothers, now, so to speak.

As one day dissolved into the next Douglas repeated the words of Moses and Solomon, Joseph and Isaac, not knowing what they meant or who had said them. And forgot even the simplest of phrases. Yet Zaida plowed on unaffected by his student's gross failures or small successes, when, at last, a few did come. He never turned back to look.

Andy snickered, hooted and peppered with buckshot every chance he could from across the huge kitchen. Unruffled, with four thousand years of patience,

Zaida moved his pencil across the pages that were on the verge of disintegration through age and use. Douglas remembered wondering, that last spring before the war, why the old man kept silent, as Andy's steady barrage of abuse grew more intense, its dispenser more animated, more involved. It took little intelligence to realize that it was no mere coincidence that Andy was in the rocker while Douglas studied with Zaida. And if Douglas knew, then surely the old man must know that his grandson was not sending him bouquets even if he spoke none of Zaida's nine languages. But it never varied, those two hours a day, listening to Andy's undirected atheism, watching Zaida's indifference.

"God, and I use the word the way I use 'shit,' is this boring! How can anyone stand it? And from *him*? How do you drill it into his thick head that there is no God? God is a cartoon character the capitalists invented to entertain and police the masses. At least those idiot Reds are right about that. Now look at this damned fool. He pissed his whole life away on a book of fairy tales. Just like they expect me to piss away my whole life on a two-by-nothing chicken farm. I'll be goddamned if I will. First chance I get it's up and out. Anyplace, anywhere but here."

Douglas decided that it was exciting to watch and see how much the old man could take before he would finally react. He was constantly braced for a clap of thunder or a bolt of lightning from a God they both denied since Zaida refused to defend himself or how he spent his life.

Nothing happened. It was all so strange. Yet something was occurring that he did not understand, like a card game in which he was the dummy. Neither of them spoke to him, but bar-mitzvah lesson aside, he was providing some twisted, arcane line of communication between a bearded lunatic and a ranting, raving maniac. And after August the two of them would probably never sit in the same room again. If that blessed month ever arrived.

The lessons continued, however, in the same manner, day after day. April and May vanished easily enough, but June was tough on Douglas. So many things to do. Yet, despite the lack of time and weeks of wet weather he had perfected a curve ball that would give Ted Williams nightmares. Douglas was anxious to hold the stitching and slice down hard, then watch the ball act crazy as it nicked the strike zone of the makeshift batters' cage he had set up behind the coal shed. Zaida would never understand why he fidgeted on the smooth bench, suffering each minute away from the pitcher's mound.

"*Boray, p'ree, ha-gofen,*" Zaida said, completing the prayer over wine.

And that triggered Andy. He threw his Parker against the stove, the writing tool separating into its component parts. The tubular rubber well sizzled on the iron monster that raged even though it was June. First the odor of burning rubber, then the hiss of the ink as it evaporated in little puffs of blue smoke. The words flew from Andy's mouth as if someone were inside throwing them out.

"What a dumb old man. Not just dumb, stupid. Dumb you can outgrow. Stupid is for life. To sit and read that damned gibberish all day and smoke those stinking cigars after. And where the hell does it get him? A moron, a nitwit. Oh, God, if anyone is up there, strike me dead right now if this is what I've got to look forward to. Even hell is better than stealing eggs from under chickens' asses."

Andy stood up from his chair and choked the thin arms of the rocker, a little more bowlegged than usual. He looked as if he felt awkward, like standing in a crowd while everyone else was seated. He sat down, too, and stared at the stove.

And that triggered Douglas, that and the airless, heated kitchen, compounded by Zaida's gruff monotone.

"Goddamn you, old man, let me alone. Stop torturing me. I can't wait until you're the hell out of my life."

After Douglas had finished he realized that he was doing the shouting and not Andy. He grew dizzy, glanced at Zaida's face and tried to read it as he never had during Andy's wildest assaults. The old man looked at him with elephant eyes, narrowing one of them. It happened so fast that it almost didn't happen at all. Zaida quickly returned to the page.

Instead of returning there, too, Douglas looked at Andy. He expected a big-brotherly smile, a secret signal of acceptance in their exclusive society of atheists and shakers of authority's rotten foundation. It shook Douglas when Andy rose slowly, was about to say something, hesitated and walked to them. Looking concerned, Andy placed his hand on Zaida's shoulder. Without glancing up the old man patted Andy's hand and continued the lesson. The boy, confused, sought answers in Andy's face.

"Kid, you ever do that again and I'll kick your ass out of here so fast it'll take a week for the rest of you to catch up."

Andy's jaw looked as if it had been nailed shut and his eyes raked Douglas with the kind of intensity that might melt cast iron. There were no further outbursts from either end of the room for the rest of the summer.

Arlene took her seat on the high wooden chair close to the register. She sent Douglas a cold-fish stare that evaporated his reverie. He grew busier. Eggshells he had saved were the first thing he threw into a fresh coffee urn. They absorbed the fusel oil that gave coffee its bitter taste. It was one of Phil's secrets that he shared with his protégé.

This time Andy took a prune danish with a fresh cup from the fresh urn, and traded glances with Arlene, slowly, carefully. She looked for Douglas's eyes before submitting to Andy's. Slowly she crossed and uncrossed her legs while sending the tip of her tongue along her upper lip. Douglas ignored everything while Andy, drinking her all in, missed nothing.

It became busy in the store but Andy was oblivious to the afternoon crowd. He had retreated into the sanctuary of himself.

It was almost nostalgic for Andy to sort things out, to piece together internal and external history and remember how it was politically in Sullivan County before the Japs attacked. A time of clean and simple issues. Capitalism was corrupt and in an advanced state of decay; labor was saintly. Every liberal worth the price of the *Nation* knew that the South was one big lynch mob and only the Soviet Union held high the beacon of freedom and democracy in the world. It was so deceptively simple then that he must have been simple-minded not to doubt it. Politics and simplicities—they never really go hand in hand.

He remembered how his across-the-road neighbors, the Ostermans, had shaped his thoughts at the beginning of the forties. Nice people, most thought. Lilly and Paul Osterman raised eggs, like everyone else, to survive, but they practiced Marxism to live. Country Marxists are different from city Marxists, Andy soon learned. The urban variety were sharp-tongued, strident. They moved at a rapid pace. They were always having meetings, strike committees, protests, fund-raising rallies; they had little time for nonsense. Their country cousins, Lil and Paul, were the friendly smile, sit-awhile-and-have-a-cup-of-coffee, what-do-you-think-of-the-rotten-weather kind of Marxists. They oozed friendliness the way maple trees exude sap in the spring. And they caught flies by the droves—himself, Douglas, and the top ten percent of the high school graduating class. Meetings at their house were always large, noisy affairs. Glasses clinking, a fire eating up pine knots, voices warm and friendly. Hayseed politics. Who's who in Sullivan County and nobody important queuing up for Lilly's deep-dish apple pie which was always prelude to supporting the Abraham Lincoln Brigade—those American idealists who fought the Fascists in Spain—or the setting up of a committee to organize the steam laundry or the hotel workers, or some other neglected group.

The Ostermans probably thought they had struck oil with him. He remembered brooding, being noticeably dissatisfied. And he was already going out with

Delilah O'Brien, one of the colored girls who emptied the giant tumblers at the laundry. It was a baby step in Lilly's lithe and seductive mind from sleeping with Delilah to the struggle for racial equality.

They stuffed him with literature as if he were a Sunday roaster. The Ostermans had Moscow-leaning pamphlets on every conceivable subject: *Farm Cooperatives in the Soviet Union, Sex—The Leninist View, Hollywood and Fascism, The Hoax of the New Deal, The Capitalist Exploitation of Motherhood.* Andy wondered if there was a Marxist-Leninist way to move his bowels.

One Friday night, after a most difficult soiree, during which the patently simple had suddenly grown complex, hosts and guest mutually decided to give each other up. With malice and forethought Andy asked the smiling, well-fed, well-liquored audience of doctors, students, Negroes and housewives the definition of an act whereby two countries agree to divvy a third one situated between them. Before being shouted down he asked if they saw Comrade Molotov of the U.S.S.R. shaking hands with Von Ribbentrop, Hitler's Foreign Minister, in this morning's *Times*, both grinning like well-fed wolves.

"Obstructionist," Paul screamed, spilling good Scotch on the couch, when he realized that Andy was rubbing their noses in the Russo-German Pact of 1939 that made a doormat of Poland.

"Opportunist," a young woman shouted, whom Andy remembered from a Sunday picnic where she had openly nursed a baby.

Those two words were among the harshest in the Marxist lexicon, Andy knew, signaling his expulsion from a society in which he had never felt comfortable, anyway. He would just have to find something else to do with his Friday nights. A shame, he was making excellent progress with Lilly's sister, a ravishing brunette he felt had been especially conscripted to keep his interest in Socialism high. But they were so smug, so sure that they had all the answers, so willing to bend when the breezes from Moscow blew. He just had to tweak noses. Looking back Andy realized that that night was the high point and the end of his political life.

Afterward he still signed petitions and donated small amounts, selectively, to Lilly, who took with a seductive smile. But he also bought Girl Scout cookies without feeling committed to their cause either.

From the enormous distance of the four war years Andy realized that after the Ostermans he had narrowed his sights. He had given up searching for large, powerful enemies in Washington, in corporate boardrooms, in foreign capitals, and settled for three at arm's reach. Until the day he was drafted he believed that all that was wrong with the world lived in his father, his mother and his grandfather.

There was plenty of evidence. His father, Ben, an elfish man who gave Andy his size and shape, had a blindly cheerful disposition that condemned him.

"So what? A hunnert years from now it won't mean borscht."

Translated that meant let it all pass: your life, your mind, your ambition. The hell with bettering yourself, getting the chickenshit off your shoes. Stay and get buried alive.

And Momma. The cow, he called her. She always wore her hair in a bun that came to a point. One of two answers to anything. Often chosen at random. Both totally unacceptable.

"It'll be all right. You'll see, you'll see."

Her second answer was performed in pantomime, a shrug of the shoulders with eyes closed, that infuriating thousand-year-old *shtetl* answer of resignation to whatever happened. To starvation and the sweep of a Cossack's sword. To the torch of the Inquisition and fixed quotas for Jews in medical schools. She alternated dumb optimism with stupid body motions. Andy wanted more than that. This was 1941, the Fascists owned half the world; the other portion was in an uproar and he wanted more than one-night stands and discontented wives in awkward places.

But Zaida, his grandfather, received the most abuse in Andy's post-Osterman days. Zaida was the triumph of religion over life, of the past over the present. He was the supreme example of what happens when one fraction of human experience rises up to smother all the others. Like the Bolsheviks in Russia, like the Catholic Church during the Dark Ages. Zaida had a long beard, wore dirty clothes and carried an Old Testament that appeared to be more an extension of his left hand than an artifact. Saints breed more misery than sinners, which is probably why many of them are martyred. Andy was unable then to forgive Zaida his saintliness.

As exorcism, when Zaida walked the two miles to a *shul* that he often prayed in alone, Andy recalled racing up and down the road with Delilah in the truck and waving vigorously to the old man. Zaida had ignored them as he inched home. When he had finally reached the farm and sat on the porch reading the *Rambam*, a cube of sugar between his molars, sipping hot tea from a glass, Andy had forty-miled it up the driveway, slammed on the brakes and leaped out of the cab like a lunatic, and bolted the steps to his room to change his perfectly clean shirt. While Zaida read and calmly sipped his steaming tea.

Then Delilah would honk three or four times and Andy would perform the same act again down the steps and off the porch. Both he and Delilah laughed when he popped into the cab of the truck, rocketed out of the driveway and disappeared in a cloud of dust and smoke. While Zaida had never taken his eyes off the page or spilled a drop.

Andy went to war the first week of the new year. The Selective Service Board, composed of a group of townspeople too old to fight, decreed that the farm could carry on without him. Andy was overjoyed. This answered prayers for a way out. He had a clear picture in his mind of mock-saluting Douglas from the bus and grinning at him before they pulled out for Fort Dix. Almost four years later he returned, wondering why he had been so anxious to go. It was hardly worth the trip, personally, except for liberating the concentration camps. That made the difference. That was the part of the war that changed him.

Zaida died while he was in England practicing for D-Day, Momma the week his platoon broke out of a German trap at Saint-Lô and Ben when they marched into Aachen. He attended none of the funerals, there being greater need for his presence elsewhere.

By 1946 his restlessness and anger were gone the way some allergies disappear by adolescence. Andy did not attach a label to it. Seeing men die in combat and fleeing civilians cut down in error were explainable things, but Bergen-Belsen and Buchenwald were something else. A whole race, his, scientifically blueprinted for extermination because of some mad theory of inferiority. Contemplating that dwarfed all his ambitions, his drive, his restlessness. A general contentment to leave things as they were replaced it. Psychic paralysis, a clever friend said. He returned home and was glad to be there, happy to raise chickens and watch the seasons change. He often thought of Zaida and had his regrets. Those were his bad days. He wore the old man's sweater with the protruding suspender marks when it was cold and didn't mind the winds at all.

Andy was low on cigarettes and that gave him the excuse to approach the register without being obvious. Arlene saw him on his collision course with her and with birdlike glances quickly took measure of the store to see where Douglas and Phil stood and if they were watching.

"Something you want?" she asked him.

"How can you say that with a straight face?" he asked.

"I mean now," she said, suppressing the urge to smile.

"Now, yesterday, tomorrow—the answer's the same."

"You're making it difficult for me, Andy," she said.

"That's the *last* thing I want to do. Give me a pack of Luckies," he sighed, "and I'll get out of your hair."

"Don't go too far," she answered and handed him his change.

Part 2

BOARDING HOUSE, BUNGALOW, AND KUCHALAYN LIFE

Breezy Corners, Kiamesha Lake (above) and Five Star Cottages, Monticello (below). Two operating bungalow colonies that began as kuchalayns, 2000. The large building in each of these colonies is evidence of the earlier kuchalayn building.
PHIL BROWN

Shandalee Camp, Livingston Manor.

Boris Colony Club, Glen Wild. Martin Boris grew up on his parents' colony and got much of the material there for his book *Woodridge, 1946*.

A bungalow colony handball court overgrown with vines, 1998. Such overgrown courts
and swimming pools are common archaeological relics on the roads of the Catskills.
PHIL BROWN

Kolel Tartikov Bungalows, Thompsonville,
1998. This is one of the few orthodox
bungalow colonies that tell you what the
original name was.
PHIL BROWN

Most Catskills resorts were modest in the early days, with only a few large hotels. The familial nature of the Catskills experience was cemented in the farm/ boarding house that was an extension of a home. When boarding houses expanded into kuchalayns and bungalow colonies, they provided a milieu where people were together the entire summer, forming very close connections and a very interesting minisociety. In the kuchalayn, you rented a room and got shared cooking and eating privileges in the kitchen and dining room. In a bungalow colony, you rented a whole building, small as it usually was, and had your own privacy for cooking and eating. Some places were hybrids of both types. By the 1950s few kuchalayns remained, though many would refer to bungalow colonies as kuchalayns, even if the characterization was not accurate.

Isaac Bashevis Singer's short story, "The Yearning Heifer," is an autobiographical tale of Singer's foray to a Catskill farm in search of a quiet place to write. Rather than finding a farmhouse eager to take in boarders, Singer's character encounters a surly farmer whose wife is angry that he placed an advertisement in the paper. Singer's story illustrates the primitive conditions in which an early twentieth-century farm family lived, the relations between Jewish and Gentile farmers, and developing friendship between the boarder and his or her "farmer," as boarding house and kuchalayn renters often referred to their proprietors, even if they were no longer actively engaged in farming.

Martin Boris read from his *Woodridge 1946* (an excerpt appears in the prior section) at an early History of the Catskills Conference, and he became interested in a particularly fascinating local bungalow colony a mile down the same road, long since closed. "Grine Felder—A Place in the Country" is the outcome of Boris's research into the Yiddishist and arts-oriented colony that Isaac Bashevis Singer visited on occasion. This essay shows the importance of the arts for certain resorts. While most bungalow colonies were not so cultured, there was a tradition of high culture in a minority of colonies and hotels. The significance of the Yiddish language, seen in Grine Felder, was very widespread in the Catskills, especially before World War II.

Thane Rosenbaum has only one piece on the Catskills, "Bingo by the Bungalow," in his collection *Elijah Visible*, which he read at one of the History of the Catskills Conferences. It portrays the intimacy of daily bungalow colony life through Adam Posner, growing up the child of Holocaust survivors. At Cohen's Summer Cottages in Kiamesha Lake, Adam is the only child in the colony; his mother is a bingo addict, looking for the small tsotchkes from her own and adjoining colonies, and for the mammoth $200 Labor Day jackpot. The omnipresent doom and tragedy of the survivor shows up—Adam suffers a compound fracture learning to play baseball, and his father's heart condition puts him in the hospital at the same time. The communal caretaking by the colony residents reminds us of this important element of bungalow life. A rainstorm washes out the bingo game, though Adam needs only one more number to fill his card. As in Rosenbaum's other stories, deliverance at the end just doesn't come—we are still waiting for Elijah, for peace. And like other writers of Catskills fiction, Rosenbaum has his protagonist come back as a father, with his own boy, to scour the ruins of the colony.

Irwin Richman's "Bungalow Colony Life" comes from his definitive work on the topic, *Borscht Belt Bungalows*. Not only did Richman grow up on his family's colony, but he later worked as counselor and camp director in other colonies; his grandfather provided mortgages to many others. This selection details many of the activities in which bungalow dwellers engaged and demonstrates their close connectedness.

Arthur Tanney's "Bungalow Stories" was originally written for an Internet discussion group, and later published on the Catskills Institute Web site and read at two of the History of the Catskills Conferences. They are very moving reminiscences of Tanney's many summers living in colonies, both as a child and later as an adult with his own family. Tanney shows how significant some of the most ordinary activities and experiences of bungalow life were for the inhabitants.

The Yearning Heifer

Isaac Bashevis Singer

In those days I could find great bargains in the small advertisements in my Yiddish press newspaper. I was in need of them because I earned less than twelve dollars a week—my royalties for a weekly column of "facts" gleaned from magazines. For example: a turtle can live five hundred years; a Harvard professor published a dictionary of the language spoken by chimpanzees; Columbus was not trying to discover a route to the Indies but to find the Ten Lost Tribes of Israel.

It was during the summer of 1938. I lived in a furnished room on the fourth floor of a walk-up building. My window faced a blank wall. This particular advertisement read: "A room on a farm with food, ten dollars weekly." After having broken with my girl friend Dosha "forever," I had no reason to spend the summer in New York. I packed a large valise with my meager belongings, many pencils as well as the books and magazines from which I extracted my information, and took the Catskill Mountain bus to Mountaindale. From there I was supposed to phone the farm. My valise would not close and I had bound it together with many shoelaces which I had purchased from blind beggars. I took the 8 A.M. bus and arrived in the village at three o'clock in the afternoon. In the local stationery store I tried to make the phone call but could not get connected and lost three dimes. The first time I got the wrong number; the second time the phone began to whistle and kept on whistling for minutes. The third time I may have gotten the right number but no one answered. The dimes did not come back. I decided to take a taxi.

When I showed the driver the address, he knitted his brows and shook his head. After a while he said, "I think I know where it is." And he immediately began to drive with angry speed over the narrow road full of ditches and holes. According to the advertisement, the farm was situated five miles from the village, but he kept on driving for half an hour and it became clear to me that he was lost. There was no one to ask. I had never imagined that New York State had such uninhabited areas. Here and there we passed a burned-down house, a silo which appeared unused for many years. A hotel with boarded windows emerged from nowhere and vanished like a phantom. The grass and brambles grew wild. Bevies of crows flew around croaking. The taxi meter ticked loudly and with feverish rapidity. Every few seconds I touched the trouser pocket where I kept my money. I wanted to tell the driver that I could not afford to drive around without an aim over heather and through deserts, but I knew that he would scold me. He might even drop me off in the middle of the wilderness. He kept on grumbling and every few minutes I heard him say, "Sonofabitch."

When, after long twisting and turning, the taxi did arrive at the correct address, I knew that I had made a bad mistake. There was no sign of a farm, just an old ruined wooden house. I paid four dollars and seventy cents for the trip and I tipped him thirty cents. The driver cast a murderous look at me. I barely had time to remove my valise before he started up and shot away with suicidal speed. No one came out to meet me. I heard a cow bellowing. As a rule, a cow bellows a few times and then becomes silent, but this cow bellowed without ceasing and in the tone of a creature which has fallen into an insufferable trap. I opened a door into a room with an iron stove, an unmade bed with dirty linen, a torn sofa. Against a peeling wall stood sacks of hay and feed. On the table were a few reddish eggs with hen's dirt still stuck to them. From another room came a dark-skinned girl with a long nose, a fleshy mouth, and angry black eyes beneath thick brows. A faint black fuzz grew on her upper lip. Her hair was cut short. If she hadn't been wearing a shabby skirt, I would have taken her for a man.

"What do you want?" she asked me in a harsh voice.

I showed her the advertisement. She gave a single glance at the newspaper and said, "My father is crazy. We don't have any rooms and board, and not for this price either."

"What is the price?"

"We don't need any boarders. There is no one to cook for them."

"Why does the cow keep on screaming?" I asked.

The girl appraised me from head to foot. "That is none of your business."

A woman entered who could have been fifty-five, sixty, or sixty-five years old. She was small, broad, one shoulder higher than the other, with a huge bosom which reached to her belly. She wore tattered men's slippers, her head was wrapped in a kerchief. Below her uneven skirt I could see legs with varicose veins. Even though it was a hot summer day she had a torn sweater on. Her slanted eyes were those of a Tartar. She gazed at me with sly satisfaction as if my coming there was the result of a practical joke. "From the paper, huh, aren't you?"

"Yes."

"Tell my husband to make a fool of himself instead of others. We don't need boarders. We need them like a hole in the head."

"I told him the same thing," the girl added.

"I am sorry but I got here with a taxi and it has gone back to the village. Perhaps I could stay for one night?"

"One night, huh? We have for you neither a bed nor linen. Nothing," the woman said. "If you like, I will call you another taxi. My husband is not in his right mind and he does everything for spite. He dragged us out here. He wanted to be a farmer. There is no store or hotel here for miles and I don't have the strength to cook for you. We ourselves eat out of tin cans."

The cow did not stop bellowing, and although the girl had just given me a nasty answer, I could not restrain myself and I asked, "What's the matter with the cow?"

The woman winked at the girl. "She needs a bull."

At that moment the farmer came in, as small and broad-boned as his wife, in patched overalls, a jacket which reminded me of Poland, and a cap pushed back on his head. His sunburned cheeks sprouted white stubble. His nose was veined. He had a loose double chin. He brought in with him the smells of cow dung, fresh milk from the udder, and newly dug earth. In one hand he held a spade and, in the other, a stick. His eyes under bushy brows were yellow. When he saw me he asked, "From the paper, huh?"

"Yes."

"Why didn't you call? I would have come with my horse and buggy to meet you."

"Sam, don't make a fool of the young man," his wife interrupted. "There's no linen for him, no one to cook for him, and what are ten dollars a week? It would cost us more."

"This leave to me," the farmer answered. "I have advertised, not you, and I am responsible. Young man"—he raised his voice—"I am the boss, not they. It's my house, my ground. Everything you see here belongs to me. You should have written a card first or phoned, but since you are here, you are a welcome guest."

"I am sorry, but your wife and your daughter—"

The farmer didn't let me finish. "What they say is not worth more than the dirt under my nails [he showed me a hand with muddy fingers]. I will clean up your room. I will make your bed, cook your food, and provide you with everything. If you receive mail I will bring it to you from the village. I go there every second or third day."

"Meanwhile, perhaps I can sleep here tonight? I'm tired from the trip and—"

"Feel at home. They have nothing to say." The farmer pointed at his family. I had already realized that I had fallen into a quarrelsome house and I did not intend to be the victim. The farmer continued, "Come, I will show you your room."

"Sam, the young man won't stay here," his wife said.

"He will stay here, eat here, and be satisfied," the farmer replied, "and if you don't like it, go back to Orchard Street together with your daughter. Parasites, pigs, *paskudas!*"

The farmer put the spade and the stick into a corner, grabbed my valise, and went outside. My room had a separate entrance with its own flight of stairs. I saw a huge field overgrown with weeds. Near the house was a well and an outhouse like in a Polish shtetl. A bedraggled horse was nibbling on some grass. Farther away there was a stable, and from it came the plaintive cry of the animal, which had not stopped in all this time. I said to the farmer, "If your cow is in heat, why doesn't she get what she needs?"

"Who told you that she's in heat? It is a heifer and I just bought her. She was taken from a stable where there were thirty other cows and she misses them. She most probably has a mother or a sister there."

"I've never seen an animal that yearns so much for her kin," I said.

"There are all kinds of animals, but she will quiet down. She's not going to yell forever."

2

The steps leading into my room squeaked. One held on to a thick rope instead of a banister. The room smelled of rotting wood and bedbug spray. A stained, lumpy mattress with the filling sticking out of the holes was on the bed. It wasn't especially hot outside but inside the room the heat immediately began to hammer at my head and I became wet with perspiration. Well, one night here will not kill me, I comforted myself. The farmer set my valise down and went to bring linen. He brought a pillow in a torn pillowcase, a coarse sheet with rusty spots, and a cotton-filled blanket without a cover. He said to me, "It's warm now, but the moment the sun sets, it will be deliciously cool. Later on you will have to cover yourself."

"It will be all right."

"Are you from New York?" he asked me.

"Yes, New York."

"I can tell from your accent that you were born in Poland. What part do you come from?"

I mentioned the name of my village and Sam told me he came from a neighboring village. He said, "I'm not really a farmer. This is our second summer here in the country. Since I came from Poland I was a presser in New York. I pulled and pushed the heavy iron so long that I got a rupture. I always longed for fresh air and, how do you call it—Mother Earth—fresh vegetables, a fresh egg, green grass. I began to look for something in the newspapers and here I found a wild bargain. I bought it from the same man who sold me the heifer. He lives about three miles from here. A fine man, even though he's a Gentile. His name is Parker, John Parker. He gave me a mortgage and made everything easy for me, but the house is old and the earth is full of rocks. He did not, God forbid, fool me. He told me everything beforehand. To clean up the stones would take twenty years. And I'm not a young man any more. I'm already over seventy."

"You don't look it," I complimented him.

"It's the good air, the work. I worked hard in New York, but only here I started to work for real. There we have a union, it should live long, and it did not allow the bosses to make us slaves like the Jews in Egypt. When I arrived in America, the sweatshops were still in existence, but later on things got easier. I worked my eight hours and took the subway home. Here I toil eighteen hours a day and, believe me, if I did not get the pension from the union I could not make ends meet. But it's all right. What do we need here? We have our own tomatoes, radishes, cucumbers. We have a cow, a horse, a few chickens. The air itself makes you healthy. But how is it written in Rashi? Jacob wanted to enjoy peace but the misfortune with Joseph would not allow it. Yes, I studied once; until I was seventeen I sat in the study house and learned. Why do I tell you this? My wife, Bessie, hates the country. She misses the bargains on Orchard Street and her cronies with whom she could babble and play cards. She's waging war on me. And what a war! She went on strike. She doesn't cook, she doesn't bake, she doesn't clean the house. She refuses to budge and I do everything—milk the cow, dig in the garden, clean the outhouse. I should not tell you, but she refuses to be a wife. She wants me to move back to New York. But what will I do in New York? We have given up the rent-controlled apartment and gotten rid of the furniture. Here we have something like a home—"

"How about your daughter?"

"My Sylvia takes after her mother. She's already over thirty and she should have gotten married, but she never wanted to become anything. We tried to send her to college and she refused to study. She took all kinds of jobs but she never stuck with them. She has quite a good head, but no *sitzfleisch*. She tires of everything. She went out with all kinds of men and it always ended in nothing. The moment she meets one, she immediately begins to find fault with him. One is this way, the other one is that way. For the past eight months she's been with us on the farm, and if you think she helps me much, you are mistaken. She plays cards with her mother. That's all she does. You will not believe me, but my wife still has not unpacked her things. She has, God only knows, how many dresses and skirts, and everything is packed away like after a fire. My daughter, too, has a lot of rags but hers are also in her trunk. All this is to spite me. So I decided, Let some people move in here and I will have someone to talk to. We have two other rooms to rent. I'm not trying to get rich by offering a room and three meals a day for ten dollars weekly. I won't become a Rockefeller. What is your business? Are you a teacher or something?"

After some hesitation I decided to tell him the truth, that I write for a Yiddish newspaper as a free-lancer. The man's eyes immediately lit up.

"What is your name? What do you write there?"

"*A Bundle of Facts.*"

The farmer spread out his arms and stamped his feet. "You are the writer of *A Bundle of Facts?*"

"It's me."

"My God, I read you every week! I go to the village Friday especially to get the paper, and you won't believe me, but I read *A Bundle of Facts* before I even read the news. The news is all bad. Hitler this, Hitler that. He should burn like a fire, the bum, the no-good. What does he want from the Jews? Is it their fault that Germany lost the war? From just reading about it one could get a heart attack. But your facts are knowledge, science. Is it true that a fly has thousands of eyes?"

"Yes, it's true."

"How can it be? Why does a fly need so many eyes?"

"It seems that to nature everything comes easy."

"If you want to see the beauty of nature, stay here. Wait a minute. I must go and tell my wife who we have here."

"What for? I'm not going to stay here anyhow."

"What are you saying? Why not? They are bitter women, but when they hear who you are, they will be overjoyed. My wife reads you too. She tears the paper out of my hand because she wants to read *A Bundle of Facts* first. My daughter also knows Yiddish. She spoke Yiddish before she knew a word of English. With us she speaks mostly Yiddish because—"

The farmer dashed out. His heavy shoes pounded on the steps. The heifer kept howling. There was frenzy in her voice, an almost-human rebellion. I sat down on the mattress and dropped my head. Lately I had been committing one folly after another. I had quarreled with Dosha over a foolishness. I had already spent money to get here and tomorrow I would have to take a taxi and a bus to get back to New York. I had begun to write a novel but I got bogged down and I couldn't even decipher my own scribbling. As I sat here, the heat roasted my body. If only there were a shade to cover the window! The heifer's lamenting drove me mad. I heard in it the despair of everything that lives. All of creation was protesting through her. A wild idea ran through my mind: Perhaps during the night I should go out and kill the heifer and then myself. A murder followed by a suicide like this would be something new in the history of humanity.

I heard heavy steps on the staircase. The farmer had brought his wife over. Then began the apologies and the strange exaggerations of simple people when they encounter their beloved writer. Bessie exclaimed, "Sam, I must kiss him."

And before I managed to say a word, the woman caught my face in her rough hands, which smelled of onion, garlic, and sweat.

The farmer was saying good-naturedly, "A stranger she kisses and me she lets fast."

"You are crazy and he's a scientist, greater than a professor."

It took but a minute and the daughter came up. She stood in the open door and looked on half mockingly at the way her parents fussed over me. After a while she said, "If I have insulted you, excuse me. My father brought us here to the wasteland. We have no car and his horse is half dead. Suddenly a man with a valise drops from the sky and wants to know why the heifer is yelling. Really funny."

Sam clasped his hands together with the look of a man about to announce something which will astound everyone. His eyes filled with laughter. "If you have so much pity on animals, I am going to give back the heifer. We can do without her. Let her go back to her mother, for whom she pines."

Bessie tilted her head to one side. "John Parker won't give you back the money."

"If he won't return the whole amount, he will return ten dollars less. It's a healthy heifer."

"I will make up the difference," I said, astonished at my own words.

"What? We will not go to court," the farmer said. "I want this man in my house all summer. He won't have to pay me. For me it will be an honor and a joy."

"Really, the man is crazy. We needed the heifer like a hole in the head."

I could see that husband and wife were making peace because of me.

"If you really want to do it, why wait?" I asked. "The animal may die from yearning and then—"

"He's right," the farmer called. "I'm going to take the heifer back right now. This very minute."

Everyone became silent. As if the heifer knew that her fate was being decided this minute, she let out a howl which made me shudder. This wasn't a yearning heifer but a dybbuk.

3

The moment Sam entered the stable the heifer became quiet. It was a black heifer with large ears and huge black eyes that expressed a wisdom which only animals possess. There was no sign that she had just gone through so many hours of agony. Sam tied a rope around her neck and she followed him willingly. I followed behind with Bessie near me. The daughter stood in front of the house and said, "Really, I wouldn't believe it if I hadn't seen it with my own eyes."

We walked along and the heifer did not utter a sound. She seemed to know the way back because she tried to run and Sam had to restrain her. Meanwhile, husband and wife argued before me the way couples used to argue when they came to my father's court for a Din Torah. Bessie was saying, "The ruin stood empty for years and nobody even looked at it. I don't think someone would have taken it for nothing. Suddenly my husband appears and gets the bargain. How does the saying go? 'When a fool comes to the market, the merchants are happy.'"

"What did you have on Orchard Street? The air stank. As soon as daylight began, the crash and noise started. Our apartment was broken into. Here you don't have to lock the door. We can leave for days and weeks and no one will steal anything."

"What thief would come to such a desert?" Bessie asked. "And what could he take? American thieves are choosy. They want either money or diamonds."

"Believe me, Bessie, here you will live twenty years longer."

"Who wants to live so long? When a day is over, I thank God."

After about an hour and a half I saw John Parker's farm—the house, the granary. The heifer again tried to run and Sam had to hold her back with all his strength. John Parker was cutting grass with a crooked scythe. He was tall, blond, lean, Anglo-Saxon. He raised his eyes, amazed, but with the quiet of a person who is not easily astounded. I even imagined I saw him smiling. We had approached the pasture where the other cows were grazing and the heifer became wild and tore herself out of Sam's hands. She began to run and jump with the rope still around her neck, and a few cows slowly raised their heads and looked at her, while the others continued to rip the grass as if nothing had happened. In less than a minute the heifer, too, began to graze. I had expected, after this terrible longing, a dramatic encounter between the heifer and her mother: much nuzzling, fondling, or whatever cows do to show affection to a daughter who was lost. But it seemed that cattle didn't greet one another that way. Sam began to explain to John Parker what had happened and Bessie too chimed in. Sam was saying, "This young man is a writer. I read his articles every week and he is going to be our guest. Like all writers, he has a soft heart. He could not stand the heifer's suffering. My wife and I cherish every line he writes. When he said that the heifer might disturb his thinking, I made up my mind, come what may. So I brought the heifer back. I am ready to lose as much as you will say—"

"You will lose nothing, it's a good heifer," John Parker said. "What do you write?" he asked me.

"Oh, facts in a Yiddish newspaper. I am trying to write a novel too," I boasted.

He remarked, "Once I was a member of a book club, but they sent me too many books and I had no time to read. A farm keeps you busy, but I still get *The Saturday Evening Post*. I have piles of them."

"I know. Benjamin Franklin was one of the founders." I tried to show erudition about American literature.

"Come into the house. We'll have a drink."

The farmer's family came out. His wife, a darkish woman with short black hair, looked Italian to me. She had a bumpy nose and sharp black eyes. She was dressed city-fashion. The boy was blond like his father, the girl Mediterranean-looking like her mother. Another man appeared. He seemed to be a hired hand. Two dogs dashed out of somewhere and, after barking for a few seconds, began to wag their tails and to rub up against my legs. Sam and Bessie again tried to explain the reason for their visit, and the farmer's wife scrutinized me half wondering and half with irony. She asked us in, and soon a bottle of whiskey was opened and we clinked glasses. Mrs. Parker was saying, "When I came here from New York I missed the city so much that I almost died, but I'm not a heifer and nobody cared about my feelings. I was so lonesome that I tried to write, even though I'm not a writer. I still have a few composition books lying around and I myself don't remember what I put down in them."

The woman looked at me hesitatingly and shyly. I knew exactly what she wanted and I asked, "May I look at them?"

"What for? I have no literary talent. It is kind of a diary. Notes about my experiences."

"If you have no objections, I would like to read them, not here, but back at Sam's farm."

The woman's eyes brightened. "Why should I object? But please don't laugh at me when you read the outpourings of my emotions."

She went to look for her manuscript and John Parker opened a chest drawer and counted out the money for the heifer. The men haggled. Sam offered to take a few dollars less than what he had paid. John Parker wouldn't hear of it. I again proposed to make good the difference, but both men looked at me reproachfully and told me to mind my own business. After a while Mrs. Parker brought me a bundle of composition books in an old manila envelope that smelled of moth balls. We said goodbye and I took their phone number. When we got back, the sun had already set and the stars shone in the sky. It was a long time since I had seen such a starry sky. It hovered low, frightening and yet solemnly festive. It reminded me of Rosh Hashanah. I went up to my room. I could not believe it but Sylvia had changed my linen: a whiter sheet; a spotless blanket, and a cleaner pillowcase. She had even hung up a small picture with a windmill.

That evening I ate supper with the family. Bessie and Sylvia asked me many questions and I told them about Dosha and our recent quarrel. Both wanted to know the reason for the quarrel, and when I told them they both laughed.

"Because of foolishness like this, a love should not be broken," Bessie said.

"I'm afraid it's too late."

"Call her this very moment," Bessie commanded.

I gave Sylvia the number. She turned the crank on the wall phone. Then she screamed into the phone as if the woman at the phone company were deaf. Perhaps she was. After a while Sylvia said, "Your Dosha is on the telephone," and she winked.

I told Dosha what I had done and the story about the heifer. She said, "I am the heifer."

"What do you mean?"

"I called you all the time."

"Dosha, you can come up here. There is another room in the house. These are kind people and I already feel at home here."

"Huh? Give me the address and phone number. Perhaps this coming week."

About ten o'clock Sam and Bessie went to sleep. They bid me good night with the gay anticipation of a young couple. Sylvia proposed that we go for a walk.

There was no moon, but the summer night was bright. Fireflies lit up in the thickets. Frogs croaked, crickets chirped. The night rained meteors. I could make out the whitish luminous band which was the Milky Way. The sky, like the earth, could not rest. It yearned with a cosmic yearning for something which would take myriads of light-years to achieve. Even though Sylvia had just helped me make peace with Dosha, she took my hand. The night light made her face feminine and her black eyes emitted golden sparks. We stopped in the middle of the dirt road and kissed with fervor, as if we had been waiting for each other God knows how long. Her wide mouth bit into mine like the muzzle of a beast. The heat from her body baked my skin, not unlike the glowing roof a few hours earlier. I heard a blaring sound, mysterious and other-worldly, as though a heavenly heifer in a faraway constellation had awakened and begun a wailing not to be stilled until all life in the universe shall be redeemed.

Translated by the author and Ruth Schachner Finkel

Grine Felder—A Place in the Country

Martin Boris

It must have been quite pastoral back in July 1938 when Isaac Bashevis Singer first glimpsed the bungalow colony grounds after a long, tedious drive from Manhattan. He might have stood at the entrance off the narrow serpentine road, beneath a jade-green canopy of tall, resin-scented cedars. Ahead of him lay a flowing, even more verdant landscape rising sharply into a series of tree-studded hills. But Singer must surely have questioned what he was doing in this "wilderness" so far from his tiny, one-room flat in lower Manhattan and why he'd allowed his young friend, Zygmunt Salkin, to inveigle him into journeying up to the country.

Three years earlier, Salkin had waited at Ellis Island with I. J. [Israel Joshua] Singer, Isaac's older brother, to welcome the 39-year-old Polish immigrant to America. Since his arrival, the younger Singer hadn't fared as well as he wished in his writing career, so when Salkin, a budding theater director, approached him with a plan to move his fledgling troupe to a Woodridge, N.Y., bungalow colony to rehearse an English version of I. L. Peretz's *At Night in the Old Marketplace*, Isaac consented to oversee the project.

In his pitch to Singer, Salkin had painted a very bleak picture. "There was a time when I dreamed about reviving the Yiddish theatre. But I've convinced myself that this is a waste of time," said Salkin, as reported in Singer's memoir of his salad days in Manhattan, *Lost in America*. "Something has to be done for the theatre. . . ."

Salkin's despair was well founded. The Golden Age of serious Yiddish theater was over. Maurice Schwartz's grand and noble Yiddish Art Theatre, established in 1918 at Manhattan's Irving Place Theatre with high hopes and higher aspirations, with plays by stellar Yiddish playwrights such as Perez Hirshbein and David Pinski, had, over the next two decades, devolved into offering a menu of mostly lighter, crowd-pleasing fare—still Yiddish in language, but grandiose in production, the stage often filled chock-a-block with actors, singers, and dancers, the choreography ornate, the scenes many in order to boost attendance. Schwartz had become what noted actress Celia Adler called "a slave to spectacle."

Jacob Ben-Ami's Jewish Art Theatre, with even loftier aims, had lasted two seasons, from 1919 to 1921. By the '30s, all that remained of Yiddish theater was ARTEF (Arbeiter Teater Farband), a vibrant but leftist group more interested in propaganda than artistry.

And, of course, there was the Second Avenue fluff of sentimental comedies, overcooked melodramas and mindless musicals, known collectively and pejoratively as *shund*, which purist critics defined as trash.

In 1937, the great author-critic Alexander Mukdoiny wrote, "The Yiddish Theatre is finished. It is no longer even bad theatre. It has no actor, no repertoire, no directors and no designers. . . . Professionalism, talent and ambition are practically dead."

Zygmunt Salkin's attempt at a solution that summer of 1938 was to gather a group of stage-struck youngsters and present them with his own English translation of the I. L. Peretz play, to be produced under Singer's guidance. The practical part of his agenda was the free use by the troupe of a gathering hall in the bungalow colony known as Grine Felder (Green Fields). But this was no ordinary Catskill resort for the families of middle-class Jewish shopkeepers and businessmen who would come for a respite from Manhattan's swelter. When Salkin and Singer arrived, Grine Felder had been for two years summer home to the most concentrated assemblage of Yiddishist elite anywhere on Earth. While other groups—artists, leftists, Bohemians—organized their own colonies, none equalled the caliber of talent at Grine Felder.

Indeed, not anyone could vacation at the unique colony. Malvina Fainberg, 93, a summer resident from 1947 to 1987, describes the admission practices: "There was a long waiting list, composed of only those recommended by Grine Felders already there. I was considered because my brother-in-law [Jules Fainberg] was one of the original founders. One had to be first interviewed, parents and children alike, by the membership committee. Next, we were evaluated by the cultural committee as to his or her possible contribution to the various cultural activities going on."

The colony's origins are almost mythic. In the autumn of 1936, a delegation from nearby Mirth bungalow colony had approached Raphael Kasofsky and Meyer Arkin, owners of the popular Avon Lodge a mile outside of Woodridge. Representing 32 families dissatisfied with their present summer accommodations, the delegates asked the two owners to build them a modern enclave of approximately 40 units on 35 acres of unused Avon Lodge property. The group would then assume all aspects of managing the colony, from maintaining the grounds to collecting the rents and paying the owners' fees.

By the next spring, the spanking new colony was ready for occupancy. Its name would be Grine Felder, after the enormously successful play and movie by Perez Hirshbein, who was among the colony's founding fathers. At the eleventh hour, however, Hirshbein decided to remain at Mirth, out of loyalty to its owner.

Those making the transition couldn't have been more pleased with the two- and four-unit structures, its modern kitchens and screened porches, and the large recreational building which they promptly named the Amphion Theatre and stocked with rows of benches and three massive Melodigrand pianos. They especially appreciated the illusion of isolation and solitude, the bungalows scattered helter-skelter, each on a small hillock and hidden from the rest by stands of maples and oaks.

Among the notables who pioneered Grine Felder were David Pinski, a major Yiddish playwright whose work a decade earlier had dominated both Schwartz's Yiddish Art Theatre and Ben-Ami's Jewish Art Theatre; Mendl Elkin, one of the founders of the Bronx's Unzer Theatre and a writer, director, teacher, and lecturer also involved with Pinski and Hirshbein in various ripples of Jewish and cultural life in New York City; Nahum Stutchkoff, author and playwright, whose radio series *Tzores bei Leiten* ("Trouble Increases") ran for 20 years on WEVD in New York City, "the station that speaks your language."

Samuel Charney, who wrote under the name "S. Niger," was also an original at the colony. Editor, journalist and historian, founder of the Zionist Socialist Party and president of the Shalom Aleichem Folk Institute, Charney was considered the dean of Yiddish literary criticism.

Musical excellence was also well represented in the persons of Lazar Weiner and Moishe Rudinow. The former was a famed composer of orchestral works and the conductor of the Mendelssohn Symphony Orchestra, the latter chief cantor at prestigious Temple Emanu-El on Manhattan's Upper East Side.

And from the world of labor: Joseph Schlossberg who, in 1914, helped found the Amalgamated Clothing Workers of America and later served as a member of the New York City Board of Higher Education, as well as writing several books on the American labor movement.

In his journal as recording secretary of Grine Felder, Abraham Shiffrin, a noted poet, short story writer, and former president of New York University's School of Journalism, describes some of the day-to-day cultural activities at the colony.

He writes of Grine Felder's children putting on a performance of Robert Sherwood's *Abe Lincoln in Illinois*, followed by a more Yiddish-centered production of I. L. Peretz's *Two Brothers*.

Under Shiffrin's direction, the parents of these children presented another Peretz play, *Arendar*, a stirring three-acter. Other evenings, David Pinski would command the Amphion stage with talks about the lives and works of his fellow artists: the two Sholems, Asch and Aleichem; Peretz; and Ossip Dymov.

Wednesday evenings were especially glittering. The women's cultural committee would take charge of "Tea Parties," at which Lazar Weiner would often play an original composition or accompany an invited guest such as Alexander Zadri, the world-renowned violinist. They'd play Mozart and Brahms, but more frequently Yiddish folk music.

At another Wednesday gala Jacob Ben-Ami, the quintessential Yiddish actor, would give a dramatic reading. At another, the great Russian basso Sidor Belarsky, a recent immigrant and star of the City Center Opera Company, would sing solo or duets with Moishe Radinow to the accompaniment of the Melodigrand piano.

Refreshments would be served after, and the conversation was rich and heady—the fate of European Jewry; the tense situation in Palestine; the paintings of Marc Chagall; the German-Soviet Pact of 1939, which badly splintered the left; the American economy, still ailing from the Depression.

Rosina Fernhoff, an actress who has performed in America and Israel, recalls that her father, Dr. William Fernhoff, "would often make after-hours calls to this most unusual colony. I would be his driver, and for me, an aspiring young actress and dancer, nothing was more exciting than to be in the presence of such artistic giants as Perez Hirshbein and Lazar Weiner.

"Long after my father treated his Grine Felder patient, we'd linger to listen to the music, to absorb the poetry and drama, to speak with creative people whose common bond was the preservation of Yiddish language and culture."

During the day, Pinski would hold classes in Yiddish history for children and adults. In addition, Shiffrin noted that "we have a reading circle in Yiddish, to which about 30 residents come each Tuesday, in the open meadows, to listen to readings of works from our Yiddish classics."

In his journal, Shiffrin also tells of the colony's own weekly newsletter, *The Locust*, a breezy two-pager that he edited and to which Elkin, Pinski, Niger, and other Grine Felders were happy to contribute.

Involved in his directorial and re-editing chores, I. B. Singer nevertheless took note of his hosts. In *Lost in America* he recalls with amusement that each bungalow was named for a Yiddish writer or Socialist leader: Peretz, Sholem Ale-ichem, Rosa Luxemburg, Emma Goldman.

But, sourly, Singer carps that "when the Yiddishists learned that I was getting ready to dramatize something by Peretz . . . I became an overnight target. Yiddishism in America suffered from a lack of young forces. I was comparatively young, and my book (*Satan in Goray*) had already received some notice among the Yiddishists, even though the critics complained that I failed to follow in the path of Yiddish classicists and gave myself over exclusively to sex, as well as demonstrating a lack of concern for social problems."

This being the case, it is difficult to imagine two more antagonistic extremes in the spectrum of Yiddish literary culture. Singer, always the self-absorbed loner, demonstrated his antipathy to the Grine Felders in this acid-etched group portrait: "They seethed with those offering ready-made remedies for all the world's ills. . . . Some placed all their hopes on Freud, while others hinted that Stalin was hardly as bad as the capitalist lackeys painted him."

By summer's end, though but a novice at directing, Singer had helped whip into shape *At Night in the Old Marketplace* on the Amphion's stage, when unused by the Grine Felders. Salkin talked of receiving financial backing and booking a theater in Manhattan, but neither materialized. Peretz's anglicized play never opened.

Grine Felder, however, continued for almost 50 more years, despite the deaths or the defections of its most illustrious founders and the shift to more mainstream families. In 1973 a neighboring ski lodge bought the colony and ran it for five years; eventually it fell into bankruptcy. Finally, the town of Fallsburg took the colony in lieu of unpaid taxes.

The grandeur and glory of Grine Felder is forever gone, in ruins like so many Catskill resorts and hotels. Its Amphion Theatre, the site of so much poetry, drama, and music has collapsed into itself, only the three pianos remaining upright, their keys faded and frozen tight, their rotting hulks evidently not worth stripping or stealing.

The bungalows themselves are slowly rotting, the screened porches festooned with cobwebs, the kitchens gutted except for corkscrews of flypaper still hanging from ceiling beams, their victims long ago turned to fossils.

Nature has all but reclaimed Grine Felder, leaving scant indication of what a bountiful feast had once taken place there, summer after joyous summer: An extraordinary band of Yiddishists had endeavored to hold onto a fast vanishing world while America was struggling with its own problems of the Great Depression and later, World War II; when the stars shone a bit brighter and Grine Felder was the closest its founders would ever come to paradise on Earth.

Bingo by the Bungalow

Thane Rosenbaum

The woman was eccentric, even for the Catskills. Actually, she was crazy, but that's not the kind of silent confession a child can easily allow about his mother. It takes a measure of distance to appreciate the abnormality. Blind faith in parental credentials is a virtue of childhood, but one day it vanishes. The brittle truce that lies between the gap in generations gives way to new realities, and empathies.

But then the entire colony was filled with crazies. It was a summer loony bin of refugees from the fallen Europe, now resettled in America, spending the months of June through August in Sullivan County—"the country" as they called it. Cohen's Summer Cottages was made up of ten white-boarded bungalows scattered across a lush green field. Small boxy frames with ash roof tiles. Each cottage had a porch and swinging door that clapped firmly against the frame. A stone walkway linking the cottages—a trail for the dispossessed. A lone, rickety shed—home for a lawn mower and washing machine—rested beneath an ancient weeping willow. There was a taut clothesline that stretched from the swings to the slide. On windy afternoons, a United Nations of underwear and brassieres would flap restlessly in the breeze.

"It's over eighty-five degrees today," Hyman Cohen announced, returning from the shed, the first of many daily readings of the mercury stick. "*Ach,* imagine that, eighty-five, like an oven . . . but dry," he said, shaking his head in disbelief, and spitting to the side.

The thermometer always gave the same reading, and he the same response.

Cohen wore an oversized pair of orange cabana shorts with silver crests that trimmed the waistband. His skin was dark and rough; his hair and eyebrows thick and unruly. One of his legs appeared lifeless. He dragged it about as if chained to some burden no one could see.

It was his colony, a piece of real land, paid for in cash to mask the memories from five years before. His tenants shared in his addiction: the need to escape and forget—the smoke, the shaved heads, the ancestral remains. Each a survivor from one camp or another: Bergen-Belsen, Maidanek, Treblinka, Auschwitz. Left behind was a sacred burial ground. The geographic sacrifice. No time, or courage, to place a wreath or a tombstone. Simply too hard to go back.

The music of the colony resonated with the sounds of atonal displacement. Everyone spoke with some mangled, confused accent that had been forced on them in America. English learned in a hurry. Verbs and nouns swallowed without time to digest. Some vowels never made it into the vocabulary, abandoned heedlessly at the docks.

Where better should this horde of runaways, of phantoms, have settled in for the summer? Cohen's was strangely their home. They were safe here—well, as safe as they would ever allow themselves to feel. There was much they could never believe in again. Faith was lost. No god. No humanity. No good places to hide. Cohen's at least offered a refuge of shared cynicism.

And in doing so, it also tolerated a fair amount of dementia. All that insanity added to the atmospheric diversity of the place, like the cool mountain night air and the morning dew. The refugees could swim in Kiamisha Lake. Do as the ancient Indians: purge the sins, cleanse the soul, dive deep into the belly of the water—where it's quiet—hoping to silence the stowaway shrieks that had come along for the ride.

Cohen never liked the word *concentration camp*, preferring instead the German *lager*.

"Why a camp, they should call it? Belsen was no camp, no picnic. In America, camp is where you send the children, or where you learn to be a Communist. We shouldn't call the *lager* a camp." And then, prideful of the haven he offered, he would add: "You want to know from a camp? This is a camp . . . right here. My camp! An American camp, not for children, but for the people like us. We don't march. We play cards all day. We sing, we cry. We look out at the trees. No fences, no wires. . . . Now, who wants for pinochle?"

Written on the swinging sign at the foot of the stone road, carved into the wood in seductive script, read:

COHEN'S SUMMER COTTAGES
LEISURE MACHT FREI!

"Keep up with me, you're falling behind," Rosa said. She was wearing a black polka-dot dress with flowing chiffon lace that floated in the air. Moving smartly between branches and twigs, she cut through the woods like an animal beginning its evening hunt.

"I can't walk this fast," a whining voice trailed her brisk pace, "it's too dark. . . . I'm tripping over acorns."

The sky was seared in blackness. A few resilient stars wriggled free of the buried pack. With flashlights, mother and son made their way into the forest. Beams sliced between trees, startling mosquitoes, overexposing fireflies, scattering milky streaks through the bushes.

"We're going to be late for my game," she said. "Do you want your mama to miss her bingo game? Think what we could win."

From behind and stammering: "What can we win?"

"Let's see . . ." she ruminated, pointing the flashlight down against her side, a white mist of light dappling the ground. "They have a blender and a seltzer maker. Ida, next door, tells me there is a bagel slicer; you just put the bagel in a plastic cover, and then slice like regular. No more cutting my hand. Such good prizes, no?"

"We'll never use any of that junk—even if we do win." The child was not easily tempted by convenience, nor fooled by deceit.

"Don't argue with me," she said. "I need to practice for the big game when summer is over—the one at Cohen's. He offers a cash grand prize."

"Why do we have to go? Can't we just stay home tonight? Lucy's on television."

Rosa turned around, lifted the flashlight, and planted a perfect moon over her face. In a possessed voice she said, "What do you think puts food on our table?"

"Bingo?"

"Bingo!"

"How does a bagel slicer put food on our table?"

"Every little bit helps."

"But we went last night. . . ."

"And we go tonight. Tomorrow we will go to Krause's Colony for a movie at their concession. The Three Stooges are playing. We'll have bagels, lox, and cream cheese. That you'll like."

And with that offer she danced through the woods, waving her arms like a sorceress, skipping around each tree; then she turned swiftly to flash a ray of light on her young son, who by now had resigned himself to the night's bingo game.

Two years earlier Rosa's husband had died, suddenly. His heart stopped. Just gave up. They had been two survivors who left much behind in that European graveyard—except death, which must have been lonely, or simply wasn't yet finished with the family. With Morris's parting, the task of raising Adam fell to her, alone.

Rosa Posner, fragile, a thin face with full lips, an unforgetting purple scar molded on her forehead, feared being a widow with child in a new land. Like the other refugees, she stumbled over the language. She did not know the secret handshakes that seemed so natural for immigrants who came before the war. And of course there was the concern over money. "*Ach, geld. Ich brauch mehr geld.*" Her money worries never allowed her mind a minute's rest.

"I know from nothing except how to survive," she pondered. In the camps she had been a saboteur, a black-market organizer, an underground operator. It took years to relearn the simple etiquette of life among the living. "Who in this country needs to know from such things?"

They lived in a middle-class section of Brooklyn. Ethnics at every corner. Dark walk-up apartment houses. Trees planted at the foot of the curb, in front of some buildings, but not others. It was a borough built mostly of stone and concrete, not entirely in harmony with nature.

One day, joining a card game in Brooklyn, Rosa learned that she had a knack for recalling numbers, and a certain streakiness with luck that seemed to will the royalty of the deck in her direction.

She became a gambler, a regular shark at the neighborhood tables. During the day she worked in a stationery store off Nostrand Avenue—calendars, magazines, fancy pens, newspapers, especially the *Forward*. She knew them all. But at night, off to a neighborhood game for gin rummy or seven-card poker.

For three weeks each year, during the Christmas season running through the first part of January—the peak time for snowbirds—she would take Adam out of school, board a Greyhound bus, and head down to Florida. It was a long bus ride—almost two days. Adam would sleep for most of the time, or stare down at the pages of a book, or color in a large white pad that Rosa had picked up for him at the stationery store. He never complained about the trip. It was all part of his mother's therapy—he knew it, even then.

Rosa passed the time by staring out the window. She loved the long journey south, chasing the warm weather, anticipating the tropics, breezing through all those unfamiliar towns. "What is this Fayetteville, and Jacksonville? Where are we now?" The motion of the bus rocked her gently, but her eyes never closed as she struggled with all those solicitations posted along the highway. Her lips moved slowly, and then the billboard was gone, already well behind her.

But when the bus reached Miami, Rosa stepped on the warm asphalt on Flagler Street and was immediately reminded of why she had come. There was the dog track on First Street on Miami Beach. And jai alai in Miami. The hotels along Collins Avenue were filled with "pigeons," as she called them—a phrase picked up from late-night movies, the source of much of her English.

"Now you stay in this room until I get back," she said, her son lying in bed in his pajamas, shadows from the black-and-white TV flickering off the window. Jackie Gleason droned in the background. "If you need anything, I'll be at the Caribbean Hotel, down the street. I'll come back with lots of money tonight. We'll be rich like Rockefellers. Tomorrow, I'll buy you a stuffed alligator in the souvenir store downstairs, maybe even a painted coconut. Now go to sleep."

In the country, during the summer, the games were fewer, and the stakes lower. But there was bingo, the calling of the numbers—B23, A14, G9—which serenaded her through each night.

At the top of a road littered with pinecones the forest came to a halt. There was a light that led down to a barn, a long trailerlike edifice where the whole colony gathered for bingo. Once inside, Rosa purchased eight cards.

"You play so many cards, Mrs. Posner," the man at the concession observed. "How do you keep up with all of them?"

"I brought my little helper," she replied.

The room was filled mostly with people from the colony, but there were a few, like Rosa and Adam, who traveled from neighboring villages, playing bingo wherever it could be found. Each colony offered a game a week. For some, that was more than enough.

"You'll play these two, Adam, and I'll play the rest."

They took their seats at a long wooden table with an adjoining bench, and set the cards out in front of them.

"Oh, I like these," Rosa said, uncorking a Magic Marker that had a round sponge for a head. "You see, you just push the marker down on the card like this. Watch me, you don't want to mark the wrong number."

A giant cage filled with wooden balls readied itself for the caller's rumbling spin.

"Our first prize is the bagel slicer," the caller said. "To win you got to have an L in any direction." He let go of the crank. The balls came to a crackling halt. He then opened the cage and released the first of the night's numbers.

"B seven!"

"We got one," Adam said, patting the card with his marker, his small face alternately glowing and serious. "We live in bungalow seven—that's why they called it."

Rosa smiled down at her son but remained earnest in her own vigil. As the numbers dropped from the cage, Rosa was busy blotting her card, checking up and down the rows, hands moving methodically like a spirited conductor.

Several games passed and Rosa gathered her fortune: the bagel slicer, the blender, a summer umbrella, a walking cane, a straw hat, two ashtrays—one made into the shape of a flamingo, the other a fish.

Someone in the front row screamed "Fix!" which drew a wave a laughter from the good-natured folk.

"Who is that lady back there?"

"Check her cards! Read me back her numbers again, will yah?"

"Go back to your own bungalow colony, lady!"

Rosa smiled shyly, but paid little mind to their teasings. With each call of the numbers, her eyes—fixed and hypnotic—would light up like the brightest of moons. Adam concentrated on the pageantry of his mother's luck, the lettering on her forearm raced by him, the branded marks blurred in streaks before his eyes.

His attention faltered. A disapproving Rosa leaned over and blotted in a few of the numbers that her son had missed. "Adam, you are not watching. I cannot depend on you." He, meanwhile, checked his cards once more, trying to see if the hand dealt his mother—the one on her forearm—in any way equaled a winning card. Chasing her movements, he grew sleepy. All that kept him awake was the sound of his mother's calming refrain, the lullaby of his summers:

"Bingo!"

"Bingo!"

"Bingo!"

As the night wore on, Adam dropped off to sleep, stretched out over the bench, beside Rosa. A half-eaten hamburger remained at the table. His cards failed him. So did his stamina. "Bingo!" unaccountably soothed his slumber.

Years earlier, just a few months before Morris's death, a five iron glistened in the sun. Artie was lofting golf balls out into the open blue sky. A scuff of grass, burnished on the blade, mixed with the first moisture of the day. The flight of the ball came into view against the tall green trees that surrounded the colony. On the other side of the forest were other crazies, with their own accents.

"Fore!" he yelled.

The refugees didn't have a whole lot of experience with golf in Poland and Russia, so it took a number of summers for them to realize that the avalanche of dimpled white balls—preceded by the number "four"—was not an air raid, just conspicuous recreation.

The other half of the field was occupied by Abe. He was wearing a pair of white tennis shorts and a white undershirt. At first glance, the features of his face seemed to be getting away from him. He had a fleshy nose, prominent ears, and heavy eyelids.

Abe was holding fast to a spool of cord. A kite flew above him, scattering in the wind, looping in the airy currents.

"Get that kite out of here!" Artie yelled. "I'll punch a hole right through it! Fore!"

The launching of a retaliatory golf ball did not deter Abe.

"How much of the field do you need for that stupid game?" he asked.

Artie paused and contemplated just how valuable breathing room was to everyone at Cohen's Summer Cottages. Once imprisoned, they all now longed for space. Before coming to any conclusions on the matter, Adam, wearing blue short pants with matching suspenders and a striped blue polo shirt, circled up to him. He was pedaling a bright red fire engine, and pulling on a string that sounded a bell.

"Hey kid, come here," Artie said, his tanned face taking on a soft and tender glow.

Adam wore a red helmet that was much too large for his head. It tipped over his face like a catcher's mask.

"How's your dad?"

"He's on the porch," he replied, removing the helmet.

Artie strained his eyes and caught sight of Morris sitting on the porch of the bungalow. Artie liked Morris, considered him a real scholar, a refined and decent man, but emotionally tortured—worse even than the rest. Adam's father had survived two camps, fought in the forest as a partisan, almost died of typhus. And now a heart condition, the poor guy. Artie reached for another club—a wood this time, to satisfy his anger—and before sending the ball into fuming orbit, wondered why a man like Morris, who had suffered so much senseless pain, should not be allowed some kind of immunity from ordinary diseases, at least for a while.

"Is he feeling better?"

"Don't know," Adam said. "He can't come down from the porch."

"What do you mean?"

"Doctor said he's got to stay on the porch, or inside the bungalow. Too many steps to go up and down."

"I see. . . . Tell him I'll come by and see him later."

"Okay," and with motoring feet, the red fire engine sped away down the walking path.

Adam was the only child at Cohen's Summer Cottages. One generation removed from the awful legacy, he was their uncorrupted hope, the promise of a life unburdened by nightmare and guilt. Such a delicate compromise they were all forced to accept; all so aware of life's cruelest impulses, and yet they so desperately wanted to trust in the possibility of their renewal. But Adam gave them an alarming sense of the future. Everyone feared that something bad might one day happen to him, forcing them to recast all their hopes and dreams, start all over, amend their expectations.

The men of the colony—most of whom wished someday to have children of their own, or mourned the murdered children they left behind—took it upon themselves to act as surrogates for the Posners. The child was born and lived for most of the year in Brooklyn, but the refugees—many of whom lived in Brooklyn as well—committed themselves to year-round sentry duty. Even before Morris's illness, they undertook a shared communal responsibility to raise the boy.

Adam's actual father was never the kind of man well suited for the task, anyway. All the consolidated anguish of his life left him empty, distant, and cold.

Artie played catch with Adam. He even bought him his first baseball glove—a smooth black leather one with gold stitching and a Mickey Mantle signature. They would go out to the field and toss a pink Spalding back and forth. Artie was patient with some of Adam's erratic throws and his insistence on keeping the mitt sealed.

"Adam, open the glove," Artie would say. "You want to catch it, not knock it down!"

Morris watched from the porch, smiling and nodding occasionally—never once defying his doctor's orders. He had seen so much in his life—a great deal unspeakable and unknowable, particularly for those who existed outside the shared nightmare of Cohen's Summer Cottages. And he had come so far—as a boy in Germany; his early manhood in a concentration camp, and now, a withered and fading creature, unrecognizable to himself, spending his summers in the mountains of upstate New York, recuperating from a lifetime of distress.

Artie also taught Adam not to be afraid coming down on the slide.

"Just kick your legs through and slide."

"It's hot. I'll fall!"

"Come on, son, we've all been through worse than this, you can do it."

The bickering between Artie and Abe always came to a halt on account of Adam. On the days when Abe helped Adam build a kite from brown-paper wrapper, Artie refrained from polluting the otherwise buoyant air with lethal golf balls. In the end it didn't matter. Many a fruitless summer day passed without that reconstituted grocery bag ever getting off the ground.

Even Hyman Cohen himself helped out with the boy from time to time.

"Adam, follow me, *kind*, to the shed," he said, limping about. "We should find out the temperature for everybody."

Only five years of age, but Adam already knew the answer. He followed Cohen, and then obligingly emerged to announce: "It's eighty-five degrees!"

The last time anyone saw Morris was when Adam came running home from Krause's Cottages, crying and blowing on his wrist. Adam had been playing ball with the older boys. But they weren't throwing a soft Spalding. Adam must have been confused by the speed of their throws, or the weight of the ball. Artie's lessons didn't prepare him for life outside the colony. The children from the other edge of the forest didn't care about the *lager*, didn't reserve any special compassion for the boy with the sick father. The ball came too fast. Artie's glove didn't work.

The wrist was badly disfigured. A fleshy spike now occupied the place normally reserved for a pulse check. Panting away at the exposed bone, Adam thought only of how one soothes a burn.

"Phew, phew . . ."

He started to run, away from Krause's, in the direction of the rival colony that was his summer home. Dashing underneath the pines, through the woods, stopping every few steps to blow on the broken bone. As he got closer to the colony, he could make out the sight of his father sitting on the white porch, neat rows of picket columns off to each side. A watchtower connected to a bungalow, the only freedom Morris's doctor would allow.

Morris was sitting on an aqua beach chair, a crumpled German newspaper rested on the floorboards below him. He was perpetually on guard, expecting the worst—even here, so close to the otherwise calming influences of Kiamisha Lake. Adam reached the porch with a face filled with tears. Morris forgot all that his doctor had told him about stairs and the dangers of overexcitement. He pushed off the armrests, grabbed the railing, and then, as though he were a vital, solid man, raced down to his son.

"What happened to you, *mein sohn*?" he said, and hugged the boy as he had never done before. Adam held out his wrist—showing his father—staring down at it as though he had just brought home a wounded bird. "Oh, *mein Gott*—look at you . . ." And then, reflexively, with immediate regret, he let out, "Where can we be safe?"

Adam's lips trembled, and then, steeling himself, said, "Papa, you shouldn't have come down the stairs."

Morris embraced his son again, sobbing uncontrollably into the boy's small chest.

Moments later, a cavalry of refugees rushed to the Posner bungalow. Card games broke up suddenly. Wet laundry soaked in open baskets. A fishing pole lay dropped by the shore. No alarm had sounded, and yet somehow they knew to come. There was an intuitive sense that something was not right at bungalow 7. A people so sensitive to rescue, and the urgency to protect one of their fragile own.

"What happened?" old man Berman said.

"We came as soon as we saw the others start to run," one of the Jaffe brothers said, heaving desperately for air.

"Who is the sick one here?" Mrs. Kaplan wondered aloud. "Adam or Morris?"

Both father and son were taken to the hospital in Monticello, each in need of medical attention.

For weeks Morris lay in the hospital, connected to all sorts of life-sustaining machinery that couldn't possibly begin to heal what really ailed him. Rosa went off each day to Monticello to visit her husband. Adam, with his powdery white cast, was left in the care of one or several of the refugees, who were more than happy to do their part. There were rules at the hospital about not allowing visits by children. And after his experience with blanking out in that cold place—only to awaken with his arm fully recast in plaster—he had his own reservations about returning to the hospital as well. He wished to see his father, but only on the porch.

The bus edged up to the curb near the drugstore on Route 17, across the street from the bowling alley, just down the road from Cohen's. Up the other hill was the Concord Hotel. The door to the bus was open, the engine was running; the driver waited patiently for Rosa to get on.

"You be a good boy," Rosa said, brushing Adam's hair to one side. "Don't throw any more balls."

"I don't throw with my left arm."

"Then don't catch any more balls, and don't cause any more trouble."

She boarded, paid the fare, and slipped into the first seat. She then turned to the window to look back at her son. The bus pulled away. The roar and heavy exhaust seemed to smother the small boy. Adam remained behind, waving his heavy wrist.

With each afternoon return from Monticello, Rosa seemed different. She was edgier, more nervous than usual. Gradually she was saying good-bye to her husband—so unceremoniously, the awful finality so unjust. Each day Morris looked as though more of him had surrendered. There would be no going back to the bungalow.

Rosa would return, but never in the same way again. In sympathy with her husband's deterioration, her sanity began to leave her. She was losing her memory, her sense of place, her essential bearings, her grip on reality. Physically she was still strong, but the psychic toll had now become insurmountable—even for someone so seasoned in survival. Morris was leaving and ghosts were arriving. They took over her mind, ambushed her reason.

In what became an almost daily ritual, Rosa would retrieve her son and take him inside bungalow 7. Then the interrogation would begin:

"What did you tell the neighbors today?"

"I didn't tell them anything."

More forcefully. "What did you tell them?"

"Let go of my arm. . . ."

"Did you tell them about the box?"

"What box?"

"And the bullets?"

"What . . . ?"

"You told them about the bread, didn't you?"

"I don't know what you're talking about! . . . Mama, you're scaring me!"

"Tell me what you told them!"

She slapped Adam, who fell against the kitchen cabinet; the door panel slammed shut by the white cast. The crash caused a loud thud.

The child was too young to understand; the parent too mortified to concede the injury—to both of them.

Overwhelmed with grief, fatigue, and persevering nightmare.

It seemed like all those living near Kiamisha Lake descended on Cohen's Summer Cottages for the annual Labor Day bingo game. It started off as a bright and cloudless day. The temperature was cooling, fall was a few short weeks away. By then all the refugees would be gone, back to their respective boroughs, grateful that they had lived through another summer. Perhaps by next year, their memories of Europe would grow dimmer. But nobody actually believed that.

The bingo game was held outdoors on the grassy field. Long tables were set out. A sound system was installed to announce the numbers. People who had spent their summer traipsing from colony to colony in search of bingo by now felt fully practiced for the final game of the season—the World Series of bingo, the one with the biggest prizes.

"This is exciting," Adam said, slipping beside his mother in the last row, which was right in front of their bungalow.

Rosa was wearing one of her best dresses—a long beige sleeveless gown with a full-pleated bottom, a garment reserved for very special occasions. She was vastly overdressed—it was still summer, during the middle of the day, and hot—but nobody cared to notice. That's because there was so much else that could not be ignored. She had been given to walking around the colony late at night, howling into the woods like an animal. And, of course, there was her uncontrollable fury. Fortunately, the refugees knew to take care of her son on the days when her anger was directed at him.

"All these people," Adam continued.

Nursing his own two cards, Artie, who had become the closest thing that Adam now had to a father, sat next to him.

"I'd love to wallop a golf ball right into the middle of this place—that would get rid of everybody."

"The more people, the larger the pot," Rosa reminded him. She had instincts for these kinds of observations.

"Welcome to our end of the summer bingo tournament," Hyman announced from the podium with bravado. "The grand prize of two hundred dollars goes to the first person who can fill an entire card."

Rosa had waited all summer for this. She had a treasure trove of household trinkets to show for her preparation; now she was all geared up for the actual cash offerings.

"Mama, I have this card, right?" Adam asked.

"Don't bother me, I'm trying to concentrate."

She worked feverishly, tapping away at her cards.

"O twelve," Hyman's voiced screeched into the microphone.

"I six."

"B thirty."

Rosa blotted the appropriate boxes, scouring the rows for the letters and numbers that would win her the title and bounty she so coveted.

Minutes into the game, Artie offered, "I got nothing. Must be a bum card."

"Shsh . . ." Rosa insisted.

They paid no attention to Adam, who was diligently filling in the boxes of his one card. He feared jinxing the outcome, so he kept the card to himself, hoping that neither Rosa nor Artie would notice the streak he was riding.

Some of the players had gotten up to walk around, moving slowly, mingling, drinking soda pop and eating sandwiches. A sharp, cool wind brushed over the colony, and a faint crackle of thunder echoed in the distance. Birds scattered from trees.

Adam slowly filled in the open spaces of his card—one at a time—as though he were working on a coloring book. Many of the other contestants appeared bored, tapping their fingers, waiting anxiously for a matching bingo ball to drop. Adam never noticed the collective frustration, or even the disappointment on his own mother's face, so uncharacteristic an expression for her to have while caught up in a game of chance.

All but one number had been filled on his card when the rains came. The afternoon summer shower drenched everything. Fortunately the bingo balls, made of wood, could float. As for the cards, streaks of Magic Marker smudged them beyond recognition, making them all indistinguishable. Cohen's Summer Cottages had been transformed into a finger-painting festival.

"This is the best my card is going to look," Artie said. "We should go inside."

"No!" Adam yelled.

"It's raining," Rosa said defeatedly. "We should go in. The game is over." Arms reaching toward the sobbing heavens, "What is wrong with my life! What did I do to deserve all this?"

"I have one number to go!" Adam screamed.

"Come . . ." Artie said.

The rain fell harder. All who had gathered for the afternoon now ran for the cover of the forest, or huddled under the roof of a bungalow, trying to outlast the downpour. Adam remained seated, alone on the bench. He stared at his solitary card, trying to shield it from fading, preserving the record of his unrealized triumph. Deprived of victory at his mother's favorite summer game.

"Bingo!"

"Bingo!"

"Bingo!"

A man with a thick, silver-speckled beard cried out for his prize, but no one responded.

It was fall in Sullivan County. Brown, red, and purple leaves looked vivid but fragile, about to surrender to the inescapable gravity that comes with autumn. Cohen's Summer Cottages were empty. Not at all unusual for that time of year. Not a living soul ever stayed at the colony past Labor Day. The place looked entirely different, but it wasn't the change in season that made it so.

It had been sold years before—the new name was not really important. The sign at the foot of the road had been replaced by something that had neither the wit, nor historical gumption, of LEISURE MACHT FREI.

He toured the barren grounds. The walking path was overrun with wild weeds and moss, the kind of unkempt, tangled growth that once colonized the former owner's eyebrows. The visitor surveyed the green field. He looked in the direction of the shed, and found nothing. When he got tired, he rested his back against the sinuous spine of that same weeping willow. It was still standing. The swings were gone, as was the slide. The ground was strangely moist, as though the earth had wept, or had never quite gotten used to the change in the landscape.

Looking back toward the bungalow—his old bungalow, 7—he watched as his son stood on an overturned pail. The boy needed a lift to see inside.

"Hey Mory, what are you doing? You'll fall down and hurt yourself! You might break your arm!"

The porch had been dismantled. The entrance was now supported by stilts. Plants uprooted. The entire place had been unearthed, barren, stripped of the emblems that once made it so familiar.

Slowly, Adam walked over to where his son was peering into the kitchen window, hands cupped along the side of his face like blinders.

"You see anything?"

"Not really. Just some old furniture moved up against the wall."

Adam took out his camera and snapped a picture of the boy on the pail. There was a sheriff's warning posted on the door.

AUTHORIZED PERSONS ONLY

"'Authorized'?" Adam wondered. "If not me, who's allowed in then?"

But without the porch, how could you even enter? And once inside, what could you expect to find?

The camera clicked; he took a picture of the front door with the sheriff's sign on it. Ghosts, however, cannot be photographed. Those who he remembered would not sit still for a group picture. Only the sign would survive the eventual processing.

The colony had been transformed into a ghost town, which it had already been in a different way so many years before.

Mory turned around and jumped off the pail. Grabbing his father's hand, he ran off into the lifeless field, leaves crackling underneath each heavy step.

"So this was the place?"

"Sure is."

Looking up at the sky, hoping to pick up the sight of a brown paper kite, or a falling golf ball—some marking, something to pinch the senses and tweak the memories.

Some indication that the boy in the cast had once actually lived there.

"What are you looking for?"

"I don't know."

But he did.

"One number away from the jackpot, huh?"

"Yes. Never got the chance. Game called on account of rain."

"Bummer. Where's Krause's?"

"Over there. . . ."

Bungalow Colony Life

Irwin Richman

After paying for accommodations, the most traumatic part of the summer for most adults was getting packed and traveling to the mountains. How families arrived varied with time and economics. The trip could be quite luxurious or a crowded and uncomfortable ordeal.

Joey Adams remembered an early mountain experience, a summer at Boxer's Dairy Farm near Ellenville. Even more vivid were the memories of preparing for the trip. His family was to go to the country 15 June: "About the middle of May my father brought home the burlap sacks. Who had luggage?" They also borrowed valises. And "anyone who had a valise that closed without a rope was a millionaire." When you went to a *kuchalein*, you took your clothes and everything needed for housekeeping, except furniture, right down "to pots, pans, dishes, silverware, hammocks, and toilet paper." Joey's mother carefully packed all of the household goods. "Pots and pans were expertly stashed between pillows and blankets so they wouldn't rattle." Among other essentials were "umbrellas and seven pairs of rubbers for the rain, fly swatters, . . . netting for the baby, [and] a jar of Vicks (just in case)." The filled burlap sacks were sent ahead by Railway Express.[1]

On departure day the family, laden with valises and boxes and paper bags, took the cheapest way to the mountains, the train. Getting to the train was an unpleasant adventure in itself: "We took the trolley from Brooklyn . . . to 42nd Street, then the 42nd Street cross-town to the Hudson River. There we grabbed the Weehawken Ferry," a steamer, "which blackened your face and nostrils for a week." Arriving at the New York, Ontario, and Western terminal, and not being able to afford a redcap, the family dragged their luggage down along the train to the Ellenville car. "Of course, the damn ropes always broke and night-gowns, bloomers, and hot water bottles were always lying all over the train."[2]

Once settled aboard the train, the family started to eat the food they'd brought along. Their mother always proclaimed that it was "better to die from hunger, than you should eat from a lunch counter. Poison they give you." Along with many of her generation, like my grandparents, Adams's mother believed "restaurateurs were on a par with thieves, robbers, and dope peddlers." Lunch usually included canned salmon salad sandwiches, hard-boiled eggs, and "whatever was left over . . . from the night before . . . clamped between two pieces of bread. Maybe cold, rubbery calves' liver on rye ain't exactly a taste sensation, but who could afford to waste food?"[3]

After the long journey, which always took at least six hours, the family would be met at the local railroad station by the "farmer," often with a horse-drawn wagon. The farmer was not necessarily there out of the goodness of his heart, rather he made sure you arrived at his place. His presence guaranteed you didn't yield to the blandishments of other farmers, less fortunate, who, if they had vacancies, would even offer to give back your deposit money if only you'd stay at their place instead, at less money. "Farmers" had to be early and aggressive when meeting their tenants.

Buses were a bit more expensive, but they eventually helped drive the passenger trains out of existence. They were also more convenient in that they left from Brooklyn and the Bronx, as well as from Manhattan. But the trip along the poor roads of the time was long, and pre–World War II buses were often "smelly, gassy, cracking vehicles [that] had to detour hours out of their way." Midway on the trip there was always a stop at "The Red Apple Rest or at [Orseck's] 999," where "the restaurants, the restrooms and lunchrooms usually looked like a battle scene in *Quo Vadis*."[4]

The best public transportation to the Catskills was via hack, which, while it was more expensive, promised portal-to-portal service. While the train cost under two dollars a person, the hack was upwards of five dollars well into the 1920s and 1930s. If you had a lot of luggage you might be assessed another dollar. The hack was a large sedan that had room for seven passengers and the driver. You paid a premium for a window seat; you paid a reduced rate for children if you kept them on your lap. Hackers promised door-to-door service. "And he kept his word, he went door-to-door to door-to-door until he picked up every-one."[5] Luggage was packed in the trunk, tied to the hack's sides, and lashed onto the top. Bungalow colony fares would take everything, "even ironing boards. It was like they were going to Europe." Hackers were adept at packing. "We'd get the stuff into the car any way we could—hanging out of the trunks, tied on the roof rack with ropes. It took hours to get everything strapped in and ready to go."[6]

From the passenger's perspective, the dream trip was to be picked up last and dropped off first, for the driver it was simply to make it. "Wurtsboro Mountain was always a pain in the ass," hacker Billy Feigenbaum recalled. "We were al-ways so loaded down with crap that the Checker couldn't get over five miles an hour." In the 1950s, hacks, such as Goldy's Limousine Service, charged ten to twelve dollars for a seat in a ten-passenger stretch Buick.[7] Joey Adams describes a hacker as "a symphony in rags, his livery a pair of torn pants, and underwear, shirt and a handkerchief around his neck . . . [which] soaked up perspiration." He often smoked "a black stinky cigar."[8] This might be an extreme description, but drivers were a harried lot who worked long hours with uncomfortable peo-ple packed into a car with strangers.

Joey Adams also recalls a trip when his mother reserved the backseat of a hack for Joey, his sister Yetta, and herself. "The rest of the car contained an elderly lady and a young man who were squeezed together with the hacker in the front seat. A tubby bleached blond sat on a jump seat with most of her belongings." The other jump seat was occupied by a bald-headed man "reverently carrying a jar . . . [of] garlic pickles" that stank up the air.[9]

Since hacks were most crowded and expensive on the weekend, mothers and their children would often come up during the week with the father following on the weekend. It was not unusual for wives arriving at Richman's to say, "My husband will pay you on Friday"—and they always did. The most affluent non-car owners would rent an entire hack, and they had a quicker, safer, less crowd-ed, if more expensive trip. Hacks still exist, although today they are usually large vans and they charge thirty-five to forty-five dollars per person. My mother uses one when she needs to go into the city to see her doctor.

If you had your own car, transportation was easier. Many first-time renters would bring a load of household goods up with them when they rented. Others might do the same on Memorial Day weekend. By the mid 1950s, as competi-tion got fiercer, many larger colonies would allow tenants to come up for the long preseason holiday weekend. As people became more affluent and possessions multiplied, many people had trailers put on their cars or had much of their baggage delivered by van. At Richman's we had several well-to-do tenants who would arrive by car, usually a Cadillac, followed by a truck with their belongings, usually driven by an employee of the family business.

No matter how you traveled, when you arrived you had to unpack. On the "last Sunday in June, . . . Hector's Pond Colony, a pocket of ranch-style cottages, was undergoing heavy assault. Suitcases, cartons, bundles of bedding, groceries and assorted necessities [were] flowing feverishly into the clapboard frames."[10] At all colonies, arrival times were frantic as everyone unloaded, often helped by well-tipped handymen. On more than one occasion while working around the place, I was mistaken for a handyman by new guests. I usually helped them, but I had to decline a tip. Old-timers would mostly be embarrassed to ask a "Jewish college boy" to do such menial work. Owners hurried around attempting to resolve last minute crises and making themselves available to receive payment. All of this frenzy would, of course, be repeated in reverse in ten weeks. Once unpacked, summer was ready to begin.

A photo montage in *A Summer World* shows hotel activities and a group of people playing cards at Cutler's Cottages in South Fallsburg in the 1940s. The caption calls this "the slow track," but card playing was the single most important daytime activity at most hotels as well as at bungalow colonies.[11] During the many times I visited hotels as a kid and a young adult, I was always fascinated by how little the athletic facilities were used. This has probably changed in our fitness-conscious era, but empty swimming pools and mostly empty tennis courts are an indelible memory. On a visit to someone at a hotel or a colony, a sightseeing trip around the place was *de rigeur*. The visitor would see that card playing predominated all, and if a pool had a true function—it was to allow you to play cards next to it.

The hotel goers were truly differentiated from the bungalow people by the everyday chores of life. Hotel goers could avoid doing anything but dressing and eating, both done many times a day. *Kuchaleiners* had to literally "cook for themselves," but life went on at a more casual pace than in the city. Quarters were smaller and more simply furnished, daily dressing was informal, there was less laundry, and, with husbands gone much of the week, cooking was simpler. At Richman's, the rhythms of everyday life changed after the halcyon years of the 1940s and 1950s. Our clientele differed, or in most cases, just aged. We went from lively families to retired folks, the week and the weekend melded together, and eventually our clientele literally died away.

A mother's typical day would begin when the kids woke her up. She made breakfast, cleaned and did other chores, made lunch, fed the kids, and was outside in time for the walk down to the river. When the family came back from the river, it was time to change and get the kids changed (young kids had already been changed before the walk back), shop when Hymie the dairyman came, and then make supper for the family. Meals tended to be simple. Few Jews ate meat at each meal, especially since many kept kosher—and drinking milk (believed to be very important for children) and eating meat at the same meal is not kosher. Breakfasts of cold cereal, canned juice, and milk were very common, as were eggs and toast. Smoked fish—the bagel, cream cheese, and lox feast—was usually a weekend treat. Lunch was often a sandwich—peanut-butter-and-jelly and American-cheese-and-mustard-on-rye were favorites. Tuna fish and canned salmon were often served. A quirky kid, my favorite sandwich was cream cheese, lettuce, and caviar on a seeded roll. As a special treat, we might get spaghetti (overcooked and served with ketchup) or Aunt Jemima pancakes with syrup. All sandwiches were accompanied by milk and cakes or cookies—usually store-bought treats. Yankee Doodles and Oreo cookies were favorites. Dinners featured broiled or fried meat in big portions: hamburgers, steaks, lamb chops, and liver. Potatoes, canned vegetables, and fruits rounded out the meal. In our house, we often ate more elaborately at dinnertime, even during the week, because Grandpa really liked to eat and Grandma was a very obliging cook. She would make traditional dishes throughout the week, but even with Grandma, Friday was the major cooking day.

After dinner, the kids would have their last chance to whoop it up, while mothers cleaned up the kitchens before beginning the nightly ritual of rounding up the kids and putting them down for the night. Bedtime varied with age, and I remember hating going to bed while it was still light outside, as it was in the summer until nine o'clock or so. Mostly, the preteenage group were put down by nine; for older kids, ten to eleven was the usual time.

When the kids were in bed, the women would play cards. They'd meet in various bungalows or in the small kitchens in the Big House where they were within earshot of the children. Gin rummy was very popular in the 1940s and early 1950s—later canasta became all the rage. Occasionally, most of the women would come together in the kitchen of the Big House to play Continental rummy or Michigan rummy. Our women seldom played poker, but it was commonly played at other colonies. All the games were penny ante, and even at that many of the women, including some of our richest, hated to lose "unlimited" amounts of money that might go to a dollar fifty or two dollars if luck was incredibly bad, so they played with twenty-five cents or fifty cents "pie." After you lost that amount of money in an evening, you could play gratis, and you could still collect winnings.

Children vanished from the scene as our crowd aged, and cards became increasingly important as a time killer. Afternoons were spent playing cards, usually rummy or canasta, and in the evenings, most of the women would gather in our Big House kitchen to play cards or kibitz. Games that whole gangs could play, such as Michigan rummy, were especially valued. Although our place was small, there were always cliques, and in larger places this was even more evident. At Richman's in later years, one clique centered around our neighbors, the Puttermans and the Yustmans. Both were very affluent and both owned their own small houses. They had friends among our tenants, whom they would invite over to play cards at their houses. Increasingly, when "the 400," as the rest of the tenants called them derisively, had their card parties, Mother felt obliged to see that the other tenants were happy and so she organized card parties for them—canasta was a favorite here, too.

In larger places with day camps and freer-spending crowds, cards were played more often and for higher stakes. It was not unusual to see games that went on all day and night. Bridge, that normative middle-class pastime, was rare in Sullivan County. I only remember one group of our guests ever playing it. It was played at some of the larger places, but poker and gin rummy were much more common.

Another game, moderately popular at our place but extremely popular at the larger places, was mah-jongg. Played with tiles rather than cards, mah-jongg became a national craze in the 1920s. Considerably more expensive than cards, the sets themselves cost thirty to a hundred dollars or more. The Depression put an end to this national craze, but postwar Jewish women took to the game with a vengeance. A day of major importance came each July when the National Mah-Jongg League issued its annual new card, detailing that year's permissible "hands" or tile combinations. The click, click of tiles and phrases like "five bam" and "two cracks" filled the air many an afternoon at the large colonies. Mah-jongg was a gambling game. The stakes were usually higher than cards, and there was no "pie." In the city, my mother played mah-jongg with her group of five. As only four could play each game, one sat out each hand on a rotation basis. That way the game never had to stop for bathroom breaks. The women would meet in each others' houses on a rotation basis and see who could outdo whom in the preparation of snacks: cakes, pies, and other goodies. Other women, more fanatical about the game, belonged to several groups and could play afternoon and evening. At the larger places, a number of cliques were based on these winter mah-jongg groups whose members rented together and played the game morning, noon, and night. Emulating their mothers, teenage girls often played serious games of mah-jongg as well. Apparently, mah-jongg is still played. After not hearing of Jewish mah-jongg for years, I was mildly surprised to see an advertisement in the Lancaster Jewish Community Center newsletter announcing, "It's Time to Order Your 1997 Mah-Jongg Card!"[13]

Mothers at large colonies had the opportunity for "a real vacation," with freedom to pursue their own interests, especially in the postwar years. Day camps could make the kids disappear all day, laundry services processed their linen and clothes, and cleaning help was also available. Ann Cutler in *Bungalow Nine* complains of being tired from all of her chores. Looking to the future, she tells Jason that hopefully "you can treat me to a full-time maid like the Millers have":

JASON: Up here?

ANN: Even the Krinskys have a woman twice a week.

JASON: What would a cleaning woman do even once a week in these small matchboxes?

ANN: The Krinsky's irons one day and cleans the other. Whenever I tote our laundry to the machines, I run into someone's hired girl.[14]

Summertime help could charge a premium. Even at Richman's, while most women did their own work, several had cleaning help and a few had full-time maids.

Bingo was another diversion. In the 1940s, bingo was mostly a kids' game. Five or six kids played, taking turns at calling. By the mid 1950s the adults had started playing, and by the end of the 1950s Richman's even had a professional cage with balls for number selection. While it was extremely rare to see colony-wide card games of any kind, bingo was always integrated at our place and even "the 400" joined in. At first everyone took turns calling but, little by little, this chore fell to my mother. Bingo, thankfully, was only played once a week, and in later years it was in our garage, which doubled as a casino. By the 1950s, professional callers were common at larger places. Some callers ran the whole operation and owned the equipment. At Richman's, bingo was played with a fifty-cent pie. It could be considerably more expensive to play at other places where you typically paid for each card used and the game was a profit maker.

Women also had their "girls' night out" when they went to the movies in town. During the 1940s and 1950s, this meant walking to town—sometimes they took a cab home, but most of the tenants were in their twenties or thirties and the walk was fun. Often, they'd go on two nights, with one half watching the other half's children. Before coming home, a stop at a soda fountain for a frappe (one syllable) was a necessity. As the Richman's crowd aged, the women went to the movies by car. After my father died, Mother learned to drive and would often shuttle the ladies down in two or even three trips. In 1993, when I interviewed her, Miriam Damico was still ferrying her ladies around.[15]

Beginning in the postwar years, first hotels and then bungalow colonies started to show movies one or two nights a week—sometimes outside, but often in the casinos or playhouses. Some owners, such as the Kassacks for whom I worked in Woodbourne, owned their own projectors and showed films themselves, renting the films from catalogs. Others would hire projector, operator, and film as a package from one of several film entertainment companies that operated in the county. In the summer of 1959, Dave Burcat, who worked with me as arts-and-crafts counselor at Kassack's Day Camp and who became a life-long friend, moonlighted as a projectionist. If he were showing something interesting, I might go see the film—that summer, I saw a lot of films, and a lot of bungalow colonies and small hotels. Dave was married, had two kids, and was finishing dental school at the University of Pennsylvania. If it could be arranged, I would pick up his wife, Jessie, who ran the day camp's nursery, and take her along to see the film—then we'd all go out later. The car I drove was a very distinctive, very ratty old Chrysler. One evening, Jessie and I were riding up to see Dave, and a film, when I noticed a car following us as we turned into the hotel driveway. When the occupants of the other car saw us, they zoomed away, but not before I caught a glimpse of them. They were other counselors from the camp where we worked, and they thought Jessie and I were up to no good. After the movie, we came up with some dream scenarios, including having Dave "shoot" me at flag raising the next day. We didn't go through with it, but the next day everyone was very solicitous of Dave and very cool to Jessie and me.

The entire dynamics of the colonies changed when the men came up. For most people this was Friday night. While there was a train that ran until the early 1950s, I don't recall anyone using it—the heyday of the train had apparently been the 1920s. Most of our tenants arrived by car or bus. As Harvey Jacobs noted, most likely they had made a pit stop at the Red Apple Rest or the Orseck brothers on the way:

On the south side of Route 17 was The Orseck Boys. On the north side, the Red Apple Rest. Two restaurants practically identical.

Both oases had outdoor stands that sold hot dogs, hamburgers, lox and bagels, Cracker Jack [sic] candy, Life Savers, postcards. Both had gas pumps and plenty of sanitary toilets with signs proclaiming them inspected safe, boiled against any kind of bacteria. Both had lines of buses parked in their lots, indication [sic] that the food and comfort stations were trusted by big companies with plenty to fear from the law.

Both had multitudes of identical customers, families, young studs, old ladies, girls in shorts, teenagers in shirts that said Taft or Thomas Jefferson in block type, occasional loners who sat chewing and watching, clusters of humans from this or that bus with an eye on the driver who could pull out without them, smaller groups from the hacks, all in motion. Inside the restaurants were huge cafeterias where everybody was his own waiter. If you had time, if you could find a table, you sat. Tables were shared with strangers, as at the Automat in New York. The difference was that here the strangers were interchangeable. A father could go and support the wrong family, or a mother nurse the wrong kids, and it might never be noticed.

All were Jews on the move to and from vacations, all except those who worked behind counters or took plates and flatware from the tables. They were locals with a pale, puzzled look of overwhelm. Their faces contrasted with the pure colors of Jell-O in tall cups, mountains capped with whipped cream peaks, the favorite dessert.[16]

Stop or no-stop along the way, the men were tired on arrival, but most were also young. Dinner was waiting on the table for them. Curlers were out of their wives' hair, and they would often go out to see a late movie—and it wasn't unusual to have eleven o'clock movies on Friday nights. But the next night was the biggest entertainment night—in many ways, Saturday night was the culmination of the entire weekend. Friday night was foreplay. By the end of the 1950s, some of the bigger colonies were even offering live bands on Friday nights. Some tenants didn't go out, but played poker and gin on Friday nights.

Joey Adams's view of Friday night was that "after a little sex and a big dinner the husband took over the seat vacated only a few hours before by his wife . . . to play gin."[17] Actually, sex was reserved for late at night, after the children were asleep. I remember hearing people grousing about how late the kids were up the night before and how that hampered their plans.

When the men came up with cars, many brought food, especially fruit and vegetables from the city. With cars available, some people went shopping, some went visiting, but most stayed put and played cards. The men's game at Richman's was three-hand pinochle played with two decks. Often two games or more went simultaneously, one featuring folding money and the others, change. Some men preferred to play rummy. At my father's pinochle table, it was not unusual for several hundred dollars to change hands during the weekend. The regulars could all afford it, but I remember when a new guest joined them and lost heavily. His wife came to the regulars and berated them for taking advantage of the poor guy. They never played with him again, and his family didn't return the following year.

The fathers at Richman's were not very sports-minded, although most of them went swimming on the weekend if it was hot enough to drive them from the card tables to The Rocks. At many of the larger colonies, especially those with younger crowds in the late 1950s and 1960s, sports were very important on the weekends, and fathers took full advantage of all the facilities—except for the swimming pools, which tended to be mostly used by the kids, with parents playing cards at the poolside.

Some men also enjoyed fishing. Most went to the Neversink, while others drove to a nearby lake. Morningside Lake was especially popular in our area. Nightcrawlers were especially favored for bait. Mother's cousin Sidney, then our tenant, told a tale of bait-gathering woe from his previous colony. Anticipating Saturday fishing, Sid and a pal went out with a flashlight on a rainy Friday night. The worms were out in abundance, and as they collected them near the bungalows they enthused, "what a beauty" and "boy that's a big one." The next day an irate tenant-friend berated them. "Don't you guys have any shame?" He, perhaps egotistically, thought they were voyeurs.

After the 1950s completion of the Neversink Dam as part of New York's watershed program, and the ensuing impounding of its waters, the Neversink River became unswimmable because its flow was changed. Formerly free-flowing for many miles, the water warmed up in the summertime to a temperature in the seventies and eighties. Now, water from the bottom of the reservoir was released in a restricted flow just about nine miles above our swimming spot.[18] Water temperatures are usually in the fifties, except in the midst of a heat spell when they may rise to the low sixties. With a restricted flow, the water level was also radically lowered, rendering many swimming holes too shallow. New York City compensated those resort owners who owned riparian rights for the loss of the swimming use of the river, and many bungalow colony owners used the money to build swimming pools.

Before World War II, only hotels had swimming pools, and many of these were spring fed and so had algae in the water. I vividly remember going swimming at the Raleigh Hotel pool during the war—in a large green tank. While most tenants cheered the antiseptic blue and white modern pools, some people were nostalgic for the messier early ones. In the film *Sweet Lorraine*, the granddaughter and the handyman met at the site of the "Old Pool," which the girl "always loved."[19] But progress was at hand. Shortly after the war ended, the building of blue-painted, chlorinated pools began in earnest. Hotels advertised "Hollywood" pools, and some of the larger bungalow colonies followed suit. The river's demise as a swimming alternative stimulated the rush to pools, and, by 1960, most colonies whether they could afford it or not had a pool. The demand for nice, sanitary-looking pools was so overwhelming that even hotels and colonies on good swimming lakes put in pools. The anomaly of a pool right at lakeside became commonplace. Many of my grandfather's mortgage loans during the 1950s were made to pay for swimming pools. If you decided to go ahead with the pool, your next decision was whether to have a pool less than seven feet deep, or a deeper one capable of allowing for a diving board. Any pool under seven feet, by law, didn't require a lifeguard—deeper pools did. While lifeguard lore at hotels often involves romance, bungalow colony lifeguards were usually teenagers whose parents were staying at the colony—and the job really lacked cachet and glamour. Sometimes parents only agreed to rent on the condition that a son be made the lifeguard. It was usually the lifeguard's job to check the chlorination level of the pool, to skim leaves off the surface, and, most particularly, to remove any dead creatures—frogs or small mammals—before the guests used the pool. City people were especially squeamish about sharing their water with animal corpses. At many colonies, the pool became what one observer called an example of "conspicuous nonconsumption,"[20] where tenants, even nonswimmers, would not rent in a pool's absence. On the heels of the pool trend came the demand at hotels for indoor pools. Hotelman Carl Gilbert ruefully noted in the 1970s that, "A person will call and ask if we have an indoor pool. They may not use it, but if you don't have it, they won't come."[21] The indoor pool mania never hit the colonies, although at least one colony, Mason's in Monticello, had one. Indoor pools tended to be used even less than outdoor ones, but they were and are symbolic.

Richman's received almost fifteen thousand dollars for our riparian rights, and Grandpa and Father debated putting in a pool. I naturally wanted one. There was discussion with our neighbors the Yustmans and the Puttermans about sharing the cost, but that went nowhere. Pools were costly, not only in their structure, but because of the elaborate, massive filtration systems then used. Sensibly Grandpa and Father decided against a pool, but with the loss of swimming facilities, we could only attract a crowd not interested in swimming—that is, mostly older people or people with very small children who liked the lower rates we had to charge because we lacked a pool. Today, the Sullivan County landscape is littered with abandoned pools built for small colonies that were simply not economical.

At large colonies, athletic men would play water polo and the whole colony would stage water shows that were mock emulations of Esther Williams movies. A water show illustrated with home movies made at Lansman's is in *The Rise and Fall of the Borscht Belt*.[22] But mostly the pool was a background.

Handball courts were common and were used to play both handball and racquetball. Basketball courts—incorporated with the handball court's paving or separated in the larger colonies—were also very popular, especially with American-born fathers who had played the game in school. By the 1960s, some colonies even had tennis courts. But the single most popular game was baseball. Many of the larger colonies were league members, and the big games against other colonies were on Sunday mornings. Saturday was practice day. Women and children were expected to show up and cheer. Lansman's, our local Goliath bungalow colony, usually dominated the play. Jason Cutler, the hero of *Bungalow Nine* who is hung over after a night of partying, is rousted out of bed by other active tenants of Hector's. "Hey Cutler! Yo Cutler! The visiting team is on the field."[23] Dressing quickly and skipping breakfast and even coffee, goaded by his wife ("Musn't be a poor sport, Darling"),[24] he drags himself to the field, and—as a first-time bungalow tenant—is astounded by what he sees:

> The ball field was a human beehive. The visitors had the diamond. Along the fringes the local team was limbering up arms, batting fungos and capering about with vigor Jason found demoralizing. Hector stood by importantly wearing blue pants and a blue cap mounted rakishly over his left side tic. He was ready to umpire. The men of the colony were out in force. They had more than enough for a team; light-footed Al Miller, hoarse-voiced Buddy Berg, florid Milt Krinsky, big Jack Rappaport, smiling Joe Alfelder, Abe Barsky prancing about . . . and plenty more. The heavy drinkers, heavy dancers, and good-time-Charleys until three in the morning were out en masse, behaving as if Saturday night had never been.[25]

If sport intensity varied from colony to colony, with some colonies almost ignoring strenuous physical activity, food was another story. Meals and noshing are part of the Catskill culture. "Eating was done on an almost continuous basis—breakfast around eight, coffee and maybe a piece of cake or toasted bagel around ten-thirty, lunch at twelve-thirty, fruit, coffee and cake in the mid afternoon, dinner around six-thirty," recalls *New York Times* food and restaurant critic Mimi Sheraton of Catskill summers. "Then after card playing and other evening activities, some herring, more cake, a little of this and that around eleven, just before bed."[26]

Cramped as most bungalows were, many people had weekend or weeklong guests. (At larger places, owners tried to discourage this by charging a per-night guest fee for the use of facilities, but enforcement was difficult—short of a bed check.) Hostess gifts were expected, and "whoever came up from the city brought food, as though my mother hadn't stocked up for the new arrivals," Sheraton remembers. "The customary gift was delicatessen," and there were always "towering boxes of cake."[27]

Notes

1. Joey Adams, with Henry Tobias, *The Borscht Belt* (New York: Bobbs-Merrill, 1966), 23–24.
2. Ibid., 25.
3. Ibid., 25–26.
4. Ibid., 25. While its official name was Orseck's 999, everyone called it "Orseck's," or "the Orseck boys," or just "999." *Quo Vadis* (1951) is an epic movie known for its lavish use of extras.
5. Ibid., 26.
6. Myrna Katz Frommer and Harvey Frommer, *It Happened in the Catskills* (New York: Harcourt Brace Jovanovich, 1991), 98.
7. Ibid., 96.
8. Adams, *Borscht Belt*, 26–27.
9. Ibid., 27.
10. Norman Ober, *Bungalow Nine* (New York: Walker and Company, 1962), 1.
11. Stefan Kanfer, *A Summer World* (New York: Farrar Straus Giroux, 1989), photographs between pp. 46 and 47.
12. Adams, *Borscht Belt*, 30.
13. "It's Time to Order Your 1997 Mah-Jongg Card," Lancaster (Penn.) Jewish Community Center's *The Center News*, November 1996, 3.
14. Ober, *Bungalow Nine*, 141.
15. Miriam Damico, personal interview with the author (Loch Sheldrake, New York), 12 August 1993.

16. Harvey Jacobs, *Summer on a Mountain of Spices* (New York: Harper and Row, 1975), 13. "Taft" was a Bronx high school. Thomas Jefferson High School is in Brooklyn.

17. Adams, *Borscht Belt*, 30.

18. Robert K. Plumb, "Upstate Hydroelectric Plant Will Tap City's Water System," *New York Times*, 3 March 1954, late city edition, A20.

19. *Sweet Lorraine*, dir. Steve Gomer, Autumn Pictures/Angelika Co., 1987.

20. Robert L. Schain, "A Study of the Historical Development of the Resort Industry of the Catskills" (Ph.D. diss., New York University, 1969), 368.

21. Ibid.

22. *The Rise and Fall of the Borscht Belt*, dir. Peter Davis, 90 min., Villon Films, 1988, video-cassette; distributed by Arthur Cantor, Inc.

23. Ober, *Bungalow Nine*, 70.

24. Ibid., 71.

25. Ibid. A "fungo" is a bat with a ball attached to it by an elastic cord. You can hit at the ball endlessly.

26. Mimi Sheraton, *From My Mother's Kitchen* (New York: Harper and Row, 1979), 243.

27. Ibid.

Bungalow Stories

Arthur Janney

WHO REMEMBERS BEING YOUNG?

There was a certain stillness to the mountains. A quiet unlike what we'd ever known in the city. You felt it the first moment your parents opened the car door in the small town to pick up a few things, maybe milk, juice, and rolls, on the way to the colony that first weekend. You and your brother or sister piled out of the back of the sedan, from under a mountain of pillows and blankets, and you waited a moment while your mom went into the store. All the while the excitement bubbled inside you, like a geyser, so eager to get to the colony to see friends not heard from in almost a year. Would there be new kids this summer? Would your name still be where you wrote it on the big rock under the tree near the handball court? Would the pool, by some miracle, have given birth to a diving board during the winter? Who'd be your counselor in camp? Hopefully not the dweeby guy with the glasses and the acne. . . .

Then back in the car for the last five minutes to the colony. The anticipation unbearable. The car windows were open wide, because a/c just didn't exist, and you could smell the jasmine and the honeysuckle and the fresh-cut grass, and the small hint of pollen, and then, around the bend, through a clearing in the stand of pine and birch, you got your first glimpse of a bungalow, peeking through the branches.

Has anything since been as much fun?

HAVE YOU THANKED YOUR PARENTS?

Mid July, and it was at about this point that you had really settled into your summer. The camp softball team was pretty set, and you were doing better than you'd hoped all winter long, though not quite so well as the new kid on the colony, whose surprise presence had upset your plans on being the pitcher, having you settle, instead, for playing second base. You'd had your eye on the new kid's sister, who was a year and a half younger than you, but cute all the same, with curtly red hair and a smattering of freckles across the bridge of her nose, and you didn't half mind the half pound of steel she was carrying on her teeth, because her smile was brilliant all the same. You'd been too long in the pool earlier in the summer, when the sun was subtropical, and your shoulders had burned so badly that they'd blistered, and you were sure you'd never escape the ubiquitous scent of the Noxema that your mom gobbed onto your reddened skin every day. But there were other things that were going especially well. You'd made the record score on the colony pinball machine, winning an unheard of fifteen free games, consecutively, managed to impress even your dad in the process. Your grandparents had already completed their annual summer sojourn to the colony and left you with a tidy stash of cash that you were tapping into regularly to consume egg creams and malts in the colony concession. You had even adjusted to being a half day behind on box scores, because the *Daily News* and *Post* didn't get the late boxes upstate, and the *Record* was always a day behind, anyway. But there was news of great concerts upcoming at Monticello Raceway—Jay and the Americans, Ike and Tina, maybe even Chuck Berry—if only your parents would let you go. And in August they were throwing a big thing outside of Monticello, with a lot of groups—The Who, Santana, Hendrix—but no way your parents would let you go, at twelve. They were calling it an Aquarian Festival. Woodstock.

And you got postcards and letters from your buddies in the city, who were going to day camp or just hanging about, playing ball on the asphalt and chasing the Good Humor man, and stifling in the humidity, not knowing what it was like to slam shut the screen door of the bungalow and saunter over to the pool, your arm slung through a big, black inner tube, the world at your feet.

And have we thanked our parents for such great memories?

THE CASINO ON SATURDAY NIGHTS

On Saturday nights the parents dressed a little better than usual, and after dinner they migrated toward the casino, where they performed God only knew what kinds of pagan rituals that were guarded like holy state secrets from us, the kinder. There was a certain mystery and romance to seeing our parents act silly and laugh at foolish, inane jokes while sloppily inbibing rye and scotch and gin (who drank vodka and tequila in those days?), and munching potato chips and pretzels from those little plastic bowls that were lined with napkins and ritually refilled from huge metal tins. From a distance, through the warm, sweet Catskill summer nights, the sounds of their merriment were cloaked in velvet.

We could distinguish the band—usually a three- or four-piece combo, a collection of NYC school teachers who, on vacation, imagined themselves magically transformed into Dave Brubeck, Bill Evans, or John Coltrane. Every summer there was a stripper, and the next day there were hushed stories around the pool about which father had been foolish enough to manhandle the talent while under the influence. Each year there was a mentalist, or hypnotist, whose appearance and resulting hystrionics were fodder to embarrass at least a half dozen parents, and then, each year, there was a mock marriage—this the best of the weekends—when our parents entertained themselves by role reversal, dressing the biggest, crudest man as the bride and the smallest, meekest woman as the groom, and *La Cage aux Folles*ing it up all the way to the breaking of the glass.

I think of those nights our parents shared in those little colonies dotted all about Sullivan and Ulster counties, in the 1940s and '50s and '60s, when they fled the city for little shacks in their country, with no air conditioning, no TV, one colony phone, and little else but their desire to enjoy. And I look at our lives now—fancy cars, the Hamptons, backyard pools—and damned if I'm still not jealous.

BUNGALOW COLONY MOVIE NIGHT

The "movie guy" always showed up a little late. He wasn't tall, wasn't short, was pretty nondescript, in fact, but he usually wore a plaid short-sleeved shirt and black slacks, always black slacks, even in the dead of July when the temperature topped out past 90. He drove a beaten up blue-green station wagon, with half-bald tires and a filthy, grimy windshield that by a miracle could be seen through. Strapped to the roof of the wagon were long, metal cylinders and black, steel and iron poles that, after a little "movie guy" magic, were suddenly transformed into a giant screen, which wound up erect at the far end of the casino, in front of the stage.

Once he'd set up the screen, which invariably was more yellowish than white and somewhat stained around the edges, he adjourned to the concession for coffee. Coffee! It was 96 degrees in the casino and the guy was drinking hot coffee!

There he would endure the entreaties of 50 or more pajama-clad monsters, bags of Bon-Ton potato chips or pretzels in hand, pleading for him to finish his business and roll the film. The "kiddie films," a long reel of short cartoons, usually began at 7 or 7:30, always too early for the summer sun to have left the sky. So the shades were pulled down on all the casino windows, and we sat in semidarkness, our hair still damp from our evening bath, bathrobes pulled snug against summer pajamas, our feet encased in slippers or pool thongs, and were delighted and enthralled by Heykyl and Jekyll, Tom and Jerry, Woody Woodpecker, Daffy Duck, Elmer Fudd, and, of course, Bugs Bunny. Sometimes, maybe once or twice a summer, by some miracle, we found a Three Stooges or Little Rascals slipped in with the animation. That was a special treat.

It's been more than 30 years now, but I can still vividly remember the way the film would crackle over that screen, breaking up, as it counted down from 10 to 1, just at the moment before the color would appear. I remember the stream of white foggy light flowing out from the noisy old projector, bisecting the darkened casino, and how when the screen was still blank but for light some kid would thrust his hands into that beam and adroitly fashion his fingers into shadow puppets. I remember the sweet and tart taste of Orange Crush on my tongue, and how bits of potato chips would somehow wind up floating in the bottle. I remember sitting there in the darkness, my best friends in the world all around me, looking up to the screen and hoping against hope there were another 5 or 6 or more cartoons left on the reel.

Of course, years passed, and we all aged, and then we one summer we discovered that by some mysterious decree we were suddenly old enough to be included with the elite group of "older" kids who got to see the "adult" film. We set up our lawn chairs in the front of the row upon row of casino folding chairs and waited for the few fans to blow some stale, stagnant air our way, while watching the flickering images of Cary Grant, Rock Hudson, Marilyn Monroe, Jack Lemmon, Doris Day, et al.

There were no VCRs or cable TV. The movies were saw were truly a special amusement. There were some films that were pretty much bungalow colony movie night classics. Remember? *Charade* is one. And all the Rock Hudson–Doris Day flicks—especially *Pillow Talk*. Then there was *The Thrill of It All*. *The Apartment*. I remember seeing *Rear Window* and being scared silly by *Psycho*. Cary Grant was always big; aside from *Charade*, there was *North by Northwest*, *That Touch of Mink*, *Houseboat*, *Father Goose*. Jack Lemmon was a staple, too—*Under the Yum Yum Tree*, *Some Like It Hot*, *It Happened to Jane*. Oh, and Judy Holiday and

Paul Douglas in *The Solid Gold Cadillac.* When the film ended and the clacking of the final reel was done, we exited into the sweet summer night, startled by how the air had cooled so, brushing popcorn and pretzel crumbs off our clothing, toting our lawn chairs, and yawning, headed off for crisp, cold sheets and stacks of Supermans and Batmans and Green Lanterns, and maybe Archies, too.

You know, we never had what our kids do now—computers, video games, and 98 channels of TV, VCRs, and videos at $12.99. But maybe what we had was better. It certainly seems so in the remembering.

FRIDAY NIGHT—RETURN OF THE DADS

Looking back today, it's obvious that it was a classic matriarchal society. Close to maybe what had existed so many years before, when the senior men in the clan were out hunting and foraging and the women tended home fires and children. But in the remembering it is clear that the weekdays were devoid of fathers and husbands, except for the colony owner and maybe the camp director.

At some time between dinner Sunday and breakfast Monday, the dads vanished, banished back to "the city," where they slaved long and hard to earn the bounty that made our summer's solace possible.

Disappearing along with them were all vehicles of the internal-combustion variety. On Monday mornings the colony parking lot was as empty as a temple ten minutes after the shofar blows on Yom Kippur. From Monday through Friday, we were pretty much landlocked to that little plot of grass and asphalt—remanded to the handball court, ball field, casino, swimming pool, and rows of little shacks that were our respite from the teeming and steaming streets of Brooklyn, the Bronx, and Queens.

The weekdays were full—with day camp and ball games and swimming and horseplay; and the moms had meals to prepare and washes to do, and, more essentially, mah-jongg and canasta to play. But invariably, Friday rolled around again, and with it the much-heralded return of our the wandering dads.

Friday came, and our moms, who on other evenings would throw anything at all together for dinner, often "pot-lucking" it between two or three or more families, would suddenly emerge as Jewish Julia Childs incarnate, and spend hours preparing lavish "Friday" (or "Shabbos" to the more observant few) repasts. They roasted chickens and turkeys and made chicken soup from scratch. They made chopped liver, chopping the liver and eggs and onions and chicken fat in those old wooden bowls with a gleaming, steel, sharper-than-the-devil's-tongue hand chopper that preceded *Sling Blade* by a good three decades. They baked kugels and bought or baked fresh challah. I remember my mom would stock away jars of cold borscht, or schav—a foul-smelling, mysterious, green concoction that my dad downed with relish preceding his dinner.

They began arriving sometime after six, those that were fortunate enough to be able to leave their offices an hour or so before regular closing. The small, winding country road that for five days had been practically barren now witnessed a continuing, relentless clump-clump of tires bounding over its weary blacktop. The cars knew not from air conditioning, and the Chevys and Fords and Oldsmobiles and Dodges appeared, windows opened wide in search of a small breeze. The dads emerged from the steamy cars in short-sleeved white shirts opened at the collar, a hint of perspiration stain at the underarms, stopping to stretch, then await the rushing onslaught of their children, who, gratefully, were still young enough to be excited by the simple reappearance of an absent parent. I recall us charging my dad with the zeal of the bulls at Pamplona, eager to discover what treat or surprise he'd smuggled up from the city. One weekend it was my grandfather, replete with overstuffed valise, intent on a two-week stay, armed with enough loose change to keep me in pinball heaven for the fortnight. Another time it was a stack of new Supermans. One time it was a surprise visit from a city friend, although that one backfired, because, well, the city friends and country friends, they were two different breeds, you see, and they mixed as well as gasoline and turpentine.

I remember those Friday nights like they were last week. The promise of dusk settling around the colony as we spied my dad's car turning into the parking lot. He lumbered from the car, and you caught a hint of his smell—that dad smell. Part Old Spice, part Pepsodent, part Lucky Strikes, part perspiration. And he'd been three hours on the road, but he was anxious and eager to hear all about your week in camp, and the softball game you won with a late-inning base hit, and the movie you'd seen the other night in the casino, and the new high you'd posted on the colony pinball machine, and anything and everything else you wanted to share. Harry Chapin wrote a lot of great songs, but fortunately, "Cat's in the Cradle" didn't apply to us. We really did know when Dad was coming home, and we really did have a great time then. We really did.

VENDORS, PEDDLERS, AND KNISHMEN IN THE SUMMER

The vendors usually made their rounds midweek, which always puzzled me a little. Either they were ignorant of the fact that the husbands held most of the cash, or they were banking on the husbands' absence liberating the wives' conscience, allowing a free-spending attitude to permeate the women on the colony. Either way, I remember them arriving on weekdays, while we were in day camp, either playing softball or splashing in the pool or simply lazing around on the grass, in the shade, telling each other lies and battling a Fudgesicle to a draw—equal amounts in the mouth and drizzled down the front of our camp T-shirt.

Usually the concessionaire, or colony owner, announced the vendor's appearance on the colony PA system. Sometimes, though, it was the vendor himself. Ruby the Knishman, whose proclamations were as famous as his dreamy, greasy, sumptuous knishes, stands out above all. Ah, but I digress.

Looking back, it's truly a remarkable phenomenon—these mobile vendors, like New World descendants of the old Jewish peddlers who'd roamed the rocky dirt roads of the "old country." They pulled onto the colony grounds in their dusty station wagons or panel trucks and erected a few bridge tables on which to display their wares. There was the bathing suit guy, and the sweater guy. There was the T-shirt guy and the jeans guy. There was an assortment of anonymous shoe men. Honestly, most of the clothing vendors were forgettable, except, in the late 1960s, for an old school bus painted in psychedelic colors and covered with peace signs that had been christened "Bus Stop Boutique." It was little more than a head shop on wheels, but the time was right, and for kids marooned on a bungalow colony with little access to rolling papers and screens, it was a Godsend. They also stocked great tie-dye wear, and a varied assortment of the latest record releases. I remember buying James Taylor's seminal album, *Sweet Baby James*, for $2.99. Also the second Blood, Sweat and Tears, the faded brown cover, with "Spinning Wheel" and "You've Made Me So Very Happy."

Some of the vendors were so colorful and unique that they remain indelibly on my memory circuits even with the confounded passing of more than three decades. There was the "Knishman from Mountaindale." He would arrive on our colony each and every Thursday afternoon, his truck laden with freshly roasted chickens, brisket, soup, kishka, kugels, cholent, and, of course, those marvelous knishes—potato and kasha. A harried and hurried mom could purchase an entire Friday dinner with some mah-jongg winnings, and save Friday afternoon for sunning at the pool. And they did.

There was "Shimmy the Pickle King." He owned a huge blue truck, the side painted with giant pickles. His garlic sours were a thing of beauty, a joyous memory forever—crisp, flavorful, and tart. He also moved jars of sweet red peppers, sour tomatoes, and sauerkraut, as well as nuts and dried fruit.

There was Chow-Chow Cup, of blessed memory. We savored chicken chow mein that came in that wonderful bowl made of Chinese noodles, and the Chinese hot dogs, just corn dogs on a stick, really, that came encased in a wrapper with Chinese lettering all over. The egg rolls were loaded with enough oil to slick the hair of the entire Lincoln High School football team. On the first bite the grease saturated the flimsy napkin and stained every article of clothing within 200 yards.

There was an unending and countless assortment of peddlers—honest men and women hustling hard in the heat to make a buck. They hawked everything from pocketbooks to kids' sweatshirts, cheap watches to fresh fruit. But no matter what it was they were pushing, one thing was a constant—the rushing tide of the mothers from their mah-jongg and canasta games, and from their poolside sun perches, just to "look, I'm just looking, sweetheart." Of course, suffice to say that God has yet to create a Jewish woman who could "just look," and inevitably, you'd return from camp at day's end to discover some new, hideous, and utterly unnecessary addition to your bungalow, or worse, your summer wardrobe, an item your mom was certain was "just perfect" for you. Then you did your best to relegate the item to the back and bottom of your dresser drawer, hoping it would be forgotten until well after Labor Day, when, in the rush to pack the bungalow, you might succeed in misplacing it forever.

Of all the vendors that came and went through all those enchanted summers, my favorite, an authentic Mountains character, was Ruby the Knishman. I close my eyes and see his long, thin face, three days' salt-and-pepper stubble riding his gaunt cheeks. His fingers are long and thin and crooked, and he doesn't walk so much as lope, a little stooped, until, standing in the concession as he announces his presence on the microphone, you see him stretch and realize he is actually tall. He wears a soiled old sport shirt and a pair of beaten trousers, a baseball cap on his head, and he speaks to the microphone in a voice part gravel, part velvet. I only wish I'd once thought to record his announcements, because they were rich in ad libs and merriment.

"Ladies and gentlemen," he would intone, "I am back! Ruby the Knishman is now on the premises, with my delicious and nutritious, hot, homogenized, pasteurized, and recently circumcised kosher knishes. We got today for you potato, onion, kasha, mushroom, and pizza knishes. Come on, folks, I need the money. I gotta send my wife to Florida. She's killing me! Oy! Have some *rachmunis* on an old man and buy a dozen. Buy two dozen!"

The knishes, at half a buck each, were the best buy in 100 miles. They were unlike any other kind of knish I've had before or since—a fried covering, like a pouch, inside filled with cloudy dollops of potato, or potato and mushroom, or, for the adventurous few who also desired to fulfill some dubious dietary necessity—broccoli. I haven't had a Ruby's knish—he called them "Mom's Knishes" because his wife, "Mom," was their sainted creator—in more than ten years now, but the taste is just beyond my tongue as if it were yesterday.

Ruby is gone now. After he passed on, his wife and kids operated a store in Woodbourne, turning out the same remarkable product. That lasted a few summers. I've heard rumors of a place in Loch Sheldrake stocking a knish somewhat akin to what Ruby once fed us. But it wouldn't be the same. Not without the battered truck he had, held together with spit and a prayer; not without his glorious and memorable announcements on the colony loudspeaker; and certainly not without being touched by the hands of Ruby himself, the true Pied Piper of knishes from my childhood, all those years ago.

Enchanted Summer Nights

"Night" was always late arriving. The days stretched on forever, refusing to surrender the sunlight, so that even after nine o'clock there were traces of pink and crimson in the western sky, the horizon flaming with the promise of another glorious summer day.

Actually, what just constituted "night" was open to wide and varied interpretation. As far as our parents were concerned, "night" was anytime after we returned home, ragged and ragamuffin, from day camp. Certainly, for their purposes, it commenced with the conclusion of dinner, when we would bound from bungalows like stampeding livestock. Of course, as kids, we contended that for the "night" to be officially under way, a few requirements needed to be fulfilled. First was the absence of the pajama-clad "little kids." Second was the mandatory appearance of at least three stars in the inky sky. Finally, and most important, was the beginning of a game we called "Ring-a-leevio."

The group divided equally, each team took a turn being "it." The team that was "it" had to scatter to all corners of the colony. The other team secured an area as the "jail," and after a period of time allowing the "it" team to hide, they began seeking out the enemy. When a member of the adversarial team was sighted, he had to be stopped—often with a flying, leaping tackle—and secured to the count of "Ring-a-leevio, one two three, one two three!" That accomplished, the "caught" man was escorted to jail, where he waited, with the other unfortunates of his team, to be "rescued" or until the entire team was jailed. Rescue occurred when a team member succeeded in breaching the outer barrier of the "jail" area to touch the hands of his imprisoned teammates before he himself was apprehended.

Ring-a-leevio was the passion of our summer's evenings. We played from dusk till our mothers, on a break from their mah-jongg and canasta games, shouted us into our bungalows. On Friday nights, with a camp-free day to follow, we played deep into the night. As experienced ring-a-leevio players we became familiar with each corner, nook, and cranny of the colony, filing away new hiding places and reworking mysterious routes and passageways.

It's been thirty years since my last game of ring-a-leevio. Yet, sitting here now, eyes closed, I can recall waiting in the tall grass, bent to one knee, the ground damp, the night air icy cold in my lungs, breath short as I struggled to be quiet and assess if I might succeed in a mad dash across the open lawn to the rear corner of the handball court, where my teammates were in "jail." To be the last free man on a captured team and manage to vanquish all the competition then guarding one's teammates, thus setting companions free for another round, was an accomplishment akin to winning a game with a grand slam in the bottom of the ninth.

Ring-a-leevio was a passion, but it was hardly all we played. There was "Johnny on the Pony," or "Buck-Buck." Two teams, equally divided, took turns leaping onto each others' prostrate backs and, once supported for the required time, reversed position. Here, the heaviest kid, usually a late selection when choosing up teams for baseball and other games, became a hot commodity, often the first round draft pick.

The summer nights were filled with camaraderie. Our bungalows were without TVs, let alone VCRs, cable, video games, computers, air conditioners, or phones. In place of electronic advancements we were stuck with, well, each other. If we were fortunate enough to have lights on the handball court, we could play stickball well into the night. Basketball, too.

As the years matured us, we graduated from organized games to "hanging out." Sitting in a wide circle on painted Adirondack chairs and lawn chairs made of woven straps, we bundled up in winter coats against the cool evenings. The stars illuminated our friends' faces, and we talked of our lives at a time when we were young and cocky, and so ignorant and self-absorbed and wonderfully foolish, that the future lay before us like a great, wide boulevard on which options were innumerable and anything seemed possible.

On those nights we took our first tentative steps toward being adults. We sampled cigarettes and pot and wine, and a girl's soft, sweet mouth (or a boy's, as the case might be). Under a canopy of Catskills stars we pulled grass from the ground and playfully tossed it at one another, as James Taylor, the Beatles, the Rascals, or Tommy James and the Shondells played softly in the darkness. We laughed and kidded and plotted and planned, and we swore we'd know one another forever. And life was so full and easy and simple that we felt no pressure or stress or strain, and we were convinced we would all live forever.

THE IDES OF AUGUST

By mid-August came the chill. The nights, which previously had held a blessed respite from the torrid days, now snapped cold. Your mom dug deep into the closet, behind the broken lawn chairs, to pull out the reliable old bungalow heater. The heaters were of two varieties, really. There were the kerosene heaters, of which I hold little memory; then there was the electric coiled type. This heater was plugged in and soon its tightly wrapped coils glowed red, like the inside workings of a giant toaster. These heaters, not much bigger than a small TV, gave off a surprising amount of warmth. But your mom wasn't satisfied. She proceeded to ignite all four of the stovetop burners, and on very frigid nights the oven, too, with its door swung open. The bungalow retained a small hint of gas, but it was warm and toasty as you came in from a fierce game of ring-a-leevio or tag, the night air icy in your chest, to sit at the linoleum kitchen table and devour hot chocolate and a sleeve of Oreos.

If the dawn of August marked summer's midpoint, then halfway through August began the death watch. The vacation rapidly diminished, and you began counting off the days on your fingers. The evening cold now invaded the days. You dressed in sweatshirts and jeans, your T-shirts and shorts abandoned in the drawer, or worse, sent home with your dad in the first or second shipment of "cleaning out" for summer's end. You found yourself walking by the deserted swimming pool with longing in your eyes, hoping against hope for a late summer heat wave that would convince your mom it was swimming weather again. You noticed that when the air moved through the trees, the leaves would not only rustle and bend in the breeze, but many would begin their slow descent to the ground. Around the perimeter of the colony you could distinguish small touches of yellow and red and bronze on the branches. The small stand of apple trees near the play area had birthed an avalanche of apples—small, green, and sour. They were great for war games, but hell to eat.

Your letter writing to home began to slacken off. You'd see them all soon enough. You began to cling ever closer to your summer friends, forging bonds you believed were sacrosanct, decreed to survive a long ten-month winter. Day camp wound down, as the camp play loomed a week away, to be followed by the prom. Then, invariably, came the last hurrah—the final week of summer, no camp, no supervision, all freedom for play as your mom hurried against the clock to complete packing up the bungalow.

You hated seeing the bungalow that final week. When you entered the kitchen and discovered Mom had removed the "good" cover from the high-riser, replacing it with the "winter spread," you knew it was as good as over. Slowly but inexorably, your summer dream was being dismantled. Just days to go and so much to do.

You didn't know, couldn't know, how quickly the ensuing ten months would leave the calendar, and that in an eye's blink you'd be back there again, in June, the trees verdant and the days long and warm and the promise of the summer lush and alive. All you knew was that it had gone too fast, had fled like a thief in the night, leaving a long winter to stand before the return. Foolish, how we pushed the days away to get back to those fleeting ten weeks. If only all our days had been like summer. But then, if so, would they have held such magic and wonder?

DON'T CALL THEM "BIMMIES"

They were mostly anonymous men. Often they'd be gathered in late spring from the county jail, having been arrested for drunk and disorderly. Not bad men, just guys who were older and weary and down on their luck for so long that it had managed to become a chronic condition. Where our parents had friends, family, jobs, and community, these guys had the weekly paycheck and what solace there was at the bottom of a bottle. It might not have been much, but it was dependable and affordable.

Too often they caught crap from the colony kids, but it wasn't warranted and it wasn't pretty. The older kids called them "bimmies" and winos. But, for the most part, what drinking they did they did on their own, in their cramped dingy quarters, or in local shot and beer joints we had been instructed to avoid at all costs. Mostly they did their jobs with little or no notice—repairs to bungalow roofs, minor plumbing, routine carpentry, groundskeeping, pool maintenance.

Of all the faceless and nameless men that filled these thankless jobs over so many summers, two stand out in memory. In our small Mountaindale bungalow colony the owner's right-hand men were Paul and Martin. Both were tall, strong, and weather-beaten men. They gave the appearance of being as old as the mountains, though in looking back I realize they were likely no older than I am today—late thirties, early forties. I remember them always in soiled T-shirts and khaki work pants. They wore beaten-up lace-up boots, even in the dog days of summer, and each man owned a tattered and faded baseball cap that was his daily guard against the sun burning a balding scalp. Paul had various tattoos over his biceps, but now I can't quite recall what any were. Martin, though, carried a vibrant tattoo of a warship, the USS something or other, on which he had dutifully served during World War II.

Paul had had a family. My dad had told me that, one day after we'd seen him in town, sucking on a can of Schlitz outside the local grocery. For some reason I failed to ascertain at the ripe age of nine, my dad held a special affinity for both Paul and Martin. I remember my mom berating him for lending money to the men, because she was certain the cash would do little else but contribute to their almost constant off-duty state of inebriation.

Yet, for whatever their shortcomings, each June we returned to find Paul and Martin dutifully at work painting bungalows, repairing lawn furniture, seeding gardens, prepping the pool, and apparently genuinely happy to see the return of the summer guests. Where they dispersed to each autumn, and how they passed their winters, was a never-answered mystery. One time, when we were returning from visiting a maiden aunt in Manhattan, I imagined seeing them among the lost and lonely roaming the Bowery, but I am now certain that was youthful whimsy.

In the summer I was to turn twelve, I secured steady weekend employment baby-sitting the Goldstein twins in bungalow 12. The twins were three, and usually asleep before I arrived to take charge from the casino-bound parents. It was an easy gig. Janet Goldstein was a nice lady, not too tall, with generous hips and an easy smile, and her kitchen was often better stocked with junk food than the local grocery. I'd arrive with an armful of comic books and sports magazines, and on the umbrella table outside the bungalow I'd arrange myself a small banquet of potato chips, pretzels, M&Ms, Raisinettes, cookies, and soda. Then I'd wipe a lawn chair free of dew, switch on my flashlight, and start in on my reading material, cognizant of the seventy-five cents I was earning as each hour ticked off the clock. It was one Saturday night just like that, under a speckled night sky, amid the incessant din of the crickets and cicadas, that Martin decided to keep me company.

I couldn't tell if he was drunk. He certainly seemed sober enough, and there was no telltale scent of liquor. He ambled out of the darkness and pulled up a wooden lawn chair. He stretched out, crossing his long, lean legs and placing his muddy boots up on the metal table. Squinting in the moonlight, he reached into his T-shirt pocket for a pair of grimy eyeglasses, placed them on the bridge of his nose, and began examining my reading material, pausing at the most recent issues of *Baseball Digest*.

"Ya a baseball fan, huh?" he said. It was more words than I'd ever heard him speak at one time. His voice had the feel of gravel, deep and husky and rumbling. I thought it might have hurt his throat to speak.

"Uh-huh," I said.

"Seen ya playing softball," he said, still perusing the magazine. "Ya play third base?"

"Uh-huh," I said.

"Hard spot, the corner. That's why they call it the hot corner. Ya know?"

"Uh-huh," I said.

"Played third base myself," he said.

"Uh-huh."

"Before I became a pitcher." Then he hawked a bit, twisted his head, and spit into the night.

"Baseball and softball be two different animals," he said. "Softball like an old ladies' game. Ball up there big as a watermelon. How kin ya not hit it?"

Then he hawked again and spit again and reached into his trousers pocket to take a cigarette from a crumbled pack of Camels, which he lit with a shiny, steel Zippo lighter.

"Ya play baseball?" he said.

I nodded that I did. He nodded. The smoke snaked out from his nostrils in a long, spiraling helix, then disappeared into the night. He was quiet for a long time. I said nothing. After a while his breathing settled into a quiet cadence, his chest moving so slightly he might be taken for dead. The cigarette burned down to a stub, and softly dropped from his mangled fingers. I leaned forward to see that his eyes had shut, and I noticed, too, that his mouth had moved slightly, so that in his sleep there was just the trace of a smile about his lips.

There were other nights that Martin visited me as I sat under the Catskills stars, standing watch over the Goldstein twins. He told me stories of having seen

Babe Ruth and Lou Gehrig, Ted Williams, and Jackie Robinson. One night he brought a baseball and, in the quiet evening, he began instructing me on the proper grips for throwing a curveball, and a knuckleball, too. I began experimenting with these pitches, to become both exhilarated and bewildered when the ball commenced breaking and arching, moving to some mysterious heretofore-unknown music that I was suddenly able to master by the simple placement of my fingers on the horsehide.

Sitting near the pool one Sunday late in August, an atypically warm day for so deep into summer, I became aware of a small commotion on the central lawn. The parents had fled the pool to assemble in a small mob, gesturing and arguing with great animation. Then, on top of the hill, at the front entrance to the colony, from behind the colony store, a red and white ambulance rolled onto the grounds. It slowly moved across the center of the grounds, passing between two bungalows to the rear, where I knew only the laundry room, clotheslines, and handymen's quarters stood.

I raced from the pool with my friends David and Joel, to be cut off by our moms just feet from the water. No one was volunteering any information to the kids, but somehow, intuitively, we knew. Someone either was very, very ill, or worse. Judging by the meandering pace of the ambulance, we would bet on the latter.

I don't remember anyone actually telling me Martin had died. He'd been found lying in his bed, still clothed, a half-empty bottle of gin and the latest *Sports Illustrated* propped next to his stiffening body. I remember very little else from that day or the few that followed. I remember sitting behind my bungalow and crying. I remember my dad, and a few of the other dads, returning from the city midweek, something they'd never done before, to be present at a small, sparsely attended graveside service. I remember developing circuitous routes about the colony so I might avoid passing by Martin's now vacant shack. I remember babysitting those last weeks of summer, after his demise, and being afraid to sit by myself in the night, retreating inside the Goldstein bungalow.

A few weeks later the summer ended, and we said our good-byes to friends and neighbors, returning to the city, where, in a few days, our lives resumed their normal cadence and routine. The ensuing ten months passed quickly, and the following June we returned to the bungalow colony. Martin was gone, of course, and Paul, we were informed, had moved to Florida, to be closer to his adult children, with whom he'd reunited during the winter. In their place were two new men, one black, one Hispanic. They were good workers, polite, easygoing, friendly, and they managed to last the entire season. But that was all, and the following summer they were replaced by a parade of unreliable drunkards and sinners.

In the years that followed I sharpened my skills with the hardball, succeeding in baffling my peers with a sharp breaking curve and an unpredictable, but infuriating knuckler. I suspect I was the only high school kid throwing the knuckler in all of New York. And oftentimes, standing alone on the mound, peering in and waiting for my catcher to flash a signal, I would think of Martin and those sweet, lost summer nights when he'd taken the time to pass me his legacy, such as it was.

Part 3

HOTEL LIFE

"GOLDBERG'S," Loch Sheldrake, N.Y.

E-11470

HOTEL SEVEN GABLES Greenfield Park, N.Y. Tel. ELLENVILLE 449

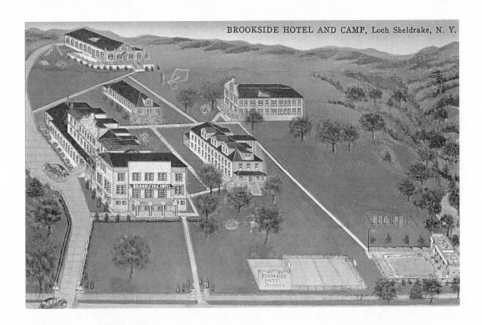

BROOKSIDE HOTEL AND CAMP, Loch Sheldrake, N. Y.

FOUNTAIN HILL HOUSE, Inc., Ellenville, N. Y.

Four postcards by Alfred Landis, the great artist of the genre.

CATSKILLS INSTITUTE

Landis watercolor of the Hollywood Hotel, Livingston Manor. Landis painted watercolors of his clients' hotels and bungalow colonies and used them as models for the postcards he produced back in his studio in Wurtsboro. Often, Landis gave the hotel a package price for the painting and the cards, allowing the owner to keep the watercolor. The Sullivan County Historical Society has several of these in their collection.

KATE HYDEN

Ruins of the Main House of the Youngs Gap Hotel, Parksville, 1999.

PHIL BROWN

Rainbow Hotel, Ulster Heights, 2000. The Rainbow, previously the Alpine Hotel, has been run for about a decade by Russian Jews. The unmodernized shape and stucco front retain the original style of a small Catskills hotel from the 1920s to the 1950s. This is the probably the best preserved small hotel in the Catskills.
PHIL BROWN

Old hotel, now private home, Ulster Heights, 2000. Many old hotels are now the residences of individuals. Ulster Heights has an especially large number of them.   PHIL BROWN

Comparison of small and large hotels. The owners and staff in the kitchen of the Maple Court Hotel, Dairyland, 1941. This small hotel had a maximum capacity of eighty guests and was clearly run with a very small labor force, though they certainly worked hard.
ALICE GUTTER

Brickman Hotel, South Fallsburg, 1960s. In contrast to the Maple Court, Brickman's could hold about 750 people. It had two baseball fields, a dozen tennis courts, and a riding academy. The aerial view shows much of the original shape, despite extensive modernization. BEBE TOOR

The Eldorado
FALLSBURG • NEW YORK

Executive Office

FAMILY RATE SCHEDULE

TYPE OF ACCOMMODATION	1 adult & 1 child, plus husband's 2-day week-end	1 adult & 2 children, plus husband's 2-day week-end	2 adults and 1 child	2 adults and 2 children
HALLWAY BATH AND SHOWER	$160.00 172.50 185.00	$190.00 205.00 220.00	$185.00 195.00 215.00	$225.00 240.00 260.00
SEMI-PRIVATE BATH AND SHOWER	$186.00 202.50 210.00	$215.00 230.00 250.00	$220.00 227.50 235.00	$260.00 275.00 290.00
PRIVATE DE-LUXE ACCOMMODATIONS	$220.00 240.00 260.00	$255.00 275.00 310.00	$250.00 275.00 290.00	$290.00 325.00 350.00

FOR CHILD IN MAIN DINING-ROOM ADD $15.00 WEEKLY TO ABOVE RATES.

WHEN ONE ADULT AND ONE CHILD OCCUPY A ROOM ALONE, THE RATE FOR TWO ADULTS APPLIES.

EXACT RATE IS DETERMINED BY LOCATION.

COMPLETE FACILITIES AND ACTIVITIES FOR CHILDREN OF ALL AGES. SPECIAL PROGRAMS PLANNED FOR DIFFERENT AGE GROUPS. NIGHT PATROL IN ALL BUILDINGS.

TEEN-AGE ACTIVITIES INCLUDE GOLF, BOATING, BOWLING, HAY RIDES, ETC.

RESERVATIONS PLANNED FOR SUNDAY ARRIVAL.

NO RESERVATION IS DEFINITE UNTIL CONFIRMED IN WRITING.

Rate sheet for Eldorado, Fallsburg, 1960s. The prevalence of weekend husbands can be seen in the rate categories. This medium-sized hotel could hold perhaps 300 people.   CATSKILLS INSTITUTE

INTRODUCTION

Catskills hotelkeepers pioneered the all-inclusive vacation, with three meals plus a nighttime tea room, entertainment, many sports and activities, and eventually day camps for children. Because they often began as boarding houses and small family-style hotels, even larger hotels retained a certain intimate feeling. The owners were always present, often as a pair of in-law couples, and they all worked in various capacities. They mingled with guests, many of whom were relatives, friends, and acquaintances, and provided a familial environment. This milieu was safe but also contained the pros and cons of intimate contact. More than 1,000 boarding houses and hotels existed over the century, the latter making up the vast majority. At least 500 operated at any one time, and they ranged from small places holding 40 people to large ones with 500–900 guests, Grossinger's with more than 1,000, and the Concord with 2,000.

Abraham Cahan, founder of the *Jewish Daily Forward* newspaper, was one of the major Jewish writers in the early decades of the twentieth century. His 1917 novel, *The Rise of David Levinsky*, was the first piece of fiction to take up the Catskills. This excerpt, "Dinner at the Rigi Kulm House," is a literary look at the life of an elegant Catskills hotel and its elaborate food, served to the accompaniment of a band. Cahan captures the tumult of the dining rooms, even in this fine hotel, that can still be observed today.

Hortense Calisher's short story "Old Stock" is unique in telling the story of a Jewish family at a Gentile-owned boarding house that now has Jewish clientele. German Jews who have recently had a financial downturn, this family is displeased at staying with Eastern European Jews. That conflict was significant throughout America, and clearly in the Catskills, where German Jews typically stayed in a different area, around Fleischmann's. Calisher's fifteen-year-old protagonist, Hester Elkin, and her mother visit a nearby woman they have come to know, but are surprised to hear this neighbor of Dutch descent make an anti-Semitic remark, apparently unaware of her guests' background. That casts a shadow on Hester's vacation, as she keeps expecting anti-Semitism to surface in others at the boarding house.

"Young Workers in the Hotels," an excerpt from my *Catskill Culture: A Mountain Rat's Memories of the Great Jewish Resort Area*, is a description of my own and other young workers' experiences as waiters, busboys, bellhops, and counselors. I describe our work life, the staff quarters, ways we entertained ourselves, and the importance of this experience in terms of both income and learning key work skills.

Eileen Pollack's "The Pool" comes from her novel *Paradise, New York*, in which young Lucy grows up in her grandparents' and parents' hotel. Later, when her grandmother is trying to sell it to Hasidim, Lucy tries to salvage it. While not autobiographical, Pollack's novel draws on her experience in the hotel business until she left for college. In this excerpt, nine-year-old Lucy describes her life as an owner's child, using the pool setting to examine her fascination with the dining room staff and observe the guests.

Tania Grossinger's "Growing up at Grossinger's" derives from her book of the same title. Grossinger's mother, a relative of the Grossingers who owned the famous resort, worked as the social hostess there for many years. This gave Tania a wonderful insight into the workings of the hotel, and she treats us to a glimpse of the famous entertainers who played there and of how the staff lived and entertained themselves.

Sidney Offit's "Five and Three House" comes from his 1959 novel *He Had It Made*, just republished in 1999. Offit's original title for his book was *Five and Three House*, but it was changed before publication. "Five and three" refers to the typical tip level of the hotel—five dollars a week for the waiter and three for the busboy. The lead character, Al Brodie, talks himself into a waiter's job and makes his way as best he can in the tense atmosphere. Offit presents the best account yet of life in the dining room and kitchen, full of humor and sex.

Jerry Jacobs wrote "Reflections on the Delmar Hotel and the Demise of the Catskills" especially for this anthology. Jacobs is a sociologist whose family owned a small hotel near Liberty, and who only later in life came to realize that his experiences there were worthy of sociological attention. He notes that most of the Jewish academics he knows have no interest in studying Jewish life, and that this has meant that we have hardly any exploration or documentation of the importance of this unique culture. He provides a vivid view of the inside of the hotel business, including the many different jobs he had; explores some of the reasons for the decline of the Catskills; and mourns the loss of the sense of community it provided.

Dinner at the Rigi Kulm House

Abraham Cahan

D inner at the Rigi Kulm on a Saturday evening was not merely a meal. It was, in addition, or chiefly, a great social function and a gown contest. The band was playing. As each matron or girl made her appearance in the vast dining-room the female boarders already seated would look her over with feverish interest, comparing her gown and diamonds with their own. It was as though it were especially for this parade of dresses and finery that the band was playing. As the women came trooping in, arrayed for the exhibition, some timid, others brazenly self-confident, they seemed to be marching in time to the music, like so many chorus-girls tripping before a theater audience, or like a procession of model-girls at a style-display in a big department store. Many of the women strutted affectedly, with "refined" mien. Indeed, I knew that most of them had a feeling as though wearing a hundred-and-fifty-dollar dress was in itself culture and education.

Mrs. Kalch kept talking to me, now aloud, now in whispers. She was passing judgment on the gowns and incidentally initiating me into some of the innermost details of the gown race. It appeared that the women kept tab on one another's dresses, shirt-waists, shoes, ribbons, pins, earrings. She pointed out two matrons who had never been seen twice in the same dress, waist, or skirt, although they had lived in the hotel for more than five weeks. Of one woman she informed me that she could afford to wear a new gown every hour in the year, but that she was "too big a slob to dress up and too lazy to undress even when she went to bed"; of another, that she would owe her grocer and butcher rather than go to the country with less than ten big trunks full of duds; of a third, that she was repeatedly threatening to leave the hotel because its bills of fare were typewritten, whereas "for the money she paid she could go to a place with print-ed menu-cards."

"Must have been brought up on printed menu-cards," one of the other women at our table commented, with a laugh.

"That's right," Mrs. Kalch assented, appreciatively. "I could not say whether her father was a horse-driver or stoker in a bath-house, but I do know that her husband kept a coal-and-ice cellar a few years ago."

"That'll do," her bewhiskered husband snarled. "It's about time you gave your tongue a rest."

Auntie Yetta's golden teeth glittered good-humoredly. The next instant she called my attention to a woman who was driven to despair by the superiority of her "bosom friend's" gowns, had gone to the city for a fortnight, ostensibly to look for a new flat, but in reality to replenish her wardrobe. She had just re-turned, on the big "husband train," and now "her bosom friend won't be able to eat or sleep trying to guess what kind of dresses she brought back."

Nor was this the only kind of gossip upon which Mrs. Kalch regaled me. She told me, for example, of some sensational discoveries made by several boarders regarding a certain mother of five children, of her sister who was "not a bit bet-ter," and of a couple who were supposed to be man and wife, but who seemed to be "somebody else's man and somebody else's wife."

At last Miss Tevkin and Miss Siegel entered the dining room. Something like a thrill passed through me. I felt like exclaiming, "At last!"

"That's the one I met you with, isn't it? Not bad-looking," said Mrs. Kalch. "Which do you mean?"

" 'Which do you mean'! The tall one, of course; the one you were so sweet on. Not the dwarf with the horse face."

"They're fine, educated girls, both of them," I rejoined.

"Both of them! As if it was all the same to you!" At this she bent over and gave me a glare and a smile that brought the color to my face. "The tall one is certainly not bad-looking, but we don't call that pretty in this place."

"Are there many prettier ones?" I asked, gaily.

"I haven't counted them, but I can show you some girls who shine like the sun. There is one!" she said, pointing at a girl on the other side of the aisle. "A regular princess. Don't you think so?"

"She's a pretty girl, all right," I replied, "but in comparison with that tall one she's like a nice piece of cotton goods alongside of a piece of imported silk."

"Look at him! He's stuck on her. Does she know it? If she does not, I'll tell her and collect a marriage-broker's commission."

I loathed myself for having talked too much.

"I was joking, of course," I tried to mend matters. "All girls are pretty."

Luckily Mrs. Kalch's attention was at this point diverted by the arrival of the waiter with a huge platter laden with roast chicken, which he placed in the middle of the table. There ensued a silent race for the best portions. One of the other two women at the table was the first to obtain possession of the platter. Taking her time about it, she first made a careful examination of its contents and then attacked what she evidently considered a choice piece. By way of calling my attention to the proceeding, Auntie Yetta stepped on my foot under the table and gave me a knowing glance.

The noise in the dining-room was unendurable. It seemed as though everybody was talking at the top of his voice. The musicians—a pianist and two violinists—found it difficult to make themselves heard. They were pounding and sawing frantically in a vain effort to beat the bedlam of conversation and laughter. It was quite touching. The better to take in the effect of the turmoil, I shut my eyes for a moment, whereupon the noise reminded me of the Stock Exchange.

The conductor, who played the first violin, was a fiery little fellow with a high crown of black hair. He was working every muscle and nerve in his body. He played selections from "Aida," the favorite opera of the Ghetto; he played the popular American songs of the day; he played celebrated "hits" of the Yiddish stage. All to no purpose. Finally, he had recourse to what was apparently his last resort. He struck up the "Star-spangled Banner." The effect was overwhelming. The few hundred diners rose like one man, applauding. The children and many of the adults caught up the tune joyously, passionately. It was an interesting scene. Men and women were offering thanksgiving to the flag under which they were eating this good dinner, wearing these expensive clothes. There was the jingle of newly-acquired dollars in our applause. But there was something else in it as well. Many of those who were now paying tribute to the Stars and Stripes were listening to the tune with grave, solemn mien. It was as if they were saying: "We are not persecuted under this flag. At last we have found a home."

Love for America blazed up in my soul. I shouted to the musicians, "My Country," and the cry spread like wild fire. The musicians obeyed and we all sang the anthem from the bottom of our souls.

Old Stock

Hortense Calisher

The train creaked through the soft, heat-promising morning like an elderly, ambulatory sofa. Nosing along, it pushed its corridor of paper-spattered floors and old plush seats through towns whose names—Crystal Run, Mamakating—were as soft as the morning, and whose dusty little central hearts—all livery stable, freight depot, and yard buildings with bricked-up windows and faded sides that said "Purina Chows"—were as down-at-the-heel as the train that strung them together.

Hester, feeling the rocking stir of the journey between her thighs, hanging her head out of the window with her face snubbed against the hot breeze, tried to seize and fix each picture as it passed. At fifteen, everything she watched and heard seemed like a footprint on the trail of some eventuality she rode to meet, which never resolved but filled her world with a verve of waiting.

Opposite her, her mother sat with the shuttered, conscious look she always assumed in public places. Today there was that added look Hester also knew well, that prim display of extra restraint her mother always wore in the presence of other Jews whose grosser features, voices, manners offended her sense of gentility all the more out of her resentful fear that she might be identified with them. Today the train rang with their mobile gestures, and at each station crowds of them got off—great-breasted, starched mothers trailing mincing children and shopping bags stuffed with food, gawky couples digging each other in the side with their elbows, girls in beach pajamas, already making the farthest use of their smiles and great, effulgent eyes. At each station, they were met by the battered Fords and wagons that serviced the farms which would accommodate them, where for a week or two they would litter the tight Catskill towns with their swooping gaiety and their weary, rapacious hope.

"Wild!" said Mrs. Elkin, sotto voce, pursing her mouth and tucking her chin in her neck. "Your hair and that getup! Always so wild." Hester, injured, understood that the indictment was as much for the rest of the train as for herself. Each summer for the past three years, ever since Mr. Elkin's business had been doing poorly and the family had been unable to afford the summer rental in Westchester, Mrs. Elkin had resisted the idea of Old Corner Farm, and each year she had given in, for they were still of a status which made it unthinkable that they would not leave New York for some part of the season. This year and last, they had not been able to manage it until September, with its lowered rates, but it would have been a confession of defeat for Mr. Elkin had he not been able to say during the week to casual business acquaintants, "Family's up in the country. I go up weekends." Once at the farm—although the guests there were of a somewhat different class from the people in this train, most of them arriving in their own cars and one or two with nursegirls for the children—Mrs. Elkin would hold herself aloof at first, bending over her embroidery hoop on the veranda, receiving the complimentary "What gorgeous work you do!" with a *moue* of distaste for the flamboyant word that was a hallmark of what she hated in her own race, politely refusing proffered rides to the village, finally settling the delicate choice of summer intimacy on some cowed spinster or recessive widow whom life had dampened to the necessary refinement. For Mrs. Elkin walked through the world swinging the twangy words "refined," "refinement," like a purifying censer before her.

Hester, roused momentarily from her dream of the towns, looked idly across at her mother's neat navy-and-white version of the late-summer uniform of the unadventurous and the well bred. Under any hat, in any setting, her mother always looked enviably right, and her face, purged of those youthful exoticisms it once might well have had, had at last attained a welcomed anonymity, so that now it was like a medallion whose blurred handsomeness bore no denomination other than the patent, accessible one of "lady." Recently, Hester had begun to doubt the very gentility of her mother's exorcistic term itself, but she was still afraid to say so, to put a finger on this one of the many ambiguities that confronted her on every side. For nowadays it seemed to her that she was like someone forming a piece of crude statuary which had to be reshaped each day—that it was not her own character which was being formed but that she was putting together, from whatever clues people would let her have, the shifty, elusive character of the world.

"Summitville!" the conductor called, poking his head into the car.

Hester and her mother got off the train with a crowd of others. Their feet crunched in the cinders of the path. The shabby snake of the train moved forward through its rut in the checkerboard hills. Several men who had been leaning on battered Chevvies ran forward, hawking persistently, but Mrs. Elkin shook her head. "There's Mr. Smith!" She waved daintily at an old man standing beside a truck. They were repeat visitors. They were being met.

Mrs. Elkin climbed into the high seat and sat tight-elbowed between Mr. Smith and Hester, denying the dusty indignity of the truck. The Smiths, people with hard faces the color of snuff, made no concession to boarders other than clean lodging and massive food. Mr. Smith, whose conversation and clothing were equally gnarled, drove silently on. At the first sight of him, of old Mr. Smith, with his drooping scythe of mustache, Hester, in one jolt, had remembered everything from the summers before.

The farm they travelled toward lay in a valley off the road from Kerhonkson to Accord. The house, of weather-beaten stone, was low and thick, like a blockhouse still retreating suspiciously behind a stockade long since gone; upstairs, beaverboard had partitioned it into many molasses-tinted rooms. In front of it would be the covered well, where the summer people made a ceremony of their dilettante thirst, the children forever sawing on the pulley, the grown-ups smacking their lips over the tonic water not drawn from pipes. Mornings, after breakfast, the city children gravitated to the barn with the indecipherable date over its lintel and stood silent watching the cows, hearing their soft droppings, smelling the fecund smell that was like the perspiration the earth made in moving. Afterward, Hester, usually alone, followed the path down to the point where the brown waters of Schoharie Creek, which featherstitched the countryside for miles, ran, darkly overhung, across a great fan of ledges holding in their center one deep, minnow-flecked pool, like a large hazel eye.

"There's Miss Onderdonk's!" Hester said suddenly. They were passing a small, square house that still preserved the printlike, economical look of order of old red brick houses, although its once-white window frames were weathered and shutterless, and berry bushes, advancing from the great thorny bower of them at the back, scraggled at the first-floor windows and scratched at the three stone steps that brinked the rough-cut patch of lawn. A collie, red-gold and white, lay on the top step. "There's Margaret!" she added. "Oh, let's go see them after lunch!"

A minute before, if asked, Hester could not have told the name of the dog, but now she remembered everything: Miss Onderdonk, deaf as her two white cats, which she seemed to prize for their affliction (saying often how it was related in some way to their blue eyes and stainless fur), and Miss Onderdonk's parlor, with a peculiar, sooty darkness in its air that Hester had never seen anywhere else, as if shoe blacking had been mixed with it, or as if the only sources of light in it were the luminous reflections from the horsehair chairs. Two portraits faced you as you entered from the bare, poor wood of the kitchen; in fact, you had only to turn on your heel from the splintered drainboard or the match-cluttered oilstove to see them—Miss Onderdonk's "great-greats"—staring nastily from their unlashed eyes, their pale faces and hands emerging from their needle-fine ruffles. The left one, the man, with a face so wide and full it must surely have been redder in life, kept his sneer directly on you, but the woman, her long chin resting in the ruffle, one forefinger and thumb pinching at the lush green velvet of her dress as if to draw it away, stared past you into the kitchen, at the bare drainboard and the broken-paned window above it.

Last year, Hester had spent much of her time "helping Miss Onderdonk," partly because there was no one her own age at the farm with whom to while away the long afternoons, partly because Miss Onderdonk's tasks were so different from anyone else's, since she lived, as she said, "offen the land." Miss Onderdonk was one of those deaf persons who do not chatter; her remarks hung singly, like aphorisms, in Hester's mind. "All white cats are deaf." "Sugar, salt, lard—bacon, flour, tea. The rest is offen the land." The articles thus enumerated lodged firmly in Hester's memory, shaped like the canisters so marked that contained the only groceries Miss Onderdonk seemed to have. Most of the time, when Hester appeared, Miss Onderdonk did not spare a greeting but drew her by an ignoring silence into the task at hand—setting out pans of berries to ferment in the hot sun, culling the warty carrots and spotted tomatoes from her dry garden. Once, when she and Hester were picking blackberries from bushes so laden that, turning slowly, they could pick a quart in one spot, Hester, plucking a fat berry, had also plucked a bee on its other side.

"Best go home. Best go home and mud it," Miss Onderdonk had said, and had turned back to the tinny plop of berries in her greedy pail. She had not offered mud. Hester, returning the next day, had not even felt resentment, for there was something about Miss Onderdonk, even if one did not quite like her, that compelled. As she worked at her endless ministrations to herself in her faded kitchen and garden, she was just like any other old maid, city or country, whose cottony hair was prigged tight from nightly crimpings never brushed free, whose figure, boarded up in an arid dress, made Hester gratefully, uneasily aware of her own body, fresh and moist. But when Miss Onderdonk stepped into her parlor, when she sat with her hands at rest on the carved knurls of the rocker or, standing near the open calf-bound book that chronicled the Onderdonk descent from De Witt Clinton, clasped her hands before her on some invisible pommel—then her role changed. When she stepped into her parlor, Miss Onderdonk swelled.

"How *is* Miss Onderdonk, Mr. Smith?" Mrs. Elkin asked lightly.

"The same." Mr. Smith kept his eyes on the road.

They turned in to the narrow dirt road that led off the highway down to the farm. Hester recognized a familiar curve in the sweep of surrounding hills, patch-quilted with crops. "There are hardly any white patches this year," she said.

Mr. Smith flicked a look at her, almost as if she had said something sensible. "People don't eat much buckwheat any more," he said, and brought the truck to a bumpy stop in front of the covered well.

Hester and her mother ran the gauntlet of interested glances on the porch and went up to their room. The room had a mail-order austerity, with nothing in it that was not neutralized for the transient except the dim cross-stitch doily on the dresser. Hester was glad to see their clothing shut away in the tar-paper wardrobe, sorry to see their toilet articles, the beginning of clutter, ranged on the dresser. This was the most exciting moment of all, before the room settled down with your own coloration, before the people you would get to know were explored.

"I saw that Mrs. Garfunkel on the porch," she said.

Her mother said "Yes" as if she had pins in her mouth, and went on putting things in drawers.

Mrs. Garfunkel was one of the ones who said "gorgeous"; it was perhaps her favorite word. A young matron with reddish hair, chunky, snub features, and skin tawnied over with freckles, she had the look of a Teddy bear fresh from the shop. Up here, she dressed very quietly, with an absence of heels and floppy sun-wear that, with her pug features, might have satisfied certain requirements in Mrs. Elkin's category of refinement. Neither did she talk with her hands, touch your clothing with them, or openly give the prices of things. But it was with her eyes that she estimated, with her tongue that she preened, and it was not long before you discovered that her admiring comment on some detail of your equipment was really only a springboard for the description of one or the other of her own incomparable possessions. Her satisfaction in these rested in their being not only the best but the best acquired for the least: the furs bought in August, the West Indian nursegirl who would work a year or so before realizing that the passage money Mrs. Garfunkel had advanced was more than underwritten by her inequitable salary, the compliant, self-effacing Mr. Garfunkel, who would probably go on working forever without realizing anything—even the languid, six-year-old Arline, who was so exactly suitable that she might have been acquired, after the canniest negotiation, from someone in that line to whom Mrs. Garfunkel had had a card of introduction. Perhaps, Hester thought now, her mother could better have borne Mrs. Garfunkel and her bargains if all of them had not been so successful.

When Hester and her mother, freshly washed and diffidently late, entered the dining room for dinner, which was in the middle of the day here, Mrs. Garfunkel hailed them, called them over to her table, pressed them to sit there, and introduced them to the others already seated. "Mrs. Elkin's an old-timer, like Mel and me. Meet Mr. and Mrs. Brod, and Mr. Brod's mother. And my brother Wally, Mrs. Elkin and daughter. What's your name again, dear?" She paid no heed to Hester's muttered response but dug her arm affectionately against the side of the rickety young man with slick hair who sat next to her, doggedly accumulating food on his plate. "Wally ran up here to get away from half the girls in Brooklyn."

The young man gave her a look of brotherly distaste. "Couldn't have come to a better place," he said, and returned to his plate. Great platters of sliced beefsteak tomatoes and fricasseed chicken were passed, nubs of Country Gentleman corn were snatched and snatched again; the table was one flashing activity of reaching arms, although there was much more food upon it than the few of them could possibly eat. This amplitude was what one came for, after all, and this was its high point, after which there would be nothing much to look forward to through the afternoon daze of heat but supper, which was good, though not like this.

Eating busily, Hester, from under the wing of her mother's monosyllabic chilliness, watched Mr. and Mrs. Brod. They were newly married, it developed, but this was not the honeymoon. The honeymoon, as almost every turn in the conversation indicated, had been in California; they were at the farm to visit old Mrs. Brod, a little leathery grandmother of a woman, dressed in a jaunty Roman-stripe jumper and wearing a ribbon tied around hair that had been bobbed and blued. The young Mrs. Brod had a sleepy melon face with a fat mouth, dark-red nails, and black hair cut Buster Brown. Mr. Brod, a bald young man in fawn-colored jacket and knickers, said almost nothing, but every so often he did an extraordinary thing. At intervals, his wife, talking busily, would extend her hand sidewise, palm upward, without even looking at him, and in one convulsive movement that seemed to start somewhere outside him and end at his extremities, as if he were the tip of a smartly cracked whip, a gold case would be miraculously there in his hand, and he would place a cigarette tenderly in her palm. A second but lesser convulsion produced a lighter for the negligently held cigarette. He did not smoke.

The two Mrs. Brods were discussing the dress worn by the younger, evidently a California purchase. "Right away, I said, 'This one I take!' " said the bride. "Definitely a knockout!"

"Vunt vash," said her mother-in-law, munching on an ear of corn.

The bride shrugged. "So I'll give to cleaners."

"Give to clean, give to ket." The mother put down her ear of corn, rolling it over reflectively.

"Don't have a cat, Ma."

Mrs. Brod the elder turned away momentarily from her plate. "Sah yull *buy* ah ket!" she said, and one lean brown arm whipped out and took another ear of corn.

The bride looked miffed, then put out the cigarette-seeking hand. Flex, flash from the solicitous Mr. Brod and the cigarette, lit, was between her lips, smoke curling from her scornful nostrils.

"Sweet, isn't it, the way he does that? And not a smoke for himself," said Mrs. Garfunkel in an aside to Hester's mother. "You better watch out, Syl," she called across the table to the bride. "He forgets to do that, then the honeymoon is over."

Mrs. Elkin smiled, a little rigid but perfectly cordial, unless you knew the signs, and stood up, reaching around for her big knitting bag, which was hung on the back of her chair. "Come, dear," she said to Hester, in accents at which no purist could cavil. "Suppose you and I go out on the porch."

On the empty porch, Mrs. Elkin selected a chair far down at the end. "Those people!" she said, and blew her breath sharply between set teeth. "I told your father this place was getting rundown."

"Sah yull *buy* ah ket," said Hester dreamily, and chuckled. It was the illogic of the remark that charmed.

"Must you *imitate*?" said her mother.

"But it's funny, Mother."

"Oh, you're just like your father. Absolutely without discrimination."

Hester found nothing to answer. "I think I'll walk down to the creek," she said.

"Take a towel."

Hester ran upstairs. Suddenly it was urgent that she get down to the creek alone, before the others, digestion accomplished, went there to bathe. Upstairs, she shed her clothes swiftly and crammed herself into last year's bathing suit—tight and faded, but it would not matter here. She ran downstairs, crossed the porch without looking at her mother, and ran across the lawn into the safety of the path, which had a wall of weeds on either side. Once there, she walked on, slow and happy. The wire tangle of weeds was alive with stalks and pods and beadlets of bright green whose shapes she knew well but could not, need not, name. Above all, it was the same.

She pushed through the bushes that fringed the creek. It, too, was the same. In the past year, it must have gone through all the calendar changes. She imagined each of them—the freeze, the thaw, the spring running, like conventionalized paper pictures torn off one by one—but they were as unreal as the imagined private dishabille of a friend. Even the bushes that ran for miles along its edge were at the same stage of their bloom, their small, cone-shaped orange flowers dotted along the leaves for as far as she could see. The people around the farm called them "scarlet runners," although their flowers were as orange as a color could be.

She trod carefully across the slippery ledges out to the wide, flat slab that rose in the middle of the stream, and stretched out on her stomach on its broad, moss-slimed back. She lay there for a long time looking into the eye of the pool. One need not have an appointment with minnows, she thought. They are always the same, too.

At a crackling sound in the brush, she looked up. Mrs. Garfunkel's head appeared above the greenery, which ended in a ruff at her neck, like the painted backdrops behind which people pose at amusement parks. "Your mother says to tell you she's gone on down to Miss Onderdonk's." She waited while Hester picked her way back to shore. Until Hester gained the high weeds of the path, she felt the Teddy-bear eyes watching idly, calculating and squint.

In her room once more, Hester changed to a paper-dry cotton dress, then hurried out again, down the dirt road this time, and onto the state highway, slowing down only when she was in sight of Miss Onderdonk's house, and saw her mother and Miss Onderdonk sitting facing one another, one on each of the two butterfly-winged wooden benches built on the top step at either side of the door, forming the only porch there was.

"Why that dress?" asked her mother, with fair reason, for it was Hester's best. "You remember Hester, Miss Onderdonk?" she added.

Miss Onderdonk looked briefly at Hester with her watery, time-eclipsing stare. There was no indication that she knew Hester's name, or ever had. One of the white cats lay resiliently on her lap, with the warning look of toleration common to cats when held. Miss Onderdonk, like the creek, might have lived suspended from last September to this, untouched by the flowing year, every crimp in her hair the same. And the parlor? It would have to be seen, for certain.

Hester sat down quietly next to her mother, whose sewing went on and on, a mild substitute for conversation. For a while, Hester watched the long, important-looking shadows that encroached upon the hills, like enigmas stated every afternoon but never fully solved. Then she leaned carefully toward Miss Onderdonk. "May I go see your parlor?" she asked.

Miss Onderdonk gave no sign that she had heard. It might have been merely the uncanny luck of the partly deaf that prompted her remark. "People come by here this morning," she said. "From down to your place. Walk right into the parlor, no by-your-leave. Want to buy my antiques!"

Mrs. Elkin, needle uplifted, shook her head, commiserating, gave a quick, consolatory mew of understanding, and plunged the needle into the next stitch.

"Two women—and a man all ninnied out for town," said Miss Onderdonk. "Old woman had doctored hair. Grape-colored! Hollers at me as if I'm the foreign one. Picks up my Leather-Bound Onderdonk History!" Her explosive breath capitalized the words. The cat, squirting suddenly from her twitching hand, settled itself, an aggrieved white tippet, at a safe distance on the lawn. "'Put that down,' I said," said Miss Onderdonk, her eyes as narrow as the cat's. "'I don't have no antiques,' I said. 'These here are my belongings.'"

Mrs. Elkin put down her sewing. Her broad hands, with the silver-and-gold thimble on one middle finger, moved uncertainly, unlike Miss Onderdonk's hands, which were pressed flat, in triumph, on her faded flour-sack lap.

"I told Elizabeth Smith," Miss Onderdonk said. "I told her she'd rue the day she ever started taking in Jews."

The short word soared in an arc across Hester's vision and hit the remembered, stereopticon picture of the parlor. The parlor sank and disappeared, a view in an album snapped shut. Now her stare was for her mother's face, which was pink but inconclusive.

Mrs. Elkin, raising her brows, made a helpless face at Hester, as if to say, "After all, the vagaries of the deaf . . ." She permitted herself a minimal shrug, even a slight spreading of palms. Under Hester's stare, she lowered her eyes and turned toward Miss Onderdonk again.

"I thought you knew, Miss Onderdonk," said her mother. "I thought you knew that we were—Hebrews." The word, the ultimate refinement, slid out of her mother's soft voice as if it were on runners.

"Eh?" said Miss Onderdonk.

Say it, Hester prayed. She had never before felt the sensation of prayer. Please say it, Mother. *Say "Jew."* She heard the word in her own mind, double-voiced, like the ram's horn at Yom Kippur, with an ugly present bray but with a long, urgent echo as time-spanning as Roland's horn.

Her mother leaned forward. Perhaps she had heard it, too—the echo. "But we are Jewish," she said in a stronger voice. "Mr. Elkin and I are Jewish."

Miss Onderdonk shook her head, with the smirk of one who knew better. "Never seen the Mister. The girl here has the look, maybe. But not you."

"But—" Mrs. Elkin, her lower lip caught by her teeth, made a sound like a stifled, chiding sigh. "Oh, yes," she said, and nodded, smiling, as if she had been caught out in a fault.

"Does you credit," said Miss Onderdonk. "Don't say it don't. Make your bed, lie on it. Don't have to pretend with me, though."

With another baffled sigh, Mrs. Elkin gave up, flumping her hands down on her sewing. She was pinker, not with anger but, somehow, as if she had been cajoled.

"Had your reasons, maybe." Miss Onderdonk tittered, high and henlike. "Ain't no Jew, though. Good blood shows, any day."

Hester stood up. "We're in a book at home, too," she said loudly. " 'The History of the Jews of Richmond, 1769–1917.' " Then she turned her back on Miss Onderdonk, who might or might not have heard, on her mother, who had, and stomped down the steps.

At the foot of the lawn, she stopped behind a bush that hid her from the steps, feeling sick and let-down. She had somehow used Miss Onderdonk's language. She hadn't said what she meant at all. She heard her father's words, amused and sad, as she had heard them once, over her shoulder, when he had come upon her poring over the red-bound book, counting up the references to her grandfather. "That Herbert Ezekiel's book?" He had looked over her shoulder, twirling the gold cigar-clipper on his watch chain. "Well, guess it

won't hurt the sons of Moses any if they want to tally up some newer ances-
tors now and then."

Miss Onderdonk's voice, with its little, cut-off chicken laugh, travelled down
to her from the steps. "Can't say it didn't cross my mind, though, that the girl
does have the look."

Hester went out onto the highway and walked quickly back to the farmhouse. Skirting the porch, she tiptoed around to one side, over to an old fringed
hammock slung between two trees whose broad bottom fronds almost hid it. She
swung herself into it, covered herself over with the side flaps, and held herself stiff
until the hammock was almost motionless.

Mrs. Garfunkel and Arline could be heard on the porch, evidently alone, for
now and then Mrs. Garfunkel made one of the fretful, absent remarks mothers
make to children when no one else is around. Arline had some kind of wooden
toy that rumbled back and forth across the porch. Now and then, a bell on it
went "ping."

After a while, someone came along the path and up on the porch. Hester lay
still, the hammock fringe tickling her face. "Almost time for supper," she heard
Mrs. Garfunkel say.

"Yes," said her mother's voice. "Did Hester come back this way?"

"I was laying down for a while. Arline, dear, did you see Hester?"

"No, Mummy." "Ping, ping" went Arline's voice.

" 'Mummy'!" said Mrs. Garfunkel. "That's that school she goes to—you
know the Kemp-Willard School, on Eighty-sixth?"

"Oh, yes," said Mrs. Elkin. "Quite good, I've heard."

"Good!" Mrs. Garfunkel sighed, on a sleek note of outrage. "What they soak
you, they ought to be."

Arline's toy rumbled across the porch again and was still.

"She'll come back when she's hungry, I suppose," said Mrs. Elkin. "There
was a rather unfortunate little—incident, down the road."

"Shush, Arline. You don't say?"

Chairs scraped confidentially closer. Mrs. Elkin's voice dropped to the low,
gemütlich whisper reserved for obstetrics, cancer, and the peculations of servant
girls. Once or twice, the whisper, flurrying higher, shook out a gaily audible
phrase. "Absolutely wouldn't believe—" "Can you imagine anything so silly?"
Then, in her normal voice, "Of course, she's part deaf, and probably a little crazy
from being alone so much."

"Scratch any of them and you're sure to find it," said Mrs. Garfunkel.

"Ah, well," said Mrs. Elkin. "But it certainly was funny," she added, in a voice velveted over now with a certain savor of reminiscence, "the way she kept *insisting*."

"Uh-huh," said Mrs. Garfunkel rather flatly. "Yeah. Sure."

Someone came out on the back porch and vigorously swung the big bell that meant supper in fifteen minutes.

"Care for a little drive in the Buick after supper?" asked Mrs. Garfunkel.

"Why—why, yes," said Mrs. Elkin, her tones warmer now with the generosity of one whose equipment went beyond the realm of bargains. "Why, I think that would be very nice."

"Any time," said Mrs. Garfunkel. "Any time you want stamps or anything. Thought you might enjoy a little ride. Not having the use of a car."

The chairs scraped back, the screen door creaked, and the two voices, linked in their sudden, dubious rapprochement, went inside. The scuffling toy followed them.

Hester rolled herself out of the hammock and stood up. She looked for comfort at the reasonable hills, whose pattern changed only according to what people ate; at the path, down which there was nothing more ambiguous than the hazel-eyed water or the flower that should be scarlet but was orange. While she had been in the hammock, the dusk had covered them over. It had settled over everything with its rapt, misleading veil.

She walked around to the foot of the front steps. A thin, emery edge of autumn was in the air now. Inside, they must all be at supper; no one else had come by. When she walked into the dining room, they would all lift their heads for a moment, the way they always did when someone walked in late, all of them regarding her for just a minute with their equivocal adult eyes. Something would rise from them all like a warning odor, confusing and corrupt, and she knew now what it was. Miss Onderdonk sat at their table, too. Wherever any of them sat publicly at table, Miss Onderdonk sat at his side. Only, some of them set a place for her and some of them did not.

Young Workers in the Hotels

Phil Brown

I grew up in hotel kitchens and dining rooms. To be near my parents between the ages of five and ten, I sat at the "owners' table" in the Seven Gables kitchen where the bosses held court, and where my mother as chef sat during the rare moments she was not working. Even though the hotel had an office in the Main House, it seemed that most business was conducted from this round table in the corner of the kitchen. Deliverymen came to get their orders signed, the talent booker came by to arrange entertainment, and key staff people sat down to go over work issues. Guests who were friendly with the owners, from years of vacationing there, would even walk in to chat. All sorts of food popped up there, especially bits of whatever was currently being prepared at the stove.

I was fascinated by the bustle of the place, and learned hotel life as a preadolescent ethnographer. I learned to set tables by helping out the waiters. Running errands for Paul the salad man taught me the rudiments of "garmigiere" (typically pronounced "garmazhay," and probably a corruption of "garde de manger") work—artful food presentation. Watching food dished out at the range showed me how the kitchen ran. When my father had the concession at the Seven Gables I sold soda and beer in the dining room at dinner. Helping at the soda fountain while still under ten gave me a talent for fast work in the short-order mode.

Being a "staff kid" was a mixed bag. I had the run of the hotel, and by about age ten ate in the main dining room at the "staff table"—lifeguard, camp director, bookkeeper and band members, who were always my favorite. One Labor Day when I was around ten, after everyone checked out, the bookkeeper's daughter and I decided to rummage through all the guest rooms to see what people had left behind. We turned up tennis rackets, baseballs, and other little treasures in several hours of hunting. This seemed our due after tolerating a whole season of the guests dominating our lives.

But no matter how much fun, I felt an outsider—neither guest nor staff, and of a lower class; even if many people at this hotel were of modest means, we were the ones having to work there to serve them. Tania Grossinger, whose mother worked as a social hostess at the relatives' hotel, writes extensively of the in-betweenness of this staff child status. Even being an owner's child or relative had drawbacks:

> At the end of every week, the counselors at the day camp used to have a little ceremony, and give out a "Camper of the Week" award. I used to cry every time I did not get it (which was, of course, every time). No matter how carefully it was explained to me that I could not get the award because I was "one of the owners," my competitive nature compelled me to try to win that little trophy.

I always yearned to get into a dining room job, where I would be my own person. When I was thirteen at the Cherry Hill, a busboy missing at the last moment on a busy weekend late in the season gave me the opportunity of a lifetime—a half hour before dinner, I grabbed a cutaway jacket and bow tie, and went to work full-time for the remaining two weeks of the season. From then on, I worked the Mountains every summer, till the end of college. At the age of fourteen I felt I knew enough to be a waiter, having helped out the other dining room staff for years, but no hotel owner could swallow the idea of a fourteen-year-old waiter. Given my connections, I only needed a year of that apprenticeship, and at fifteen was a waiter.

WORKING THE DINING ROOM

Every meal had a "shape," a way that it went—a good meal, a bomb, a breeze. A "good meal" was what you could usually hope for—a fairly routine event. When the meal was a "breeze," you had waltzed through it without a care, always being ahead of the pack, with no complaints from guests. The worst, a "bomb," was when you were "hung up" and could never catch up with the guests' demands or the kitchen schedule. One of the measures of how well a meal went was how early you got out of the dining room. If you could "check out" with the waiter captain and the maitre d' while most others had as much as fifteen minutes' more labor in setting up, you felt you had done well. The amount of sweat was also a good way to judge how well the meal went—if you were excessively drenched in sweat, compared to what you usually were, then you had run too fast, made too many extra trips, worried too much about being "hung up." A gauge of success, in the middle of the meal, was how close you were to the front of the line to pick up each course, especially main dishes.

Serving lunch, and even more so dinner, the key thing was to get on the "main line" early. Guests might have drifted in and leisurely eaten appetizers and soups, easy to pick up in the kitchen. Busboys were not allowed to pick up these appetizers and soups themselves, as captured in Sidney Offit's novel, *He Had It Made*: "Danny Rose picked up the mushroom and barley soup. The chef knew he was not a waiter and shouted loud enough for everyone to hear, 'I'll cut off the hands of the next busboy I see picking up on this side of the stove.' " If you didn't get caught by an irate owner who felt the waiter should be doing the serving, you could even pick the food up and hand it immediately to your busboy, poised beside you, for delivery to the guests. The chef and steward might be tolerant with soups and appetizers, but they got frenetic and deadly serious with mains, which only waiters could handle. Partly this was because they were more expensive, there were more choices, various options about how well cooked, and what vegetables and garnishes were accompanying. Mains were large, and unlike soup, you couldn't get enough on your tray to serve your whole station at once. If you were at the head of the line for your first trip, you'd be back quickly for the next trip or two. You wanted to get mains out early since you didn't want your guests complaining that other people were being served first.

It was possible to get "hung up" during any course, but once you were late with mains, you completely lost control of the meal. Some waiters routinely got hung up because they couldn't organize their work habits and let guests send them to the kitchen too often. The trick was to not make extra trips for a single request, since you'd never stop running. You bided time until several requests were pending or you had finished serving the current course. Waiters prone to getting hung up never learned to manage themselves or others. The frenzy of a hung-up waiter was pathetic; they would be running around, dripping sweat, asking other waiters for any extra dishes, whining at their busboys to help out.

Waiting at the Karmel in Loch Sheldrake, I had to put up with Julie, one of the owners. As in many hotels, two couples owned the place, typically in-laws. Julie's fiefdom as the quasi-steward was the kitchen, where he supervised meals, dressed in a white apron over his regular office clothes, brandishing a giant serving spoon for dishing out vegetables. He yelled all the time, and when really angry waved the spoon threateningly; the prominent vein on his forehead throbbed and we joked he was on the way to a stroke before dessert. Julie and his brother-in-law, Perry, could not stand that we hung out in the kitchen waiting for the main line to open, while our guests presumably were left without our attention—as if our busboys patrolling for us were not sufficient. When, in the course of the season-long civil war of bosses and waiters, Julie and Perry managed to scare us out of the kitchen, we resorted to leaving our trays standing silent sentinel, to hold our places for when the main line opened. Then we merely kept popping in to see when the race was really on, at which point we'd take our positions where the trays stood. When this outrageous tactic got to Julie, he outlawed tray placing, and we were back to the original status of putting our bodies on line, chatting and joking, listening to Julie's and Perry's nonstop harangues to at least stand straight and not slouch over the counter.

Some of our best efforts at pleasing the guests ran up against the bosses' attempts to control us. For instance, to keep the guests happy by serving them quickly, we tried to put lots of mains on our trays. Four dishes, with metal (meat meals) or plastic (dairy meals) covers fit on a tray. The acceptable limit was three stacks of plates, allowing for only twelve mains. This often meant splitting up tables, which often had eight or ten guests; guests at one table couldn't stand to see others at their table eat while they might have to wait ten more minutes to get theirs. A fourth stack would give you two tables' worth of guests in many instances. But bosses and stewards often prevented that for fear that we would drop the whole tray, no matter how experienced and strong we were. One strategy was to have your busboy next to you, hand him some mains, and then meet up with him between the kitchen and the dining room to add them to the stack. Often enough this backfired when we were caught—the owner would halt us, yell, and take away the top stack.

Even if you got out early with mains, some guests would invariably gripe, "How come the other tables [in your station] always get served first?" Standing in our shoes, wearing our cummerbunds, we perceived the guests as always complaining. Picture the Passover seder recounted by a man of seventy:

> One person said, "I don't want this matzoh, I want Manischewitz egg matzoh!" Another says, "I weant Horowitz Margareten!," another one says, "I want Streit's! I want Streit's!" so the guy [waiter] quit on the floor!

We viewed the guests as "altecackers" (literally, old shits) who wanted to eat all they could (rates included all meals). We mocked their accents and ridiculed their habits. To them, we were adorable college kids whom they always wanted to engage about where we lived and went to school, our career choices and sweethearts. In response, waiters tried to fool the guests:

> I remember going taking orders for things for like steak which they wanted medium rare; everybody I gave mediums. That was a trick my mother told me, "Just get everyone mediums and no one ever says anything," and they didn't.

We did try to be pleasant, both because we were trained to be and because our tips depended on it. As one waiter recalled, "I would thrown in two Jewish phrases which made people feel comfortable." But sometimes, people got so much on your nerves that you couldn't hold in your emotions. One troublesome guest told me there was too much water in the teacup, no matter how much I titrated the amount. Unable to please her, I poured some out in my busbox, and she still complained, so I poured half of that right onto the floor in front of her. Another guest insisted on only a half cup of coffee, and whenever I brought it it was always too much. So I went to the cup bin and got a broken cup and poured a bit of coffee into the depression in the piece and gave it to her. An owner's son recounted a story about a guest who disliked herring so much he demanded that the waiter who served it family style put it at the far end of the table, as distant as possible from him. So difficult was this guest that someone tied a herring to the pull-chain of the light in his room, which scared him enormously when he entered one dark night.

Strategically, the best thing to do was to "train" your guests. You didn't want them to send you back and forth to the kitchen for little side dishes of sour cream, then bananas. So you told them that it would be "easier" to ask for everything at once. To preclude their choosing from too many possible selections, you brought out what you thought would be the preferred soup, and simply started dishing it out. If they wanted the other choice, you told them that it meant waiting until you could get back to the kitchen, after you served the rest of the table (who *were* behaving by accepting *your* choice). Similarly, it was common practice at breakfast to stockpile an assortment of plates of lox, pickled herring, steweed prunes, grapefruits. When a guest requested something, you retrieved it quickly, both saving a trip and impressing them with your speed. This approach to waiting was termed "speculating"; bosses and stewards (who ran the kitchen) hated it because food might get messed up from being piled up in your sidestand. Worse, if you didn't get orders for the speculated food, you might conveniently ditch it in the busbox rather than returning it to the kitchen where you'd get yelled at for speculating.

Another big sin was "scarfing," eating guest food, especially at your sidestand. Everyone did this, so it was mainly a matter of circumspection. At breakfast, while waiting for guests to amble in, you could move a chair beside your sidestand, hidden from the view of the maitre d', and eat in peace, even if briefly. If time was short, you just stooped down and gobbled up a whole honeydew slice in a big gliding-mouthed swallow. Scarfing was also possible on the way from the kitchen to the dining room, when you passed through hallways and anterooms containing toasters, egg-boiling machines, breadboxes, and bathrooms. We scarfed because the staff food was so bad, though I'm sure we would have done it even if that were not the case. They served us leftovers of food that we'd have rejected even if fresh—like flanken, boiled short ribs of beef whose gray color made you think of putrefaction. In her memoir of waiting in the Mountains, Vivian Gornick writes, "The mountains were always one long siege of vitamin deprivation. No one ever wanted to feed the help; the agony on an owner's face if his eye fell on a busboy drinking orange juice or eating a lamb chop was palpable." In the memory of an ex-waiter:

> I was a skinny kid and came home fifteen pounds lighter. We were always hungry, and we would grab whatever we could in the walk-in refrigerator. When they sent you in for something, you'd take whatever you could find. In the dining room, you grabbed some extra dessert and went to a corner, someone covered for you, and you ate it.

At the Karmel, the owners grew tired of having the kitchen crowded with staff picking up their own meals one hour before the guest meal. You could understand that two dozen waiters and busboys, four bellhops, two lifeguards, the chauffeur, and assorted others hovering at the range could get messy. So the next season started with a staff waiter, Willie, serving us all in a tightly packed ante-room to the kitchen. Willie was a veteran waiter, old and hobbled, who could no longer make the fast pace of a main dining room, so he was stuck with this sad job. We felt bad for him, and meant no particular disrespect, but one day after a whole week of leftover chicken, dried-out potato pancakes, and other such food that we found truly inedible, we decided we wanted real meat. One wait-er began spontaneously, and in a moment a chorus rose from the whole group: "Beef, Willie! Beef!" Our chant continued till the owners came running in from assorted locations, fearful that we would embarrass them to the guests. I think we got maybe one decent meal out of this the next day.

If you worked the "teenage station," you could even get one kid at each table to take orders, and you could dish out food for everyone to pass around. Busboys could get a whole table's dishes collected and stacked without lifting a finger until the pile reached the end of the table nearest your busbox. Teenagers mostly did not like soup and appetizers, so serving was quicker. They also enjoyed helping you set up tables after the meal. On the romance end, "working teenage" meant you usually got the first opportunity to meet new arrivals on Friday night, and make a date for afterward. This, plus the ease of noncomplaining guests, made it worth the lower tips you got from the teens' parents.

Our tasks seemed always to expand. Besides cleaning and setting our tables after meals, we had to wash our own silverware. This was done in a fairly slop-py way. During the meal, silver was put in a slot in the sidestand, to fall into a galvanized bucket of soapy water. At the end of the meal, we took the bucket to the sinks off to the side of the kitchen, poured out that water, added new soap and hot water, twisted this heavy load about ten times, rinsed it twice, and returned with it to the dining room—often with some burned skin and a sweaty face from the ferociously hot steam that came on top of an already hot meal. There we dumped the steaming silver—with occasional food pieces—onto a tablecloth already too soiled to keep on the table, bundled four corners togeth-er, and rubbed the whole assemblage till it was dry. For $10 a week, at some hotels, you could get your busboy to take over this task. We also had to wash our own goblets, since the bosses feared the glasswasher would break them. They also feared the busboys' carelessness, and yelled at us if we tried to unload that duty.

Everyone had a "side job" as well: refilling all the salt and pepper shakers weekly, wiping off ketchup bottles, delivering hundreds of dishes from the dish room to the chef or the baker, cutting bread in the industrial-size slicer before the meal, storing sliced bread under damp cloth napkins afterward, sorting the soiled linen for the laundry truck. There was so much laundry that several staff had this task. It was so boring that we often had spoon fights, throwing silverware across the room at each other—I still have a forehead scar from one of these episodes. About every three weeks we would have to spend an extra couple of hours between lunch and dinner burnishing the silverware. This miserable task involved waiting our turn to place our silver in a revolving round chamber filled with a viscous, gloppy soap and thousands of BBs that made a terrible sound as it removed egg stains, scratches, and tarnish, and shined the silverware. You lost your whole afternoon. I recently visited the Aladdin Hotel in Woodbourne, where an old burnishing machine without its brass top serves as a flower planter in front of the main entrance. A similar problem occurred with a periodic major task of buffing the floors with a heavy power buffer. This required putting all the chairs in the dining room up on the tabletops, hence being unable to set up for the next meal. By the time the buffing was done and the tables were set, little time remained for rest—another afternoon lost. At least this was very occasional—some hotels had busboys mopping and buffing floors every day.

Like many elements of Catskills life, dining room staff relations had something of a cutthroat attitude. Waiters would steal silverware from each other's drawers, goblets from their trays, and even food from their sidestands. It was often necessary to make sure that either you or your busboy was always present at the station to protect the sidestand from marauders. Inexperienced waiters would find more seasoned ones cutting in front of them on the line in the kitchen. One of the worst offenses was stealing toast. We had to make our own toast in large revolving machines that held ten rows of four slices each. The best way to save time was to thrown toast in on the way from the dining room to the kitchen, pick up egg orders, and fetch the toast to add to the eggs on the way back. Lots of toast was stolen in that interim, and the excuse was always, "Hey, I put that in before. Someone else took yours." The exact same thing held for boiled eggs, which we had to make ourselves. A large vat contained a number of egg machines hovering over the boiling water. You placed your eggs in the basket and pulled the chain down according to a marker indicating the number of minutes for that type of egg. When the time was up the chain returned the basket for you to extract your order. Eggs were stolen less frequently than toast, but only because many waiters couldn't tell how well the eggs were done by merely shaking them.

We played around a lot in the dining room, before and after meals. We did animal imitations and performed impromptu skits satirizing the chef, maitre d', and owners. We called make-believe harness races. We roughhoused with each other. A busboy recalled:

> While working as a busboy we had contests after everyone left the dining room to see who could carry the heaviest tray. You would pack it all around on the tray and then see who could carry it into the kitchen without dropping it. I was carrying one of these heavy trays into the kitchen when the owner walked in and said to me, "If you drop a dish, you're fired. Even if you don't, you're putting on the amateur show on Wednesday."

THE STAFF AT PLAY

For the money, we worked long hours. We got up at 7 to serve breakfast. With luck you could be done by 10 or 10:15 if your guests finished trekking in early enough. Then back at 12 for lunch, and out again at 2 or 2:30. Free until 6 for supper. Time enough to go cruising other hotels or the streets of Liberty or Monticello in search of girls. Maybe just hang out poolside, play basketball, baseball, tennis. The advantage of smaller hotels was that you could use all the guest facilities; many larger ones segregated the staff. By hustling, it was possible to get out of the dining room by 8:30 at night. Almost everyone was after some fun. Sunday night was often poker, since we had just gotten the week's tips. Once a week at Paul's Hotel we hoarded food from the kitchen and rowed across the lake for late-night cookouts. But the best of times were at Monticello Raceway, local pubs, and rock shows at some of the larger medium-size hotels like the Eldorado in South Fallsburg, where you could hear groups like the Four Seasons. A waitress at the Homowack in Spring Glen recounted how the dining room staff would celebrate the end of the season by going glider flying in Wurtsboro.

The best tavern I ever patronized was Kilcoin's in Swan Lake, just down the hill from town. Al McCoy, owner and bartender, was a jolly man and a great card trickster. To see Allie's tricks the unspoken rule was that you had to sit at the bar and drink liquor, not draft. Draft beer, sitting at the table, was fifteen cents for a small glass, a quarter for a mug pulled from a freezer and then filled with the coldest beer anywhere in the world (New York's drinking age was then eighteen, and poorly enforced). Kilcoin's was pure roadhouse—hard wood benches, jukebox, coin-op pool table, and no decor save brewery clocks with electric bubbling froth. I worked several years in Paul's Hotel in Swan Lake, and had ample time to visit Kilcoin's. During the year I worked at SGS Bungalows, and another year at the Commodore Hotel, most nights when I finished work at midnight in the coffee shop, I'd drive down for an hour of sanity. Even the years I worked far from Swan Lake, I was drawn back to this spot.

My friends from the Cherry Hill Hotel band got a great job at the Raleigh's smaller bar, where they could specialize in mainstream and Latin jazz instead of endless repetitions of Catskill warhorses ("Hello Dolly,' "Havenu Sholem Aleichem," "Sunrise Sunset"). This was one of the few places where you could hear good jazz, apart from jam sessions held after the shows were over—when hotel owners allowed it.

Monticello Raceway was a major fun spot. "The Track" drew everyone—locals, staff, and guests. It was impossible for dining room staff to get there at post time, but a mad dash could get you in by the second or third race if you worked close enough to Monticello. When we got tired of rushing and frustrated by losing money, we often opted for the free admission to the last two races. The Track exerted a pervasive effect. Guests often requested fast service, with all the courses delivered at once, so they could make the daily double. At one place I worked, a busboy, Nathan, would grab the dining room mike and announce make-believe races during set-up time, only to be shut up by the maitre d', lest guests in the lobby hear it.

The whole Catskills were full of thousands of other workers our age, and that contributed to a partylike atmosphere. You could go anywhere—laundromat, restaurant, bar, sidewalk fruit stand—and you'd find compatriots with whom to compare working notes, make new friends, line up dates, and learn of job openings if you wanted to make a switch. Most—probably 90 to 95 percent—of these young workers were Jewish, up until the middle 1970s. This was logical, since the milieu was so Jewish that the guests would best be understood by Jewish staff. Also, many staff got their jobs through family connections or via relatives who were guests. It was always noticeable who was gentile, but Jewish staff did not generally exclude people from social interaction. One hotel I worked in had some Polish waiters and busboys from Carbondale, nearby in Pennsylvania, and it was actually refreshing to have some people who were dissimilar from the rest of us. In another hotel, during Passover one gentile bellhop didn't know what to call the rabbi's wife when he served her in the tearoom, so he addressed her as "Mrs. Rabbi" until we corrected him.

THE SHLOCK HOUSE

What waiters and busboys really feared the most was working in a shlock house. How can I describe a shlock house? In Yiddish, "shlock" means junk, but the colloquial usage refers to something of poor quality, especially if it has pretentions. In the Catskills, what many people termed a shlock house was a run-down hotel which, if full, held maybe 75 to 150 guests. Above all, the shlock house was disorganized and crude. It had no real facilities beyond a pool, handball court (often with many cracks on the pavement), perhaps a decayed tennis court, sometimes a hoop and backboard on crumbly pavement. Entertainment in some of the very small hotels might be quite circumscribed—some didn't even have a band, and hence couldn't present singers. Not all small hotels were shlock houses. Some were run very well and tastefully, without the disorganization and cheapness of a shlock house.

You'd know a shlock house just by seeing it. One night some of us went down the road to pick up a friend for a night out. We had finished serving dinner, showered, changed, and gotten to the shlock house, and they were still serving! Everything was out of control, waiters and busboys aimlessly running about, helplessly behind. At any other hotel, outsiders like ourselves would be thrown out of a dining room for entering in the middle of a meal. Here, there was no one to notice, no authority or direction. Often, food in a true shlock house was served "family style," with large bowls and platters in the center of the table. You wanted bananas and sour cream at lunch, your waiter brought bananas and you added the sour cream from the big *shissel*. At night, the waiter served your chicken, and you added vegetables from a common plate. One salad man proudly told how he started working at a hotel that served family style, and gradually weaned them to the more modern, less shlocky a la carte service.

Why would you wind up working in a shlock house? Maybe your parents knew an owner to give you your first job. Sometimes you could make just as good money as elsewhere, with lower tips but more guests. Perhaps you screwed up badly in your job, and there were no other jobs around. Maybe you just never got good enough to work anywhere else—I knew such guys. A high school friend from Florida wound up in a shlock house with his trumpet, but no real band to play it with. Many talent agencies put together pick-up bands, but they at least rehearsed them once to see that they could play. Not so in this case. The opening night of the season, I came to visit after I finished serving supper. Howard showed up, along with a piano player and drummer. None had ever seen the others before, and try as they might they could not play for the waiting guests. There were these three musicians basically pretending to play music for people who were fated to stay in shlock houses where they got this kind of treatment. Howard asked for help—he knew I played piano in the lounge at the Karmel after finishing a day waiting tables, then driving twenty miles to help my father in his concession, then returning. But I declined—this situation was beyond salvage. It was the essence of the shlock house.

What might have been a small but somewhat fancy hotel in the 1940s and 1950s could become a shlock house by virtue of neglect, or even failure to expand. Those of us in the small- and small-to-medium-size hotels were sometimes just a category above the shlock house, working in what we called "2–250 houses," hotels holding between 200 and 250 guests. Guys we knew in larger places even told us *we* were working in shlock houses. Shlock was always a measure of superiority over the next lowest rung on the ladder, whether it be working in the Catskills or one's choice of clothing or furniture.

The Pool

Eileen Pollack

I always suspected I had been chosen by God for some special fate, but I didn't receive proof until I was nine. It was summer, mid June. Where could death hide on such a bright morning? Nowhere, I thought, and poked one bare foot out the bungalow door. How soft the grass looked! I longed to turn cartwheels, climb the old oak, perform a few miracles to take up the hour until the pool opened and I could show off my new lime-green two-piece.

"No," my mother told me. Her fingers closed around my suit straps.

"Why not?" I demanded.

"Put on your shoes first."

I wrinkled my nose.

"You heard me, Miss Piss."

In my mother's opinion, deadly microbes were breeding in every warm puddle. The germs of paralysis were tiny sharks teeming in each muddy drop.

"If you go around barefoot, you might pick up TB."

For years I had assumed she was saying Tee *Vee*. The current ran through the earth like a snake of hot sparks. If you stepped on the snake with bare feet, the pictures shot to your brain. One afternoon, when my mother wasn't looking, I took off my sneakers and searched for the spot. I planted my right foot, paused, saw no pictures, planted my left foot a few inches over, stepping and pausing until I had signed every patch of the Eden with my footprints. But I couldn't find the current. I even tried pressing my ear to the ground and listening for voices—

Fred, Ethel, Rickie, and the red-headed Lucy for whom I had been named, or so my brother told me.

I kept doing this until Arthur discovered me down on all fours, ear to the ground. He jumped on my back and wouldn't let me up until I admitted what I was doing. Then he laughed so convulsively I could feel my body shake beneath his. He sputtered his last laugh and took pity on me, explaining the truth: that our family's hotel once had been a refuge for patients who coughed furiously and spat blood until they choked, eyes bulging, tongues black. Their mucus, Arthur told me, still wriggled with germs, which waited to crawl in the blisters on my feet. He thought this would scare me, but it excited me to think that the Eden was haunted with dead people's germs, and these lived on, unseen, awaiting a chance to make contact with me, inhabit my blood.

"Put your shoes on this minute," my mother ordered, "or no swimming for a month."

I didn't bother to tell her that I wasn't afraid of catching tuberculosis. What would that matter? TB was only one of a hundred virulent devils waiting to prey on a girl in bare feet.

"If you step on a rusted nail you'll get lockjaw."

I savored this tragedy. Arthur would be chasing me across the front lawn. I would step on a nail and stumble. He would catch me and threaten to pull down my bathing suit, as he often had done before, and when I tried to beg for mercy my jaw would lock shut. Slowly, he would realize what dreadful affliction had silenced his sister. He would beg my forgiveness, which of course I wouldn't grant.

Not that I believed I would die. How could such puny villains—a microbe, a nail—strike down a girl of rare visions and dreams? If anything, I sensed on that brilliant June morning not death but a challenge, an occasion to prove my powers at last.

I put on my flip-flops and dodged past my mother.

"Come back here!" she shouted. "Those things are so flimsy, a piece of glass could go through!"

But she didn't have time to run after me and tie real shoes on my feet. Flip-flops smacking against my heels, I ran to the camp house, an unpainted shack with a dozen old mattresses piled high inside. The raw wooden walls were inscribed with the signatures of campers now in their fifties: YUDEL LOVES EDITH; SHEL CLOBBERED MILTIE 8/10/32. Standing on my toes, I was just able to reach the top cubbyholes. Wasps dove from the eaves, but I wasn't afraid. I had given them instructions to strafe all intruders and leave me unstung. From the only cubbyhole with a door I withdrew a shabby book—a present from my Grandpa Abe the year before, on my eighth birthday. He had bought it for himself when he arrived in America; he wanted to own a copy of the Bible in English, and the bibles for adults were too hard to read. OLD TESTAMENT FOR CHILDREN, EDITED, ABRIDGED the title said in block letters. A smiling man and woman posed behind a tree; I recognized them as the couple tossing the beach ball on the Eden's main arch. In his soft stumbling voice, my grandfather started to read aloud the story of Moses. I interrupted to ask why he pronounced the *w*'s as *v*'s.

"Vell," he said. A troubled look passed his face. He leaned forward, the book slipping from his lap. He opened his mouth to speak, and I sat waiting for an answer until my parents appeared in the doorway with a cake, which we didn't get to eat. Though my grandfather lived on another eleven years, he couldn't move or talk, so it seemed to me as if God bestowed the Torah, not on Moses, but on me, Lucy Appelbaum, then He lay down to sleep while I studied His gift, preparing for a test I knew would come soon.

The more I read the Bible, the more I believed that Moses and I were two of a kind. Hadn't a bush with flame-red leaves ordered me to kneel beside the shuffleboard court because the ground there was holy? And that same afternoon, hadn't a radio emitted a wail, after which the announcer, in his resonant voice, commanded me to await instructions regarding the mission God had reserved especially for me? I heard God speaking often, praising my deeds. In return, I asked Him favors: *Please, God, let the sun stand still so I can swim one more hour.* My prayers sometimes worked, but never when any witness was near.

And this was the puzzle that occupied my mind in the camp house that morning: How could I prove how special I was if no one required the knowledge I had gleaned from my book? I lay on my back, studying the baffling words above the toilet, preparing for the day I would be called upon to translate some other warning God had written on a wall, as Daniel, my hero, had been asked to explain MENE MENE TEKEL UPHARSIN to wicked King Belshazzar.

"Attention, attention!" My mother's voice rang from loudspeakers on poles all over the Eden's grounds. "Ladies and gentlemen, the pool is now open for your aquatic enjoyment."

I replaced my book in its cubbyhole and jumped down the four steps. Slowed by my flip-flops, I left these behind, two bright crimson footprints in the middle of the walk. Beside the pool, I paused on the hot concrete deck—good training, in case I was ever flung into a burning furnace, like Daniel. Then, with a cry, I raced to the edge and threw myself over.

Cold as perfection. I frog-kicked underwater. When I emerged I felt cleansed, though of what I wasn't sure. Maybe the chlorine would sterilize my skin so no ugly hair would sprout between my legs, as it did from the crotches of the women on the lounge chairs, black tendrils creeping down puckery thighs. I levered my body to the deck, exalting in the strength of my lean, freckled arms. I pinched my nose, rubbed it—if Arthur saw snot, he would blow his whistle and call out his findings to the busboys. The pool walls were painted turquoise, the water reflecting the sun like an enormous gem sunk in the pillowed acres of the Eden. The pool didn't have a lifeguard (SWIM AT OWN RISK warned a sign), but my brother had the job of keeping the water clean, and he cleared debris from the surface as obsessively as he scrubbed blackheads from his face. He dumped in chlorine until any moth or beetle fluttering too near dropped like a stone.

I breathed deeply, then dove. Emptying my lungs, I sank to the bottom, where I lay with the rough concrete scraping my belly. My blood throbbed loudly in my ears, the watery world pulsated with the question: *How long can you stay here, how long, how long . . .*

Forever, I answered, I could live without breathing, explore the world's oceans with no need for tanks. I flipped onto my back and floated there, between the bottom and the surface, the sunlight a spatter of gold drops above, the fir trees curved wings. I told myself that no one had seen the world *this* way.

When I grew bored with floating, I climbed from the pool and tossed a penny over my shoulder. "Arthur! Hey, Arthur! I bet I can find it in less than a minute!"

Not that my brother ever would time me. Not that he ever paid attention. Like most children, I equated attention with love. But my brother thought the highest form of attention a brother could bestow was relentless correction. And because he did love me, he feared that I would become what he most hated: a woman who thought she was special. He classified people according to whether they demanded special treatment—"Waiter, make sure the fish has no bones!" "I want colder water!" "Artie, get me a fork whose tines aren't bent!"—or whether they sat quietly and ate what they were given. I knew I couldn't please him. From my orange hair to my feet, whose nails I painted red, I was too loud, too brash. But praise is most precious when given by those who dispense it most rarely. If my brother had commended me for finding that penny, I might have become a pearl diver. And when I rose from the depths and saw his turned head, I felt cheaper than the coppery coin in my fist. With no special talents, I must be the same as every other girl, as one drop of water is exactly like the other drops. This scared me so profoundly I had no other choice but to turn to the staff, who paid me attention because my last name was Appelbaum, a fact I tried hard to forget.

I climbed from the pool and shouted insults at the busboys until two of them grabbed me by the ankles and the wrists and—one, two, *three*—tossed me in the depths so water rose from the pool and flattened the hairdos of the women playing cards.

"Lucy! Don't splash!"

To protect their bouffants these women wore kerchiefs with hundreds of petals or tall hats whose filaments waved in the wind like the tentacles of spiny sea creatures. Some women played canasta, tapping spiky heels as they waited for their cards. (Their legs were shot blue, like the celery stalks my teacher had propped in an inkwell the year before, in third grade.) Other women played mahjongg—fast fingers, fast tongues, the ivory tiles clicking: "Two bam," "Red," "Two dot." But if I drew too near their table, one of these women would grab me by the shoulders, exclaiming *zise mammele tayere*—sweet, dear little mother!—while the other women chimed:

"What bottle did that red hair come from!"

"Someone is going to wake up and find herself with a lovely little shape any day now!"

I was desperate to grow up, but the crêpe-papier skin hanging from their necks made me queasy, and I had to admit that growing up didn't stop at fifteen, or even at my parents' age, but kept on and on until you began to grow *down*, the women's spines curving until they were shorter than I was.

My only hope that old age needn't be frightening came from the Feidels. Each afternoon they appeared at the pool, Shirley in a trim maroon one-piece, Nathan in trunks neither baggy nor too tight. Shirley had the figure of a much younger woman, with smooth skin and long white hair, which she wore in a bun. Nathan had a thick square-cut silver mustache, a cleft chin and a nose that came straight from his brow. He and his wife would step down the ladders on opposite sides of the pool and, without hesitation, even on the chilliest day, slip into the water and swim toward one another, pass and keep swimming, twenty laps in counterpoint, strong rhythmic strokes, as the numbers on their wrists, written in an ink that never washed off, rose, from the water again and again.

When they finished their swim, Nathan and Shirley climbed from the pool. Nathan draped his wife's shoulders with a thick purple towel they must have brought from home since the towels at the Eden were threadbare and white.

Then Nat kissed his wife. No parts of their bodies touched except their lips, but I felt so unsettled that after they had gone I was attracted more strongly than ever to the waiters sunning on the deck.

An outsider might have thought the boys were sleeping, but I knew that they were actually using the sun's rays to recharge their batteries. How else could they find the energy to work seven days a week: out of bed at six to get ready for breakfast, clear the tables, serve lunch, set up for the next meal, a few hours' break before serving dinner, which took until eleven-thirty to clear? The steel trays they brandished might have been shields for an army of knights. Loaded with dishes, such a tray couldn't be lifted by two ordinary men. But a waiter could swing a tray to his shoulder and dart between the tables so the steaming soup flew above the heads of the indifferent diners. I didn't think it fair that the guests, who did no work, should lounge on cushioned chairs while the staff were forced to lie on the concrete deck. When I ran the Eden—and I never doubted that I would—things would be fair.

I stood above Herbie, the knight I loved best, Sir Herbie the Scrub-brush, bristling with black hairs. Beside him lay Larry, with a pink hairless chest and two tiny nipples like pink candy dots, and Steve, Michael, Bruce, all of them sleeping so soundly that I almost regretted what I had to do.

Almost. Not quite. The night before, the busboys had finished work early and decided to hitch-hike to town for ice cream. When I begged to go with them, Herbie said, "Loose, you won't miss much. The waitress at HoJo's will bring us our sundaes. We'll try to imagine what she looks like without that hair net, we'll pass out in our butterscotch syrup, and when the place closes, we'll get up and crawl home."

So why didn't they stay at the Eden, with me, and go to sleep early?

"We have to, that's all." He rubbed the bristles on his chin. "When guys get together, they do certain things. Maybe those things aren't so great. But it's worse for a person to be alone."

This I understood. When no one was watching me, I felt as if my life were a movie projected on thin air.

I scooped icy water from the pool, then uncupped my hands above Herbie's belly. Though he tightened his muscles, his eyes remained shut. I hated myself, but I had to keep going.

The third scoop of water made Herbie reach out and pass me on to Larry, who, in his sleep, passed me on to Steve, who passed me on to Michael, who passed me on to Bruce, whose arms closed around me, a carnivorous plant with a fly in its leaves. I squealed and squirmed with pleasure, flesh to hot flesh, until I heard a whistle.

"Stop that!" Arthur commanded from his lounge near the diving board. "Don't pester them, Lucy. Go and play with your dolls."

His voice stung as smartly as if he had squirted chlorine in my eyes. I told myself again that my brother didn't hate me, he hated the hotel. He was always complaining that the Eden was ruining his health and souring "his chances." He couldn't take time off to visit his roommate from his first year at Princeton, though this roommate's family owned a house at a place called Martha's Vineyard. No, Arthur was just too tired to let his love show. Seeing him now, twisting to massage his own knotted back, it came to me that he truly did need me.

I freed myself from Bruce, who immediately rolled over and dropped back to sleep. I took a few steps toward Arthur. I would rub his back and tell him the jokes that Maxxie Fox, the Eden's new comedian, had taught me the day before. *I was wrong*, he would say. *The minute you touched me, the pain disappeared.*

I had just reached the diving board when Linda Brush scooted past and settled on the lounge right next to Arthur. How could he stand to have her that near? Linda Brush was one of the middle-aged mothers who brought their children to the Eden for two or three months, leaving their husbands to work and sweat in New York. Her hair was a shiny black ball; a person could poke two fingers in those black-circled eyes, a thumb in that round mouth, and send that head rolling. She wore a two-piece bathing suit much like my own, except black. A scar crawled down her belly. I grew ill, thinking where that scar led and how the two Brush twins had lived in that stomach until the doctor slit it open and lifted them out.

The twins were identical. As a younger child I had thought this meant they were alike not only on the surface but the same through and through. I couldn't see them lying next to each other without feeling compelled to draw a blanket over one baby's face. Having a twin cheapened your worth; for all anyone could tell, your twin was the real you and you were the fake.

As the Brush twins grew older, I saw, to my relief, that they weren't the same. Samuel, the younger twin, followed Mitchell wherever he went, so dreamy and slow he seemed to be mocking Mitchell the way Arthur mocked me, repeating everything I said with a retarded child's slur. ("Stop doing that!" I would scream, and Arthur, thick tongued, would mimic "thtop doing that.") For as long as I knew him, Sam Brush retained an infant's blank face, whereas even by six Mitchell had hardened his features, sharpened his gaze, as though to help people tell them apart. Today, he was pressing a scalloped bottle cap into Sam's bare arm, as though cutting dough for cookies. Sam sat there and smiled.

Their mother didn't notice. She was squeezing white lotion across my brother's chest, teasing him about his dark skin and kinky hair. "Why, if Ah didn't know bet-tah, Ah'd think one of the Appelbahms had slept with they-ah dah-kies."

Why didn't my brother slap her? He just grunted, and I saw Linda slip her pink nails beneath the waistband of his trunks.

I jumped in the water and started swimming. I wouldn't touch the bottom or the sides. At four o'clock, my mother came to the pool for her one-hour break between managing the reception desk and managing the dining room. She stood beside the water in her rumpled yellow housedress.

"You're chattering like a skeleton," she said.

"Oh, Mom, how can a skeleton chatter? A skeleton is *dead*."

"And you will be, too, if you catch pneumonia."

I swam to the shallow end and climbed the steps as slowly as it is possible to climb steps.

"Quick! Go and change! If you stay in a damp suit you'll end up a cripple."

I rolled my eyes. "How could a damp suit—"

"Sylvia Siskind's daughter got polio from just a quick dip. Of course, that was a public pool. But we don't have to ask for trouble by walking around in damp suits."

I had no intention of changing to dry clothes. I would get a snack. By the time I returned to the pool, my mother would have left or forgotten her order. I hitched up my bottoms, marched across the lawn and right through the lobby, defying a sign that said

NO WET SUITS,

then I marched out the side door and up to a window in a ramshackle booth called The Concession.

"The usual," I said.

Mrs. Grieben, the concessionaire and sister of the cook, who was also Mrs. Grieben, since the sisters had married brothers, reached one flabby arm into the freezer and brought out a chocolate-covered marshmallow stick so frigid it hurt my teeth to bite it. Then she opened the cooler.

"Orange hair, orange soda," Mrs. Grieben said sagely, as if God had decreed that dark-haired children must drink Coke and blond ones cream soda.

The Orange Crush tasted like summer itself. I gulped half without stopping.

"Who gave you that *chazeray!*"

The voice made the bottle shake in my hand.

"Who gave you that pig food!" My grandmother raised a fist at Mrs. Grieben. "You want her to get fat as a pig, as a *chazer* like you?"

"You don't call me pig!"

"Pig! *Chazer*! Pig!" Nana whirled. "And you! Don't run around barefoot!" She said this in Yiddish—*gey nit arum borves*—and I wanted to laugh because this last word sounded like "boobas," but I knew what was coming.

"You go without shoes, your feet get stepped on!"

I jumped back in time to prevent Nana's heel from grinding my toes. As far as I could tell, this was the only real risk of not wearing shoes.

Nearly everyone I knew was terrified of Nana. As a toddler, Arthur had picked up a block and hurled it at her. He missed; she retrieved it and hurled it right back. Though the block split his scalp, Arthur was too stunned to cry, even when the doctor was stitching shut the wound.

My grandmother couldn't hear a word of bad news my parents shouted in her ear, but let an enemy whisper a disparaging word across the hotel and Nana would scream: "You should burn in Gehenna for such a lie!"

She didn't speak, she ranted, punctuating her sentences with goaty snorts—*naah, naah*—which made me believe this was how she had come to be called Nana in the first place.

"Don't run with that bottle in your mouth, you might trip, naah, naah, you'll knock your teeth out."

"I don't *have* any teeth."

But even when confronted with the gaping truth, my grandmother wouldn't relent. "Stay here until you're finished, naah. You don't walk, you can't fall."

I guzzled my soda and set the bottle on the counter. "I don't think you look like a pig," I assured Mrs. Grieben, then ran back to the pool.

What luck! My mother was playing canasta. I slipped quietly down the steps, but the waves spread like radar.

"Lucy, you'll get cramps!" She turned in her chair. "You need to wait an hour after eating, at least."

"But I only ate soda!"

"Then why is your face covered with chocolate?" She unrolled a tissue from her sleeve. "Here, spit."

I refused; she spit for me, scrubbing my cheeks and the skin under my nose until I could smell my mother's sour saliva. I squirmed free. Had Herbie and the other boys witnessed my shame? No, they had already left to set up for dinner.

"Come on, Mom," I pleaded. "Just a little while? Can I?" I was whining, I knew, but the sun already was touching the hill behind the Eden. "Now? Can I? Please?"

My mother's eyes strayed to the new hand of cards on the table. The other women's heels were tapping the deck. "Oh, all right. Just don't go into the deep end."

"I promise," I said. But even before she had played her first card I had ducked beneath the floats and was heading toward the marker that proclaimed

7 FEET.

The sunbathers were the first to pack up. The pinochle players stubbed out their stogies and hectored their wives into bidding their last hands. The canasta games ended. My mother stood and stretched. She saw me in the water. "Lucy, come out of there this instant!"

"Just one more lap."

"I can't stand here arguing."

Though Nana ruled the kitchen and my father served as her steward, my mother's job was hardest since she mixed with the guests, scurrying from table to table and enduring their complaints about cold soup and spoiled liver. They had paid a flat sum, which earned them the right to gobble all they could, three meals a day. Most of them tried to wolf down enough food to recoup their investment, and, if they could, accumulate interest.

"You're old enough to understand," my mother said. "Even with all our work. . . . The prices these days! And how can we pay off our debts if we're only a quarter full? What will your father do, at his age. . . . All I ask is, please, don't do so much to aggravate me."

Growing Up at Grossinger's

Tania Grossinger

The Grossinger staff was very large. Sometimes at the height of the season there were almost as many people who were paid to be at the hotel as there were those who paid to be there. It was not uncommon, in summer, to find nine hundred and fifty employees on the payroll and one thousand guests on the register.

There were a great many jobs to fill. In addition to augmenting the departments whose staffers had direct contact with guests, i.e., waiters, waitresses, bellhops, bartenders, pool staff, social staff, athletic staff, camp counselors, office help, and the like, there was a whole staff world behind the scenes. The guests never saw them, but their stay could not have run as smoothly without the cleaning help, kitchen stewards, pantry help, gardeners, plumbers, electricians, engineers, security men, maintenance men, laundrymen, florists, greenskeepers, and others I can't even remember.

Most of the "back of the house" staff worked at the hotel year round and many of them made their homes in Liberty. Many had been with the hotel for twenty or thirty years, some even longer.

In the summer, many college students applied for jobs as busboys, waitresses, or bellhops where they could conceivably make $1,500 during the season in tips and salary, have virtually no expenses, and have a heck of a good time to boot. Competition was tough. Dave Geiver was never particularly disposed to hiring collegiates for the summer as he considered his dining room organization professional and didn't like the idea of having to train new people from scratch. Not for naught was he nicknamed "Dave Geiver, the Slave Driver." But he had little choice because who else but college kids could afford to take a job for just three months a year. So he culled the best from the applications he received. Whenever possible he demanded experience, at best from other hotels, at least from summer camps. Sometimes it became sticky when guests tried to use their influence to get a job for a relative or friend of the family. Geiver had one stock question: "Would you want him to wait on your table?" Not surprisingly, many withdrew their requests.

Off season, there were at least four hundred permanent employees. They took jobs for a variety of reasons, making money usually the least of them. No hotel in the mountains paid very well, though I assume Grossinger's paid better than most. But working there had several advantages in addition to the free room and board and few expenses.

The major reason most of the single women worked there was to meet rich men and get married. While others paid for the privilege, they, because they were there for a long time, would be exposed to all the "good catches" and pocket a salary as well. And they were very highly motivated.

I remember one girl who was nicknamed "How much?" because the first question she'd ask a fellow she was snuggling up to on the dance floor was "How much money do you make?" If the answer wasn't to her liking, as far as she was concerned, the dance was over.

Interestingly enough most of the girls, especially those in the front and back offices, did marry as a result of working at the hotel. But they married fellow staffers.

Some boarded the Shortline bus from New York City just to get away from home . . . to be part of the "glamorous, exciting, swinging life" they read about in the gossip columns. Others were escaping an unhappy love affair or marriage. And, of course, there were those who just had nothing else to do and thought they'd try it out as a lark.

Youngsters who wanted to make it big in show business were always applying for jobs. The girls would take jobs as file clerks or switchboard operators, the guys as bellhops or chair movers on the athletic staff, hoping to get the chance to sing a song or two some evening with the dance band or do their "thing" in front of a live audience.

It wasn't always easy to achieve such ambitions. When I was ten years old I became friendly with a roly-poly fellow on the athletic staff named Butch. Early that winter he had gone to see Morty Curtis, the man in New York who booked the entertainment for the hotel, introduced himself as Butch Hacker, and explained he wanted a job in the mountains. Asked what he could do, he gave an imitation of Lou Costello. Mort knew he had his man. He had finally found the one person qualified for the last position left open on staff. He gave him a one-way bus ticket to Liberty and wished him well. Buddy Hackett, né Butch Hacker, spent the next three months freezing, pushing people down the toboggan slide, and fixing them up with snow sleds. When spring came and he began to thaw out, he left for greener pastures.

In the beginning I was astounded at the singleness of purpose among the staffers who wanted to be "discovered." The men would do anything they thought would brighten their chances of getting ahead. If a top agent's wife was alone during the week, you can rest assured she wasn't alone for long. If a talent booker for a nightclub had any worries about his homely daughter finding someone to keep her company, he need worry no more. She had company. The women were just as aggressive as the men. It was not uncommon, any day of the year, to overhear the following conversation, or variations thereof: HE: "Can you really sing?" SHE: "Can you help me?" HE: "It depends." SHE: "Baby, not only can I sing, but take me back to your room and I'll make your mattress sing!"

One thing for sure. The hotel offered employees a life-style that no 9 to 5 job back in the city could equal. Not everybody lasted. Some couldn't adjust. Others couldn't keep up with the pace. They became part of the "We hire, they tire, we fire" cycle.

It was not uncommon for some to come up for a short time, a season perhaps, and stay five or six years. It was a way of life they quickly grew used to. No chores. No grocery shopping. No cleaning the rooms. Everything was done for them. It was what I called "the convenient rut."

Of course there also was fun—and inside jokes—that made getting through the tough days tolerable. I remember one bellhop, Joey, who was a master at double-talk. He'd start speaking to a guest in his own impeccable slang, insulting him with every outrageous epithet in the book, and the poor guest, not understanding a word that was said, and afraid to show his ignorance, made up for it by double tipping.

New page boys at the pool always had to pass a test. A call would come in and the head lifeguard would instruct him to walk around the pool paging "Mr. Cocken. Mr. Gay Cocken, please" (which is Yiddish for what one tells someone else to do in his hat). One summer a guest, who was trying to be a bigshot and didn't understand what the words meant, got up and answered the page.

And there was always some clown in the dining room who, on the busiest Saturday night of the season, would organize all the busboys to carry their trays of dirty dishes at precisely the same moment into the kitchen and dump them simultaneously, insuring a nervous breakdown for at least two dishwashers.

Sometimes the experience taught one how to think on her feet—and fast. One friend of mine at the front desk received an emergency call from a guest early on a Sunday afternoon. She had checked out that morning after breakfast and had just discovered she had left her diaphragm in the room. The problem was that she needed it later that evening. Seriously. What to do? My friend thought fast. She told the guest to meet the 3:00 P.M. bus arriving at Port Authority bus terminal in New York City at 6:00 P.M. and she guaranteed her package would be on it. It was.

There were side benefits as well for those who worked at the hotel. One young staffer was about to be insulted when she was asked if she would baby-sit for some pickled herring, lox, and bagels. Before she had a chance to protest, she was told it would involve a little more than just sitting. Dinah Shore was opening at the Paramount Theater in New York City and Bob Weitman, the manager and a summer seasonal, decided to surprise her. He called Abe Friedman and asked to have a huge basket of Jewish delicacies prepared, then called the hotel airport and arranged for the pilot to fly them to Teterboro airport in New Jersey, where they would be met by car and driven directly backstage to the theater. As Ethel told her friends afterward, when she had awakened that morning, the last thing in the world she expected to be doing was sharing a corned beef and pastrami sandwich with Dinah Shore in her dressing room that same afternoon.

The girls weren't the only ones to have fun. The guys came in for their share, too. One bellhop's claim to fame occurred at the height of a taxi strike in Manhattan. Eddie Fisher had flown in from California for an appearance at the Waldorf and someone at the "G" had arranged for the bellhop to meet him with a car at the airport and drive him there. On the way in, Eddie told him that there were a few girls in an apartment on the upper East Side he had heard about and, after he had showered and changed, wanted the bellhop to pick him up and bring them over to his suite. "But try them out first," he ordered. "If they're good enough for you, they're good enough for me. If not, forget them."

It was this same bellhop, Meyer, who checked out a rather eccentric elderly man who, instead of a tip, presented him with a check made out for $500 because "I like you. You're a nice bellhop." When Meyer got back to the front office, the Superintendent of Service told him he had been had. The gentleman had pulled the same stunt with his dining room waiter, who didn't even bother to check it out. He just ripped the check up. Meyer wasn't so sure. He went right down to the bank, and much to his and everyone else's amazement, he was notified a week later that the check was legitimate. It had cleared with no complications whatsoever.

The fun and games notwithstanding, however, the staff took their work seriously. And even though it didn't always look so, it was hard work. I know how exhausted my mother and many others were at the end of each and every day. One of the captains in the dining room summed it up beautifully when asked what he considered to be the hardest part of his job. "Keeping the smile on my face," he answered. "Do you think it's easy to always walk around with a smile?"

Everybody on the staff in their own way accepted the unwritten maxim that "If a guest isn't having a good time, no matter what the reason, it is the fault of the hotel. Something must be done to rectify it." Which prompted one executive to put a sign in his office which read: "Everyone entering this place makes us happy. Some when they arrive. Some when they leave."

One thing that separated the Grossinger staff from staff at many of the other hotels was the "personal touch." As much as possible, they really were treated as if they were members of the family. Jennie tried to take their problems to heart whenever she could. Abe Friedman always had an available shoulder to cry on. And my mother was always seeing to it that the girls on the staff, and the men as well, didn't spend too much time alone against their will.

For the most part, staff were given complete use of the facilities, both athletic and social, as well as discounts at the concessions. There was one period when some guests complained that the female staffers were monopolizing the eligible males in the Terrace Room so they were asked to refrain from coming in. But someone soon wisely pointed out to Jennie that today's staffer was tomorrow's paying guest, so the employees were just told to use their judgment—translated as "Give the guest an even break!"

The hotel threw marvelous staff parties at least twice a year. The big one was held in August, immediately following the long looked forward to Staff Show. This was the staff's answer to the Guest Show held each July, but the Staff Show was a thoroughly professional job. Upcoming Broadway and television writers were hired to put the skits together. Mel Brooks moonlighted one August when he was working for Sid Caesar and "Your Show of Shows." Jerry Ross and Dick Adler, Eddie Fisher's boyhood friends from Philadelphia, took the job the summer before *Pajama Game* and then *Damn Yankees* became Broadway hits. Carl

Reiner and Howard Morris also made frequent contributions. Rehearsals began five weeks before the big night, with all of us—kids, waitresses, bellhops, busboys, lifeguards, office help, switchboard operators, musicians—giving up off-duty time to put together what, after the Labor Day Extravaganza, even the guests acknowledged was the highlight of the summer entertainment season.

After the show an all-night bash, courtesy of the family, would begin for staff only, with endless champagne, open bar, hors d'oeuvres, dancing, and every kind of merriment one could think of. Then at the end of the season there'd be another get-together, this informal, down at the lake, with square dancing, beer, hot dogs, rowboats, and whatever fun and frivolity one could come up with. An outsider looking in would swear that the place was more like a summer camp run for the staff than a structured business operation run for guests.

Rare was the employee who seriously complained about the food—or lodging. Unlike the policy at many other hotels, the Grossinger staff always ate the same food as the guests, the only difference being that the staff didn't have the variety of choices. But the food was always fresh—and first rate.

The accommodations, though nothing to write home about, were acceptable, especially since one rarely did anything more in them than sleep. Many cottages, the Farm House, Hibscher's, the Playhouse upstairs and downstairs were turned over to staff completely. Some staff lived in less expensive rooms in buildings that served guests, but not many. And to make summer jobs more attractive to college students, in the late fifties the hotel purchased a smaller place, the Lakeside Inn, a mile from the Main House, with swimming pool and athletic field especially for them.

Not many staff lived in private rooms, and those who did were "up" in the hierarchy. Competition for these rooms was intense not only because they represented status but because, since roommates were assigned indiscriminately, problems often arose. It was difficult, for example, when a dance teacher who came home at 3:00 A.M. was matched up with a file clerk who had to be up at 7:00. Sometimes the situation was impossible. When Jack Shor, now the public relations director for Clairol, Inc., first came to Grossinger's to put together the *Tattler*, he was assigned a room with a security guard who was habitually inebriated. This guard's favorite pastime, next to boozing, was using a dresser drawer as his toilet, thus saving himself a trip to bathroom at the end of the hall. Sometimes people quit as a result of roommate problems, but usually, somehow or other, things managed to work out, and most would openly acknowledge that they certainly got as much out of their jobs as they put in—if not more.

Five and Three House

Sidney Offit

"The way it works," the proprietor of the knish stand said, "you got first of all your bungalows. They'll give you a place you'll have where to sleep, the mountain air, maybe a little pool you can swim. Your wife is a good cook, you'll have what to eat. You say you don't want your wife she should schlep? So you'll go by a hotel. They'll give you three meals, a porch, a rocker.

"Not fancy enough for you? Some place famous? You mean they should know where you've been when you tell them about it at home? Why not? So you'll take the family to the Aladdin, a Brickman's, a Laurels, a Nemerson's, a Pines, a Kutsher's, a Windsor. They have everything new, everything modern. You should only live and be well, you'll have a wonderful time.

"You want the best, the best in the world? From Paris I wouldn't know. To London I've never been. But you'll go to Grossinger's, the Concord, the Nevele—you couldn't want for nothing better. They've got night clubs, health clubs, golf courses. It rains, already they got an indoor swimming pool—you wouldn't even get wet."

Audrey Grier didn't wear stockings. It was June but her legs were already tanned. She wore shoes with open toes that displayed her brightly polished red toenails. Every part of her that could be rouged or polished was done up carefully. She had full, thick lips and a heavy-set body that came off as a good figure because her hips and bust were larger than her waist. It was her nose that spoiled her. Broad and flat, it spread out across her face like a young fighter's.

She tried to talk like a drill sergeant but her voice was thin and feminine. "I want my stations spotlessly clean," she said. "Every meal I'll inspect. There's no excuse for dirty goblets, and little things like the sugar bowl and salt and pepper shakers, I expect them to be perfect. Every waiter and busboy that works my room has to be a walking advertisement for the hotel. Polished shoes, clean shirts, and I don't want anybody coming in here needing a shave or a haircut. And another thing, I want the mats by each server picked up and cleaned every day." She liked that point and she dwelt on it for a few minutes. When she was finished she consulted a small pad in her hand.

"Watch yourself in the kitchen," she said. "No busboys pick up anything from the stove, unless it's a special, and then they have to have a note from me."

She wasn't all business. She could be sisterly. "I know the going gets tough when we're busy. I've worked the mountains for ten years. The guests will get under your skin, but don't panic. When you run into a tough one—well, they require a special technique." She bobbed the bun at the back of her head. "That's what I'm here for. I want to help you."

She could be tough, too. "I'm not trying to win any popularity contests. There are twenty boys waiting around the agencies, dying for a job. And I'm not afraid to fire. The boys who've worked with me before know I don't take less than a hundred per cent."

They were sitting in the dining room, a tremendous hall with a huge plate glass window along one side. The tables and chairs were painted coral, and there was a paper that looked like a jungle scene against the far wall. The floor was highly polished, and a thin wall trimmed with redwood and artificial flowers concealed an air-conditioning unit.

For the meeting, the nine waiters and eight busboys were gathered around a small table that acted as a desk for the hostess. It was next to the concealed unit and near the dining-room entrance. Most of the boys were sitting with the chairs swung around backwards. Audrey was the only one standing.

"Audrey"—it was Stan, the Mong—"tell 'em about chasing tips."

"I'm coming to that."

"Nobody chases tips, right? You take what you get and shut up. The good make up for the stiffs, right?"

"Thanks, Stan, that's right. The first boy I catch or hear about chasing the guests for tips—out. No questions—just out."

"Tell 'em about busboys' side jobs," Stan said.

"Wait a minute, Stan. I'm coming to that later."

Stan said, "She puts the list up in the kitchen and that's it. No bitching. You got complaints, see me."

"Two months on the breadbox for Joe," one of the boys said.

Joe, the red-haired boy who had announced the meeting, blushed and said, "Not this year. I'm a waiter, I hope."

"Also, you'll be wearing special shirts this year. No more white jackets. I think they're very attractive and should give the dining room color. Naturally, you'll be expected to buy these shirts. Three for each boy. Mrs. Mandheimer is selling them at cost—two dollars apiece. And that's cheap, believe me."

"Right away money," Mike Heimer said.

"Knock it off," Stan said. "Tell 'em about the stations, Audrey."

"I'm coming to that." She inspected her notes, skipping over the reminders to talk about punctuality, place settings, and how to serve. "Of course, everybody wants a window station. Unfortunately, there just aren't enough to go around. The window stations will go to the most deserving. I like to reward the boys who do a good job, but I go hard on the ones who don't. We'll start off by giving priority to the boys who have worked here the longest. I think that's the fairest way." She was looking at the notes when she said, "Stan Macht will work station one, and I'm putting Mike Heimer on station two . . ."

"Oh, no," Joe said. "You promised me a window station last year, Audrey, remember? I was a waiter before I came here and I only agreed to bus for a season with the understanding—"

"Understanding—hell," Stan Macht said. "You go where you're put and shut up."

"I wasn't talking to you," Joe said.

"But I was talking to you," Macht said. "Don't you go telling the Mong what to do. Not you or anybody else around here is giving this boy any crap."

"Hail the great Mong," Mike Heimer said.

"Long live the Mong's schlong," another waiter said.

"Quiet—all of you." The girl's face flushed. "I don't want any vulgarity— let's get that straight right from the start. If you can't act like gentlemen, get out."

"Let's hear the rest of the stations," Stan said.

"Stop interrupting me." She looked at him angrily and then went back to her notes. "This is a tentative list. If anybody has a complaint, see me after the meeting. I'll check with the office, and the final list will be posted on the bulletin board tonight." Her voice was softer when she said, "You should all know by now that I try to be fair."

After the list was read, the meeting broke up. Joe, Stan Macht, and Al were the only boys who stayed in the room.

"I don't want to gripe," Joe said, "but it cost me a couple hundred dollars bussing instead of waiting last year. I need that window station to make it up."

"Why don't you shut up and give her a chance?" Stan said. "You and your damn crying towel—"

"I wasn't talking to you, Jock Strap."

"Somebody around here is going to get their jaw broken."

"All right. That's enough." Audrey Grier sat down on the chair in front of her small desk. She crossed her legs and was very careful to pull her skirt over her knees. The three boys watched. "Now I fully sympathize with you, Joe, but don't let your red-haired temper get the best of you." She thought that was cute and she smiled. Her teeth were even and white, but widely spaced. "I did promise you a window station, but I thought Mike Heimer might be a little stronger."

"I carried the biggest station in the house last year," Joe said, "and I had an inexperienced waiter. Did you have any trouble, any trouble at all from my station?"

"Why don't you shut up and listen to her?" Stan said.

Al Brodie stood far enough off to the side to be out of the way. He made no effort to look as if he wasn't listening.

"I could be wrong. I'm not perfect," Audrey Grier said. "I'll tell you what— you let Mike have the station for the first two weeks. Then I'll try you. Maybe we'll rotate like that all summer."

Joe's face flushed. He wheeled in his chair and turned away from her. "That won't work, Audrey. What would we do about season guests? I can see right now I'm going to get screwed."

"You won't get screwed," the hostess said. "You have my word for that. You just let Mike Heimer work the window station for two weeks. We'll see after that—O.K.?" She put out her hand as if she was going to touch him, but she quickly drew it back, jangled her loose bracelets, and adjusted the chignon at the back of her head.

Joe shrugged. "All right. There's nothing I can do about it anyway." He looked over at Stan Macht, who was smiling. "But you, you son of a bitch, don't you think you can push me around. Damn basketball players think they own this hotel."

"Why don't you drop dead," Stan said.

Joe left and Audrey said, "Stan, take it easy, will you? I know what I'm doing. You only make it harder for me."

"What about this jerk?" He motioned over his shoulder toward Brodie.

Al stepped closer to the table. "I'm Al Brodie. Did Mrs. Mandheimer tell you about me?"

"You a busboy?"

"No, ma'am, I'm a waiter. Mrs. Mandheimer promised me a job."

"She did? She shouldn't have done that. We already have a full staff. Maybe she wanted you to work in the children's dining room. We might need two waiters in there."

"She said the main dining room."

"That's funny. Well, she has so many things on her mind. I'll tell you what— I'll talk to her and see you later."

"I'd appreciate that. I certainly would," Al said.

"Oh, balls," Stan said.

"Stan, will you stop that! There's nothing wrong with acting like a gentleman." She lifted her chin and seemed to tighten her nostrils. "You say your name's Al Brodie?"

"I don't want this guy working here," Stan said. "He's no good. He's an eight ball. I could see it the first time I looked at him. He's a goddamned phony."

"Suppose you let me decide that," Audrey Grier said.

"O.K., you decide," Stan the Mong said, "but he don't work here."

"Stan, I think you'd better leave," Audrey said.

"Where the hell did you ever work before?" Stan asked Al. "Did you ever work as a waiter? Name the place. Give us a reference."

Al looked at Audrey as if it was all he could do to restrain himself.

"All right, Stan, you've said your little piece, now suppose we leave the rest up to me."

"You don't shift none of the regulars for him," Stan said. "I don't want my boys getting the shaft because of a yes-ma'am-no-ma'am phony like him." He made a loud noise with his chair as he got up. "I'm leaving it up to you, Audrey. The old man wants a basketball team this year. He wants to put this place on the map. You better do what's right."

After Stan left, Audrey touched the bun in back of her head three times in a row. She uncrossed and then recrossed her legs. "He's just about impossible," she said. "But he is strong and he carries his station very well. You see, I never let my personal sentiments interfere with my work. I may like a person very much, but that doesn't mean I'll show him any favoritism. The same thing is true if I don't like a person. I mean if I think they are crude and uncouth. I wouldn't let a thing like that keep me from hiring him or treating him with all the respect due because of his professional competence. I tried to make that very clear to the boys. In my speech, I mean—I thought it came through."

"I got it perfectly," Al said.

"Now, about you, Brodie." She folded her hands on her lap and got right down to business. "Have you ever worked a house this size?"

"I'll be honest with you. You strike me as the kind of person I can talk to straight. I mean without trying to impress you. Like the way you talked to the boys. It came through. It was right to the point. A person has to be pretty sure of themselves and really know what they're talking about to lay it on the line like that."

"You're not answering my question," she said.

"The fact is there's nobody up here I could call up and get a reference from just like that," he snapped his fingers. "I'd rather tell you that than make up some phony names and back it up with a lot of lies."

"I think you'd do very well in the children's dining room," she said. "Children require a special kind of handling. I've got a hunch you'd do nicely, very nicely—"

"The thing is—" Al said. He paused and let out his breath and then said very gravely, "I've got to make a thousand dollars this summer. If you think I can make it in the children's dining room—well, I have confidence in you. I think you understand people very well. If you think that's the place for me, I'll just tell Mrs. Mandheimer I won't be working the main dining room. After all you're the boss."

"Did Mrs. Mandheimer promise you a station in the main dining room?"

"She said something about shifting one of the other boys. But then again I don't think she consulted this fellow they call the Mong."

"Don't worry about Stan. I just let him talk. Half the time I don't even listen to him."

"Well—whatever you say—"

"Let me tell you this, Al." She uncrossed her legs, set both her feet firmly on the floor and leaned forward in the chair. She balanced her weight forward on her toes. "This is a five-and-three house—the toughest kind of house in the mountains. You really have to know the ropes to work a house like this. In the height of the season you have to carry a station of thirty or maybe more. We have a menu, but anything that's off the menu that a guest asks for we try to get for them. In that respect our service is à la carte, like it is at the best hotels. But our people are all over you. They keep you running like it's a hash house. There's no sense in our trying to kid ourselves. If I see you can't do it, I'll save you a lot of aggravation and the house a lot of embarrassment. I can be tough when I have to be. I'd fire you like that." She snapped her fingers, just the way he had a few moments before.

"I'll take my chances," Al said. "And thanks."

"Hold on a minute. It's not settled. You haven't got the job yet, not by a long shot. I have a lot of thinking to do."

"I have confidence in you," Al said. "I just hope you have some in me." It didn't come off the way he wanted, and he smiled.

"You'll know tonight," Audrey said. "I'll post the final station assignments on the bulletin board in the kitchen."

"Gee, I don't believe I know where that is," Al said.

"Here, I'll show you," she said. She stood up slowly, and was careful to hold herself straight and tall as she walked across the room toward the entrance to the kitchen. To be a good hostess, she'd often thought, you have to possess the grace and aloofness of a professional model. But there had to be just enough action in the back to keep the men's minds off the food.

Al Brodie was right behind her.

The coffee urns and the glass-washing section were in the passageway leading from the dining room into the kitchen. The kitchen itself was large, divided down the center by long stoves, back to back. On either side of the stoves were serving counters. One side was used for lunch and dinner, the other for breakfast. At intervals along the walls were doors leading to the pantry, bakery, pot-washing tubs and dishwashing machine.

There was a twenty-by-twenty bulletin board nailed to the wall beside the coffee urns. It had a redwood border and the name *Hotel Edgemoore* in black script across the front. Mrs. Mandheimer had bought it at an auction three years ago. She was very persistent about having her hostess use it. The Workmen's Compensation laws were posted along one side, and there was a notice to all the help that said, "This is Your Kitchen. Keep it Clean." The headwaiter who had preceded Audrey Grier had written and posted it the first day the bulletin board was put up. It had hung through summer and winter for three years. There was seldom a day during the season when some waiter or busboy didn't pass it and say, "Yeah, my kitchen!"

"Isn't this a mess!" Audrey Grier said. The table beneath the coffee urns was wet with hot water and leaking coffee. She pulled out a dish towel from under the urns and wiped up the puddles. Her voice lowered. "You know the kind of help we have in the kitchen."

"Let me do that," Al said.

"No, it's all right." She concentrated on the table. "I hate filth. I don't know why. That's just the way I am."

"I don't blame you, Miss Grier. Especially where food is concerned."

"Sometimes it takes a woman. We're naturally more concerned with neatness." She held the wet towel out in front of her, away from her dress.

"Here, let me take that," Al said. "Where can I wring it out?"

She gave up the towel easily. "Over there, where the boys do their trays." She pointed to a big washbasin on one side of the wall.

Al Brodie wrung the towel out carefully. Then he rinsed it and wrung it out again. "Any place in particular you want this?"

"Just put it under the urns. The next person who notices a mess can wipe it up. Big joke." She tightened the handles of the urns and said, "Well, there's the bulletin board. You can get the feel of the rest of the kitchen from here."

"Oh yeah," Al said. "I'm beginning to feel at home already."

"The children's dining room is over on the other side," she said. "You better take a look at it. You'll probably be working in there."

"I hope not," he said. "I'm counting on that job in the main. Maybe I shouldn't say this, Miss Grier. I know it sounds like polishing and all, but I knew right off that I could work with you. Really. I'm not kidding. You put everything so nice and clear, right to the point. I know I can work a station the way you'd want it worked."

She winced. "Come on now, Brodie, you're laying it on a little thick."

"No, really. I'm telling the truth."

"We'll see."

Mr. Mandheimer came in. He was with a portly man in a sport shirt and a roomy blue jacket. The man was carrying a wooden clipboard in one hand and a pencil in the other.

"Nobody keeps this place clean. I have to do everything myself," Audrey Grier said so that Mr. Mandheimer could hear. She pulled the towel out from under the urn and started wiping the table again.

"The local wholesalers can't compete with us," the man with Mr. Mandheimer was saying. "They're trying to get rich in ten weeks. How can they meet our prices?"

"So what d'you want for number-ten fruit cocktail?" Mr. Mandheimer said.

"Right now it's seven ninety-five. Later in the season, I can't guarantee."

"You'll give me six cases." They were in front of the coffee urn. Mr. Mandheimer saw Al Brodie. "Boy, come with me."

"Remember what I was saying," Al said to the hostess. "I'm counting on you, Miss Grier." He followed the two men.

"What d'you get for oil?" Mr. Mandheimer asked.

The salesman walked quickly to get in front of Mr. Mandheimer. There was an expression on his face that it was important for Mr. Mandheimer to see. "We could give you a cheap oil, sure, and steal it back on the rest of the order. We don't do business that way. I got a pure soybean oil, it's right for you."

"You'll give me six cases prune juice, three cases apricot nectar, three cases pineapple juice," Mr. Mandheimer said.

The man made a quick notation on his clipboard. "And the oil?"

They walked through a swinging door that led out of the kitchen past the outside refrigerator and the garbage room. They came to a small graveled area where a station wagon was parked. "Boy, you'll take the eggs out from the car and put them in the cellar," Mr. Mandheimer said to Al Brodie. "Be careful you don't break any."

"Where you get your eggs?" the salesman asked socially. "Pick them up from a local farmer? That's a good idea. What do they get for eggs when you deliver them yourself?"

"Prices fluctuate," Mr. Mandheimer said.

Al Brodie latched his hands into the holders on both sides of the egg crate. He rested the weight on his thighs and carried the first one over to a door leading down a flight of stairs. "Where did you say you wanted these, Mr. Mandheimer?"

Mr. Mandheimer came over, followed by the salesman. There was a light switch on the wall and he snapped it on. "Here, go back, get another case," he said to Al. "Follow me."

"Let me help you," the salesman said. He put his clipboard down on the ledge beside the stairs.

"You want to help, go get a case," Mr. Mandheimer said.

"You think I won't?" the salesman said. "When we're rushed, you think I don't load the trucks at our warehouse?"

"Something's got to be done right, you do it yourself," Mr. Mandheimer said.

They each carried down two cases before the salesman asked, "Did you decide about that oil?"

Mr. Mandheimer looked around the cellar. "This place is a mess. I got to get a man down here to clean it up."

"I was wondering," the salesman said. "I didn't see many outside men—"

"This morning," Mr. Mandheimer said. "Two of the boys who helped open the house, three weeks they worked good as gold. This morning one's drunk and the other's carrying him down the road."

"Gets worse each year," the salesman said.

Al brought the last case down to the cellar. "Is there anything else I can do, sir?"

Mr. Mandheimer wiped his hands on his handkerchief. As they started up the steps, he said, "An unusual busboy. In August he wouldn't be so courteous."

"Beg pardon, sir?" Al Brodie said.

The salesman picked up his clipboard. "What'll it be on that oil, now?"

"Don't rush me," Mr. Mandheimer said. "I can get the same oil a quarter a can cheaper, why shouldn't I?"

"You'd be a fool not to," the salesman said. "I want you to. Why shouldn't you save a quarter a can? It adds up. Look, Sam, you know me long enough. How long has it been? Ten years?"

"Are you through with me, sir?" Al asked. He shifted his weight from foot to foot and rubbed his back.

"Back hurt, boy?" Mr. Mandheimer asked.

"No, sir. It's nothing. Glad to have been of help."

"Look, your back hurts, tell me. The season isn't even started, more or less I should have a compensation case."

"You're covered for that," the salesman said.

"That don't mean they can't increase the premiums."

"I'm perfectly all right," Al Brodie said. He made a muscle. "Strong as an ox, see?"

Mr. Mandheimer laughed. "Crazy college kids we get up here," he said to the salesman.

Al started back into the kitchen.

"Look, Sam, you know me. I don't believe in high pressure," the salesman said. "If you've got the right product, they'll come to you. And needless to say . . ."

Mr. Mandheimer was nodding his head. It was funny he couldn't remember
ever having seen that boy before. And he had a good memory for faces.

"How come we never have a mock wedding?" the woman asked the social director. "I
don't know, last year I went to a place was half this size, things were always going on.
The tumler, he was dressed up in my skirt, with pillows and everything. He married the
bass player from the band—it was a riot."

It was the third week of July and the hotel was filled to capacity. Mr. Mandheimer
had to call the agency for another second cook. The chef claimed the Chinese cook
was all right on breakfast, but no help to him for lunch and dinner. It was a rough
crowd. They were always calling for specials, and if the Mandheimers wanted
everybody to be happy, they'd better get him another second.

The chef was getting four hundred dollars a week. In their winter conference he'd told them he could handle a house of three hundred by himself. He
had said he didn't trust anybody else to cook for him. He didn't want any griddle man ruining his works of art and he asked a big price, but he assured the
Mandheimers he was worth every cent of it.

Now it was the height of the season. You couldn't get a decent chef for any
price, and he was threatening to quit if he didn't get help. The agency sent over
a colored man who wore a tall white chef's hat and worked at a New York steak
house in the winter. He was very flashy on the griddle. When he put the Sunday steaks on to sear, he bathed them in so much grease they let up spouts of
flame. He was a fast man with the spatula, turning them over flames and all.

The chef didn't like that.

He seared the steaks himself. He did all the cooking for the children as well
as the main dining room, and the day he caught the colored cook pouring as-
paragus into a pot instead of spreading it in a pan, he told him to stand around
and watch until he got the feel of it.

The colored cook stood around and watched, kidded with the chambermaids,
and collected a hundred and fifty dollars a week, which was a cheap price, at that,
for an experienced second.

Calvin told Mrs. Mandheimer she was throwing her gelt away, but Mrs. Mandheimer was too busy showing rooms and checking people in to hear him. Calvin was smoking a pure Havana cigar Mrs. Leiderkopf had given him. Mrs. Mandheimer told him to stop smoking cigars in the lobby and trying to look like a big shot.

Al Brodie deposited a hundred and seventy dollars in the safe at the end of the second week of July. He hadn't received anything from the Erlangs. They would tip later in a lump sum. The Gersons and Miss Mantell had each come through with five and three.

On the third Saturday night in July, Audrey Grier asked the chef for chicken livers. She had a table of old people who had been coming to the hotel for years, and they couldn't eat spicy appetizers. They had to have chicken livers.

The chef was turning his roast chickens at the time. He was down on the floor in front of the oven and he didn't stand up when he asked, "What's spicy about my gefilte fish?"

"I think it's perfect," Audrey said, "but what am I going to do with them?"

"That's your problem," the chef said and there were no chicken livers that night.

On Sunday, Audrey Grier made a note on the blackboard near the stove. She printed the word *Specials*, and next to it wrote, *four orders of chicken livers.*

Mr. Mandheimer was dishing out French fried potatoes when Audrey came in for the chicken livers. The chef had them in a small pan on the warming shelf and he gave them to her.

They were hot and she burned her fingers putting them on serving dishes, but she was happy.

Before she left the chef said, "Go ahead, make money. You run the specials and I break my back." He was sweaty and tired, and there wasn't a soul in the kitchen who would have argued with him.

Mr. Mandheimer had been with the electrician all morning, tracking down a short circuit in one of the cottages. He had a date with a produce man for right after lunch, and he had been up until three o'clock the night before, answering inquiries for the first two weeks of August, while his wife put their grandchild to sleep. He put six big French fries on a plate and said nothing.

The steaks were going out smoothly. The colored second with the big hat was fast, and the Chinese cook kept up with him. The chef was pulling them out of the oven, calling "Rare, medium, and well done," and blessing the days they served steak. It was a popular dish, after all, and gave him a breather from worrying about whether or not he would run out of the alternate choices on the menu. (He'd had veal cutlets, hamburgers, and breast of beef on Thursday, and the pain was still fresh. There'd been a rush on the breast of beef. He'd run out, and ten angry guests had stomped to the main desk to know why.)

Each of the waiters had been around twice when Al Brodie came back with a steak in his hand. It was the filet of the rib, cut two inches thick and then sliced in half. Each portion weighed as close to fourteen ounces as the chef's eye could judge. This one looked a little smaller than the rest. It had been hacked into by an angry fork and was coming back.

Al had ten more mains to pick up. He put this one on the counter as quietly as possible and told the colored second he wanted an exchange.

The second was slicing and dishing out. He tried to exchange it but the chef saw.

"What's the matter with that steak?" He left the oven doors open, broke the rhythmical flow of steaks from the ovens to the dining room, and picked up the piece of meat.

Mr. Mandheimer was working with the Chinese second, and he told him to keep dishing out on his station before the steaks got cold.

"It looks good to me," Al said, "but it is a little small."

"You get steak like this at home?" the chef asked. He held the piece of meat up in front of Al's face. The blood dripped down his arm.

"It looks delicious," Al said. "I'll be glad to eat it right now."

"You goddamn wise guy," the chef yelled. "You take this steak back and make 'em eat it."

Al tried to be reasonable. "I can't do that." He looked toward Mr. Mandheimer. "They want another piece of steak. What am I supposed to do?"

"What are you talking to him for? I'm the boss in here," the chef said.

"You're right, goddamn it," Al said. "I'll ram it down their filthy throats." He reached for the steak and the chef handed it to him.

Al plunked it down on a plate and put on his own French frieds and vegetables. "They'll eat it and like it, the dirty bastards."

The chef went back to the oven. "How do you like that, boss," he said to Mr. Mandheimer. "He thinks he gives them a big steak, he gets a big tip. Costs you a dollar a pound, and he wants a quarter tip."

Mr. Mandheimer nodded and went back to the French frieds.

Al Brodie picked up eleven mains in addition to the one with the small steak. Audrey had come in for a side order of French frieds and had seen the whole thing. It was her rule that the boys were only supposed to take out ten mains at a time but she let it go.

When the chef saw Audrey, he said, "Look at her in her fancy dress, making all the money, while I sweat my balls off. Get the hell out of here, bitch."

Audrey tried to laugh. She picked up the French fries, cleaned off the corner of the plate where some steak juice had spilled, and left.

Mr. Mandheimer told the chef to "Take it easy. You got half a summer to go yet. You'll have high blood pressure."

"I don't like no bitch to put it over on me," the chef said. "The guests tell me about her. She's the one put them up to that breast of beef. Who ever heard of a headwaiter couldn't sell veal cutlets and hamburgers?"

"Those things happen," Mr. Mandheimer said softly.

"Sure they happen," the chef said. He put the final tray of steaks on the table, and the two cooks dished them out. "But they don't have to happen. Listen to me, boss, I been in this business all my life. You get yourself a good headwaiter, get a man in the dining room, and you'll see your food costs drop. I'll bet you my salary, you'll save ten thousand dollars in a season."

"That's a lot of money," Mr. Mandheimer said.

One of the waiters came over to the stove and asked if there were seconds on steaks.

"No seconds. Seconds, yet," the chef said. "Get out."

"Come back later," Mr. Mandheimer said eyeing the tray of steaks, "if there's any left, we'll give you."

"What d'you think that veal cutlet cost you?" the chef said. "She don't serve them. That's a total waste. Ain't a chef in the world can do anything with cold veal cutlet. I had to give them to the help."

"You couldn't give them to the kids?"

"Ah, now boss, you think I'd give the children what's left over?"

"There's nothing wrong with putting it in the refrigerator. They don't eat frozen food at home?"

"So what did you tell me at the beginning of the season? The best for the kids. That's your very words."

"Veal cutlets, the best."

"All right, so tomorrow I'll give them what's left over from the chicken à la king appetizer today."

"No. Please, forget it," Mr. Mandheimer said.

Audrey Grier came in and stood through the last part of their conversation. When they were finished, she spoke to Mr. Mandheimer. Her voice was as soft and controlled as she could manage. "All the firsts have been served, Mr. Mandheimer. Do you think I could have a second for Mr. Golden on table one?" Her eyes dropped to the tray of steaks. There were four left.

"What d'you mean, seconds?" the chef roared. "What'd he give you, a dollar? Give me the dollar. Give me the dollar. I'll give you the steak."

"Look, I haven't seen a penny from him," Audrey Grier said. She was getting bold. "Do I get the second or don't I? I'm sick and tired of all this aggravation—aggravation in the kitchen, aggravation in the dining room—"

"You're aggravated. You're aggravated," the chef screamed. His head jutted forward and he beat his fists hard against his breast. "I sweat my goddamn balls off. I kill myself behind this goddamn stove, and *she's* aggravated. Goddamn you, get out of here! Get out of here before I kill you."

Audrey Grier's face paled. She trembled and rubbed her hands together. Al Brodie was on his way to pick up desserts when he saw her. For a moment it looked as if she were going to faint. He came over to her and took her by the arm.

"I got some trouble on table thirty. I need you," he said.

He could feel her body shaking as he led her back to the dining room.

Mr. Mandheimer gave a busboy a steak two minutes later, with instructions to give it to Audrey.

Reflections on the Delmar Hotel and the Demise of the Catskills

Jerry A. Jacobs

For many years I rarely discussed my parents' hotel, but lately I find myself mentioning it more often. As I settle into my forties and watch my two little girls grow up, I wonder how to tell them what it meant to me to grow up in the Catskills. I also want to understand how the Catskills vanished so quickly and so completely that an archive had to be established to ensure that some traces survive.

In our family there was often talk about writing a book about the hotel. But how to capture the zaniness, the colorful characters, the exhausting routine, and the special camaraderie that made up the Delmar Hotel? We would try organizing it around a day in the life. My mom rose at six to begin to prepare for breakfast, first for the staff, then for the guests. My dad bantered with a guest who was up at dawn waiting to complain about something askew. The day ended at 11 P.M. as the nightly performance in the casino drew to a close and the last trays in the tearoom, where guests would repair after the show, were put away. Then we would try a year in the life, trying to evoke the rhythm of preparing for the summer onslaught, the rush of the first guests arriving, and the long, slow process of shutting the hotel down after "the season."

But neither of these schemes left room for some of the best stories. Like the time the owner of the hotel across the street hired a man to burn down his place. The arsonist got drunk, mixed up the directions, and ended up burning down the main building of what was then the Jacob Inn. Or the story about the man who walked up to the front desk and told my dad, "I bet you don't remember me." Dad replied, "Your name is Epstein, right? You were here about thirty-five years ago, am I right?" And he was. Or the way the guests would come to the bakery to ask for a care package for the trip home. "I'm going to an empty house," they would say. "Perhaps you have a *bissel* cake and a few cookies for me?" A reasonable enough request, except that 150 guests were all going home to an empty house, and a sorcerer's apprentice was needed to keep the take-home bags filled. And where would we profile Sadie Cohen, the ultimate irrepressible *yenta*, who would insist on special-ordering every element in a Hawaiian salad? And Theodosha "Terry" Jones, the steady chambermaid who served tea to the guests after the show, after a full day of straightening up the rooms. We all thought that Terry's son, Doug Jones, beat Cassius Clay in their 1965 professional boxing bout, but he was robbed of the decision.

We never could come up with the right way to capture it all. So here I won't even try to paint a full portrait. Instead I'll recall a few things that evoke the later years of the Catskills, much later than Herman Wouk's *Marjorie Morningstar* and the rise of Jerry Lewis and the other Borscht Belt comedians. And I'll take a stab at explaining the demise of the Catskills.

GROWING UP

I grew up in the Delmar Hotel, located just east of Liberty, New York on Route 52, between Grossinger's and Brown's. The hotel was started by my grandfather, who opened it for guests in the summer of 1929, just before the stock market crash that would plunge the nation into a sustained depression. After the Second World War, the hotel was run by my dad and mom, Max and Claire Jacobs. My parents met in Paris during the war, and my French mother was responsible for the names of the buildings at the hotel—Biarritz, Capri, Deauville, Lido, and Riviera. Our place could accommodate about 150 guests, but this was considered a small hotel.

My first recollection of the hotel is from when I was three or four. I walked into the kitchen naked, holding my clothes in front of me, dodging the waiters rushing to bring their breakfast orders to the guests. "Mommy, get me dressed!" I called out over the din, as I slid in between the steam table and the big serving table. The steam table was hot enough to burn your fingers, and the serving table was the center of traffic. I knew that you had to watch your step during meal time—steer clear of the busboys who were not too sure of their balance while hauling the busboxes overstuffed with dishes, the dishwashers swinging the newly cleaned kettles around, the people rushing from the pantry to the bakery to the walk-in refrigerator. But I felt I knew my way around well enough.

My mother was busy pouring pancakes onto the griddle. Everyone laughed to see the buck-naked little boy wandering around the bustling kitchen. "You are going to have to learn to put your pants on," one of the waiters pointed out. I felt a little embarrassed, although at first I didn't quite see what all the fuss was about. So people could see my tush—so what? I held my clothes in front of my privates—why was everyone laughing at me? My mom put down her pitcher of pancake batter, scooped me up, dressed me, and ushered me into the children's dining room, where I ordered my usual, French toast "with a stick of jelly."

I did learn to put my pants on, of course, and before long I was one of the waiters rushing around the kitchen, carrying trays and trying to keep all of the orders straight. I remember standing in the very same spot one Passover breakfast, next to the steam table, putting the finishing touches on a tray of matzoh-brie, medium-boiled eggs, and farfel cereal when my father burst in, just back from picking up the mail, waving two thick envelopes in his hand. "Harvard and Yale—both with scholarships!" I smiled to myself as I lifted my tray and walked with measured steps out to my station in the dining room. I collected my hugs after I had finished serving breakfast. When you had thirty or more people waiting for their breakfast, family celebrations had to wait.

Working at the hotel had always been about saving money for college. My dad even posted signs in the lobby:

SUGGESTED TIPS: WAITERS, $6 PER WEEK,
BUSBOYS, $4 PER WEEK, CHAMBERMAIDS, $3 PER WEEK.

We then made the standard even more brazen by amending the sign to read

SUGGESTED MINIMUM TIPS.

Dad's loyalty seemed perfectly divided between the guests, whose comfort and satisfaction we had to cultivate, and the staff, including his sons, who were working three meals a day, seven days a week, saving up money for college. With about 30 guests per station, one could earn $180 per week as a waiter, and over the course of 10 weeks save perhaps $1,500 toward college. During the inflationary 1970s we hiked the rates up to $8 per week for the waiters, and I think even $10 for the 8-day Passover holiday. With college room and board costing around $5,000, it took a couple of summers to earn enough to pay for one year of college.

But I've gotten a little ahead of the story, because the dining room was the last rung, not the first, on the hotel employment ladder. As a little child, I had a lot of room to roam. We had a swimming pool, a merry-go-round, and an awesome metal slide that could get quite hot in the midday sun. As a teenager I could practice my tennis swing on the backboard of the handball court. And I certainly had more freedom than most kids my age. But I soon had to go to work, an experience that many children of small-business owners know well. Following my older brother, Howie, my first job was taking care of the pool. At eleven I added the candy store to my portfolio, again following in my brother's footsteps. At first it was a great thrill to go to the candy wholesalers—Briker Brothers in Liberty—to order cases of pretzels, potato chips, and candies. Sodas were delivered by trucks decked out in Coca-Cola and Seven-Up logos. My dad liked to joke that I was my own best customer. And next to the store was a pinball machine that I got to know intimately.

But the clientele of the hotel was in the midst of a rapid change. Just a few years earlier the children's dining room had been filled to the brim with 40 boisterous youngsters and nearly as many mothers hovering, making sure that their little Mark or Janet had eaten dinner. But suddenly the families stopped coming. The Marks and Janets went to summer camps, many of which were themselves located in the Catskills. So my candy store made $200 for the whole summer when I was 11, and only $150 when I was 12. The long hours and sparse customers eventually wore on me, although I did get to read a lot. I thought I would have enough free time to complete a correspondence law program then advertised on matchbook covers. When a representative called me, he suggested that I finish high school and college first.

Near the end of that summer, the pantry man quit, and my parents and I decided to close the candy store and put me in charge of the pantry. I learned the basics quickly enough—I could make an attractive "Hawaiian" salad and even cut up the 3-pound blocks of cream cheese into presentable portions. Shredding vats of cole slaw, filleting the *matjes* herring—the specific tasks were hardly difficult. I remember betting my friend Matt Bessen that I could cut up 7 lemons in a minute—I think I lost, but it was close. There was plenty of variety, but a fair amount of drudgery as well. Putting away the food ("the livestock") was a tedious chore after every meal. And preparing for the meals could take considerable time. Preparation was everything, for during meal time the requests would pour in faster than one could keep up with. I remember having to section grapefruits for an overflow crowd of 175 guests at Passover, and it seemed that every other night's dinner opened with grapefruit. *Dayenu!*

After a full summer in the pantry it was on to the dining room. At fourteen I was a bit young to be a busboy, but I worked with my older brother Howie. At eighteen he was a seasoned veteran and could show me the ropes. I promised not to overfill the busboxes. After dinner, I would do Howie's set-up for him, because he had to change quickly in order to play saxophone and clarinet for the evening shows. I filled in for him once, played terribly, and the piano player (who doubled as an art instructor) refused to work with me again. And thus I avoided working five nights a week in the band in addition to my three-meals-a-day, seven-days-a-week day job.

At sixteen I moved up from busboy to waiter. My busboy was older and much bigger than me, and at first it was a bit awkward. But I knew the routine pretty well and was able to give the guests a sense of confidence in me. I remembered the special details about each guest's preferences, and I delivered the food pleasantly and promptly. Once I got into Harvard, the guests would often volunteer that they had a granddaughter for me. I learned many important life lessons in the dining room.

- In the chaos of the meal, slow down, take a deep breath, stay focused.

- When things seem to be too slow, speed up, get ahead of the curve, or else you will find yourself crushed when everyone finishes at the same time.

- When on the way to the bakery, it's OK to steal a taste of the chocolate cake batter, but always turn the electric mixer off first (and turn it back on afterward).

These are lessons that have guided me through the years.

Living at a hotel meant learning many useful skills, such as hanging wallpaper and fixing toilets (my college classmates were amazed on more than one occasion at this talent). I learned to skip pebbles on the water of the pool, practicing with a ready supply of chlorine tablets. But there were chores that I dreaded. We would put up newspaper on the windows in the winter to keep the sun from fading the rooms. In the spring one of the first tasks was taking down the paper and dusting the windowsills (vacuuming if necessary). In addition to the accumulation of dead flies, we would occasionally encounter a hornet's nest. This prospect would fill me with dread, and I did my best to persuade my brother to take the lead on this.

Having a hotel in the family seemed perfectly normal to me—many of my friends had their own. Marc Stier's family ran Stier's hotel, Eileen Pollack's family ran Pollack's, Stanley Lipkowitz's family ran Lipkowitz's Bungalows. The only difference was that our hotel no longer bore the family name. In the late 1940s my parents decided that the Jacob Inn was no longer a fitting title, and they came up with Delmar as their Americanized replacement. A few friends grew up on chicken farms, but these were in decline even before the hotels faded from the scene.

WHO KILLED THE CATSKILLS? AGING AND AMERICANIZATION

As a sociologist I wonder, "What happened to the Catskills? How could it unravel so quickly and so completely?" Sociologists often discuss the way one generation passes its culture, values, and rituals to the next generation through a process called socialization. I have never placed as much stock in socialization as some of my colleagues, and perhaps the Catskills experience explains why. In the course of three generations, Catskills culture was born, flourished, and vanished. So much for the standard socialization story.

Most of the Jewish academics I know want to study the world; they don't feel any special need to devote their academic careers to studying the Jewish experience. African American social scientists continue to feel an obligation to study the oppression of their people, as do many Hispanic and Native American scholars. Perhaps we Jewish academics have unduly neglected our own experiences. For the untimely demise of the Catskills is a perfect sociological "whodunit," no less deserving of serious scholarly analysis than the mating rituals of the Canela (a tribe in the Brazilian Amazon) or the earnings patterns of Asian American engineers, topics that some of my graduate students have found perfectly irresistible.

Surely the success of Jewish immigrants to America is an important part of the explanation. Large numbers of Jews moved out of the hot tenements of New York City to the surrounding suburbs of Long Island and New Jersey. Air conditioning made summers more tolerable, so escaping the city for the mountains became less of an imperative. The decline of anti-Semitism also played a role. The blatant refusal to accept Jews as guests in many resorts, which gave rise to the Jewish Catskills, has dissipated. Today we can take it for granted that no Sheraton, Marriott, or Hyatt will refuse a reservation from someone because their last name is Cohen or Goldstein or Scheinbaum. As Jews became more affluent, they sought a broader range of vacation experiences than the Catskills could provide.

At the same time, the children of the hotel owners went off to Ivy League colleges and were no longer interested in running the family business. Marc Stier attended Wesleyan on his way to a Ph.D. in political theory, Eileen Pollack went to Yale and landed a faculty position in English at the University of Michigan, and Stanley Lipkowitz went to Cornell before earning his M.D. and Ph.D.

But the immigrant success story is not enough. Other groups have been successful and have maintained more identifiable ethnic enclaves. Chinese Americans come to mind as a comparison group. In recent years, Chinese Americans have achieved tremendous social and economic success, attending elite colleges and entering the mainstream professions. Both Jews and Chinese intermarry with white, Anglo-Saxon Americans at remarkable rates. But many major cities still have a Chinatown. Why have the Chinese succeeded in maintaining this nexus of ethnic institutions while the Jews were unable to keep the Catskills in business?

The answer I have come to believe is that my parent's generation (but not my parents in particular) put the first nail in the coffin by starting a rapid exodus from the boisterous hotels and bungalow colonies. By the early sixties, success and the Americanization of the Jews of New York had put the Catskills in mortal jeopardy. As families stopped coming for the summer, the Catskills experience no longer evolved to conform to what were becoming increasingly American tastes. The hotels continued to adapt, but in response to the changing needs of an aging clientele. As youth culture began to take hold in the late 1960s, the gap between the experiences and outlook of my generation and the vacation experience offered at Catskills resorts had become a deep chasm. I don't know from personal experience why families stopped coming—that was happening offstage, from my perspective. What I do know was that the aging of the guests made the demise of the hotels much more likely, because they came to represent a vacation experience that was increasingly removed from what younger, more Americanized Jews would seek out.

In other words, affluence, suburbanization, and expanding vacation opportunities explain some of the decline in the popularity of the Catskills, but they are not enough to explain why interest in this type of resort experience completely evaporated. I am suggesting that a tipping process changed the basic character of the resorts. Tipping is a concept familiar to sociologists who study residential segregation. An example: once a neighborhood becomes predominantly black—reaches the tipping point—whites generally avoid buying new homes there and the public definition of the neighborhood changes. I am suggesting that aging guests played a similar role in defining the character of a resort. Once hotels and bungalow colonies were predominantly oriented to elderly customers, families with children began to seek other vacation destinations. This explains the fact that the change from family resort to retirement resort took place so quickly and so completely.

At the Delmar, the timing of this transition is quite easy to pinpoint. When I was five years old, in 1960, the Delmar was very much a family resort. The children's dining room was packed with forty or more children. The day camp employed as many as four full-time counselors, and the vast caches of arts and crafts supplies my parents bought never seemed to last into August. Husbands would often join their wives and children on Friday evening, and the kitchen was prepared for a number of late arrivals. The day camp closed in 1965, when I was ten, and the candy store two years later. The hotel remained open for twenty more years, but in retrospect the fate of the Jewish resorts was sealed the year the camp was converted into a storage room.

The Catskills melted away from the bottom up. The bungalow colonies were the first to go, then the smaller hotels, with some of the largest and fanciest hotels hanging on the longest. The Concord just closed, lasting nearly a decade longer than Grossinger's. The larger hotels were able to offer amenities that enabled them to maintain a mixed clientele longer.

By the time I was a teenager, the guests were largely retired—much older than my parents. We would discuss how to attract a younger clientele—would a tennis court help? A putting green? Or maybe a shuttle van to the golf course? Of course many of these ideas were impractical, too expensive; and in the end they might have delayed but would not have reversed the inexorable exodus of families from the Catskills.

My parents wanted a "middle-aged" clientele, but their definition of "middle-aged" was forced to change as the guests grew older. At one point, our working definition meant someone who was still able to use the shuffleboard court; then it was someone able to walk to the court, then someone able to see it from the dining room window, then someone able to remember what shuffleboard was, then . . .

This division by age may seem peculiar, even unkind, but remember that this was just the moment when youth culture was coalescing, with demonstrations against the Vietnam War and the emergence of the generation gap. We didn't subscribe to Mario Savio's dictum, "Don't trust anyone over thirty," but we knew just what he meant. It was a time of moonwalks. Reminiscing about the *shtetl* would have to wait.

The Catskills were in the hospice by the time I was in college. By then an age gulf separated me from the allure of the Catskills. For me, *Yiddishkeit* was more about the trials and tribulations of the geriatric set than it was about my own heritage. The aging clientele chose prunes over lox and eggs, and *Fiddler on the Roof* over the samba. By the time I graduated from college, the Catskills were literally dying of neglect. I was too busy writing my dissertation to go to the funeral. The transformation of the character of the Catskills from a vibrant center of family life to a quiet vacation locale for retired Jews can be traced through entertainment and food, two of the hallmarks of the Catskills experience.

SHOWTIME IN THE CASINO AND THE GENERATIONAL DIVIDE

The aging of the guests revealed itself first in the entertainment. Every night there was something: movie night, bingo night, talent night, and shows four times a week. This separated the small hotel from the bungalow colony, which often had just a weekly show on Saturday night.

At the Delmar we would have three singers for every comic, because singers were lower risk. Most were good enough to help the crowd pass an enjoyable evening, but many comics bombed miserably—the element of surprise had long since gone out of the same old jokes. And it was usually a bad idea to have more than one hypnotist per summer.

The music at the hotel was a mix of Broadway show tunes and old Yiddish songs. My dad liked to play Broadway scores on the hotel's loudspeaker—*Pal Joey, Guys and Dolls, Camelot*. When it was still a family resort, the music was contemporary, popular music, with some older Yiddish favorites mixed in. Of course the most popular was the score from *Fiddler on the Roof*, with its beautiful songs that evoked the shtetl. Most of the singers felt they needed to include one or more songs from *Fiddler* in their song set.

I can still map out a typical singer's set: an upbeat welcome song or two followed by a few Broadway show tunes. Then a sentimental turn toward Yiddish classics, perhaps "*Shein vi di L'vone*" "*Belz*," or "*Tsena, Tsena*." Some of the more athletic singers would dance the kazatska while singing the lively "Rumania, Rumania." A singer aiming straight at the guests' heartstrings could add some of the more sentimental Yiddish favorites, like "My Yiddishe Mama," or songs directed at Jewish identity itself—"Tell Me Where I Should Go" or "*Hatikva*," the Israeli national anthem. A few songs, like "*Bei Mir Bistu Shen*," were sung half in English and half in Yiddish, since by the 1960s Yiddish competence was disappearing among the younger parents and certainly among the children.

Running the candy store meant going to the show every night. And two years of singers, comedians, magicians, and hypnotists surely constituted an overdose. How much *Rozhinkes mit Mandlen* could you take? By the late 1960s I was thoroughly sick of *Fiddler on the Roof*. I had heard every song a few hundred times too often. *Dayenu!*

But who could forget the high drama of talent night? Countless skits were performed by the guests and staff, making gentle fun of the Catskills experience, and often involving elaborate productions of Broadway show tunes with modified lyrics. And talent night could turn into a pitched battle. One former cantor once tried to sing all of the verses to some interminable Yiddish song. People begged him to stop, but he wouldn't. He was on a mission to preserve Yiddish songs, while the audience just wanted to have a good time.

Many original numbers were composed for talent night. These typically took the form of new lyrics for familiar show tunes. One that sticks in my mind is "Delmar Time," sung to the tune of "Summertime." The chorus went like this:

> *I've got the blues, from working at Delmar.*
> *I've got the blues, from serving food.*
> *I've got the blues, from working at Delmar.*
> *So take what you ordered and come in to eat on time.*

This song was performed live by the waiters in front of the guests, and went on for many verses. The singer would talk over the musical backdrop, complaining about the trials and tribulations of being a waiter. "Everyone wants the end piece of roast beef. But there are only two end pieces. What is a waiter to do?"

When I was young I would sing on talent night. One disastrous evening my selection was "Maria," from *West Side Story*. Somewhere along the way I got the lyrics confused and I found myself stuck singing "I'll never stop saying 'Maria.' " When it became clear that I couldn't figure out how to get past this point, the audience burst into laughter, and the band brought the song to a merciful conclusion. Later I would stick to playing the saxophone—no lyrics to worry about. Eventually Howie and I would play saxophone–piano duets, most notably Dave Brubeck's rhythmically complex "Take Five."

But talent night itself changed as the clientele changed. When the hotel was filled with families with children, talent night was a wild and unpredictable affair, with elaborate skits, stage-struck tykes, and aging wannabes grabbing a moment in the spotlight. As the supply of precocious children playing accordion or performing tap dances dried up, talent night become more a show of staff members, along with fewer and fewer aging divas. Bingo night eventually displaced it.

The great divide came at the end of the sixties, when youth music turned firmly to rock and roll at the same time that the guests became much older. As a young teen, I was drawn to the Doors, Jimi Hendrix, Cream, and Simon and Garfunkel. Steve Lawrence and Edie Gorme just didn't cut it anymore. There was no longer any middle ground, no Ed Sullivan mainstream to claim any allegiance on the part of the staff in their teens and early twenties.

Out with Yiddishkeit, in with Woodstock. We did manage to get to the Woodstock festival, which took place not more than fifteen miles from the Delmar. My cousin Karen and her husband Alan just happened to be at the hotel. They were much older, perhaps in their late twenties at the time. We had to wait until Howie was done playing after the show, and at 11:15 P.M. Karen, Alan, Howie, and I hopped in the car and took off for Woodstock. Being locals, we knew the back way. The main roads had long since been closed, but we were able to park no more than a mile or so away. The scene of more than 300,000 young men and women camping out in the mud, listening to the greatest bands of the day was remarkable, even at one in the morning. We wedged ourselves into a little spot and spread out a blanket to keep the worst of the mud at bay. Creedence Clearwater Revival played a nice set from about 1:30 to 3:00 A.M. We decided not to wait for Janis Joplin, who was scheduled to come on at 4:00 or 5:00 A.M. We had to get back to the hotel, get whatever sleep we could, and be ready to set up for breakfast at 7:30 A.M. But we made it to Woodstock!

THE KITCHEN AND THE DINING ROOM

Jewish food was central to the hotel experience. At first the aging clientele clung to the traditional foods. But eventually the salty and greasy dishes no longer suited the older guests. Broiled flounder, not Big Macs, spelled the end of potato latkes.

The times I remember most fondly at the hotel were the quiet times, preparing for the season. As a little boy, in the bakery with my mom, my job was to put the sprinkles on the cookies before they went in the oven. I imagine all kids like to put sprinkles on cookies, but I got to decorate hundreds and hundreds. I remember finally being old enough to be in charge of the maraschino cherries. I felt very grown up.

And the blintz blitzes. We would prepare the blintzes before the season and freeze them. Through some interpretation of the "no cooking on Sabbath" rule, warming up blintzes on a stove that had already been lit before sundown on Friday didn't exactly count as cooking. Thus frying blintzes was OK, but frying an egg was not. This didn't make the slightest sense to me, but I could accept the fact that the hotel was advertised as following kosher rules, so we had to stay within the limits of what was accepted. In any event, we would set up a blintz assembly line on the kitchen table. Mom would make a vat of batter, and would have five or six skillets going at once. My brother (and sometimes my father) and I would take it from there: stuff the blintzes, roll them up, and line them on an industrial-size baking sheet. We would need about 125 servings of cheese and 25 potato (my preference) for each Saturday in the summer, and we would knock off two or three Saturdays' worth in one of our sessions. Of course the participants were first in line for spoils of the blintz blitzes. Now and then Howie and I would declare a blintz irreparably broken, and we would get to munch on it then and there.

Aging, not Americanization, displaced many of the most traditional staples on the menu. Prunes and cottage cheese replaced lox and eggs at breakfast, broiled flounder was awarded the slot previously held by baked whitefish at lunch, and boiled chicken and flanken came to rival brisket of beef as a choice for dinner. We had to stop serving potato latkes because our guests could no longer eat fried foods.

My mother and I quarreled about ending our lox-on-demand policy. I said "That's what people come here for!" But she was right—salt-free diets were becoming increasingly common, and rotating lox and herring every day or two made perfect sense. One alumnus of the Delmar dining room staff opened his own restaurant, but it was yuppie food, not shtetl cuisine, that was his specialty (although I am told that noodle kugel and a lox and eggs combination called "The Catskill Scrambler" have made it onto the menu).

I managed to have my friends hired as waiters and busboys. This made work in the dining room much more tolerable. The camaraderie of the dining room staff was among the most enduring pleasures of the hotel. We would regale each other with the latest outrageous request a guest had made and exchange tips on how to persuade people to accept the less popular main dishes. We would nickname the guests (whom we got to know quite well, since they typically stayed at least two weeks, and not infrequently six or eight weeks). When the routine got to us, we would escape by doing charades with food themes. Our lame efforts to imitate smoked whitefish or brisket of beef with *tsimes* would help pass the time while we cleaned up after dinner.

We even managed to establish a day-off policy. Until that time, being a waiter meant working three meals a day, seven days a week from late June until Labor Day. It could become quite a grind. Preparation for breakfast started at 7:30 A.M. and setting up after dinner usually wasn't done until 9 P.M. Of course there were breaks between breakfast and lunch and lunch and dinner, but the next meal was never more than a few waking hours away.

I still like a good bagel, but none of this blueberry bagel nonsense. Real bagels are traditional plain bagels, or poppyseed, or maybe pumpernickel. But when we moved to Philadelphia we were more worried about finding a flaky croissant than finding a good bagel. I enjoy a good corned-beef sandwich, but I'm more likely to seek out a pad Thai than kugel. I do miss a number of the dishes from the hotel, and I plan to get my mother's recipes one day. But this is not so easy. Many were not written down, and the rest require downscaling from a batch designed for 150 people to a batch intended for a family of 4.

I had borscht nearly every day for lunch for four or five years straight. When my Catskills roots come up in conversation, I volunteer "Yes, I have borscht in my veins." But the bottled borscht in the store is not the same, and making my own is out of the question. I was never especially fond of gefilte fish, but now it represents the Catskills for me and I try to buy some during Jewish holidays. Unfortunately, my Italian American wife, Sharon, prefers not to be in the house when I'm eating it.

Travel

The idea of going to a Jewish hotel, eating Jewish food, and watching Jewish entertainment was never something I even considered. Jews no longer faced restrictions in pursuing the vacation of their choice. Not that we would necessarily blend in right away. Far from it. We knew that "they" lived in a separate world, and we were not especially keen to pass for Gentiles. I remember, as a child traveling with my family, finding ourselves in a proper Virginia restaurant on our way to visit the Luray Caverns one Christmas vacation. A solemn version of the Christmas carol "Greensleeves" was playing in the background, while a fire filled the huge stone fireplace trimmed with pine wreaths. I suddenly recognized the tune from Alan Sherman's riotous version of it on his satiric/comic album.

My dad and I whispered our Jewish version of "Greensleeves" until my mom told us to be quiet. We sensed that we were not among our people, and that our sacrilegious version of the song might land us in a serious spot.

A college education fed the thirst for world travel. Since finishing graduate school, Sharon and I have traveled to Europe, Latin America, and Asia, and we have a long list of places we would like to visit someday. Go to a resort? Preposterous. But not so preposterous anymore, now that we have young children. But of course there are few resorts left in the Catskills.

On one trip, Sharon and I saw a performance of Chinese acrobats in Shanghai, while on a tour the year before the Tiananmen Square massacre. There was a contortionist who balanced a wine glass on his nose, on top of which a tray was placed. He quickly added more glasses and more trays until there was an amazing tower of glassware, still balanced on his nose. At this point, he was handed a clarinet, and he belted out an enthusiastic version of "*Hava Nagila.*" I remember laughing hysterically, but I could hear my Aunt Sarah whispering in my ear, "So, you have to travel six thousand miles to hear '*Hava Nagila.*' You could have heard it for free in the casino, whenever you wanted. But then you weren't interested."

So going to a Catskills hotel was pretty much out of the question. And running one made no sense to me, as a professional with what I considered to be loftier goals. And why run a hotel if there are no guests? If I would not consider a Catskills vacation, which of my peers would? So we let the Catskills die of neglect. But I wish some of it remained, because it was a special place and a special time. And it was full of life, especially when whole families came up for much of the summer.

So, in my view, it was not my generation, the Woodstock generation, that killed the Catskills, although we certainly share the responsibility. The generation that came of age in the late fifties and early sixties had long since departed. The gulf between my world and that of the Delmar's aging guests widened steadily. My friends were far more preoccupied with Watergate than with the Holocaust. We were all bar mitzvahed, all recited our *haftorahs* more than adequately, but being a success meant succeeding on American terms, not in some Jewish corner of America.

Law, medicine, and academics were the most obvious paths ahead. I didn't know anyone who seriously considered emigrating to Israel, becoming a rabbi, or running a hotel. My dear friend Eileen Pollack wrote a wonderful novel about the Catskills, *Paradise New York*, which drew on her experiences at her family's hotel (Pollack's) and, I like to think, a few Delmar stories she heard on long drives to debate tournaments as well. Yet I was astonished that the protagonist in *Paradise* decides to take over her grandparents' hotel. So much of her story reflects a penetrating insight into the reality of Catskills life, but this twist is surely just a plot device. We felt no special need to apply to Brandeis because we expected a fair enough shot at Ivy League and other top colleges. If we were worried about having Jewish classmates, we would find no shortage at Columbia or even Yale and Princeton.

WITHOUT A TRACE

Sharon and I were married at the hotel, in 1983, on a sunny October afternoon with the autumn foliage nearing its peak. All went well—the right bride, the right place. I wasn't sure how my friends from college would react to the hotel, but a few said it was much nicer than I had described. And I think my parents were pleased to have it as the setting for this life milestone. At the last minute, we decided that it was warm enough to hold the ceremony outside. So we rolled up our sleeves and carried the folding chairs from the casino to the front lawn of the hotel. A caterer would not have been as flexible.

My parents were ambivalent about whether the hotel should feature in their sons' lives. They felt the Delmar was a good thing because it enabled their sons to earn money for college. But college was always the future, and how long could they realistically expect their college-educated sons to run the place? And opportunities for professional positions were few in the Catskills. The last conversation we had about taking over the hotel occurred when I was finishing up my Ph.D. "When you are teaching in a university, you will have your summers off. Would you want to think about running the hotel during the summer, as a backup?" "Dad!" was all I could manage in reply. We had always scorned those absentee hotel owners who would scurry up to the Mountains just before the season. Surely he wouldn't want his son to adopt this halfhearted approach. But I suppose it is natural to want to pass along your life's work to your children. A few short years later the hotel was sold to Italian owners, and a year later it was recycled into a drug-rehabilitation center (as had happened to a number of other hotels before it).

The problem is that the Catskills are gone, now that we might like to return and to taste it, to show our children, to spend a weekend or a week in a family resort. Say what you will, the hotel was full of life, with amateur comedians, singers, and social critics. That life could be chaotic and challenging, like the day that nearly half the staff quit at the same time, but by and large it was festive. The Delmar was warm and homey and American Jews could be themselves there, in the fresh air and rolling hills of the Catskill Mountains. We let that world die of neglect, and we haven't built anything like it that can take its place.

Part 4

ENTERTAINMENT

The Flagler

— Social and Athletic —

Staff

Season 1929

MOSS HART
Director of Activities

Jack Goldbert .... *Assistant Director*
Irving Ephron .... *Athletic Director*
Violet Shulman .... *Musical Director*
Emanuel Rosenfeld .... *Scenic Director*
Anita Span .... *Dance Director*
Oscar Lasdon .... *Cameraman*
Bernard Hart .... *Stage Manager*
Frank Phillips .... *Stage Effects*
Dora Rosenfeld .... *Costumes*
Doris Abeles .... *Artist*
Helen Afsensky .... *Artist*
Bernetta Glucksman .... *Artist*
Benjamin Hirschberg .... *Artist*
Sam Solodor .... *Artist*
Henry Wolf .... *Swimming Instructor*
Donald Wolf .... *Tennis Instructor*
Charles Yacht .... *Golf Instructor*
Harvey Fleischer .... *Assistant Instructor*
Ruth Daitz .... *Kindergartner*
Janet Simon .... *Kindergartner*

The FLAGLER ORCHESTRA

"THE SERENADERS"

Violet Shulman .... *Director—Pianist*
Albert Weinstein .... *Saxaphonist*
Jules Harrison .... *2nd Saxaphonist*
Harry Robins .... *Trombonist*
Myron Robins .... *Trumpeter*
Harold Wolfers .... *Drummer*
Benedict Lupica .... *Banjoist*
Jerome Sachs .... *Violin*
Allan Schulman .... *Cellist*

Guests desiring instruction in any athletic sport will be cheerfully accommodated by any of the Staff Specialists listed above, free of any charge (golf excluded). Golf instruction is available to beginnners at a nominal charge. Golf supplies can be rented or purchased at the golf house.

A fine string of saddle horses is available at our stables. A special rate may be obtained for party canters.

Enlist your talents in our theatrical activities. If you sing, dance or perform in any way, MOSS HART wants to see you!!

Flagler News, Flagler Hotel, South Fallsburg, 1929. In the 1920s and 1930s, hotels large enough to provide entertainment did so with in-house entertainment staffs, often numbering twenty people. The Flagler was one of the largest hotels in this era, and for a number of those years, Moss Hart was the director of entertainment, with Dory Schary as his assistant.   CATSKILLS INSTITUTE

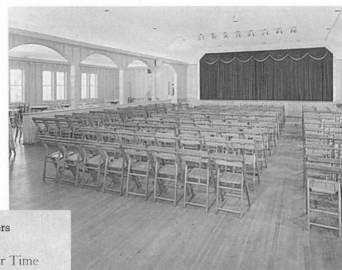

Casino, Plaza Hotel, South Fallsburg. This is a typical casino, with folding wooden chairs on a wood floor. Even in a hotel that could hold 200 guests, this was a common form. Hotels in this size range often went broke building fancier nightclubs.

The Grossinger Players

present

In The Good Old Summer Time

Entire Presentation Under The Direction of
HENRY TOBIAS

Billy Reed........................*Introduces*
Zinn Arthur............. ....*And The Orchestra*
Robinson Twins......*Red Headed Rascals of Rythm*
Siggy Lanno.........*Paramount's Romantic Voice*
Prof. Joe "Carstairs" Tucker . .*Dangers of Matrimony*
    WITH JUDY LANE and MOE HARWAY
Viola Philo...*Singing Star of Radio City Music Hall*
Lowe, Hite and Stanley........*Extremes In Fun*
Willie "The Lion" Smith
and
Hot Lips Page...*The Stuff Is Here and It's Mellow*
Finale........................*Entire Company*

●

SATURDAY EVENING, AUGUST 5th, 1939
at the
GROSSINGER PLAYHOUSE

Program from Grossinger's, 1939. Henry Tobias ran the entertainment here, and well-known jazz musicians Willie "The Lion" Smith and Hot Lips Paige played.

Champagne Hour at the Waldemere Hotel, Livingston Manor, 1954. Cuban band leader Emilio Reyes and dance team Pedro Aguilar and Millie Donay running the weekly dance contest. Latin music was extremely popular in Catskills hotels in this period.
IRA GOLDWASSER

The **Eldorado**
FALLSBURG, N. Y.
— PRESENTS —
"THE SHIRELLES"
TUESDAY, AUG. 25, 1964
2 - SHOWS ✦ 8:30 P. M. and 10:30 P. M.
$1.50 (Inc. Tax) IN ADVANCE
$2.00 (Inc. Tax) AT DOOR
No. 240

LATE SHOW - 11:00 p.m.
THE DRIFTERS
TUES., AUG. 8, 1967
at THE ELDORADO
FALLSBURG, N. Y.
ADMISSION: $2.00
(Including Tax)
No. 47

Rock and roll show tickets, Eldorado
Hotel. In the 1960s, some hotels like
the Eldorado made extra money
running midweek rock shows with
top groups.

The **Eldorado**
FALLSBURG, N. Y.
— PRESENTS —
"JAY and THE AMERICANS"
TUESDAY, JULY 14, 1964
2 - SHOWS BLUE TICKET 8:30 P.M. GOLD TICKET 10:30 P.M.
$1.50 (Inc. Tax) IN ADVANCE
$2.50 (Inc. Tax) AT DOOR
No. 780

KIAMESHA FAIRMOUNT
KIAMESHA, N. Y.
ADMISSION TICKET TO
Playtorium
NOT TRANSFERABLE
TO BE USED BY GUESTS ONLY

Stevensville Lake Hotel
PLAYHOUSE
SWAN LAKE - NEW YORK
FRIDAY
❖ Admit One ❖

Nightclub admission tickets, Kiamesha Fairmount and Stevensville
Lake Hotel. Many hotels gave out these tickets to guests at dinner,
to prevent bungalow colony residents and guests from other
hotels from sneaking into the show.

INTRODUCTION

In the early years, Catskills entertainment was all home-grown, ranging from literature readings and discussions to amateur nights. As larger and all-inclusive hotels promising everything, Catskills resorts had to continually entertain their guests. The Mountains quickly became famous for entertainment, especially the comedians who began their careers there. But the classic entertainment figure is the tummler, a regular fixture at the hotel who performed, emceed, and directed a wide range of activities. His humor was often developed out of the daily life of the people he associated with, so that much of the Catskills comedy was an organic product of its own fermentation. That locally based entertainment remained, even in medium-sized and some larger hotels, as a part of the overall package. And in bungalow colonies it was very central, since only the larger colonies provided any regular shows, and then only on one or two weekend nights.

Joey Adams's "Comics, Singers, and Tummlers" comes from *The Borscht Belt* (written with Henry Tobias), his autobiographical account of life in the Catskills entertainment world. He details the many things the social director/tummler had to do to keep the guests happy, and brings us right into showtime.

Adams also recounts stories of many of the world-famous comics who began their careers in such positions. The tone of his account echoes the vaudevillian style that predominated in the hotels.

Moss Hart's excerpt from his book *Act One*, "The Social Director in the Adult Summer Camp," gives another account of the social director's life, but from the vantage point of the adult summer camp, and mostly from an earlier era when social directors had large staffs that produced full-length variety shows and musicals every week. The adult summer camp, like the South Wind of *Marjorie Morningstar*, was a place where many people, especially men, sometimes actually slept in tents.

Harvey Jacobs's "The Casino" is from his coming-of-age novel, *Summer on a Mountain of Spices*. Jacobs describes the hotel owner's fascination with building a modern casino (the Catskills casino was a social hall, not a gambling place), and also leads us through a variety of the activities that went on there. He treats us to the antics of the emcee and the show he introduces, a song-and-dance team, followed by a magician. It is a very realistic account of small hotel entertainment.

Joyce Wadler's essay, "The Fine Art of Mountain *Tummling*," steps back and situates the performances of people like Adams and Hart in a broader context. She introduces many of the comics who built careers in the Catskills, spices her story with the jokes they told, and explains some of the underlying assumptions of Jewish humor (like the Jewish view of the universe: "Always keep one eye on the exit."). Wadler also points to the overall hilarity of the Catskills experience that went far beyond the tummlers and comedians who were paid to be funny.

I also include two songs written about the Catskills. My "Yener Welt" had its Sullivan County premiere at the Third History of the Catskills Conference in 1997, and was repeated at the Sixth conference in 2000, sung both times by myself and my son, Michael. *Yener welt* in Yiddish means "the other world." It's sort of like: "you'll get it in the afterlife," but it's not morbid or even sacrilegious; it's just Yiddish sarcasm. The only other Yiddish you need to know for this song is "*Ich hab nisht gelt,*" "I don't have any money." Grammatically, it should be "*Ich hab nisht kayn gelt,*" but it doesn't fit into the music that way, so let's not make a *megillah.*

Henry Foner sang his "Shoot the Shtrudel to Me, Yudel!" at the Third History of the Catskills Conference in 1997, and repeated it at the Sixth Conference in 2000. He had written this and other songs in the 1940s when he and his brothers played in the band at the Arrowhead Lodge. This comic song, true to the shtick so prevalent in the Catskills, was written to celebrate the delicious apple shtrudel of Yudel Slutsky, the hotel owner.

Comics, Singers, and Tummlers

Joey Adams (with Henry Tobias)

BORSCHT IN THEIR BLOOD

It was the annual *Night of Stars* benefit at Madison Square Garden. Twenty thousand people had paid in a million dollars to see David Kaminsky, Aaron Chwatt, Al Dabruzio, Philip Feldman, Pinky Perlmut, Moishe Miller, Jerome Levitch, Bernie Schwartz, Milton Berlinger and Murray Janofsky with Joseph Abramowitz as Master of Ceremonies.

Maybe these names don't sound like they could jazz up a marquee or cop a million bucks at the box office. David Kaminsky, however, has won not only theatrical awards but international awards for his work with UNICEF. Aaron Chwatt boasts an Oscar bigger than himself. Al Dabruzio starred in the movie of George Gershwin's life, *Rhapsody in Blue*, and in the Broadway productions of *Guys and Dolls* and *What Makes Sammy Run*. Philip Feldman, the curly-haired guy with glasses, is our ambassador from Brooklyn. Pinky Perlmut and Moishe Miller are fixtures at the Metropolitan, and I don't mean the insurance company. Jerome Levitch, who lives in a $500,000 bungalow in Bel Air, piled up millions for himself and Paramount. Good old Bernie Schwartz is one of the sexpots of the screen today. Milton Berlinger just gave his wife a full-length sable coat to replace the old one that was stolen—and he took it out of petty cash yet. Murray Janofsky crept into your living room for years via his daily TV show. Joseph Abramowitz roughs it on Fifth Avenue when he isn't potting around the globe on a cultural exchange tour for the President, or entertaining our soldiers on the island of Crete, or performing at a Bar Mitzvah in the Bronx.

All these fellows have something in common. A few lean years ago you could have bought any one of them for a buck and a quarter apiece. That's when they first took to the hills—an area some ninety miles north of the George Washington Bridge called the Catskill Mountains, alias the Borscht Belt.

This same neighborhood also spawned another gent named Rip Van Winkle, who hollered between snoozes that "The Kaatskill Mountains always has been haunted by strange beings." I don't know what put him to sleep, but I know he must have been awakened by the Social Directors who first came to the Catskills to make funny for the people.

It figures that if old Rip ever found out what happened to those kosher Kaatskill Social Directors, he is still revolving someplace. Some of them changed their material, a few even changed their noses, but all of them changed their names.

David Kaminsky is Danny Kaye, Aaron Chwatt is Red Buttons, Al Dabruzio is Robert Alda, Philip Feldman is Phil Foster, Pinky Perlmut is Jan Peerce, Moishe became Merrill Miller then Robert Merrill, Jerome Levitch is Jerry Lewis, Bernie Schwartz is Tony Curtis, Milton Berlinger is Milton Berle, Murray Janofsky is Jan Murray, and I changed my name from Joseph Abramowitz to Joey Adams.

I don't think I know anybody from those days who kept his own name.

When I appeared on my first TV show, a Madison Avenue agency executive approached me. He was wearing the ad man's uniform: gray flannel suit, black tie and homburg hat—a typical New England Gentile. A fine-looking man.

"You're Joey Adams," he said politely. "My name is Wendell Adams. I've seen your name in the papers lately and I've wondered if we are related in any way."

"I don't know," I yawned nonchalantly. "What was your name before?"

The Borscht Belt, which cradled some of the biggest names in show business, was a handsome ghetto unto itself that consisted of a string of summer camps, hotels and bungalows in the Catskill and Adirondack mountains. The resort owners were really farmers who boarded a few city folk come summer and made good before they knew it. They were experts on cows and chickens but they knew from borscht about show business.

As the roomers increased and manure turned into paydirt, these farmers resented having to hire musicians and entertainers to amuse their guests. To the farmers, entertainers were "the free eaters" who were necessary evils needed to keep up with their competitors on the next farm.

In the early days, when Moss Hart "starred" at Camp Copake, Dore Schary jazzed up Grossinger's, and Danny Kaye was more important to White Roe Lake than pumpernickel on a Sunday morning, the Social Director had to be producer, director, writer, actor, song-and-dance man, emcee, comedian, scenic designer, electrician, stage manager, stagehand and sometimes waiter. After the show he had to mingle with the guests, dance with the fat old women and romance the "dogs." In addition, he was the *shadchon,* or marriage broker.

But these were only his evening chores. During daylight he doubled as sports and activities director. If he was a big shot he had a permanent staff to help him out, consisting of one other skinny fella, who also doubled in such jobs as tennis pro, basketball player, lifeguard, and busboy. Most of these "stars" got paid off in meals and a place to sleep, usually cozily situated in a basement storeroom or—if they were at the top of their profession—in a stuffy attic. Alan King's bedroom at the White Roe Hotel was a cot onstage.

The theatrical unions, like the American Guild of Variety Artists and the American Federation of Musicians, have subsequently required that certain rules and regulations be observed in hiring talent for summer resorts.

Today these lettuce patches are billion-dollar, year-round resorts and they boast million-dollar show budgets on a par with Miami Beach and Las Vegas. The Concord Hotel recently paid Judy Garland more money for one night than the combined weekly salaries that Eddie Cantor, Will Rogers, W. C. Fields, Bert Williams and Fanny Brice got for doing the *Ziegfeld Follies of 1925.*

As I introduced each one of these stars at that Madison Square Garden benefit, I kept thinking of their beginnings in the huts, farms and lean-tos of the Catskills.

Red Buttons, for instance, started with me at a place called Beerkill Lodge in Greenfield Park, N.Y., where he quadrupled as entertainer, bellboy, prop boy and waiter on busy weekends. As an apprentice Borscht Belter his salary was a dollar and a half each and every week, but he found a way to make a little extra on the side.

Like the other hotels, our place was strictly kosher. That means you can't mix meat and dairy at the same meal. This upset the digestive juices of many of the younger people who wanted cream in their coffee, even after a pot-roast dinner. But it was against the kosher laws. That's where our little red-headed bootlegger came into the picture. He got the ingenious idea of buying a brand-new fountain pen, filling it with sweet cream, smuggling it to the dinner table and charging twenty-five cents a squirt to the rebels who wanted *café au lait*.

Robert Alda worked with me for six summers in the Catskills. His salary was fifteen dollars a week, which was pretty high for a singer, but Bob was a rare commodity. He was a good-looking Italian who resembled Cary Grant and could sing Jewish songs. What a prize to place before the love-starved females left on the doorsteps of summer resorts by anguished husbands (who regretted that they had but one wife to give to the country).

Bob was a good singer, a good actor and a good guy. He helped paint the scenery and write the lyrics for our shows. He learned Jewish songs and Hebrew dances, and was a smash onstage. But Bob Alda's big job was to keep the women happy. The trouble was that our Italian troubadour was married. And with a six-month-old son yet.

The owner of Beerkill insisted that Bob's wife and child take a room off the premises so that he could carry on his mingling and mixing with the romantic old bores without interruption. Robert danced with them, held their pudgy hands and sometimes even walked with them in the moonlight. But always he would run home to mama at the witching hour, like all good Italian singers do.

One poor soul, a bride of about thirty years from Jersey City, took Bob's job seriously and followed him to his room. She waited until all the lights were out so she wouldn't be recognized. Then she opened the door to his room, and quietly slipped into bed, only to find herself entangled with a family of three.

On a night when opera singer Merrill Miller was going good, a fellow called Moe Gale wandered into Grossinger's, became his manager, got him his first break on NBC's *Opera of the Air*, and changed his name to Robert Merrill. From there it was straight to the Met. Ever since, the Nevele Hotel, the President Hotel, the Laurels Country Club and at least half a dozen others lay claim to Bob making his debut in their hallowed barns.

Wolfie Olkin of Youngs Gap Hotel in Liberty recalls when Bob worked for him in 1941. It seems he was supposed to be the exclusive property of the Gap, but Bob used to sneak out between shows and make a few extra bucks singing at nearby hotels. Wolfie, upon learning of Merrill's moonlighting, docked his pay and lectured him: "I don't mind you sneaking out and entertaining at my competitor's but if you must be that greedy, why do you eat here and run? Why don't you run and eat elsewhere?"

Jan Peerce, another Met star, was discovered behind a fiddle. "I started as a violinist at the Breezy Hill Hotel, where I got five bucks more than the other musicians because I also did vocals," chuckles Jan when you quiz him about those early days.

Following summer after summer at the President, the Waldmere and the Kiamesha Lake Inn, Jan finally gave up his career as a future Heifitz. As he tells it, "I was one of three violinists working with Abe Pizik's band at a benefit at the Astor Hotel. It was the fiftieth-anniversary party for Weber and Fields and all the top show people were present. Suddenly there was a swollen lull and Abe convinced the emcee to let me sing one song, '*La donna è mobile.*' A few minutes later, a waiter told me, 'Roxy wants to see you.' He had asked me to come to his office the next day. Right away he threw away my fiddle, canceled my plans to work for Joe Slutsky at the Nevele that summer and immediately put me in the Roxy Theatre. Soon after that, I was at the Met."

Danny Kaye still retains the undisputed title "King of the Catskills." His first job was as a part of the entertainment staff at White Roe Lake in 1933. The staff was headed by "Fishel" Goldfarb, now a very successful businessman, and still a pal of Danny's. Twenty-year-old Danny learned his trade the hard way, appearing in one play a week and a different variety show every evening. He entertained at breakfast, lunch, and dinner and then rehearsed all through the night.

During Danny's fifth season fate stepped in. A dance duo decided they needed a third artist. "With a little training we can teach Danny where to put his feet," the ballerina commented with mild enthusiasm. That's how Danny became a dancer. The group was given the elite title "The Three Terpsichoreans."

With the addition of this new dimension, Danny leaped from White Roe Lake to Camp Tamiment as chief emcee, under the direction of Max Liebman. He worked as singer, dancer, juvenile lead, character actor, villain, comic and all-around Toomler. A Toomler, derived from tumult-maker, is Castilian Yiddish for a fool or noisemaker who does anything and everything to entertain the customers so that they won't squawk about their rooms or food.

In answer to his father's query "What do you really do up there?" Danny once answered: "I'm helping the manager prevent the bored guests from moving out on rainy days."

"How do you do that?" his father wanted to know.

"It ain't easy," he explained. "We play games, amuse the paying guests by falling into the swimming pool fully clothed, straw hat and all. When the going gets rough, Fishel and I chase each other through the halls with meat cleavers and make a final graceful lunge into the fishpond."

Although it was hardly a training ground for a future movie star, Danny has the Catskills to thank for everything. He segued from stooging in theatres to playing in Abe Lyman's orchestra; from traveling to Japan, China, Siam and points east as a dancer in 1934 to begging two-week bookings in third-rate Greenwich Village night clubs. But David Daniel Kaminsky's name and luck changed only when he met Max Liebman, a former resort bookkeeper then in charge of entertainment at Camp Tamiment.

It was Max who also took an ambitious saxophone player from the Vacationland Hotel in Swan Lake and refined him into the big-time, high-class TV comicker Sid Caesar. It was also Max Liebman who first unleashed Danny Kaye's comedic talents by casting him in the Yiddish version of *The Mikado*.

Danny owes not only his public success but also much of his private happiness to the mountains. During the winter, he worked for Dr. Samuel Fine, a dentist in the Brownsville section of Brooklyn to which Danny had migrated from Russia with his parents. He never noticed the boss's bright-eyed daughter Sylvia until he found her slaving over a hot piano writing special material for a production at Camp Tamiment. In 1940 Danny Kaye and Sylvia Fine were married.

It was still another mountaineer who handed Danny his first chance on Broadway. Moss Hart saw his performance at La Martinique night club on 57th Street and wrote in a part for him in Kurt Weill's *Lady in the Dark*, starring Gertrude Lawrence. Danny, Moss Hart and Broadway clicked from their very first meeting.

Jackie Mason started his career under the name of Jacob Masler. Jackie always found a way to get fired even years before he gave the finger to Ed Sullivan. Agent George Kuttin booked him on his first Catskills job at a haven called Sunrise Manor in Ellenville. Jackie loped out onstage and his first words were: "This place stinks." They were also his last words. The boss tore backstage and threw him off the premises before he could say "A funny thing happened to me on the way to the synagogue."

Before long Jackie, who comes from a rabbinical family and studied to be a rabbi himself, quickly became afflicted with an occupational disease. He fast developed an acute case of spotlight-hogging. When he served as master of ceremonies at the Pioneer Hotel for one full season and had to introduce other comedians better known than himself, he would sometimes do a half-hour routine before presenting the guest star. And he'd very often borrow the guest's own material. One Saturday night, before bringing on Phil Foster, the star of the show, he proceeded to knock off forty-five minutes of Phil's best bits. When Phil was finally introduced, he shuffled slowly to the center of the stage and said, "How do you do, ladies and gentlemen. You just heard my act, so good night," and walked off the stage and out of the hotel.

Leonard Hacker began his professional life in the Coney Island striptease act "Tirza and Her Wine Bath" because the boss let him drink the leftover grape. He became Buddy Hackett about twenty-five years ago when "my agent, Abby Greshler, changed my name at the time I auditioned for the part of 'Henry Aldrich' and lost out to Ezra Stone. I don't know why he changed it. It was a perfectly good name and my father was a good upholsterer."

Buddy and his père worked the Catskills together. He still remembers a hotel owner who paid his father $13 for 13 hours' work as an upholsterer and tossed in a buck for Buddy's efforts. Years later, that same proprietor wanted the roly-poly comic to play his hacienda. Buddy's going rate at the time was $500 a night. He wouldn't take the booking until he got $600—"plus $12 more for the lousy buck he paid me as a kid."

Like everybody else, Buddy doubled in the dining room during those lean summers. "I never was a good waiter," he insists. "If there was a long line in the kitchen I'd go back to my station and say, 'We ain't got it. Pick sumptin' else.' Or I'd start toomling in the kitchen and the waiters would forget the customers were waiting."

Our hero made the transition to comedian when a regularly scheduled comic failed to show up. "I was sixteen and the five dollars looked good," Hackett grins. "It was a disaster. They not only didn't laugh, but it looked as though they were comin' up onstage to kill me. I finished out the season in another hotel—but as a waiter!"

The following Memorial Day he rammed a car into a hotel porch in Swan Lake just to get attention. On July Fourth he stuffed dry cereal into the dining room fan and roared when the maître d' turned it on and created an indoor snowstorm. His string of triumphs was broken only by the arrival of winter, which Buddy spent as caretaker of skis, skates and toboggans at Grossinger's.

Came the first thaw, he talked another inn into hiring a friend as a lifeguard. The friend couldn't swim and they both got fired.

If Mary Martin's heart belongs to Daddy, Buddy Hackett's belongs to the Concord. That's the spot that gave him his first break as a five-dollar-a-night comic. Many scrapbooks later that's where he met Sherry Dubois, a mambo instructor, and where he married her.

Out of the summer camps in the twenties and thirties emerged such illustrious figures as Don Hartman, Dore Schary, Lorenz Hart, Garson Kanin, Arthur Kober and Moss Hart. Moss Hart had painful memories of his Catskill apprenticeship. "Social directing," he wrote, in his book *Act One*, "provided me with a lifelong disdain and a lasting horror of people in the mass seeking pleasure and release in packaged doses. Perhaps the real triumph of these summers was the fact that I survived them at all; not so much in terms of emergency with whatever creative faculties I possess unimpaired, but in the sense that my physical constitution withstood the strain, for at the end of each camp season I was always fifteen to twenty pounds lighter and my outlook in life just about that much more heavily misanthropic."

He hated the campfire nights because he had to lead the community sing and drag out blankets and wood for the fire as well as franks and marshmallows. But what made him want to sink into the earth was the "boy-and-girl" number he had to do, complete with ukulele and fat female guest on his knee.

Game nights killed him altogether. "It is not easy to feel the proper compassion for a shy girl or an ugly duckling when you are tied into a sack with her and are hobbling down the social hall to the finish line," Hart recalled. "On the contrary, rolling a peanut along the floor side by side with a bad-complexioned girl with thick glasses and unfortunate front teeth does nothing to kindle the fires of pity within you, but instead makes you want to kick her right in her unfortunate teeth."

Another torment for Hart was the forced nightly gallantry. One rule that could never be broken under any circumstance was that the male members of the social staff had to dance *only* with the ugly females. There were sound reasons for this. Every summer camp had two or three women to every man, so the shrewd camp owners met the problem head-on by hiring help whose prime qualification was that they were good dancers. If a musician didn't know his sax from a hole in the ground and if the waiter sloshed hot cabbage soup down the neck of a guest who was staying ten weeks, it didn't matter so long as he "mixed and mingled" well in the social hall.

The big trouble lay in the fact that these college kids, our future doctors, lawyers and dentists, disliked dancing with the "pots" or "beasts," as they called them. This meant that the full responsibility for the love life and social life of the "beasts" was in the hands of the Social Directors. This was what forever spoiled the pleasure of dancing for Moss Hart. "For six whole years," Moss complained, "I danced with nothing but the pots, and that was enough to make me welcome the glorious choice of sitting down for the rest of my life."

Certain of Hart's friends suspect that those grueling hot-weather sessions, forcibly entertaining lonesome, sweaty young things, bred in him a deep distaste for marriage. He finally did get married to Kitty Carlisle—but not until he was forty-five.

When Francine Lassman divorced Xavier Cugat, she retained custody of her stage name, Abbe Lane. After all, how would it look for an alumna of the Jewish Alps, who comes from Brooklyn, to be billed as Francine Lassman, the Latin Bombshell?

Abbe's first appearance on stage had far from a Latin beat—it had more of a Borscht Belt. Gracie and Abby Lassman were friends of Henry Tobias, the songwriter-producer, then the impresario of Totem Lodge. Henry arranged for them to manage the canteen concession for the summer, and naturally their luggage included their daughter. Fourteen-year-old Francine was overdeveloped for her age—in fact, for *any* age. Mommy was anxious for her to become a star, but the kid showed more cleavage than talent. At any rate, you can't keep a good stage mother down, and Gracie was the best.

She nagged away until finally Henry stuck Francine into one of his amateur shows. Gracie arranged for her "wee baby Francey" to gurgle one of his songs, and hammy Henry, who was always scratching around for somebody to plug his tunes, immediately set her for his Saturday Night extravaganza.

Although it took Cugat to make her, a *star* that is, Henry still claims he developed her—*talent*, that is. Or maybe it was just that the borscht and sour cream went to her chest.

Jerome Levitch's birth certificate was written with a stick of greasepaint, and his playpen was the hills of Fallsburgh and Loch Sheldrake. His father, Danny Levitch (alias Lewis), was a Jolson-type singer, and mama Rae was a piano player.

Every summer when his father answered the call of the mountains, the little son of Levitch was included in the deal. At fourteen he was a tearoom boy at Brown's. And while the world didn't yet know of Jerome's existence, it's for sure that the owners of Brown's did. Born with a fractured funny bone, he would drop a whole tray of peach melbas or make a three-point landing in a pot of mashed potatoes just for a snicker. On a cold night he might even start a fire in the tearoom—and it didn't have a fireplace!

At fifteen the skinny kid who needed help to lift his toothbrush signed on as athletic director at the Majestic Hotel in Fallsburgh. The patent dissimilarity between Jerry—who might have posed for the poster "Send this child to camp"—

and any physical culturist living or dead was purely hysterical. The job was cus-
tom-tailored to Jerry's sense of humor.

He pestered his father all summer for jokes and by Labor Day was set to make
his mark on immortality. Mom and Pop tried keeping him out of show business
as long as they could, but that's like trying to keep Bobby Kennedy down on the
farm. So the kid adopted his parents' name to become Jerry Lewis the record-
pantomime act, and Danny and Rae gave in and got him booked into a saloon
in Jersey for a fin a night.

On opening night they decided to telephone the club to find out how he did.
They didn't want to say who was calling lest they make Jerry nervous, but they
knew they could tell how things had gone by the way he sounded. So Danny hit
on the idea of disguising his voice and pretending to be a booker who wanted to
offer Jerry a job.

"Hello," he crooned into the receiver. "Is this Jerry Lewis? This is Al Rock,
the agent. I liked your act tonight and would like to use you on some of my dates."

"Gee, thanks a lot, mister," Jerry breathed excitedly. "But how can you like
my act? I haven't been on yet."

It was a long road for Joey Gottlieb, who first wormed into the mountains
during the summer of 1938. At a cockomaimie Loch Sheldrake hacienda, the
Gottlieb Trio was offered eight dollars a head, plus room and scraps. The morning after Labor Day they went to collect their salary and found the place deserted—office, kitchen, everything. "I was glad I had taken a stand," says Joey. "I
had insisted laundry had to be included. They said okay because they knew they
weren't going to pony up anyway. In the end it worked out about even."

A few flops later, Joey Gottlieb changed his name to Joey Bishop. "If it
weren't for the few laughs I got," he says, "I might have been a rabbi. But it's
just as well I'm not. How would that sound: Rabbi Bishop?"

Sam Levenson was one of the few who made it without bobbing his name.
He figured that if Gentiles like Danny Thomas and Jimmy Durante didn't change
their noses, he could stick with his inheritance.

The recollections of this ex-schoolteacher who worked his way through college as a musician at summer resorts are only beautiful: "Even in those days the
mountains had everything: girls, bedbugs, handball, chicken (for ten weeks
straight one summer), milk hot from the hot cow, swimming in a pool about the
same size as in the picture postcard, and nature—manure at my window.

"It seemed to me at the time that I was immortal. Guests came and went but
I stayed on forever. I listened each Sunday to the great debate: 'If we leave at

seven in the morning we can beat the afternoon rush.' 'But we are entitled to lunch' . . . 'but after lunch the rush starts' . . . 'so we can stay till the evening.' 'But that means we may have to wait till dinner, and they'll charge us five dollars for dinner. Besides, at night you meet the rush that stayed on to beat the rush, so let's stay on 'til Monday' . . . 'What! And pay them for an extra day? Besides, the longer you stay the bigger the tip!' "

Funny lines Sam remembers:

1. Bellhop: "You're not going to forget me, Mr. Harris?"
Mr. Harris: "No, I'll write you regularly."

2. Proud Mother: "My daughter won a cha cha scholarship at the Nevele."

3. "The place is just what I expected: soft breezes, beautiful evenings, soft music—and no men."

4. Sign in bathroom: "Watch your children, don't throw anything in the bowl."

Says Sam, "I remember my father wrote me twice a week and as part of the address (he copied it from the ad), he included, "LG RMS . . . ALL IMPMTS, ALL SPTS, 75 M.N.Y. RSNBLE."

Sam adds, "I don't think I did much for the mountains but they did plenty for me. They took me out of the tenements for several summers, provided me with tuition for college and much good subject matter for my unanticipated career in comedy.

"Let's give the little hills a big hand."

As I watched star after star take his turn on the mammoth Madison Square Garden stage, each a product of the Catskills, U.S.A., I kept wondering what there was about that place that manufactured so many big theatrical names. What kind of food did they have that brought out a Van Johnson, an Earl Wrightson, a Gene Barry, a John Garfield, a Shelley Winters? What kind of air did they breathe at Swan Lake that turned erstwhile violin players Henny Youngman and Jan Peerce into stars? What kind of water did Sid Caesar, Phil Silvers and Jackie Miles drink that helped to develop their funny bones? What was it that inspired Arthur Kober to write *Having a Wonderful Time* and Herman Wouk to scribble *Marjorie Morningstar*?

The Borscht Belt not only spawned Clifford Odets, Morrie Ryskind and Yip Harburg, but it also gave birth to Bob Cousy, and it groomed Barney Ross and other top sports figures. Then, too, the hills are filled with the sound of music made by those successful doctors and lawyers who worked their way through college serving as busboys, bellhops and Romeos to the love-starved file clerks. And for those whose life-long ambition was matrimony, Mountaindale, Monticello and South Fallsburgh proved the greatest Garden of Eden since Eve propositioned Adam.

How did it all start? How did we go from borscht to bouillabaisse in one short lifetime? Like some feller said before me: "There's gold in them thar hills!"

The Social Director at the Adult Summer Camp

Moss Hart

To understand the stresses and strains a camp season entailed, and which a social director of those days labored under, it is necessary, I think, to set down an actual week's schedule of camp activity, which was repeated, though with different material of course, every week of the entire camp season.

Monday was campfire night. This was presumably an informal get-together, for the new guests usually arrived on Sunday; and a campfire in the woods, with entertainment provided while marshmallows and hot dogs were being roasted over the fire, was supposed to initiate the new arrival into the carefree camp spirit. I suppose it did—but since the wood for the fire, as well as the hot dogs, marshmallows and the blankets to sit on, had to be dragged out into the woods by the social director and his staff, it did not hold quite the same easygoing informality and gaiety for us that it did for the guests, to say nothing of the fact that the entertainment around the fire had to be devised and rehearsed, and was not informal at all.

Campfire night always held a special kind of torment for me, for Eddie had delegated to me at the beginning of the season the task of leading the community singing that opened the festivities as the campfire was lit, a job that I was unfortunately good at and which I whole-heartedly loathed. There was always a good deal of heckling, actually quite good-natured, as I stood up in front of the fire to start the singing off, and it had to be answered with equally good-natured banter in return on my part. It was a rare campfire night that I did not devoutly wish that I could disappear into the air or sink into the earth.

I had two other regular spots in the campfire programs. One, a Shakespeare-an recitation, usually a soliloquy out of *Hamlet, Macbeth* or *Romeo and Juliet,* and a "boy and girl" number complete with ukulele, which I strummed and sang to while a female guest, carefully selected that afternoon as the best of a bad lot, sat on my knee and sang along with me. The fact that the crowd was usually insis-tent that we encore the number by doing the Charleston together did nothing to minimize the deep hatred I held for each Monday night that stretched from June to September.

Tuesday night was costume or dress-up night. Depending upon the whim of the social director and the kind of costumes at hand, the night was designated and proclaimed as "Greenwich Village Night," "A Night in Old Montmartre" or "The Beaux Arts Ball." The social hall had to be decorated by the staff to simu-late old Montmartre or Greenwich Village, and tables and chairs were set around the hall in night-club fashion. It was imperative, moreover, that the guests, both male and female, turn out in appropriate costumes, for the evening was a failure if they did not; so most of Tuesday afternoon from after lunchtime on was spent in going from cabin to cabin and helping guests prepare their costumes or cajol-ing them into getting themselves up in one if they showed a disinclination to do so.

Most girls arrived in camp with some sort of catch-all costume for dress-up night, as advised in the camp brochure; but the men usually brought along noth-ing but the inevitable white flannel trousers and blue sport jackets. We had a sup-ply of costumes in the camp wardrobe that could be used for just such emergen-cies week after week, and I have yet to see a figure of a French apache on the stage or in the movies that does not give me a shudder as I recall how many un-willing male guests I badgered into being an apache from old Montmartre. We seemed always to have had more apache costumes in the wardrobe trunk than any other kind, though "A Night in Old Japan" was a close runner-up for the male contingent for reasons that now escape me.

For "A Night in Old Montmartre" one or possibly two Grand Guignol sketches were usually presented—with the result that there was almost never any catsup to be had in camp the next day because we used it to simulate the streams of blood always necessary in the Guignol sketches, and the social staff's hair was usually matted or streaked with catsup that would not come out for the next two days.

On "Greenwich Village Night" there was a good deal of candle-lit free-verse poetry reading, usually done by Eddie, and a good deal of Edna St. Vincent Millay usually read by me. No one was ever more weary of hearing, "My candle burns at both ends, it will not last the night" than I was by the end of that first summer. And there were quite a few evenings when I was not quite sure that I would last the night myself, Edna St. Vincent Millay or no Edna St. Vincent Millay!

For "A Night in Old Japan" we presented our own version, complete with local jokes and lyrics, of *The Mikado*, and for "Beaux Arts Night" there were tableaux of guests, decked out in silver and gold gilt paint, gilded and arranged, of course, by a sweating and cursing social staff.

Wednesday evening was "Games Night," and between dances, potato races, sack races, one-legged races and peanut relay races were run off for prizes, and though no entertainment was deemed necessary by the management for this care-free evening, it was thought essential, nevertheless, for the social staff to encourage participation in the games by setting the example of being the first ones out on the floor for each game and seeing to it that the shy or unattractive girls in particular were included in at least one game during the evening. It is not easy to feel the proper compassion for a shy girl or an ugly duckling when you are tied into a sack with her and are hobbling down the social hall to the finish line. On the contrary, rolling a peanut along the floor side by side with a bad-complexioned girl with thick glasses and unfortunate front teeth does nothing to kindle the fires of pity within you, but instead makes you want to kick her right in her unfortunate teeth.

There was no escape possible from this nightly gallantry, however, for the one camp rule that was inviolate—that could never be broken under any consideration—was that the male members of the social staff dance only with the girls who were not being danced with, and that the shy and ugly ones be "socialized" with first. It was up to the social staff and to the social director and his assistant to set the example for this, not only so far as dancing was concerned, but in every other aspect of camp activity.

There was actually a sound reason for this. The population of every summer camp was always predominantly female—the girls sometimes outnumbering the men two to one—and this thorny problem the wily camp owners met by hiring college boys instead of professional waiters to wait on tables, for these college boys were part of the social staff after their duties in the dining room were finished.

Indeed, it mattered very little how sloppy a waiter a young medical or legal student might be if he was a good dancer and "mixed and mingled" well in the social hall. The trouble, of course, lay in the fact that the college boys disliked dancing with "the pots," as they called them, quite as much as we did, and de-vised all sorts of stratagems to be out on the floor with an attractive girl in their arms almost before the first note of each dance number sounded from the or-chestra. It was always necessary to make a blanket rule at the beginning of each season that if a girl was not dancing after the first sixteen bars of music, she must be danced with forthwith. And there was a further ironclad rule that no one girl was to be danced with more than once in an evening, for it was the boys' prac-tice to latch onto a pretty girl and dance every dance with her, proclaiming loud-ly and innocently that they had danced every dance that evening and had not sat out one!

By the middle of July in every season, it was always necessary to ship one or two insubordinate waiters home for flouting this rule, for inevitably love blos-somed between a waiter and a guest, and when that happened, he would defi-antly dance every dance with his beloved. There was nothing to do but ship him home as a stern example to the others. I was not always certain that it was ex-actly love that blossomed in a waiter's bosom, for once a waiter glimpsed that un-mistakable light in a girl's eyes, it almost inevitably followed that the hapless girl, for the entire span of her two weeks' vacation, barely saw the sunlight from then on. Instead, she was in the kitchen most of the time helping him polish silver and make salads, and then setting his tables for him. These poor creatures would ar-rive in camp with a decent glow of health on their cheeks and leave two weeks later hollow-eyed wrecks.

Curiously enough, this practice of guests' helping waiters in their work was not frowned upon by camp owners, but in a way had their blessing, for I don't suppose the waiters could have gone on moonlight canoe rides night after night and been up at six thirty every morning to prepare for breakfast without some sort of unpaid slave labor to help them. And I am certain it was love by and large that kept the camp silverware as clean as it generally was. Week by week one could very often tell whether or not love was rampant among the waiters by the way the tables were set or how the salads were decorated, and when love ran riot in the kitchen, it played hell with the dancing in the social hall at night.

I am certain, too, those camp years ruined the pleasure of dancing for me for-ever. It is seldom now that I will venture out onto a dance floor. For six whole years I danced with nothing but "the pots," and that was enough to make me welcome the glorious choice of sitting down for the rest of my life.

The one night in camp when there was no dancing at all was Thursday night, and it may be imagined that sometimes it seemed to the social staff that Thursday was terribly slow in arriving or had disappeared out of the week entirely. That was the night for basketball, played by a team of our own waiters against a team of waiters from a neighboring camp, sometimes in our own social hall and sometimes in theirs.

This night was always held up with a great show of largesse by camp owners as the night that the social staff was entirely free to rehearse the weekend's play and musical, but it was not entirely as generous as it sounded. Thursday night after the game was the night that the owners always chose to give a party in their own quarters for specially selected guests, and to this party the social staff was not only invited but more or less *ordered* to appear, for they were expected to supply the necessary entertainment for the festivities. The idea was, I suppose, that since the social staff had not entertained guests for the entire evening, they must now be panting to do so, beginning at midnight.

Another occupational hazard of camp life, and a dire hazard it was, was the parties tossed two or three times each week by the guests themselves in their own cabins after the social hall closed, and to which the social staff was always bidden. It seemed to be taken for granted by any and every guest that included in his weekly rate, was the right to the private as well as the public services of the social staff, a conclusion that most camp owners concurred in, and if you refused to appear at parties, either in self-defense or out of sheer exhaustion, there were always loud and long protests the next morning that the social staff refused to "socialize" and that next summer they would certainly go to a camp that had a social staff that did.

We could escape only some of the parties and the others we suffered through as best we could, for if there was one thing worse than entertaining the guests ourselves, it was being entertained by them at their own parties. Almost every guest who gave parties had a sneaking suspicion that he or she was equally as talented as the social staff. This was their chance to prove it—and the remembrance of various young men, a salami sandwich in one hand and a glass of celery tonic in the other, bellowing out "I'm the Sheik of Araby" can still chill my blood; or the recollection of countless ill-advised girls giving their own rendition of "Dardanella" is enough even now to make me wonder how I lived through six solid years of it, without entering the realm of the demented.

There was one hazard of camp life, however, that the social staff did not share. It was faced exclusively by the guests themselves, and it provided the staff with an endless source of entertainment and pleasure. The hazard was a simple one, but it was unfailing and constant in every camp I ever worked at. Both male and female guests always arrived in complete anonymity except for the initials on their luggage; and when they decked themselves out in their summer finery for their first appearance in the social hall or the dining room, it was impossible to tell whether a shipping clerk or the boss's son had arrived in camp. By the same token, it was impossible to tell whether a private secretary to a Wall Street broker or a steel executive was making her first appearance, or, what was more likely, a salesgirl from behind the glove counter at Bloomingdale's was beginning her two-week vacation.

Each suitcase bulged with a hard winter's saving of every penny that could be spared and strategically spent on a series of flamboyant sport shirts and doeskin trousers, or flowered prints and organdy dresses, to say nothing of the very latest in the way of bathing suits and costumes *pour le sport* for every hour of the day that might dazzle and titillate a member of the opposite sex. There were, of course, some well-heeled boys and girls among the guests, and I suppose even a boss's son or a private secretary to a Wall Street broker occasionally turned up. But in the main, the bulk of the contingent that descended on the camps every summer was composed largely of shipping clerks, bookkeepers, law clerks, receptionists, and what-not, who spill out of New York City and it environs for their annual two-week vacation.

And since part of that vacation at camp had as its goal sex on the part of the boys and marriage on the part of the girls, there was better chance for the achievement of these goals if both partners gave no hint of their true status while in camp, but played the game of letting the other one assume that each was heir to a junior executive's job or a wealthy father. It was a game of endless variations—a stately minuet of lying and pretense, and the social staff watched it flower and blossom every two weeks with no little delight and a good deal of malice.

We even aided and abetted the masquerade whenever we could, not only as a method of revenge against our mortal enemies—the guests—but because it was uncommonly instructive and somehow wonderfully comic to see the citadel of virginity being stormed each day and wavering uncertainly every evening before a pair of white flannel trousers. It was impossible to tell, of course, if those trousers encased a young man on his way up the executive ladder, or a packer who worked in Gimbel's basement. Nor could the white flannel trousers themselves tell if the girl beneath the flowered chiffon he held in his arms as he danced around the social-hall floor was really the young lady of means she seemed to be.

We made bets on the outcome of the more spectacular stormings of the fort and we listened with unending pleasure to the lies that blew through camp like thistledown in a field of clover. It was one of the few outlets we had for anything approximating glee as the camp season rolled on. Even this source of amusement was apt to wear a little thin by the time Friday morning came around, for Friday evening was "Drama Night"; and with Eddie's staggering lack of organization, both Friday and Saturday nights—Saturday being "Musical Comedy Night"—were always torturous and exhausting beyond belief or necessity. It was, of course, no easy task to present two one-act plays each week, as well as what we called "An Original Musical Comedy" on the following night, in addition to all our other activities.

The Casino

Harvey Jacobs

arpenters from Monticello went to work in the spring following Al
Berman's blueprint. A long flight of wooden steps was built leading to
a long porch held by white columns. The interior of the building was
left hollow to the roof beams. A smooth wood floor, waxed and mellow, led to
the stage. Two dressing rooms, stage right, stage left, were added and under the
stage a storage room accessible by trapdoor was a final inspiration. The concession
was placed to the left of the stairs with its front serving the porch, its side serving
the inside of the casino through a large window. The result was a Catskill master-
piece, a local wonder. The casino itself was a handsome structure. The idea of so
much empty air with walls around it, not a church or synagogue, was totally
unique. Naturally on the busy weekends the dressing rooms held paying guests
and the dance floor hosted rows of army cots for bachelors, so all was not lost.

"We had a casino practically before Jennie Grossinger," Al Berman said many
times over twenty-two years. And it was true.

Since its creation in 1924 the Willow Spring casino held up nicely. Carvings
were added to the columns, initials, hearts, designs, but they kept their circular dignity. The high barn ceiling became a haven for bats but they usually stayed out of
the social whirl. The dressing rooms, inhabited by post-adolescent musicians and assorted social directors, were covered in graffiti that immortalized their transient occupants. The velvet curtain on the stage snagged on its rope pulls. The room under
the stage was a home to small insects and animals who lived on kosher crumbs. The
stage had a half-moon of lights installed around its arc and along its base. The con-

cession's inside serving window was enlarged to a counter. Movable wooden benches were arranged before the stage for shows, shoved back for dancing. An upright piano was placed on the floor, stage right, where the band set up. A jukebox with obsolete hits was plugged in on stage left. An electric amplifier with a standing mike, cousin to the PA in the main house, was nailed down to stage center.

The latest addition, far back in the room, was a spotlight on a pedestal. This touch of class was added in 1944 at the urging of Joe Kamin, the social director for seven years.

Joe Kamin, formerly of the Yiddish theater, was the casino *mavin*. He produced and directed the shows, except the kiddie shows. He booked the movies and acts from Monticello agents to supplement his homemade entertainment. He chased bats, killed mice, changed failed light bulbs, opened and shut windows, hung bunting and confetti on the walls, swatted wasps, hung flypaper, even swept after the *klutz* handyman.

His easy night was Friday. All he had to do was introduce Essie Poritz and she brought on the kiddies, followed by dancing. During the kiddie shows Joe Kamin sat with the guests watching the clumsy *shloomping* on stage while parents and relatives *kvelled*. Some of the cockers were showstoppers, but art it was not. Joe Kamin applauded with the rest and yelled *bravo bravo*. A vacation.

"Applesauce," Joe Kamin yelled from the casino stage while Richie Schwartz gave him a drum roll.

He began Saturday show time by holding up a batch of tickets that said WILLOW SPRING HOTEL. ANNUAL BENEFIT FOR THE SOCIAL DIRECTOR AND THE BAND. PRICE ONE DOLLAR. ADMIT ONE. CHILDREN FIFTY CENTS.

"Dear people," Joe Kamin said, "that time has come again. Every year I ask you to do yourself a big favor and buy a ticket to the benefit. The proceeds go to the band of music over there and to a certain party over here, you know his name, a wonderful person, Joe Kamin."

A *tsa tsa tsa* from Richie Schwartz stroking a metal brush over brass cymbals.

"It's a long winter, so please open your heart and your wallet. You won't regret it. I promise a night to remember, the best since you got married. Tickets can be purchased from me, the musicians or by the concession. *Gott helfen* if you buy or don't buy. But if you don't buy he shouldn't *helfen* so much. I'm only kidding. Seriously, ladies and gentlemen, we hope you will support our cause.

"Now, this week we have great talent here at the Willow Spring, the best money could buy, Broadway acts who work in top places where you would pay more to see it than it costs for a week right here. Presenting that international song-and-dance team, Happy And Tappy."

Ta-da.

Al Berman went to bed early, so Harry Craft ran the spotlight. He chased Tappy, who clicked around the stage while Happy sang the Monticello top ten, a list that stayed constant for a few thousand years.

Yiddish hymns from a jungle face fractured the audience. Happy And Tappy did encores.

This time Tappy tapped down on the floor and Happy joined him. They tapped between benches, finished at the door and ran for their car. They had another show at Henderson's and one after that in Zupker's Farm.

"Wonderful, boys," Joe Kamin said to the microphone. "Not too much, not too little, just enough. Ladies and gentlemen, Happy And Tappy have another show to do down the road in Henderson's. Let's hear it for the Bermans and Ferinskys, who bring us fresh acts first, always the absolute best."

A fanfare from the band of music.

Now the casino darkened. Red Toritz And His Boys cued up an eerie refrain. Joe Kamin told Harry Craft to turn off the spotlight. He pulled a flashlight from his pants and lit himself from under his double chin.

"Next, ladies and gentlemen, we have for you the world-famous magic of Hara The Great. Give a big hand. The performers appreciate it, I know. Hara The Great, ladies and gentlemen."

Hara The Great came out of the curtain with splendid energy. He did card tricks. He made flowers come and go. Ribbons came from his ears and his nose. They vanished in his mouth. They came again from his assistant's mouth and fled through his navel. A rabbit, drooping, gave a jump from Hara's hat.

"I saw how he did it," said a voice from the dark. "A false bottom. Any kid could do that."

"You expect Houdini?" said another voice.

The audience rode Hara's back. It was expected. Hara The Great knew magic made such audiences nervous. They had to be led by the nose to the unknown. Some in the casino grew up believing firmly in ghosts, goblins and dark spirits, all cousins of death. They were committed to the practical and the real. It was the American way. They could be had, but gradually. In the way of Monticello magicians, Hara The Great kept coming, saving his best for last.

"Give him a chance. He's trying."

"Look in the sleeve. He got some kind of rubber band."

Ernie Pincus, who collected Hara's garbage, the ribbons, the flowers, the rabbit, a candle that lit by itself, was now called to stage center. Hara asked for two chairs. He placed the chairs back to back, five feet apart. Between his gestures and the wispy music a mood was building.

Joe Kamin smashed the mood when he stood in the audience.

"The chairs remind me of a story, you should excuse the interruption. There was this couple, Benny and Becky. They were married sixty years, it should happen to you. Sixty years. On the anniversary Becky says to Benny, I'm tired of how you do it. You're tired of how I do it? Benny says. So how should I do it? Try a new position, says Becky. What position, says Benny. Back to back, says Becky. Why not, says Benny. So they take off the clothes, my dear, and lay down back to back. Tell me, dollink, says Benny, how do we do it back to back? It's not hard, says Becky. But we got to get another couple."

Son of a bitch.

Hara The Great worked to regain his moment. He gazed into Ernie Pincus' eyes waving his arms. Ernie Pincus stiffened and went into a trance.

"You are a rock, a board, a piece of steel, the Brooklyn Bridge," Hara said.

Ernie Pincus agreed. He was totally rigid.

"I need assistance," Hara said.

Wilbur and Buddy Schneitzel came to the stage. The waiters helped lift Ernie's body onto the backs of the separated chairs. One chair held shoulders, the second chair held legs. Underneath was only air.

"Who will be first to cross this human span?" Hara said.

He started small. Charlie Mandel volunteered by reflex. He was lifted onto Ernie Pincus' knotted stomach and balanced up there.

Charlie was joined by Aaron Bunyik, a hefty guest. The final amazement came when Zalik Boulak climbed aboard with Leslie Quint. Charlie, Aaron, Zalik and Leslie stood on Ernie Pincus, who didn't seem to mind.

The Willow Spring casino cheered for a minute.

"Don't hurt him," Ida Berman yelled. "You'll rupture his spleen."

"Fear not," Hara said. "He feels no pain or anguish. The power of Hara The Great has transformed this man to a hunk of cement."

"It's on you," Ida Berman said. "I'm not responsible."

Vinnie Berman watched Hara The Great from in back where she sat with her family. He made her jumpy. She held two fingers in front of her eyes. It was a trick she learned in the movies. When the thing that scared you fit between your two fingers you could pretend to put it in your pocket like a doll.

Hara The Great and Vinnie Berman had talked before the show. He had a gentle manner and a commanding way. He was working for college money. He wanted to be a veterinarian. He loved animals. Magic was only his hobby turned to profit through his clever head. He got Ernie Pincus through a magic store in Times Square. Ernie was a susceptible, pre-hypnotized. Hara turned him on and off with a certain noise he made with his mouth. The hand waving was hocus-pocus. While they talked he turned Ernie off to show Vinnie. When Ernie was off Hara The Great gave Vinnie Berman a quick kiss on the nose. Some character.

Now Ernie Pincus, restored to normal, took bows, standing with the guests who walked over him.

"No harm done," Hara The Great told the casino.

Between Happy And Tappy, Hara and Ernie the Saturday special was a hit. With Bunny Bernice on Friday and this on Saturday there could be no complaints about Willow Spring's entertainment.

The band played "Star Dust" while the curtain closed and benches were moved to the walls. While dancing commenced, Harry Craft rushed to his concession. Orders poured in.

The first dancers were Arnie and Sandy Berman. Cute.

Leslie Quint dragged Marvin Katz to the floor and made him try the rumba. Phil and Fay Katz watched their son Marvin struggle with the *shiksa* with beaming faces.

Zalik Boulak took both his daughters, Eve and Lila, to the floor.

Inside a small circle made up of the Schneitzel twins, the Rifkins and the immediate family, Vinnie Berman danced with herself. From outside the circle Barry Guerfin felt a pull at his genitals. Watching Vinnie move gave him terrific sensations.

The honeymooning Blitzes did a fox-trot, holding close.

Howard Moskol danced with Manya, counting to himself the way he learned it from Arthur Murray. Manya's ears burned. Her number-two lover was in the room. She could feel him watching and thinking shitty thoughts. She could feel his mind grabbing her ass.

Hara The Great and Ernie Pincus left for their next performance at the Elsmere Arms, but not until Vinnie Berman had agreed to a meeting later in the week.

Everybody danced.

The Fine Art of Mountain *Tummling*

Joyce Wadler

This is what it was like, in the Borscht Belt, from a survivor: full of noise, full of Jews, and the jokes grew on trees.

You have perhaps in some long-ago supper club seen Myron Cohen; you think perhaps this is the way it was, five dozen over-the-hill comics wandering around the Catskills shouting, "Cut velvet!" But this was only part of the mountains, rich and lunatic and green.

"The mountains": a collection of wood frame boardinghouses and farmhouses, already collapsing when acquired, with names like the Palace and Paradise and Little Budapest and more often than not a cow on the lawn and some chickens in the back. "The season": that period from Memorial Day weekend to Labor Day weekend—for the hotels are never heated—during which the guests arrive and the family, if business is good, gives up its own rooms and pitches a tent on the front lawn. "The lemosene": an ancient vehicle—usually an Oldsmobile, with the name of the hotel painted on the side—that goes to the train station to pick up the guests. "The casino": the dining room, after dinner, when the tables have been pulled away to make room for a show.

The jokes. All over. Yes, really all over. You do not now believe it, but such was the surreal and marvelous nature of the mountains, of the extraordinary combination of Jewish refugees in the American mountains, that everyone, from the busboys in the kitchen to the ladies around the pool, had the timing of Benny, the delivery of Berle.

"Her mink coat don't keep me warm," sings *Gussie Aronowitz, in the bakery shop in Fleischmanns.*

"What you knowed in your whole life about garments, I already forgot," an old lady actually says at the *Lebowitz Pine View in Fallsburg.*

Or maybe she does not.

There are no footlights, you see, separating the amateurs from the professionals in the green Jewish mountains.

In the mountains, it will always be difficult to tell the players from the fans.

Which reminds me, in case there is someone who *doesn't* know the "Cut velvet" joke: Business is going bad at the factory of Schwartz and Ziegel. It gets so bad, Schwartz finally can't stand it. He goes to the window. He jumps. On the way down, he passes the shop of his archrival, Fierstein: hundreds and hundreds of racks of dresses. Schwartz checks out the fabric. Then, with the last words he'll ever speak, he hollers up to his partner.

"Cuuuuuut veeeelvet!"

How do you like your definitions, by the way, geography or state of mind? Geography puts the Borscht Belt three hours out of New York City, in Sullivan and Ulster counties. State of mind could put the Borscht Belt, or Borscht Belt humor, in Bensonhurst, Brooklyn, or in pockets of Lakewood, New Jersey, in the Thirties, or in Miami Beach in the Fifties. Though of course if you wanted to get to the root of Borscht Belt, you would dateline it Minsk.

Minsk, Feb. 23—Rabbi, give us a prayer for the czar.

Rabbi: Keep the czar well . . . and far away from us.

Time? Maybe the turn of the century. A hilarious time for the Jewish people. My own great-grandfather, for instance, takes medicine to make him sick to keep him out of the Russian army. He dies from the medicine, but not in vain, giving me, four generations later, the material to make him the punch line of a Jewish joke. My father's father, a tailor, comes to America and buys a share in a boardinghouse in the Catskills so he can enjoy the country air. He enjoys it for approximately twenty years before being clobbered to death by a falling tree, thus making his own contribution to Jewish humor: the absurdity of Jews in nature, which you see running so often through Woody Allen's work. Nonetheless, by this time my grandfather is part of a trend. The Catskills are scattered with boardinghouses. Grossinger's, in 1914, begins as a seven-room farmhouse, with cow.

By 1942 in Sullivan and Ulster counties alone there are literally hundreds of small boardinghouses, and more than five hundred of them use entertainers—even if it's only once a week.

They called them *tummlers*, Yiddish for "noise" or "merrymaker," and what they liked to pay them, in the late Thirties, early Forties, was room and board, and maybe fifteen dollars a week. What the guests generally paid in a boarding-house was perhaps twenty or twenty-five dollars weekly, all you could eat. They would lie around the pool, with maple leaves on their noses, and in the afternoon they gathered on the lawn to wait for the social director—who in the case of our establishment, the Maplewood House, was cousin Bernie, an English teacher from the city—to give them cha-cha lessons on the porch. Wood frame board-inghouses around them; the shadow of Hitler behind them; but everybody on the floor when the social director hollers, "CHA-CHA-CHA!"

You ask me my memories of the Borscht Belt. I can tell you, again, the first thing is noise. Noise at canasta; noise in the dining room; noise (this is only the-ory) at the astonishment and joy of being alive. They dried the silverware in the kitchen by putting it in pillowcases and shaking it, to give you an idea.

The second thing—it cannot be repeated often enough, and repetition is the signature of the worrisome Jewish soul—it was funny in the mountains. The bosses yelling at the help were funny. The busboys spitting in the soup were funny. The social directors chasing the weekday widows were funny. Morris the goddamn *butcher* was funny. You want to know the essential spirit of the Borscht Belt, I give you Morris the Butcher, philosopher and refugee, who never saw the stage.

Morris the Butcher on life: "Anyone can sell a steak. To move hamburger, that's something."

Morris the Butcher on the hotel owner who sent back an order of eight dozen eggs because they were green: "When business is slow, they got time to look at the eggs."

What the crowd in the mountains really liked, by the way, was comics throwing themselves, fully clothed, into the pool. Once, after bombing at the Nevele, Jan Murray warmed up the crowd during the day by sliding down the hill on his *tuchis*, and that night, sure enough, he knocks 'em dead.

What can you say—it was very broad humor. Jerry Lewis in the main dining room pouring soup on his head to get a few laughs. Buddy Hackett, doubling as a busboy and comic, scratching his ass through supper all week to provide the setup for one lousy joke. *(Waiter, in front of the guests: "Busboy, I noticed you been standing with your hand on your ass all week. Do you have hemorrhoids?" Hackett: "We only have what's on the menu.")* Crude stuff, rough stuff. Humor of the working class.

Also—and this is perhaps why so many people these days turn away from it, want to make you believe they were never a part of it—it wasn't just crude humor, it was Jew Humor. Shtetl Humor. Unassimilated Humor. Them-and-Us kind of humor. Humor that made fun of the affectations of Jews trying desperately to become part of the middle class. Humor that pointed out the barriers between Jew and Gentile rather than making believe they did not exist. Humor that not only addressed itself to the Jewish long view of the universe (briefly put: Always keep one eye on the exit) but also dealt with areas that some Jews did not want to look at: aggression and self-hatred and overstriving and pain.

Jewish man gets a boat, gets the outfit, gets the captain's hat, takes his mother out for a spin. "So, Ma," he says. "Whattaya think of the captain?" His mother checks him out. "Son," she says, "by me you're a captain. By your father you're a captain. But by a captain, you're no captain."

Have I mentioned, by the way, how many comics who came out of the Borscht Belt refuse even to discuss that life? I believe it is because of the aforementioned lowbrow nature of the joints. Also because *borscht* is a buzz word for "Hebe"—that is to say, for a comic who can play only to Jews.

"Dah premise is insulting," says one man who made his career in the mountains. "I consider myself a *univoisal* comedian."

"Borscht Belt? Rodney was never in the Borscht Belt," somebody else's publicist says. "He played a few *dates*, but they never went for him. His background was strictly the clubs in New York."

What a pity, to remove oneself from a scene so rich and wild.

Consider: in two counties alone, 524 hotels that require entertainment, which translates into new material *seven nights* a week—guests stay on the average at least two weeks. What a lure for comics, what a pressure cooker, what a pull!

And the excitement, in those days before Beverly Hills. Henny Youngman and his band getting into food fights in the dining room or turning a fire hose on a guest. Gas rationing, during the war, when the comic who had a decent car could get himself a job—provided he schlepped along a few other acts—and when Jack Carter, going to the mountains, would pray, *"Please*, not another dance act, to have to sit five hours under a pile of dresses; *please*, not another magician, to have to sit in the back with the goddamn birds."

Picture it: Singer's Restaurant, which is still there, where Dick Shawn and Jackie Mason and Jerry Lewis and Myron Cohen and Don Rickles and Red Buttons and Joey Bishop hung out after a show and you could always tell, according to Milt Ross, a veteran mountain comic, who was doing good and who was not according to what was on their plate. ("If they were eating a sandwich which was not so expensive, they were not doing so good; if they were having Chinese, which cost, they were doing okay.")

Their acts, within Borscht Belt parameters, are varied, though perhaps it is best to let Ross, who began his career in the Yiddish theater in New York City and now works out of Miami, call the shots.

"Jerry Lewis, whose father, Danny Lewis, was a comedian and his mother was the accompanist, did a mime record act, Jerry in those days wasn't so great," says Ross. "Dick Shawn didn't do any Jewish at all except he sang 'Roumania.' Eddie Schaeffer did a good mountain act, but a good mountain act isn't that good; always talking about fire escapes, and what did people not from New York know about fire escapes? Jack Carter did just jokes, one after the other; he'd either kill them or he'd die. Myron Cohen was a wonderful storyteller, wonderful; the Yidluch *loved* him," he says.

The *Yidluch*—the first generation; the Jews just off the boat. But the majority of Borscht Belt comics were second-generation, and they were a restless crew. They ripped off hit movies and Broadway shows, writing their own versions. ("*Awake and Sing!, The Informer*—we'd take a play and chop it up. . . . Imagine how ridiculous it must have looked," says Murray. "We had the nerve of burglars in those years.") They tired of doing the same old gags from burlesque and worked up their own material. Sid Caesar begins doing his double-talk routines; Milt Ross picks up some social satire from Max Liebman. And of course there are the mountain classics, some of them very painful, born who knows where on the stage or around the pool.

Two Polish Jews, captured by the Nazis, are about to be executed. Very smooth SS officer approaches. Asks the first Jew about to die if he can offer him anything: a blindfold, a brandy, a cigarette. First Jew starts cursing him out. "Nazi Pig," he begins, "I spit in your face. I spit on your blindfold and cigarette and brandy. You are mindless scum now. You will be remembered as scum by history. You—" His friend grabs him and interrupts him.

"Abie," he says, "why look for trouble?"

With the Fifties, the area is changing. The New York State Thruway is making the mountains more accessible, and comics are coming up for one-nighters and weekend dates rather than for the whole season. Air travel is becoming available to the middle class, and small hotels are folding, and the large ones, such as the Concord, Grossinger's, the Nevele, and Brown's, can make a Zero Mostel, an Eddie Fisher, an Alan King.

And there is something else that is going on and that is important: television. It will, as it disseminates everything, spread the mysteries of the Borscht Belt across America. Sid Caesar, with producer Max Liebman and former Borscht Belt social director Mel Brooks, will score a television hit in 1949 with the *Admiral Broadway Revue* show, then really make his name with *Your Show of Shows*. Milton Berle, a Borscht Belt comic in spirit, though he comes out of the burlesque houses of New York, will spread New York Jew into everyone's living room— will, according to some, be the fellow who makes Jewish humor safe and takes it into the mainstream.

"Jewish humor didn't change. The country changed," says Alan King.

"Mel Brooks," he says, "The Twelve Thousand Year Old Man, that was about as Borscht Circuit as you could get, and was a terrific success: *"How many children do you have?" "Sixty-five hundred and forty—four hundred doctors."*

"And the Two Thousand Year Old man talks like an old Jewish man, y'-know," says King. "He didn't talk like John Gielgud."

And so, in its old incarnation, the Borscht Belt is finished. Perhaps a half dozen big hotels remain in the Catskills, with stars flying in for dates the way they'd go to Vegas. The old hotels were burned down for insurance money; the young comics are getting their start in comedy clubs and their break on TV.

And you ask some of the people in comedy today about the mountains, they sound pained.

"I don't even think of it as show business," says George Schultz, the owner of Pips in Brooklyn. "It's an anachronism, a closed-shop kind of thing; none of these guys could go anywhere with it . . . go, say, on *The Tonight Show*."

Likewise, some of the people who came out of the mountains see little of value in comedy today.

"Today everybody's doing the same act," says Jack Carter. "They have no performance value. In the Catskills they demanded more showmanship—to dance, to sing, to do improv. . . ."

"You had to *give* to an audience up there," says Joey Adams. "Woody Allen would die there. . . . He just hasn't got the warmth. A Berle is a giver; a Jackie Mason is a giver. . . ."

But you know, this is really superficial, a confusion of content and style. Woody Allen wouldn't play in the mountains, maybe. *Maybe*. His style is more the third

generation, the college-educated professional, while most of the Borscht Belt veterans were of the working class that came before. But when you look at the content of the thing, the attitude, they are not so far apart.

Jackie Mason, a brainy and traditional Borscht comic, doing his routine on
the bad nerves of Jews in boats, is not so far from Woody Allen's Broadway
Danny Rose faced with a trip across the Hudson. "I don't travel by water," says
Danny. "It's against my religion. I'm a landlocked Hebrew." Shtetl humor.

Jackie Mason doing his bit about the eating and drinking habits of Jewish people—"Ya see a Jew in a bar, he's lost; ya see a Jew in a bar, he's looking for a
piece of cake"—is not so far from Allen's hero in *Annie Hall* trembling at the
sight of lobsters on the loose. "Talk to him," Alvy says to Annie. "You speak
shellfish." And Carson, in his timing, in that look when he misses a joke, is pure
Benny. And Benny, though he only played the mountains later, was Borscht.
And Pryor, when he does his bit about the heart attack, when he clutches his
heart and falls to the floor and starts hollering, "You didn't think about it when
you was eating all that pork," is, in his attitude (expectant of disaster: Keep your
eye on the exit), pure Borscht.

It's style, often, that separates Allen from Mason—a figure of speech, a veneer
that comes from education, a gloss. The basic attitude of Borscht Belt—which is
to be an outsider with all the conflict of the outsider; which is to expect the worst
because the worst is what outsiders often get; which is to be funny because funny
is the only strength the powerless have—remains.

A great part of it does not translate to other cultures, is True-blue Jew, making performers fear it; but the heart of it, should you change an ethnic detail here
and there, can be made universal, translating to any alienated outsider group:

Two old Polish ladies sitting on the stoop talking. "Ya see what happened with Soli-
darity this week?" asks one.

"I don't see nothing," the other one says. "I live in the back."

A continuum, you see. Borscht has always been a continuum; an attitude that
began, most likely, when the first Jew, at about the time of the destruction of the
Second Temple, looked up and said, "Y'know, I think I'm beginning to see a
pattern. . . ."

And if there seemed a golden time of Borscht in the Thirties, Forties, and
Fifties in the Catskills, it was not because these were the decades when Borscht
was invented; it was because the number of small hotels, the coming together of
the comics at that time, made the mountains such a conspicuous, fertile field, a
seeming mother lode.

With the disappearance of the hotels, it seems diminished. Though, if you are curious, some of the essential flavor remains. Go to Kutsher's on a weekend: the same busboys will be hustling for tips on the floor; the same gang will be on the lawns, playing gin; the band will play the same goddamn music—"Yellow Bird," "More," "Matilda"—and when they play "Matilda" they will make the same ("My Zelda") awful joke. And when the master of ceremonies, somebody's moonlighting cousin, surely, hollers "Merengue," the same crowd of Jews will thunder to the floor. And you, outcast hoodlum, whatever the specifics of your great sorrow, you, the next time they shout it, will get up with the people, and show your joy of the mountains, and shake it, shake it, shake it across the floor.

Yener Welt

Phil Brown

Yener Welt

At Cohen's Shady Grove a guest came to the boss one day
To make requests for breakfast he'd like served a different way.
Dear Cohen, I pay you good for room and board, more than you rate;
I'm tired of herring every day; some sturgeon would taste great.
Dear Mendel, said the boss, I know you come here every year,
But sturgeon costs too much, and even nova lox is dear.
So try the herring salad, maybe pickled lox or prunes
There's plenty else to grace your forks and satisfy your spoons.

You want sturgeon, ich hab nisht gelt
You'll get sturgeon in yener welt
Yener welt, yener welt
You'll get sturgeon in yener welt

Mister Cohen, I'd like a window station where the tips are grand
My college fees and books and things have gotten out of hand.
I'll serve the guests with friendly smiles, a Yiddish phrase or two.
So give me this, dear Mister Cohen, I kindly ask of you.
You want a window station, but you're slow to serve the mains;
Your shoes have drops of schav and your pants are full of stains.

You've got to have more class, you've got to have more style,
So keep your station by the kitchen door a little while.

Shine your shoes, fix your belt
You'll get a window station in yener welt.
Yener welt, yener welt,
You'll get a window station in yener welt.

Late August came, the guests were sparse, and Cohen let out a shriek.
My mortgage never stops for sluggish end-of-season weeks.
The meat will spoil, the fish will smell, potatoes will grow eyes
How can they go to Bernstein's Lodge or Schwartz's Paradise?
The busboys and the waiters thought how all that season long
Cohen had served them week-old flanken, fed them for a song
They didn't care if Shady Grove went bankrupt, broke, and dead
The dining staff stared right at Cohen, and this is what they said:

Hold your horses, tighten your belt
You'll get more guests in yener welt.
Yener welt, yener welt,
You'll get more guests in yener welt.

Now Cohen was not the only owner in the Catskill Mounts
And Shady Grove was not the only schlock house that we count.
Some were better, some were worse, and most were in between,
But said to say, the Mountains died, we lost the whole damned scene.
So join us as we recollect the golden years we spent
And shed a tear and give a laugh at how they paid the rent.
When people ask about the Catskills, tell them it was tops,
And lift your glass to make a toast with Mister Cohen's schnapps.

A song you'll sing, a tale you'll tell
We'll have another hotel in yener welt.
Yener welt, yener welt
We'll have another hotel in yener welt.

(repeat last chorus)

Shoot the Shtrudel To Me, Yudel

Shoot the Shtrudel to Me, Yudel! (1941)

Words and music by Henry Foner

Dedicated to Yudel Slutsky
of Arrowhead Lodge, Ellenville, NY

Verse:

Ev'ry Sunday afternoon,
Up at the Arrowhead—
We sharpen up each knife and spoon,
Get ready to be fed.

We polish off the entree,
Our throats with soup refresh—
The main dish comes, the main dish goes,
The way of all the flesh.

The meat may be a potted roast,
The soup green pea or noodle—
But the one dish that we love the most
Is Yudel's Apple Shtrudel.

Chorus:

Shoot the shtrudel to me, Yudel—
Watch my tongue hang out with glee.
'Cause I know that kind of food'll
Brighten up the day for me.

Let me grapple with that apple,
Let me taste those flakes sublime.
Raisin filling's very thrilling
In Apple Shtrudel Time.

Interlude:
 I'll be with you in Apple Shtrudel Time.
 I'll be with you where all the Slutskys dine.

 Ev'rybody's eating the Big Apple,
 The Big Apple Shtrudel Pie,
 When Yudel shoots that shtrudel to me,
 I could eat 'til I die. Oh—

(repeat chorus)

Part 5

ROMANCE

Sha-Wan-Ga Lodge, High View. Sha-Wan-Ga Lodge had such a reputation as a singles place that many Mountains people called it "Shwenga" Lodge, Yiddish for "pregnant."

Postcard from Delmar Hotel, Loch Sheldrake. Although this was a small, family-oriented hotel, it shared the common Catskills postcard feature of attractive young people meeting at the pool.
CATSKILLS INSTITUTE

Postcard of lobby lounge at Laurels Country Club, Sackett Lake. The Laurels was another hotel known as a singles spot. This boat-shaped bar was very glitzy, even for the Catskills.
CATSKILLS INSTITUTE

The Catskills were great for romance, since they provided more freedom than Jews usually had in their tight-knit communities back home in New York. Some resorts catered to singles looking to meet others. Hotels and bungalow colonies where husbands only joined their wives on weekends provided the potential for midweek romance. And young staff members could meet other staff or guests for romantic liaisons. It is no surprise that sex has figured prominently in all the fiction that is centered in the Mountains.

From Abraham Cahan's *The Rise of David Levinsky* comes "Miss Tevkin," about the first glimpses of a romantic attachment during Levinksy's brief visit to the Rigi Kulm House in the Fleischmanns area of the northern Catskills. There, Cahan writes, "the air was redolent of grass, flowers, ozone, and sex." For people looking to meet a potential spouse, the Catskills was prime territory, as we see in Cahan's depiction of the singles. The "bewitching azure of the sky and the divine taste of the air seemed to bear out a feeling that it was exempt from any law of nature with which I was familiar," showing how romance could blossom in such a special location. Even though Levinsky is supposed to be en route to his fiancée, he attracts the attention of young women at the hotel, and he winds up involved with Miss Tevkin.

We return to Harvey Jacobs's *Summer on a Mountain of Spices* for the next selection, "Forbidden Fruit." Jacobs's novel is a coming-of-age piece, and by definition must be full of sex for lead character Harry Craft and many others, including the beautiful mistress stashed in the hotel for the summer by a gangster on the run from competition. In this selection, young Marvin Katz winds up a surrogate partner for counselor Essie Poritz, whose fiancé Burton Zomkin is fighting in Europe.

"Marjorie at South Wind" is excerpted from Herman Wouk's *Marjorie Morningstar*. This novel, made into a popular film starring Natalie Wood and Gene Kelly, centers on the romance between Marjorie Morningstar (the assimilationist name taken by Marjorie Morganstern) and Noel Airman (originally Ehrman). Working as a counselor at a girl's camp across the lake from the sexually infamous adult camp, South Wind, Marjorie rows over and meets Noel, the social director who puts on Broadway-type shows reminiscent of the ones Moss Hart wrote about in the previous section. The next year Marjorie returns as a staff member at South Wind itself, despite her mother's fears that she will lose her virginity. Indeed, Marjorie's parents send her uncle along to work as a dishwasher, in the hope that he will protect her, but he tolerates her affair with Noel. Noel ultimately cannot conceive of Marjorie or of any other woman as wanting more than a domestic, suburban life, which he finds unimportant.

Terry Kay's novel *Shadow Song*, from which "Amy Lourie" is taken, is unique in that it was written by a Gentile from Georgia who worked two summers in the northern Catskills. The protagonist, Bobo Murphy, is waiting tables at a hotel when he falls in love with a Jewish girl, Amy Lourie, whose family is staying there. Her parents prohibit the relationship. After his few years working at the hotel, Bobo returns every year to visit an eccentric Jewish man he befriended, Avrum, while the lifelong unrequited love stays in the background. Many years later, Bobo returns to the Catskills when Avrum dies and arranges his very untraditional Kaddish, to the consternation of the local rabbi. In the part included here, we see Bobo in the old hotel where others are having affairs, and the action is interwoven with his memories of how he first met Amy and learned of the strikes against their potential relationship.

Miss Tevkin

Abraham Cahan

On a Saturday morning in August I took a train for Tannersville, Catskill Mountains, where the Kaplan family had a cottage. I was to stay with them over Sunday. I had been expected to be there the day before, but had been detained, August being part of our busiest season. While in the smoking-car it came over me that from Kaplan's point of view my journey was a flagrant violation of the Sabbath and that it was sure to make things awkward. Whether my riding on Saturday would actually offend his religious sensibilities or not (for in America one gets used to seeing such sins committed even by the faithful), it was certain to offend his sense of the respect I owed him. And so, to avoid a sullen reception I decided to stop overnight in another Catskill town and not to make my appearance at Tannersville until the following day.

The insignificant change was pregnant with momentous results.

It was lunch-time when I alighted from the train, amid a hubbub of gay voices. Women and children were greeting their husbands and fathers who had come from the city to join them for the week-end. I had never been to the mountains before, nor practically ever taken a day's vacation. It was so full of ozone, so full of health-giving balm, it was almost overpowering. I was inhaling it in deep, intoxicating gulps. It gave me a pleasure so keen it seemed to verge on pain. It was so unlike the air I had left in the sweltering city that the place seemed to belong to another planet.

I stopped at the Rigi Kulm House. There were several other hotels or boarding-houses in the village, and all of them except one were occupied by our people, the Rigi Kulm being the largest and most expensive hostelry in the neighborhood. It was crowded, and I had to content myself with sleeping-accommodations in one of the near-by cottages, in which the hotel-keeper hired rooms for his overflow business, taking my meals in the hotel.

The Rigi Kulm stood at the end of the village and my cottage was across the main country road from it. Both were on high ground. Viewed from the veranda of the hotel, the village lay to the right and the open country—a fascinating landscape of meadowland, timbered hills, and a brook that lost itself in a grove—to the left. The mountains rose in two ranges, one in front of the hotel and one in the rear.

The bulk of the boarders at the Rigi Kulm was made up of families of cloak-manufacturers, shirt-manufacturers, ladies'-waist-manufacturers, cigar-manufacturers, clothiers, furriers, jewelers, leather-goods men, real-estate men, physicians, dentists, lawyers—in most cases people who had blossomed out into nabobs in the course of the last few years. The crowd was ablaze with diamonds, painted cheeks, and bright-colored silks. It was a babel of blatant self-consciousness, a miniature of the parvenu smugness that had spread like wildfire over the country after a period of need and low spirits.

In addition to families who were there for the whole season—that is, from the Fourth of July to the first Monday in October—the hotel contained a considerable number of single young people, of both sexes—salesmen, stenographers, bookkeepers, librarians—who came for a fortnight's vacation. These were known as "two-weekers." They occupied tiny rooms, usually two girls or two men in a room. Each of these girls had a large supply of dresses and shirt-waists of the latest style, and altogether the two weeks' vacation ate up, in many cases, the savings of months.

To be sure, the "two-weekers" of the gentle sex were not the only marriageable young women in the place. They had a number of heiresses to compete with.

I was too conspicuous a figure in the needle industries for my name to be unknown to the guests of a hotel like the Rigi Kulm House. Moreover, several of the people I found there were my personal acquaintances. One of these was Nodelman's cousin, Mrs. Kalch, or Auntie Yetta, the gaunt, childless woman of the solemn countenance and the gay disposition, of the huge gold teeth, and the fingers heavily laden with diamonds. I had not seen her for months. As the lessee of the hotel marched me into his great dining-room she rushed out to me, her teeth aglitter with hospitality, and made me take a seat at a table which she shared with her husband, the moving-van man, and two middle-aged women. I could see that she had not heard of my engagement, and to avoid awkward interrogations concerning the whereabouts of my fiancée I omitted to announce it.

"I know what you have come here for," she said, archly. "You can't fool Auntie Yetta. But you have come to the right place. I can tell you that a larger assortment of beautiful young ladies you never saw, Mr. Levinsky. And they're educated, too. If you don't find your predestined one here you'll never find her. What do you say, Mr. Rivesman?" she addressed the proprietor of the hotel, who stood by and whom I had known for many years.

"I agree with you thoroughly, Mrs. Kalch," he answered, smilingly. "But Mr. Levinsky tells me he can stay only one day with us."

"Plenty of time for a smart man to pick a girl in a place like this. Besides, you just tell him that you have a lot of fine, educated young ladies, Mr. Rivesman. He is an educated gentleman, Mr. Levinsky is, and if he knows the kind of boarders you have he'll stay longer."

"I know Mr. Levinsky is an educated man," Rivesman answered. "As for our boarders, they're all fine—superfine."

"So you've got to find your predestined one here," she resumed, turning to me again. "Otherwise you can't leave this place. See?"

"But suppose I have found her already—elsewhere?"

"You had no business to. Anyhow, if she doesn't know enough to hold you tight and you are here to spend a weekend with other girls, she does not deserve to have you."

"But I am not spending it with other girls."

"What else did you come here for?" And she screwed up one-half of her face into a wink so grotesque that I could not help bursting into laughter.

About an hour after lunch I sat in a rocking-chair on the front porch, gazing at the landscape. The sky was a blue so subtle and so noble that it seemed as though I had never seen such a sky before. "This is just the kind of place for God to live in," I mused. Whereupon I decided that this was what was meant by the word heaven, whereas the blue overhanging the city was a "mere sky." The village was full of blinding, scorching sunshine, yet the air was entrancingly refreshing. The veranda was almost deserted, most of the women being in their rooms, gossiping or dressing for the arrival of their husbands, fathers, sweethearts, or possible sweethearts. Birds were embroidering the silence of the hour with a silvery whisper that spoke of rest and good-will. The slender brook to the left of me was droning like a bee. Everything was charged with peace and soothing mystery. A feeling of lassitude descended upon me. I was too lazy even to think, but the landscape was continually forcing images on my mind. A hollow in the slope of one of the mountains in front of me looked for all the world like a huge spoon. Half of it was dark, while the other half was full of golden light. It seemed as though it was the sun's favorite spot. "The enchanted spot," I named it. I tried to imagine that oval-shaped hollow at night. I visioned a company of ghosts tiptoeing their way to it and stealing a night's lodging in the "spoon," and later, at the approach of dawn, behold! the ghosts were fleeing to the woods near by.

Rising behind that mountain was the timbered peak of another one. It looked like the fur cap of a monster, and I wondered what that monster was thinking of.

When I gazed at the mountain directly opposite the hotel I had a feeling of disappointment. I knew that it was very high, that it took hours to climb it, but I failed to realize it. It was seemingly quite low and commonplace. Darkling at the foot of it was what looked like a moat choked with underbrush and weeds. The spot was about a mile and a half from the hotel, yet it seemed to be only a minute's walk from me. But then a bird that was flying over that moat at the moment, winging its way straight across it, was apparently making no progress. Was this region exempt from the laws of space and distance? The bewitching azure of the sky and the divine taste of the air seemed to bear out a feeling that it was exempt from any law of nature with which I was familiar. The mountain-peak directly opposite the hotel looked weird now. Was it peopled with Lilliputians?

Another bird made itself heard somewhere in the underbrush flanking the brook. It was saying something in querulous accents. I knew nothing of birds, and the song or call of this one sounded so queer to me that I was almost frightened. All of which tended to enhance the uncanny majesty of the whole landscape.

Presently I heard Mrs. Kalch calling to me. She was coming along the veranda, resplendent in a purple dress, a huge diamond breastpin, and huge diamond earrings.

"All alone? All alone?" she exclaimed, as she paused, interlocking her bediamonded fingers in a posture of mock amazement. "All alone? Aren't you ashamed of yourself to sit moping out here, when there are so many pretty young ladies around? Come along; I'll find you one or two as sweet as sugar," kissing the tips of her fingers.

"Thank you, Mrs. Kalch, but I like it here."

"Mrs. Kalch! Auntie Yetta, you mean." And the lumps of gold in her mouth glinted good-naturedly.

"Very well. Auntie Yetta."

"That's better. Wait! Wait'll I come back."

She vanished. Presently she returned and, grabbing me by an arm, stood me up and convoyed me half-way around the hotel to a secluded spot on the rear porch where four girls were chatting quietly.

"Perhaps you'll find your predestined one among these," she said.

"But I have found her already," I protested, with ill-concealed annoyance.

She took no heed of my words. After introducing me to two of the girls and causing them to introduce me to the other two, she said:

"And now go for him, young ladies! You know who Mr. Levinsky is, don't you? It isn't some kike. It's David Levinsky, the cloak-manufacturer. Don't miss your chance. Try to catch him."

"I'm ready," said Miss Lazar, a pretty brunette in white.

"She's all right," declared Auntie Yetta. "Her tongue cuts like a knife that has just been sharpened, but she's as good as gold."

"Am I? I ain't so sure about it. You had better look out, Mr. Levinsky," the brunette in white warned me.

"Why, that just makes it interesting," I returned. "Danger is tempting, you know. How are you going to catch me—with a net or a trap?"

Auntie Yetta interrupted us. "I'm off," she said, rising to go. "I can safely leave you in their hands, Mr. Levinsky. They'll take care of you," she said, with a wink, as she departed.

"You haven't answered my question," I said to Miss Lazar.

"What was it?"

"She has a poor memory, don't you know," laughed a girl in a yellow shirt-waist. She was not pretty, but she had winning blue eyes and her yellow waist became her. "Mr. Levinsky wants to know if you're going to catch him with a net or with a trap."

"And how about yourself?" I demanded. "What sort of tools have you?"

"Oh, I don't think I have a chance with a big fish like yourself," she replied. Her companions laughed.

"Well, that's only her way of fishing," said Miss Lazar. "She tells every fellow she has no chance with him. That's her way of getting started. You'd better look out, Mr. Levinsky."

"And her way is to put on airs and look as if she could have anybody she wanted," retorted the one of the blue eyes.

"Stop, girls," said a third, who was also interesting. "If we are going to give away one another's secrets there'll be no chance for any of us."

I could see that their thrusts contained more fact than fiction and more venom than gaiety, but it was all laughed off and everybody seemed to be on the best of terms with everybody else. I looked at this bevy of girls, each attractive in her way, and I became aware of the fact that I was not in the least tempted to flirt with them. "I am a well-behaved, sedate man now, and all because I am engaged," I congratulated myself. "There is only one woman in the world for me, and that is Fanny, my Fanny, the girl that is going to be my wife in a few weeks from to-day."

Directly in front of us and only a few yards off was a tennis-court. It was unoccupied at first, but presently there appeared two girls with rackets and balls and they started to play. One of these arrested my attention violently, as it were. I thought her strikingly interesting and pretty. I could not help gazing at her in spite of the eyes that were watching me, and she was growing on me rapidly. It seemed as though absolutely everything about her made a strong appeal to me. She was tall and stately, with a fine pink complexion and an effective mass of chestnut hair. I found that her face attested intellectual dignity and a kindly disposition. I liked her white, strong teeth. I liked the way she closed her lips and I liked the way she opened them into a smile; the way she ran to meet the ball and the way she betrayed disappointment when she missed it. I still seemed to be congratulating myself upon my indifference to women other than the one who was soon to bear my name, when I became conscious of a mighty interest in this girl. I said to myself that she looked refined from head to foot and that her movements had a peculiar rhythm that was irresistible.

Physically her cast of features was scarcely prettier than Fanny's, for my betrothed was really a good-looking girl, but spiritually there was a world of difference between their faces, the difference between a Greek statue and one of those lay figures that one used to see in front of cigar-stores.

The other tennis-player was a short girl with a long face. I reflected that if she were a little taller or her face were not so long she might not be uninteresting, and that by contrast with her companion she looked homelier than she actually was.

Miss Lazar watched me closely.

"Playing tennis is one way of fishing for fellows," she remarked.

"So the racket is really a fishing-tackle in disguise, is it?" I returned. "But where are the fellows?"

"Aren't you one?"

"No."

"Oh, these two girls go in for highbrow fellows," said a young woman who had hitherto contented herself with smiling and laughing. "They're highbrow themselves."

"Do they use big words?" I asked.

"Well, they're well read. I'll say that for them," observed Miss Lazar, with a fine display of fairness.

"College girls?"

"Only one of them."

"Which?"

"Guess."

"The tall one."

"I thought she'd be the one you'd pick. You'll have to guess again."

"What made you think I'd pick her for a college girl?"

"You'll have to guess that, too. Well, she is an educated girl, all the same."

She volunteered the further information that the tall girl's father was a writer, and, as though anxious lest I should take him too seriously, she hastened to add:

"He doesn't write English, though. It's Jewish, or Hebrew, or something."

"What's his name?" I asked.

"Tevkin," she answered, under her breath.

The name sounded remotely familiar to me. Had I seen it in some Yiddish paper? Had I heard it somewhere? The intellectual East Side was practically a foreign country to me, and I was proud of the fact. I knew something of its orthodox Talmudists, but scarcely anything of its modern men of letters, poets, thinkers, humorists, whether they wrote in Yiddish, in Hebrew, in Russian, or in English. If I took an occasional look at the socialist Yiddish daily it was chiefly to see what was going on in the Cloak-makers' Union. Otherwise I regarded everything that was written for the East Side with contempt, and "East Side writer" was synonymous with "greenhorn" and "tramp." Worse than that, it was identified in my mind with socialism, anarchism, and trade-unionism. It was something sinister, absurd, and uncouth.

But Miss Tevkin was a beautiful girl, nevertheless. So I pitied her for being the daughter of an East Side writer.

The tennis game did not last long. Miss Tevkin and her companion soon went indoors. I went out for a stroll by myself. I was thinking of my journey to Tannersville the next morning. The enforced loss of time chafed me. Of the strong impression which the tall girl had produced on me not a trace seemed to have been left. She bothered me no more than any other pretty girl I might have recently come across. Young women with strikingly interesting faces and figures were not rare in New York.

I had not been walking five minutes when I impatiently returned to the hotel to consult the time-tables.

Forbidden Fruit

Harvey Jacobs

Free of the children two hours before Nite Patrol, Essie Poritz sat on the lawn in weak light and finished a letter to Burton Zomkin.

First she thanked him for the copy of *This Is My Beloved* that was mail-ordered to her home address. It was Essie's first copy of the love poems. She knew girls who had two, five, one who had twelve copies of the epic of World War II. The verse, Hallmark with hormones, was written in honey from sick bees.

Essie and Burton had talked about how the book made them vomit. He sent it for a joke. Essie wrote how her mother opened the package and read the poems. She got so upset by the sex she called the Willow Spring to ask Essie what was between the lines. Did they "do it"?

Next she wrote about the lady at the Italian farm, a frozen life behind glass watching seasons change from her own final season. Which was why it was important to make hay in sunshine. Please hurry home.

Essie wrote about news of the bomb and the imminent end of the war. While she wrote it came to her that by the same hour next year she would be Essie Zomkin. Burton would be climbing the gangplank of a troopship in a matter of days. What was left to do over there?

Ray Stein walked past. There was a good-looking woman. She didn't peek through closed windows guarding well water. On the other hand, Hannah Craft wasn't so different from the lady at the farm. And they were all young girls once, all brides, all went through life's dance. Who knew how anybody would end up. In the woods with a shovel like Mendel Berman.

Mrs. Essie Zomkin saw herself return to the Willow Spring with her own kids. She turned off the fantasy. No. Let her kids sweat. She would never go away for the summer while her husband worked in the city, waiting for weekends.

In her letter Essie Poritz wrote how she would fill Burton in on the culture he missed. Books, movies, songs. In his last letter he said he felt alienated. Out of touch. No wonder.

Essie wondered if Burton Zomkin ever killed anybody. He saw some action but never gave details. It must be an impossible subject to write in a letter. Dear Essie, today I blew the brains out of a German. Would he ever tell her? He would some night. Returning veterans had to share their experiences. But it was wrong to rush them.

How fast the summer had flown. Here it was, August. Here she sat, under young constellations, with soft wind combing the lawn.

Soon the same girl would stand under the *huppa* with civilian Burton Zomkin. Next August would blow its breezes at a very different girl. A woman, a finished person with a determined pattern of days and nights, months, years.

Essie shivered. It wasn't true. Nothing is that predictable. Marriage must be full of surprises for those open to receive them.

In that moment Essie forgot Burton Zomkin's look. She opened her bag and found his picture.

Hello, smiley. Hello, darling.

"More letters?" Marvin Katz said from behind her.

Essie jumped.

"More letters," she said. "Don't think I'm not sick of writing. How would you like to walk to Monticello with me to mail this fellow?"

"Walk? More walking?"

"I still have more than an hour. We can make it. Come on, lazy."

Marvin glowed in the dark.

"Sure, why not," he said. "I only walked ten thousand miles today."

"Come, Gunga Din. We'll take a brisk walk and have a talk about life. Marvin, who should get the Outstanding Camper Button this week? Help me decide."

As they went along the Old Liberty a slash of russet split a violet sky. Color flowed from behind the Elsmere Arms as if a volcano there spit marvels. The color changed Essie and Marvin to golden souls from outer space.

"All this magnificence makes one wonder," Essie said.

"You have that feeling?"

"Oh yes. Am I a stone?"

"Essie, do you believe in God? I don't."

"Sometimes yes, sometimes no. What other artist could mix such a palette?"

"The color comes from grains of wheat and oats in the air," Marvin said. "The light bounces off them."

"Wheat and oats? Cereal? Is that what we're really seeing? Is that what a sensitive boy like you believes in his inner heart?"

Essie, feeling happy, tickled Marvin Katz on his T-shirt. He returned the favor. They went along laughing.

"Don't crinkle my letter to Burton," Essie said.

"Burton Shmerton," Marvin said.

"Oh, the green-eyed monster of jealousy."

It had never occurred to Marvin Katz that he had the right to be jealous of a soldier, a man, a fiancé. He was uplifted by the comment.

They talked easily on the way to Monticello.

Marvin told Essie he didn't know who he was or what he wanted to be. Essie told Marvin she used to feel that but when she decided to become Mrs. Burton Zomkin the uncertainty melted away.

They held hands while these secrets were exchanged. Marvin confessed nameless fears. Essie said that was common. Then Essie told Marvin the story of how she wouldn't sleep with Burton Zomkin before he went overseas.

Why did she tell him that?

"Whoops. I said too much. I hope you are mature enough to keep a confidence. I have faith in you."

"You could tell me anything," Marvin said.

"And you can tell me anything," Essie said. "We're friends, Marvin. Isn't that exciting?"

"Yes," Marvin said, under red and orange lights.

They stopped at the post office.

"The mailbox looks like a pregnant lady," Marvin said.

"You know, it just really does."

Essie got her envelope.

"The letter is open," Marvin said.

"I know. I know."

She took Charlie Mandel's snapshot out of her bag, dropped it in with the folded pages and sealed the flap.

"So? Mail it."

She mailed it.

Heading back for the Willow Spring, they refused a lift from a passing truck. Throwing away a ride made the two of them feel closer. They didn't want to hurry the walk.

"Back to patrol," Essie said. "You know who gives me the biggest trouble?"

"Lolly Edel?"

"Guess again," Essie said.

"I give up."

"Gerald Tish."

"He's a very *shleppy* child. Now at least he's got the dog."

"Those aunts of his. Marvin, you know what I actually saw? I saw his Aunt Tanya walking with the puppy down by the handball court."

"So what?"

"So what? No leash. You know who lives across the road, don't you?"

"I don't get it."

"The vicious police dog. Lindy. You should have seen Lindy watching that itty-bitty puppy. He was licking his teeth."

"Now I get it."

"I'm not saying anything definite, but it looked to me like Aunt Tanya had something in mind. What a terrible thing for me to say. I take it back. I'm drunk on the sunset."

"Sometimes hunches like that are right," Marvin said.

"You know who's big on hunches? My Burton. He has extrasensory perception."

"I didn't know he was a hunchback," Marvin said.

"That was beneath you, Marvin, that was a Charlie Mandel remark," Essie said.

Then she laughed her head off.

"Do they have hunchfronts?" Marvin Katz said, sticking his belly out.

Essie Poritz roared.

"I am drunk," she said.

They enjoyed each other's company so much Marvin Katz went on Nite Patrol with Essie Poritz. They walked through the Main House listening for tears and sniffles.

"I'll give you a nickel if you guess who pees in bed."

"Sidney Buloff."

"Wrong. Eric Frobheim."

"The politician? The one who wants to be a major?"

"That one. Marvin, don't make me laugh anymore."

They stopped at Jerry Tomato's door.

"You want to see how he sleeps with the dog in his bed? It's cute. Come in but be quiet."

Marvin followed Essie into the room. A night-light and the moon made a yellow broth, enough to show Jerry curled around his puppy.

"They look married," Marvin said.

Essie held her hand over her mouth.

They stood watching Gerald Tish sleep. He looked better out of action. A warm feeling came over both of them. They felt grateful for each other.

"Marvin, listen to something crazy. If I closed my eyes and pretended you were Burton and gave you one kiss would you laugh at me?"

"No."

Essie Poritz closed her eyes and kissed Marvin Katz on the lips. Her tongue played with his front teeth. His tongue came out and touched, then pushed. They kissed again.

"Come home safely to me," Essie said.

"He will. Don't worry," Marvin said.

"You're not supposed to talk, remember?" Essie said.

"I'm sorry. I forgot for a minute."

"Marvin, are we being silly?"

"No. We're not being silly."

Essie kissed him again. Marvin's hand was lifted to her breast. He squeezed a little.

"Burton, be careful. That's so tender. So wonderful."

Burton slipped the hand inside her blouse between buttons. Jerry Tomato snorted. The hand waited. Jerry and the puppy were contained in the circle of sleep.

"The war is done," Essie said.

"Not yet," Marvin said.

"Soon, though."

Her hand stroked his backside.

"Do we dare to lay down," Essie said. "This is naughty. I'm so drunk. It's the water you brought me."

"Enchanted water," Marvin said.

Essie helped Burton open her blouse and the catch on her brassiere. He played with her hard nipples. She played with his shocked genitals. Burton's underpants came down to his knees. Essie's panties kept them company.

"Burton, I love you," Essie said.

Burton came in her hand.

"Wow, I'm sorry," he said.

"For what, dearest?" Essie said. "It was beautiful."

Essie Poritz never held such a handful.

Love soup.

"Now that's enough, Burton. Enough for tonight."

"We could do it again tomorrow," Burton said.

"Touch me here. Oh, that's unbelievable."

It was unbelievable to Burton too.

The puppy woke first. It yelped. Jerry Tomato said, "Essie, what are you doing?"

"Doing? Nothing. We're playing. Go to sleep."

"I'm coming over there."

"No you're not, Gerald."

"Look at Essie," Jerry Tomato said.

"Turn around."

"I'm telling," Jerry said.

"You tell and I'll break your face," Marvin said.

"No, no," Essie said. "Marvin didn't mean it. Besides, this is only a game of pretend. Jerry, listen. You can play too. You don't tell and you'll get a nice present."

"What present?"

"Remember the farm? Remember those delicious tomatoes up there?"

"Yum. Yeah. Yum."

"I'll get you some. A whole lot."

"For me?"

"For only you."

"I won't tell. What are we playing again?"

"Let's pretend. Go to sleep."

"I want to watch you get dressed. My aunt lets me."

Marvin Burton pulled up his shorts and pants. Essie Poritz put on her bra and blouse after getting her panties in order.

"This is like a little dream," she said to Jerry Tomato.

"You promised," Jerry said. "I'm not dreaming."

"A promise made is a debt unpaid," Essie said.

Marvin Burton caught a look at her in the strange light. Essie breathed fast and hard while she hummed a lullaby to Jerry and the dog.

He took Essie's hand and held on.

Marjorie at South Wind

Herman Wouk

Marjorie came to South Wind on a lovely June afternoon.

There was no sheriff waiting with a subpoena to take her back to New York; and when in her bungalow (the same one Karen Blair had occupied) she opened her trunk, Mrs. Morgenstern did not pop out at her. Neither occurrence would have entirely startled the girl. The mother's defeat in the first skirmish over South Wind had been temporary; she had rallied her forces for a month of energetic nagging, snipping, fault-finding, and obstructing, only to surrender with queer docile suddenness a week before Marjorie's departure. She had seen the girl off at the train in excellent humor, even calling out her standard parting joke as Marjorie went up the steps of the coach car, "Don't do anything I wouldn't do." Marjorie had made the standard reply, "Thanks, that gives me plenty of rope," only halfheartedly, wondering what devilment her mother was up to. Mrs. Morgenstern was a last-ditch fighter by nature, and her philosophic resignation struck the girl as extremely suspicious.

Nevertheless, though Marjorie could hardly believe it, here she was in South Wind. She unpacked, still expecting the telegram, the telephone call, the sudden turn of events that would send her home. Nothing happened. She walked down to the social hall with a book under her arm, feeling more secure and more triumphant with each passing quarter hour; and at the bar she bought a pack of cigarettes for the first time in her life. She still did not enjoy smoking, so she chose

Wally's mentholated brand; and strolling out on the lawn, puffing a cigarette, she felt quite grand and grown up.

Her elation was somewhat spoiled by the seediness of the camp. Seen by daylight in June, after a winter of neglect and hard weather, South Wind radiated little of the glamor it had had a year ago by moonlight. The fountain in the center of the overgrown lawn was dry. The spout, a rusty iron pipe, stood out a foot above the cracked concrete cascade, which was splotched with sickly green moss. All the buildings needed paint. The white had gone to dirty rust-streaked gray, and the gilding had mostly peeled off, showing tin or wood underneath. The dock was being torn, sawed, and hammered at by workmen. Three tan boys in sweaters and bathing trunks were slapping red paint on the mottled canoes. Everything seemed smaller—buildings, lawn, fountain, lake, oak trees—everything. In her winter visions the lawn had been a public park, the oaks towering old monarchs, the social hall a great building marvelously transplanted from Radio City; she had honestly remembered them that way. But the lawn was just a good-sized hotel lawn, the trees were just trees; and the social hall was not much more than a big barn topped by a phony modernistic shaft, which badly needed replastering.

But there was Airman himself, coming out of the camp office! Weedy, golden-haired, long-striding, in the black turtle-neck sweater that seemed to be his badge of office, he at least, of all the attractions of South Wind, retained his first lustre. He saw her, and turned his steps across the lawn. "Hi, Marjorie. Got here at last?"

"About half an hour ago, Noel."

"Good. Welcome."

"Thanks." Her face was stiff in a smile. "How about the show this weekend? Can I help?"

"No, it's all set. Just a scratch revue, old stuff—there won't be two hundred people here. Got another cigarette?" But when she held out the pack, he fended it off. "Good God, you too? You and Wally. The younger generation certainly has depraved tastes." He pointed to the book. "What are you reading?"

She handed him Plato's *Republic* at once, glad of the chance to cover her cursed mistake of buying Wally's brand of cigarettes.

She really was reading the *Republic*. Shortly after Billy Ehrmann had informed her that his brother was interested in philosophy, she had found herself taking philosophy books out of the library. It had seemed natural to do so, just as, when George Drobes had been her god, it had seemed natural, in fact inevitable, to elect biology as her major subject in college. Biology had now become stupefyingly dull to her; Plato and John Dewey, on the other hand, seemed full of good things, and amazingly easy to read.

Airman wrinkled his nose at the book and at her. "What are you doing, catching up on next fall's homework?"

"No, I'm just reading it."

"Just reading Plato?"

"That's right."

"You're silly. Why don't you get hold of a decent mystery?" He gave back the book.

"I wish I could. I think I've read 'em all."

He rubbed his elbow, smiling at her with a trace of interest. "Seen my brother Billy lately?"

"I don't see your brother Billy." It sounded too sharp; but his kindly tone flicked her nerves. "I mean, years ago when I was a freshman we ran around in the same crowd. That's all."

He ran a knuckle over his upper lip, inspecting her. "Maybe we can use you in the show at that. Come along."

Most of the staff people were the same. Carlos Ringel, fatter and very pasty-faced, was waddling around the stage, shouting to someone in the wings, who was shouting back. The performers sat here and there on the floor of the hall, dressed in sweaters and slacks; several of the girls were knitting. The couple who had done the jungle dance last year were stomping near the piano, doing a Hindu dance. The rehearsal pianist was the same, and he seemed to be chewing the same cigar, and to need the same shave. Noel introduced her to everyone as Marjorie Morgenstern; she lacked the courage to correct him. Then he turned her over to a little plump man with tiny fluttering hands, Puddles Podell, a comedian who had exchanged some horribly coarse jokes with Marsha in the bar last year. Puddles took Marjorie out on the back porch of the hall and taught her a burlesque sketch called *Fifty Pounds of Plaster.*

"It's strictly the hotel bit, sweetheart," he said, acting out the scene with a thousand little hand gestures. "Just say whatever comes into your head. We're honeymooners, see—affa-scaffa, wasn't it a beautiful wedding, abba-dabba, at last we can be alone, abba-dabba—" The point lay in two lines at the end. The honeymooners rushed indignantly on stage, supposedly out of the bridal suite, to complain to the desk clerk.

"What's the matter with this hotel?" Marjorie had to say. "The ceiling in our room is coming down. Fifty pounds of plaster just fell on my chest." Whereupon

Puddles said, "Damn right—and if it had fallen two minutes sooner, it would have broken my back."

When the joke emerged, Marjorie turned scarlet and burst out laughing. The comedian paused and stared at her. "Are you laughing at the *bit*?"

They played the skit on the dance floor for Noel, who slouched low in a folding chair. "I guess she'll be okay," Puddles said to Noel. "What do you think?"

Noel nodded. "Marjorie, it's a longish road from *Fifty Pounds of Plaster* to *Candida*—but nobody can say you're not on your way. Try it on stage, Puddles."

Wally Wronken came into the social hall just as the sketch was starting, and squatted on the floor beside Noel's chair. Almost at once he began talking earnestly to Noel, who listened, shrugged, and raised his hand. "Hold everything—Margie, do you object to acting in this skit?"

"Object? Why, no."

"That's not the point, Noel," Wally said. "It isn't funny with her in it, *that's* the point. She looks too pretty on stage, too wholesome."

Puddles came to the footlights. "That's what's bothering me, Noel. We always used one of the strippers in this bit. Margie looks like my baby sister or something, it kills the gag."

Glaring at Wally, Marjorie exclaimed, "Look, I'm *delighted* to do it, please let's get on with it."

Noel shook his head, yawning. "I'm not very sharp today. Thanks, Wally. You're out, Margie, sorry. We'll get someone else to do this immortal scene."

She stalked off the stage and out of the social hall, humiliated, furious. When Wally tried to talk to her, she cut him dead.

It was only four o'clock; two hours before dinnertime, and nothing to do. She went up to the camp office, hoping to make herself useful there. But it was an utter chaos of tumbled furniture, strewn papers, stained cloths, and paint cans and ladders; it was being repainted a very fishy-smelling green. Greech ran here and there in his shirt sleeves, his face streaked green, snatching up a ringing telephone, bawling at the painters. He shouted when he saw her, "Get out, get out. No time for you, no use for you. Clear out. See me Sunday. Don't come in here again."

Marjorie wandered down a curving road behind the dining hall toward the tennis courts, thinking that her first day at South Wind could not have been worse if her mother had planned every detail. She was a bit of female clutter on the landscape; moreover, she was Marjorie Morgenstern—stamped, branded with the name for good, all in a few seconds. Her irritation and anger focused on

Wally Wronken; she felt quite capable of not speaking to him all summer. She lit another cigarette, but it reminded her of Wally, and it tasted awful anyway. She threw it away after one puff.

At that moment she saw the Uncle.

He was carrying a tin tub of garbage down wooden steps from the back door of the kitchen. She recognized him instantly, though he wore a kitchen uniform: small white hat, white undershirt and trousers, and an amazingly dirty apron. There couldn't be two men in the world with such a paunch; besides, as she stood frozen in surprise, watching him empty the garbage, she faintly heard him singing the song to which they had danced with the turkey leg. "Uncle! Uncle, for heaven's sake! Hello!" She ran up a slope through daisies and long grass. "What on *earth* are you doing here, Uncle?"

"Havaya, Modgerie! Vait, I come to you! Up here it don't smell so fency. Vait, vait, I come down." She halted midway on the slope. He approached, grinning broadly, mopping his streaming red face with a handkerchief. "Is a surprise, no?"

"Surprise? I'm stunned—"

"Modgerie, ve keep it a secret, no? By Modgerie and the Uncle a little secret. Better ve don't tell your mama, she'll only make a big hoo-hah. I tell you, darling, by the golf course vas too lonesome. Here is more fun, nice fellers, plenty to eat—hard vork, but vot is vork? I make plenty money, too—not like by the golf course—"

"The golf course?" she said, more and more bewildered. "What's the golf course got to do with it? Why are you here?"

The Uncle smiled in a placating way, showing the black gap in his teeth. "You vent to find me by the golf course, no? Your mama thinks I'm still there. Ve von't tell her notting different, vy does she have to know I'm a dishvasher?"

After Marjorie asked a good many questions, it came out that Mrs. Morgenstern had arranged a caretaker's job at South Wind for the Uncle, a week or so before Marjorie's departure. This explained her sudden mysterious good cheer, of course. She had succeeded in placing a chaperon of sorts over her daughter at "Sodom," after all. Greech had taken the Uncle on without salary (and with Mrs. Morgenstern paying the railroad fare) as a kind of janitor and watchman for the lodge on the golf course. But then two dishwashers had quit. Greech had offered him the kitchen job at twenty-five dollars a week, and he had accepted it gladly.

It penetrated the old man's mind very slowly that Marjorie was amazed to find him at the camp at all. "Vot? She didn't tell you notting? How is it possible?"

"She didn't, Uncle. Not a word. I swear I thought I was seeing a ghost for a minute."

"A nice fat ghost, hah?" He shook his head. "So! For you it's some disappointment, no? A fat old uncle you need around your neck, hah? Like a cholera, you need it. It's too bad, Modgerie, I'm sorry—your mama is a smart vun—"

"Uncle, it doesn't matter, really—"

"Listen, Modgerie, a mama remains a mama, she can't help it. By her it's still Friday night in the Bronx, the Uncle has to keep an eye on the baby. So vot? You think I spoil your fun, Modgerie? Have a good time, darling, vot do I know? I'm busy in the kitchen."

She had been looking at his hands uneasily. Now she caught one as he made a gesture. "Uncle, what's the matter? What are these?" There were several gaping little red wounds on his fat fingers. They were neither bleeding nor healing. They were like mouths, open, dry, and red.

With a laugh, Samson-Aaron pulled his hand away. "You vash dishes you get cut. Dishes break. Soap keeps vashing in the cuts, so they don't heal, so vot? You lay off from vashing dishes they heal up."

"I don't like the look of them. Did you see the doctor?" Marjorie stared at the red gaps.

"Modgerie please, it's notting." He put both hands behind his back. "Don't be like your mama, alvays questions."

"I just don't know if you ought to be doing this, Uncle."

"Vot, I'll disgrace you? Modgerie's uncle is Sam the dishvasher? I von't say a vord to nobody, depend on the Uncle."

She threw her arm around his neck. "It's not that. You're—It's hard, dirty work, you know—"

"So? I never vashed dishes? I vashed dishes in the Catskills, Modgerie, before you vere born. Vot is it? Caretaker, vatchman, that's the jobs I don't like. Jobs for old men, for cripples. I'm strong like a horse—Vait, I show you something." He fumbled under his apron, brought out a tattered sweat-blackened wallet, and pulled a snapshot from it. "Did you see yet a picture of Geoffrey's vife? Here, look at a doll, a sveetheart—"

Geoffrey had been married for six months. The picture showed him standing on the porch of a tiny house, in shirtsleeves, with his arm around a thin girl in flat shoes and a house dress. She was squinting into the sun, and her hair was pulled flat in a plain knot, so Marjorie could form no notion of her looks. Geoffrey, fatter and with much less hair, was grinning foolishly, his chest thrust out, a beer bottle in his hand.

"She's lovely, Uncle. What's her name?"

"Sylvia. Her father is a doctor in Albany, a big specialist. You know vot? She calls him Milton. Says it sounds more like him than Geoffrey, God bless her. A doll, hah?" He showed the black gap again in a happy grin, curiously like Geoffrey's, and lowered his voice. "Modgerie, in October they have a baby already."

"That's wonderful."

"You see vy I vash dishes maybe, Modgerie? Vy should I take money from Geoffrey ven he needs it? I send it back! Comes October I send *him* money. For the baby, a present. The baby should sleep in the finest crib money could buy. A crib from Samson-Aaron the gobbage pail. A good idea, hah?"

A voice roared from the rear of the dining hall. "Hey *Sam*, you fat old bastard, you drop dead or something?"

"Okay, okay—" yelled the Uncle. He chuckled. "That's Paul, the other dishvasher. A good feller, a Hungarian, plays good chess. So?" He caressed Marjorie's cheek lightly. "I see you sometimes, Modgerie, hah? I got a secret, you don't tell Mama, I don't tell her your secrets. It's a bargain? I see you sometimes ven nobody's looking, I give you maybe a Hershey bar." He ambled toward the kitchen, shouting, "Vot's the matter, Paul, you vash a dish good and break your back?" He toiled up the stairs, his paunch shaking, waved at Marjorie from the top stair, and disappeared.

Marjorie marched straight to the public telephone booths in the main building across the hall from the office, and put in a call to her mother. The fishy fumes of the office paint brought tears to her eyes. In the next booth Mr. Greech was alternately growling and howling incomprehensibly at his secretary in New York. The operator told her that the circuits to New York were busy. She went out on the porch to escape the fumes while she waited. The afternoon had clouded over; a dank wind was lashing the oak trees, and there was a smell of rain in the air. Marjorie dropped dejectedly on the porch steps, her chin resting on her hands.

All magic was leaking out of South Wind, like air out of a punctured tire. She liked Samson-Aaron; no, she loved him, shabby old glutton though he was. But the injection into South Wind of a family face soured the very light of day. South Wind had been, in Marjorie's visions, a new clear world, a world where a grimy Bronx childhood and a fumbling Hunter adolescence were forgotten dreams, a world where she could at last find herself and be herself—clean, fresh, alone, un-trammelled by parents. In a word, it had been the world of Marjorie Morn-ingstar. The shrinking of the camp's glamor, her own lowly status, the mischance with the name, were bad enough. And here came the Uncle, dragging behind him the long chain of all the old rusty realities. She could feel the weight of that chain; she could feel the clamp, cold on her ankle, fixed there by the invisible far-stretching hand of her mother. It was unendurable.

"Rain again, for Christ's sake!" grated Mr. Greech, making her jump. He stood directly behind her, scowling at the black sky, slapping the flashlight on his palm, looking fully as satanic as he had last year. Being on South Wind soil did something to Mr. Greech. "When in the name of hell am I going to get these buildings painted? Do you realize we've had rain for fourteen straight days?" He bellowed this last observation directly at Marjorie.

"I'm sorry," she said.

He looked at her with a blink, as though a stone had spoken. "What? What did you say?"

"Mr. Greech—pardon me, I hate to trouble you—it's a small matter—"

"What, what?"

"My uncle—he's washing dishes, I see."

"Who? Oh yes, old Sam. Well, sure, he'd rather make twenty-five a week than nothing a week. So would I, by God, and it doesn't look as though I will this season."

"It's just—well, it's hard work."

"Of course it is. That's why I pay him."

"He's—well, he's an old man—"

"What's all this, now? See here, your mother told me he's stronger than I am. He's not chained in the kitchen. He jumped at the job. He seems to be thriving. In fact, the cook tells me he's eating like ten men. I'm going to talk to him about that, by the way, I'm not running a hog-fattening farm in that kitchen. Now, what exactly are *you* fussing about? What's eating *you*?" He thrust at her with the flashlight on each *you*.

She withered under his tone and his stare. "Well, I just thought—I don't know—I suppose if it was his own idea . . ." She trailed off. Greech was walk-ing away from her into the office.

In a few minutes the telephone call went through. As Marjorie waited, re-ceiver in hand, to hear her mother's voice, this thought flashed through her mind: *When I object to her sending the Uncle here without my knowledge she'll say,*

"What's the matter, are you planning to do something up there you don't want us to know about?" She was trying to think of a crushing answer when her mother came on the line. After assuring her that she was well and the camp was splendid, Marjorie said, "Quite a surprise you prepared for me!"

"What surprise?" said Mrs. Morgenstern blandly.

"Samson-Aaron."

"Oh. The Uncle. Well, how is he?"

"Just fine."

"That's good. Give him my regards."

After a little pause Marjorie said, "Don't you think you might have told me he'd be here?"

"Didn't I?"

"Of course you didn't."

"Well, that's right, I guess it was the week when you were so busy with exams. Well, you have no objections to his being there, do you?"

"It's a little late to be asking me that, I would say."

"What's the matter," said Mrs. Morgenstern, "are you planning to do something up there that you wouldn't want us to know about?"

"I've already done it," said Marjorie. "I've been having an affair with Mr. Greech since March. How do you suppose I got the job?"

"Don't be smart."

"He's washing dishes."

"Who?"

"The Uncle."

"What! No, he isn't. He's a caretaker."

"Not any more. He makes money washing dishes. Wants to buy a nice present for his grandchild."

There was a silence. Mrs. Morgenstern said, "Well, I can see that's not too nice. Your uncle washing dishes. I'll write him to go back to caretaker."

"Let him alone! You're hopeless, Mom."

"What are you so touchy about? One of these days you'll be glad the Uncle is there."

"I'm sure that's why you did it, Mom—to accommodate me."

"What do you want of me, Marjorie? Why did you call? Do you want me to write him to come home? Say so, and I'll do it, that's all."

Several seconds went by, while Marjorie weighed the neat impasse. It would have been hard for her under any circumstances to force the Uncle out of South

Wind, once he was there. Now that she had seen his pride and pleasure in earning money, it was impossible. "Thank you, Mama, I don't want anything. I thought you might be interested to know that he's all right, and that I'm all right, and that everything couldn't be lovelier."

"It fills me with joy, dear."

"Fine. Give my love to Papa."

"I will. Goodbye. Don't do anything I wouldn't do."

"Thanks, Mom, that gives me plenty of rope. 'Bye."

Another round lost.

But once Marjorie became used to two unpleasant and very unwelcome facts: that she was still Marjorie Morgenstern, and that she was not likely to fascinate Noel Airman (at least not straight off), she perked up and began to enjoy South Wind. She hardly ever saw the Uncle; and if they did come on each other by accident they smiled and exchanged a few quick pleasant words, and that was all. It was still gratifying to look across the lake to Klabber's camp on a fresh sunny morning, and to realize how far she had come in a year. It was fun rehearsing in the shows, even if she did nothing but kick her legs in a chorus of office girls. She began to find a certain arid pleasure in the office work. Keeping her desk clean and severe, getting her work done on time, drawing a grunt of praise from Greech for letters typed up swiftly and without errors—however petty, these things were satisfying.

Every day the look of the camp improved. The weather turned fine, too. By the first of July, after a week of continual sunshine, the fountain was flowing, the grass was velvet-neat, the buildings were dazzling white and gold, and the grounds were alive with noisy merry people in summer clothes of carnival colors. They were a helter-skelter group of ordinary young New Yorkers; a few girls spoke with comic Brooklyn and Bronx grotesqueness, and a few of the men were excessively crude, but most of them were just like the young people she had known all her life. They ate, danced, drank, and played at all the sports with great gusto. Gaiety and freedom were in the air. The food Greech fed them was a curious mélange of traditional Jewish delicacies—gefilte fish, stuffed neck, chopped chicken liver—and traditional Jewish abominations, like shellfish, bacon, and ham; the guests devoured the delicacies and the abominations with equal relish. Marjorie had to comb the bacon off her eggs for the first week or so, until the waiter became used to her old-fashioned ways.

If South Wind was Sodom, it seemed to be a cheerful, outdoors sort of Sodom, where tennis, golf, steak roasts, and rumbas had replaced more classic and scandalous debaucheries. Marjorie did notice a lot of necking in canoes and on the moonlit porch outside the social hall, but there was nothing startling in that. Perhaps terrible sins were being committed on the grounds; but so far as her eyes could pierce there was nothing really wrong at South Wind. All was jocund and fair to see. She lost her curiosity about the guests after the first week or so. They were a blur of similar faces; part of the background—like the lake, the trees, the clouds—to the real life that went on among the people of the staff.

Amy Lourie

Terry Kay

My history in Arch's was Amy Lourie.

It was where I discovered her one night, following dinner, two weeks after the regular season had begun in the Inn. I had gone into Arch's to buy envelopes to mail a letter to Carolyn. Amy was sitting in a booth with Carter. He saw me and motioned me over.

"Bobo," he said, "this is Amy Lourie. You're going to be serving her breakfast in the morning. Amy, this is Bobo Murphy, your waiter and my boss, and if you understand anything he says, you'll be among the few. He's from Georgia, way down yonder in Dixieland."

Amy Lourie flicked a smile to me. She was the most beautiful girl I had ever seen.

"Hi," she said.

I nodded a reply and forced a smile.

"Why are you called Bobo?" she asked.

I blushed. "One of my sisters gave it to me. She couldn't say *brother*. She called me Bobo and it just stuck."

"You're really our waiter?"

"I—I don't know." I looked at Carter.

"You are," Carter said. "They always sit in the middle dining room." He moved in the seat of the booth. "Come on, take a load off."

I sat beside Carter and looked away from Amy Lourie. I was uncomfortable.

"They just got in," Carter explained. "Amy comes up every year with her folks. They spend the summer."

"My parents love it here," Amy said softly.

"You don't?" Carter asked.

She moved her hand to touch the milk shake in front of her. Her hand and her fingers were as beautiful as her face. She looked around the store, then said, "I like it, but it can get a little boring." Her eyes covered me. "Have you ever been here?"

"I've never been anywhere, until a few weeks ago," I said.

I could see the flash of delight in her eyes. She said, "You really are, aren't you?"

"Excuse me?" I replied.

"From the South."

"I told you he was," Carter interjected. "Come on, Bobo, say 'y'all' for Amy."

I blushed again.

"Leave him alone, Carter," Amy said. "I love the accent."

"You better get used to it," Carter told her. He grinned. "You should see the look on old Mrs. Mendelson's face when Bobo tries to speak German."

"Carter, that's mean," Amy said. She was still looking at me. "How did you get to be our waiter?"

Carter chuckled. I knew it was a tender matter with him. He had been at the Inn for two years as a busboy, and I had been promoted from dishwasher to waiter in three weeks.

"I'm not sure I know," I answered.

"Jesus, Bobo," exclaimed Carter, "don't be so uptight." He said to Amy, "Al Martin—maybe you remember him from last year—got fired and Mrs. Dowling gave his busboy job to Bobo. Then Connie Wells found out she was pregnant and her husband didn't want her to work, and that opened up a waiter's job. Bobo got it, and that's fine with me. I don't mind being his busboy. Jesus, who wants to be a waiter, anyway? People always yelling at you, giving you grief. Jesus. I didn't even think I was going to be here this summer, but I changed my mind. My car needs a new motor. Anyway, Harry Burger taught him the ropes, and you know Harry. He pulls some weight—most of it in silver dollars."

"Mr. Burger?" Amy said. "He's back?"

"Did he ever leave?" Carter said. "He's like your folks. They couldn't live without this place."

Amy smiled patiently, ignoring Carter. She said to me, "I'm glad to meet you, Bobo. Will you keep something warm for me in the morning? Sometimes I sleep late."

Carter laughed.

"I'm sure we'll find something," I said.

"Don't y'all know it," Carter drawled, mocking me.

Later, in The Cave, Carter strolled from the bathroom after his shower. A towel was wrapped around his waist and an amused smile was lodged at a crooked angle in his face. He took a cigarette from the night table and lit it, then he sat on the edge of my lower bunk bed and gazed at me through a veil of smoke that steamed from his nose. I closed the writing pad that I had balanced against my knees.

"Bobo," he said.

"Yeah."

"What color are her eyes?"

"Who?"

"You know damn well who: Amy."

"I don't know."

"Bullshit," he snorted. "You're the artist. Artists see things like that. What color, Bobo?"

"Aqua. Violet. Something like that."

Carter laughed. "Are they the prettiest eyes you've ever seen?"

"I don't know," I mumbled. "They're pretty."

"What color is her hair?"

"Brunette," I said.

"No, Bobo, black-gold," whispered Carter. "You've never seen hair like that, have you?"

"Sure, I have."

There was a pause. Carter drew from his cigarette and nudged a smoke ring from his lips. The ring twirled over my head and scrubbed against the mattress of the top bunk.

"You're lying," Carter said easily. "You've never seen eyes or hair or lips or arms or hands or fingers or legs or feet, or anything else like Amy Lourie. Wait until you catch her in a bathing suit. You're going to faint, Bobo. Arch will have to get you up off your little Rebel ass with a gallon of smelling salts. All you'll want to do is put your face between those babies, and she's got them, Bobo. She makes Elizabeth Taylor look like she's deformed. And you tell me you've seen women like her? Not on the best day of your life, Bobo. You're from Georgia, for Christ's sake. All you've ever seen are field hands."

"So?" I said. "Some of them are pretty."

"Maybe," Carter replied. He leaned close to me. "But I'm talking beautiful," he whispered conspiratorially. "There's a difference."

"She's very pretty," I admitted.

Carter flicked ash on the floor. He bobbed his head in thought. "I can see it now. In a couple of weeks, you'll be trying to get her to strip naked and pose for you."

"My God, Carter."

"If you do, I want to buy whatever you draw," Carter replied. "You can have the whole damn summer's take on my tips."

"Why are you telling me this?" I asked.

"Because, Bobo, you are going to fall in love with her, and I guarantee that. You're going to cream in your jeans over her. When you close your bloodshot eyes at night, you're going to see her looking at you." He sighed and inhaled slowly. "Yeah, yeah, you will. You're going to be staring at those little aqua-violet sunspots and you're going to want to lick them off her face. You're going to be in love, Bobo. I'm an expert at this sort of stuff, and I watched you tonight. I know the signs. I ought to. Last year, I went through the same thing you're going to go through. But I'm a politician at heart, and I know when to cut and run. You're an artist. You'll never have any sense. But I like you, Bobo. Damned if I know why, but I do, and I've got to warn you: she's got a boyfriend back home, in the big city. Adam. That's his name. He'll probably be up before the summer's over. He was last year. Comes from more money than you'll ever see, and I don't care if you take a tour of the U.S. Mint. But you know what the real pisser is? He looks like a goddamn movie star. When I saw him last year, I folded the tent, and Amy and I became friends. I figured if I couldn't have it one way, I'd settle for the next best thing—just being around her."

"So?" I said.

"So, I just wanted you to know. Don't come around whining, saying I didn't warn you. You're going to be surprised at how right I am." He stood and stretched. "What are you doing, anyway?"

I opened the cover of the writing pad. "Writing Carolyn."

Carter laughed and pulled himself up to the bunk above me. He smoked and giggled and talked aloud about Amy Lourie, talked of her beauty, of the sound of her voice, of the way she touched a napkin to her lips in the dining room. And every time he said her name, I could see her face.

"Yep," he sighed, "that's the kind of woman that scares a man to death. Too damn pretty. Take one look at her and you know you don't have an ice cube's chance in hell with her. Not her."

In my letter to Carolyn, I wrote:

I'm not sure if I can last through the summer with the boy in the bunk above me. He's my busboy. His name is Carter Fielding and he lives in a little town not far from here called Phoenicia, but he stays here during the summer. He says it's because Mrs. Dowling wants him to stay here, but I have a feeling it's because his parents don't want him around. He talks too much and he seems a little girl-crazy, if you ask me, but he's good in the dining room. He's kept me from making a fool of myself a few times. Maybe he's all right. He's just different from the people I know. By the way, if you see Coy, tell him I said he was right about Yankees being all over the place.

Above me, a snowflake of cigarette ash drifted down and landed on my writing pad. Carter said, "Yeah, Bobo, that's the kind of woman that scares a man to death."

The next morning, Nora Dowling led Amy and her parents, Joel and Evelyn Lourie, into my dining room and seated them at a circular table in the middle row. She motioned me to the table and introduced me, as she did with all new guests, telling them—or maybe warning them—that I was from the South, from Georgia.

"Oh, yes, we've heard," Joel Lourie said pleasantly, extending his hand to me. "Our Amy tells us you're quite charming, a gentleman. You must be, or she wouldn't be here for breakfast. She does like to sleep late on vacation."

Amy did not blush. She gazed at me confidently from her aqua-violet eyes and smiled. He black-gold hair hugged her face. And I knew Carter had been right in his assertion: Amy Lourie scared me to death.

At dinner, I sat with Sammy and Lila. The stockbroker and the judge's wife were not in the dining room. "Room service," Lila said with an exaggerated sigh when I asked if they had left. The other two couples were there, seated at a table near the lobby door. Both couples were older, both recently retired and traveling together, according to Sammy. "Taking the cut-rate, senior-citizens' tour of America that they've been saving for since God was a baby," he said. "They're worse than the Japanese. They take pictures of everything that moves. Talk about bored. Can you imagine their families when they get home?"

We had liver for dinner, which was only a slight improvement over the chicken for lunch. Lila cut wedges of apples for us and we drank more wine from the stockbroker's cache. Lila confided they had switched to chilled champagne. "Her choice," Lila said. "It's her turn-on. Give her a couple of bottles and she tries to tear his dinger off."

"Jesus, Lila, don't talk like that in front of a guest," Sammy complained.

"What guest? This is Bobo."

"Is he paying?"

"Of course he is."

"Then, goddamn it, he's a guest."

"And guests need some entertainment," Lila shot back. "Which is exactly what we've got in Hump and Bump upstairs."

"You make it sound like a whorehouse," Sammy mumbled.

"Honey, she ain't charging," Lila hissed. "She's giving. I call that life."

"And I call it a joke," Sammy countered.

Lila laughed cynically. "You would," she said triumphantly. She turned to me. "Am I offending you, Bobo?"

"No, of course not," I said.

"Good." She leaned to Sammy. "Then, you can kiss my ass," she whispered.

After dinner, after the running, word-swatting argument about the stockbroker and the judge's wife, I went with Lila and Sammy to the front porch of the Inn and we sat in padded rocking chairs with our wine, and I listened as Sammy talked hopefully of his Woodstock exhibit.

"All I need is a foot in the door," he said. "I'd sure like to sell something." He paused. "Well, something else."

"You've been selling some pieces?" I asked.

"A couple," Sammy said nonchalantly. "A guy down in Jersey—Vinnie Paulsen—bought a couple of things last winter when he was skiing."

I saw Sammy look at Lila. She pulled on her cigarette and stared at the empty ghost-town street. I knew she heard the accusation in Sammy's voice.

"He said he had one of those modern apartments," Sammy continued. "Said what I did would go perfect in it."

"That's good," I told him. "It's a start, a good one."

Sammy smiled painfully. "I guess. I need all the help I can get."

Lila picked up her wineglass and sipped from it. I wondered if she had bartered with Vinnie Paulsen to buy Sammy's curious sculpture, and if she had, was it for Sammy or for her? I knew she loved Sammy, but I also believed she was lonely.

"So, you're going to let me know if you want the *Old Man* for your service?" Sammy said.

"Of course," I replied. "And that's something I should go up and get started on."

Sammy tried to sound cheerful, but there was begging in his voice: "Just let me know." On the porch, in the rocker, Sammy looked tired and desperate.

"Look, why don't we put that to rest now," I suggested. "I think it'd be nice, having the piece. Something that Avrum would have liked. Let's use it."

Sammy shifted in his rocker. He nodded relief. "You're sure, Bobo? I don't want to push it on you."

"You're not doing that. I'm glad to have it." I stood and thanked them for the wine and the company at dinner.

"The company's our pleasure," Lila said. "You need to thank the stockbroker and his playmate for the wine."

"It's a good vintage. I hope they stay for a week," I replied.

Lila laughed and beckoned me to lean to her for an embrace. She whispered, "Thanks, Bobo. By the way, I've got a little surprise for you upstairs."

I knew the surprise when I saw the two empty champagne bottles at the doorway leading to the suite next to my room: by Lila's arrangement, I would be forced to listen to the stockbroker and the judge's wife making love. I knew that, downstairs, Lila was pleased, and I knew that she would greet me at breakfast with a wink.

I took paper and pen from my briefcase to make notes for Avrum's memorial service, but I knew the notes would be useless. It would be a short, informal ceremony. I would thank those who appeared—if any did—and I would tell them about meeting Avrum, and how our friendship began, and then I would tell them a story I had never told anyone. I did not know what I would say about Sammy's *Old Man*.

I began a letter to Carolyn, but the words were heavy and listless and I wadded the paper and dropped it into the trash can. In 1955, I had written to her daily—at least in the beginning—and she had written to me daily. I wondered if she ever thought of that summer of letters and of the confusion that eventually found its way into my words. The confusion was over Amy Lourie. I could not tell Carolyn about Amy. I had wanted to tell her, yet I could not. And in the years after the summer of letters and confusion, I had often wanted to say to her, "Look, there was a girl in the Catskills. Her name was Amy Lourie . . ." But I knew what Carolyn would say and how she would say it: "Oh, really? And why are you talking about the Stone Age? Did something happen I need to know about?" She would try to say it teasingly, but there would be a touch of arrogance in her voice.

That has been the one constant about Carolyn: she has an answer for every mood, and her answer can be as soft as a kiss or it can be delivered on the tip of a dagger. She permits very little silliness in her life, and maybe that is why our children have always relied on her when they needed protection. She has been—is—the warrior for them, and it did not matter if the foe was a neighbor or an umpire in a Little League baseball game. Carolyn was—is—a lioness in the face of threat against her family, including me. I have heard her bully art dealers who expressed a so-so attitude about my work, even when the work did not impress her.

Still, I think Carolyn suspected something must have happened that summer. In one of her letters, she had asked, *Are you dating anybody?*

I answered with a lie: *No*. I explained there was a group who would sometimes go to a movie or take walks together or meet in Arch's to have milk shakes and to talk. I told her the only date I had had was not a date at all, but a favor for Harry Burger, and he had paid me for the experience. And it was true. It was also the reason that I began to be with Amy.

Harry had been raving about his two teenage nieces, who were to visit him for a weekend. They were beautiful, he assured me. I would be begging to take them to a movie, he predicted, but I would agonize over which to choose. "Angels," Harry sighed with pride. "Like models in great magazines."

Carter knew them. He laughed foolishly and said, "Bobo, you are talking about the two ugliest girls in the state of New York, and, just possibly, the northeastern United States. They were here last year."

"Harry said they were beautiful."

"What did you expect him to say? They're his nieces, and he's Jewish."

"What's that got to do with it?"

"Maybe you haven't noticed, Bobo, but the Jews tend to have a little pride. If those girls weren't Harry's nieces, he'd swear they were freaks from a sideshow, but blood, like love, is blind, boy, blind. Harry thinks he's got Jane Russell and Betty Grable on their way here."

"Harry wants me to take them out," I told him. "He said to find somebody to go with me and he'd pick up the tab."

"And you're asking me?" Carter said suspiciously.

"No," I replied sarcastically. "I thought I'd ask Ben Benton."

"Ben would slit your throat," Carter said. He pondered a moment. "All right, I'll do it, but this is what you've got to tell Harry: twenty bucks apiece, plus expenses."

"I can't do that," I protested. "Not after all he's done for me."

Carter shook his head and laughed cynically. "Believe me, he's been setting you up for this little adventure since day one. That ten bucks he gave you for washing dishes, it was just a down payment. All that waiter training was for one thing: his nieces. Remember, Bobo, I've seen them. Twenty bucks. That's the deal, or find somebody else—if you think you can. I'm telling you, last year every eligible male in a twenty-mile radius went into hiding the weekend they were here. Twenty bucks apiece. All you've got to do is say it to him like you're kidding him. He'll pick up on it. You don't know Harry. He'll go for a bargain like a trout after one of Arch's flies, and that, my friend, is a bargain. Trust me."

Carter was right, as usual. The next day I said to Harry, "We need to talk about this date with your nieces."

"What's to talk?" Harry said irritably. "I offer you a night out with beautiful women and you want I should talk about it?"

"I figure twenty bucks each for me and Carter, plus expenses," I said, grinning.

Harry did his dramatic sigh, the one where he rolled his head and his eyes in exasperation. "*Ach du lieber Gott*," he muttered. He wagged his cigar like a swagger stick. "You're a thief, Bobo Murphy, an Irish *no-goodnik*, but, all right, all right. If I didn't like you so much, I'd find somebody else for two such beauties."

Harry gave me the money up front. He said it was because he was an honorable man. Carter said it was because he didn't want me to renege on the arrangement.

Carter, again, was right.

Harry Burger's nieces were beyond ugly. They were tragic. Thin, pinched faces, no chins, beaver teeth, tiny eyes behind thick eyeglasses. Coy Helms would have said of them, "You'd have to hang meat around their neck to get a dog to play with them."

They were waiting with Harry on the porch of the Inn, having arrived an hour earlier, after dinner.

"Take your pick," Carter mumbled as we approached him.

"I'll take Harry," I whispered.

Carter giggled. "Damn, Bobo, you just did a funny."

"So, boys, you're in good spirits, I see," Harry called cheerfully.

"Great," Carter said.

"Good, good," Harry chirped. He beamed a smile of joy.

We reached the porch.

"Boys, I want for you to meet Charlotte and Erin," Harry said. He indicated the girls. Then: "Girls, this is the Georgia boy I've been telling you about—Bobo Murphy. He didn't know a *schnitzel* from a *schnook* when he met me. Now, he's a waiter." He looked at Carter. "And Carter you know already. He's the one who dropped the fruit cup down your back last year, Erin."

The girls smiled.

I thought: Oh, my God.

"Hi," Carter said brightly. "You still mad at me, Erin?"

Erin tilted her head to Carter, like a long-necked bird inspecting an insect. She shook her head timidly.

"Hi," I said weakly.

"Well, boys, what's it to be?" Harry said in a loud voice. "A movie? A little stroll under the moon, maybe? Yes? Why don't you make the start down at Arch's? I told him you'd be there, to put whatever you wanted on my bill."

"Uh, I—I think we'd better get on to the movie," I said.

"So, what's the hurry?" Harry replied in a firm voice, "No, no, Bobo. The girls love Arch's. There, first."

"Suits me," Carter said flippantly. "Come on, Erin, why don't you go with me? I owe you."

"Sure," Erin said in a small voice. She stepped off the porch to stand with Carter.

"And that leaves lovely Charlotte with Bobo," Harry said proudly. He pushed at his niece. She moved hesitantly toward me.

"Have fun," Harry crowed. He wiggled his finger at her. "No hanky-panky, boys."

Carter coughed down a laugh.

"No, sir," I promised emphatically.

We began the long, tortuous walk to Arch's.

I saw Avrum on his bench. His head was tilted back and his eyes were closed and he was not aware of us. I wondered if he was listening to the ghost-voice of Amelita Galli-Curci, or if he was faking a nap.

Ben Benton was waiting to turn into the side yard of the Inn for his garbage pickup. He looked at me in astonishment, then shouted from the window, "Hey, Bobo, finally found you a woman, did you?" He ducked his head in laughter.

Mrs. Mendelson, slow-stepping up the sidewalk, paused and smiled. "*Gut, gut*," she squeaked.

We walked into Arch's. It was early and only a few people were there. One of them was Amy. She was sitting alone in a back booth, writing a letter.

Carter called to her, "Hey, Amy."

She looked up, first to Carter, then to me. She saw the girls and a shudder of surprise touched on her face. She tried to smile, but the smile faded quickly. She got up and walked past us and out of Arch's. She did not speak.

"Look, girls, why don't you grab that booth back there?" Carter said. "We'll get some Cokes and be right there with you."

The girls dipped their heads in agreement and walked away. Carter whispered, "I think you just screwed up, Bobo."

"What?"

"With Amy. She was pissed. I could tell."

"Why?"

"I was wrong, Bobo. I hate to say it, but I was," Carter sighed. "She's got a thing for you."

"Me?"

We were at the counter of the soda fountain. Carter said to Jeannie Ellis, who was Arch's daughter and occasional counter girl, "Four Cokes, Jeannie, and a pack of Marlboros. Put it on Harry Burger's bill."

"Sure," Jeannie replied. "He was in earlier. Said to give you whatever you wanted."

"Make it a carton of Marlboros," Carter said, "but, Jeannie, do me a favor: make it show up as sandwiches or something."

Jeannie smiled. "Sure." She reached for the glasses on a rack behind her.

"What do you mean, she has a thing for me?" I said to Carter.

Carter looked at me sadly. "You stupid, dumb redneck hick. The most beautiful woman you'll ever see is dragging around like she's got lead in her ass because of you, and you're out with Miss Ugly of Nineteen Fifty-five."

"It was your idea, not mine," I reminded him.

"So, I was wrong again," Carter said. "Sue me. Jesus, Bobo, it's been a year since I saw them. I thought they might improve." He took the carton of cigarettes from Jeannie and tucked them under his arm and then he picked up two of the Cokes. "Come on, let's get this over with."

It was a night I remember only in pain. In a private whisper as we were getting into his car to drive to Margaretville, Carter offered me his twenty dollars to kiss Charlotte—fifty if I would touch her breasts. I told him. "If there's any kissing going on, you can do it, and you know where you can start." He laughed maniacally.

We attended a movie in Margaretville, then drove to the base of the ski lift at Belleayre Mountain and walked in the cool air under a full moon that was like a lamp dimmed for sleeping. Carter told absurd stories about me—that Harry had almost persuaded me to convert to Judaism, that I was a great-grandson of a Confederate general who had fought at Gettysburg and lost his leg, and that my ambition in life was to be a country music star like the great Little Jimmy Dickens. He begged me to sing for them. I refused. "He's shy," Carter explained to the girls. "He knows nobody can understand him, so he doesn't say much." He looked at me and winked and he added, "You'd think his mind was somewhere else, wouldn't you?"

Carter knew.

I was thinking of Amy Lourie.

Amy did not appear for breakfast the following morning. Her parents said she had not slept well. I asked if I could prepare a plate for them to take to her, some muffins or cheese or fruit. "If she wants something, she'll come down," Evelyn Lourie said gently. "But thank you for offering, Bobo." I knew she was watching me carefully. When I served Harry and Charlotte and Erin, suffering Harry's jesting about his nieces being in love with me, I could again sense Evelyn Lourie's eyes, which were as beautiful as Amy's.

At midmorning, I looked from the back window of the kitchen and saw Amy. She was walking alone on the mountain behind the Inn, climbing toward a birch tree where I would often go at night to be alone. I had found the birch on advice from Avrum not long after meeting him. He had said, "Look up to the hill and find you a place, and go to it. Make it yours. Get a tree. A tree is best." I had selected the birch because I could look down on the village and up to the stars. For some reason, it was not so lonely to be there, at the birch, between the village and the stars.

I told Carter, "I need to get away for a few minutes. Can you cover for me?"

"Sure," Carter said. He glanced around the kitchen. Nora Dowling was not there. "I saw her, too," he added. "I don't blame you."

Amy was at the birch, under the canopy of its limbs. I knew she had seen me approaching, but she looked away, as though something in the valley, something far off, had captivated her.

I said, "Hi."

She turned to me. Her face was calm, controlled. "Hello."

"You missed breakfast," I said.

"I wasn't hungry."

I waited for her to say something else, but she did not.

"I like this tree," I told her. "Sometimes at night I come up here and look at the stars."

"I know," she said.

I was surprised. "You do? How?"

"I've watched you."

"You have?"

She said nothing. She sat on the soft grass beside the tree.

"Mind if I sit with you a couple of minutes?" I asked.

"It's your tree," she said.

I sat near her, but not near enough to touch. "It's pretty up here," I said.

"Yes, it is."

"Are you—well, mad at me, or something?" I asked.

"No. Why should I be?"

"I don't know. You act like it. I thought you were mad last night, in Arch's."

She moved her head and the wind caught the thick curl of her black-gold hair and made it flutter across her shoulder.

"How was your date?" she said after a moment.

"Date?" I said. "That wasn't a date. We were with Mr. Burger's nieces. You know that. He wanted us to take them to a movie."

"I call that a date," she said firmly.

"Well, I don't," I countered. "I'd consider it a job. He paid us."

"He did what?"

"He paid us."

"Do you know what that makes you?"

"No. What?"

"A gigolo," she said.

"I don't know what that is," I confessed. "Is it a German word?"

"No, it's not. It's English. A gigolo is someone who gets paid to—to escort women," she explained.

"Then I guess I am one," I conceded.

Amy ducked her head. The sun coated her hair. Her lips puffed into a smile. She said softly, "Bobo, it's not a compliment to be a gigolo, so don't tell anyone you are."

"I didn't know what it was," I said. "First time I've ever heard the word."

She looked at me. The brightness was back in her eyes. She asked, "Are you really an artist?"

"Did Carter tell you that?" I replied.

"He said you were good. Really good, I mean."

"I draw some. It's something to do."

"Will you draw a picture of me?" she asked.

I wondered if Carter, in his disregard for anyone's privacy, had found the pictures I had been drawing of Amy—quick sketches penciled in moments of solitude and hidden away among my things. I wondered if he had told her about them.

"Will you?" she repeated.

"I'll try," I said. "But I'm not very good at faces. Not from memory."

"I'll pose for you," she offered.

I thought of Carter, of the torment that Carter would heap on me. "I don't think that would be a good idea."

"What about a photograph?" she asked. "Would that help?"

I shrugged uncomfortably. "I guess."

"I'll get one for you. It's new, a school picture."

"Okay," I said, "but give it to me at Arch's."

Amy leaned toward me, almost close enough to touch. "You don't want my parents to know, do you?"

I looked away, to the Inn. I could see the old people moving about on the lawn, ambling to tables with umbrellas cupped open against the sun. They would sit and play their games of cards until lunch.

"Do you?" Amy said again.

"It doesn't matter to me," I told her.

"They think you like me, you know," Amy said quietly.

"Well, I—"

"They also think I like you," she added.

I did not know what to say to her. I wanted to reach and touch her hand, to feel her hand living in my hand. I could hear the easy rhythm of her breathing.

"I do," she said gently.

I looked at her. I could feel her mysteriously entering me, slipping past caution. I thought she could also feel it. She smiled at me.

"Would you take me to a movie if my father paid you?"

I could feel my heart rushing. "I wouldn't do that. I'll take you, but not for money."

"I'm glad," she said. There was a pause. "I feel better. Thank you."

In the room next to me, the stockbroker and the judge's wife were making love. She was begging, in a voice muted by the wall that separated us, "Please, please . . . Now, now . . . Oh, yes. Yes, yes yes." There was a sudden, furious slapping of the headboard against the wall. The judge's wife cried once. I could hear her inhale against the pouring from her body. The sudden, furious slapping of the headboard stopped.

I wondered if somewhere, nearby, Lila was smiling and breathing deeply, trying to catch the scent of sex.

I slept, finally, sensing that I was somehow more exhausted than the stockbroker and the judge's wife. I believed I would dream of them, see them as a voyeur watching erotic movies in a dark room. I would peer at them as they caressed and moved over one another like powerful animals at sex play. I would see the oils of their skin shining in candlelight. I would watch their mouths at feast.

I did not dream of them. I dreamed, instead, of Amy Lourie. And in the way of dreams—surreal moments so startlingly clear you know they have happened or will happen or should happen—I was sitting with her in the Galli-Curci Theater in Margaretville and her hand was in my hand, milking my fingers with her fingers. It was two days after being with her at the birch tree on the mountain.

Carter had arranged it in the bold manner that was his personality. A group of us were going to the movies on Tuesday night, he had said to Amy in the presence of her parents as we served lunch. Would she like to go?

"Why don't you?" urged Joel Lourie. "Get away from the old people for a night."

"And who would be going?" Evelyn Lourie asked quietly.

"Just a group," Carter replied. He glanced at me as I served coffee. "Me, two or three others who work at some of the other places around here. Bobo, I think. Are you still going, Bobo?"

"I don't know," I said. "Maybe."

"We do it all the time," Carter added casually and pleasantly. "We never know who's going. Whoever shows up at Arch's."

"Oh," Evelyn Lourie said. She smiled at me. Her eyes lingered, questioning.

"I'd love to," Amy said cheerfully. She did not look at me, but she knew what Carter was doing.

That night, in The Cave, Carter leaned over from his top bunk and said, "I've been thinking about it, Bobo. You owe me for tomorrow night."

"I know. And I'm sure you won't let me forget it," I replied.

"No, you don't know. Not yet," Carter said. "I plan to slit my wrists in front of both of you. You'll be sorry when I'm dead." He leaned back on his bed. I saw a cloud of smoke from his Marlboro rolling toward the ceiling.

"Carter?"

"Yeah."

"Do you think her mother believed it?"

"Believed what?"

"That story you fed her," I said.

"Of course not. She's a mother," Carter answered.

I have never remembered the movie we saw, and even in my dream I knew nothing about it. We were at the theater, holding hands, and then we were walking at the base of the Belleayre ski lift, where we had been with Harry Burger's nieces—Amy with me and a girl named Rene Wallace with Carter. Rene worked as a chambermaid at the Greenleaf Lodge. She and Carter had been dating since the first week of the summer season.

I did not know what happened to Carter and Rene. We were all walking together, and suddenly, they were no longer with us, and I said to Amy, "Maybe I should find them."

"They're all right," she said. "They just want some time alone. Are you afraid of being with me?"

"Of course not. I just wondered—"

"Bobo, it's all right," she insisted softly.

We walked past the gate leading to the ski lift. There was a sharp chill in the air, like the late-autumn nights in Georgia. I thought I heard the call of an owl somewhere from below us. Far off, I could see the feathered rim of the mountains and the murky purple of the horizon under the moon. We passed a hemlock and Amy took my hand and pulled me into its shadows. She said, "I'm cold. Will you hold me for a minute?"

She moved to me and I embraced her. She curled her arms around my waist and rested her face on my chest. I could smell the delicate scent of flowers in her black-gold hair. Her breasts were soft against me.

"This is nice," she whispered. "You're warm."

"You, too," I said.

After a moment, she asked, "Do you have a girlfriend back home?"

I knew it was a test. Carter had told Amy about Carolyn, as he had told me about Adam. Carter loved the entanglements of romance.

"There's a girl I dated when we were in school," I answered.

"What's her name?"

"Carolyn."

"Oh. Do you write to her?"

"Some. Yes, some."

"You must get lonely, being so far away from home."

"A little," I confessed. I added, "It's not as bad as it was."

"Do you think I would like your home?"

"I doubt it. It's just a farm."

"I've never been to a farm," she said. "Not a real one."

"What about you? Do you have a boyfriend?"

She lifted her face to me. "I don't know," she replied.

I tried to be flippant, as I thought Carter would be. "Did you forget?"

A tiny smile, almost a shadow, moved on her lips. "We had a fight before I left."

"Why?"

"He's spoiled. He thinks he can get anything he wants simply because he has money."

"I don't know anybody that rich," I told her.

The smile moved again, off her lips, into her face. "It's nothing special, Bobo. It's just money."

I did not speak and she again nuzzled her face against my chest. "He wouldn't do this," she said softly.

"Do what?"

"Hold me to keep me warm. He'd want to go to the car and turn on the heater. He's not a warm person."

"He'd miss a great view," I mumbled.

I felt her mouth touch my shirt. "Of what?" she asked lightly.

"Well, a lot of things," I replied. "The mountains."

She raised her face and her hand moved from my waist to my neck and she pulled me gently to her and kissed me. I could feel the heat of her tongue tipping my lips and I turned my face away.

"Carter said I would have to kiss you first," she whispered. "He said you would be afraid. Are you? Are you afraid, Bobo? Did I scare you?"

I shook my head.

"Maybe you're not," she said, "but I think I am. I think I scared me."

"Don't be," I begged. "Please—"

She kissed me again, her tongue finding my mouth. Her body trembled. She pulled back and burrowed her face against me. I could feel her heart racing.

"Do you want to date me, Bobo?"

I nodded.

"It won't be easy," she said.

"I know," I replied.

"There'll be so many things against us."

"What things?"

She did not answer. She stood close, holding me. Then she said, "I have something for you."

"What?"

"It's in the car, in my purse."

"Your picture?"

She nodded. "I hope you like it."

"Can I keep it?" I asked.

Her head moved against my shoulder.

"I mean, after you leave?"

Her head moved again.

&

Joel and Evelyn Lourie were sitting on the front porch of the Inn with Nora
Dowling when we returned. I walked with Amy across the lawn to them.

"Well, here they are now," Nora said in a relieved voice. "We were beginning to worry."

"We got a Coke in Margaretville and then Carter had to drive a couple of
the other kids to the Greenleaf," Amy lied cheerfully.

"Did you have a good time?" her father asked.

"It was great," Amy said. She turned to me. "Thanks for letting me tag
along, Bobo."

I was nervous and I knew it was obvious. I said, "Sure. Anytime."

Joel Lourie reached for his wallet. "Well, let me pay for the tickets," he said
in a kind voice.

"No, sir," I replied too quickly. "I couldn't do that."

"But I should," he said.

"No, sir, I really couldn't accept that." I glanced at Amy. She was biting a
giggle.

"Put the money away, Joel," Nora said. She looked at me tenderly. "He's a
Southerner. They're gentlemen. I think, next year, I'll have all Southerners
working for me."

Joel Lourie laughed easily. He slipped his wallet back into his pocket. "I'm
sorry," he said to me. "I didn't mean any offense."

"There wasn't any," I replied. I again glanced at Amy. "See you in the
morning."

"Good night, Bobo," Amy said.

I heard Nora Dowling say as I walked away, "Such a nice boy. So nice."

Carter was waiting for me outside The Cave. He was smoking a cigarette and watching the smoke curl in blue ribbons against the haze of the sky. "Come on," he ordered. "Let's go for a little walk."

I followed him across the street and beside the annex to the swimming pool. We sat in lounge chairs. Carter was in a languid mood and he did not speak until he had finished his cigarette and crushed it against the ground.

"Hell of a night, wasn't it?" he said, leaning his weight against the back of the chair and gazing into the sky.

"Yeah, it was nice," I agreed.

He rolled his head to look at me. "So, tell me: how did you do?"

"What do you mean?"

"I mean, what happened? Jesus, I gave you enough time, didn't I? I almost froze my balls off."

"Nothing happened," I said. "What happened to you?"

"Got my hand on it," Carter chortled. "God, Bobo, it was warm." He paused and whistled softly and twirled his lucky hand in the air above his head. "And wet. I think I'm in love, Bobo."

"I'm glad," I told him. "Look, it's late."

An evil grin crawled into his face. "Yeah, I forgot. You've still got a letter to write, haven't you?"

"What letter?" I demanded.

"To Carolyn."

"Come on, Carter, Don't bring that up."

"A joke, Bobo. Just a joke," Carter said. "Don't be so damned tense. Tell me what happened with the most beautiful woman you'll ever see."

"We walked, we talked," I said.

"That's it?"

"I hugged her."

"Did you kiss her?"

"Yes," I said after a pause.

"You son of a bitch. I hope your tongue falls out," Carter sighed. "Was it good?"

I smiled. "It was nice."

"Nice?"

"Nice," I repeated.

"That's it? Nice? You kiss that woman and you call it nice? Bullshit," he snorted. "Next thing you know, I'll be renting a tux and standing up with you before your preacher brother and some pissed-off rabbi, and you'll be seven months away from being a daddy."

"Don't start it, Carter," I said.

"Okay, okay," he mumbled. "Joke, Bobo. Joke." He laced his fingers in his lap and crossed his legs at his ankles, a pose imitating the old people who used the lounges in the heat of the day. "But we need to talk about something," he added after a moment.

"And what's that?"

"About Amy."

"What about her?"

"I haven't said anything about it, because I didn't think I'd have to, but sometimes, Bobo, you're such a goddamn hick you miss things."

"And what have I missed?" I asked.

Carter again turned his head to me. "That little remark about your brother and the rabbi. I think you missed it."

"What about it?"

"Bobo, Amy's Jewish."

His voice was uncharacteristically deliberate and serious, and it surprised and angered me.

"I know she is," I told him.

He sat up on the side of the lounge, facing me. He rested his elbows on his knees and let his hands dangle between his legs. "Do you know why I want to be a politician?" he asked.

"No, I don't."

"Part of it is because my daddy's a lawyer and I want to take it one step more up the ladder," he answered. "But the real reason is because I think I can read people. It's a little like you when you draw somebody. You see them from the outside, but I see them from the inside, see who they are. I think people who can do that should be politicians or priests, one of the two. I like politics better than pulpits."

"What does all of that mean?" I asked.

"With Amy, it means you know she's Jewish, but you don't know what being Jewish means. Not up here," he advised quietly. "And I'll bet you don't even know what it means back in Georgia. You asked me if I thought her mother believed the story about all of us going to the movies, and I told you she didn't. I meant that. Why do you think her mother's so nervous around you? She knows what's going on, Bobo. I don't know how she knows, but she does, believe me. Maybe Amy told her. But after tonight, she'll be watching you like an eagle."

Carter fumbled for another cigarette and lit it. He fell back into the lounge chair and flipped small smoke rings into the night air with his tongue. He said pleasantly, "Does it get this cold at night in Georgia?"

"Not in the summer."

"Then I think I'll move down there," he mumbled. "I hate freezing my ass off."

"Down there, you sweat it off," I told him. Then I asked, "Carter, what does it mean to you—Amy being Jewish?"

"What it means, Bobo, is that nothing is ever going to happen between the two of you. Nothing more than tonight. Oh, you may diddle with her, and love it, but that's as far as it goes. Some things just don't happen. New York Jew and Georgia redneck, that's one of those things. Not in your lifetime."

I thought of Amy's warning: "There'll be so many things against us."

Part 6

RELIGION

Passover seder at Grossinger's, 1960. Many people came to the Mountains for Passover so that they wouldn't have to kosher their homes. Large hotels like Grossinger's had famous cantors, such as Richard Tucker and Robert Merrill, and large choirs.
MARTHA MENDELSON

Passover seder at Hibsher's Hotel, Liberty. This very small hotel offered a very different kind of seder than Grossinger's.

MELVIN GUNSBERG

Yiddish ads for Catskills hotels, 1956. Even in the 1950s,
many hotels that were not religious ran ads in Yiddish.
CATSKILLS INSTITUTE

The Swan Lake/White Lake shul, 2000. This shul was built by people who lived too far away to walk to the shuls in Swan Lake or White Lake; it is right in between. The style of the façade comes from eighteenth-century Polish synagogues and is found in a huge proportion of the hotels as well.
IRWIN RICHMAN

The Ulster Heights Shul, 1999.
PHIL BROWN

Street scene in Woodbourne, 1998. Most of the stores that remain open in this small town are orthodox establishments, such as this bookstore that is open as late as 11 p.m.   Phil Brown

Hasidim loading furniture bought at Concord liquidation sale, 1999. The Catskills' largest hotel went broke and had a two-month-long liquidation sale. Hasidim were among the many people who furnished bungalow colonies and homes with that hotel's furniture, dishes, and silverware. Phil Brown

סדר

בִּרְכַּת הַמָּזוֹן

הֶחָדָשׁ

עִם זְמִירוֹת לְלֵיל שַׁבָּת.

הַדְלָקַת נֵרוֹת כָּל בִּרְכוֹת הַנֶּהֱנִין, סֵדֶר בְּרָכוֹת
אֵירוּסִין וְנִשּׂוּאִין, סֵדֶר בְּרִית מִילָה, אִיךְ דִיא נָעמָמָן ם
פוּן בְּרִית מִילָה, וּקְרִיאַת שֶׁמַע

GARTENBERG & SCHECHTER'S

Telephone for Reservations REctor 2-0150

Telephone Ellenville 668

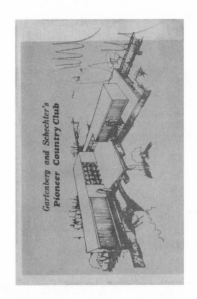

"GRACE AND BLESSINGS

Open from Passover through Succos
Kashrus and Shabbos Strictly Observed

Lebowitz
PINE VIEW HOTEL

Fallsburg, N. Y. 12733 - Tel.: (914) 434-6100
New York City Phone: (212) BRyant 9-3854

Prayer books from two orthodox hotels, the Pioneer Hotel in Greenfield Park and
Lebowitz's Pine View in Fallsburg. CATSKILLS INSTITUTE

Itinerant rabbi looking for food and a place to sleep at the Beerkill Lodge in Greenfield Park, 1930s.
ELOISE KANFER

Eloise Kanfer, whose father built the Beerkill Lodge in Greenfield Park in the 1930s, lent me a photo to copy of an itinerant rabbi who came to the hotel looking for food and a place to sleep. In that fairly typical small hotel, where kosher food was served but the clientele was not orthodox, it was not seen as odd that this rabbi would hang around. After all, if the Catskills was the Jewish resort area, then all the elements found back home—in Europe or New York—could be found there as well. Virtually all Jewish hotels were kosher. Most had at least brief Friday night services, even if not many attended. 'Most every hotel I worked at had wine and challah on Shabbos, and many women lit candles on a special table, often in the card room. Observant orthodox hotels always existed; some still do. And today there are hundreds of orthodox and Hasidic summer camps, bungalow colonies, Yeshivas, and social service agencies. Hatzalah, the orthodox volunteer rescue squad/ambulance service, maintains a full branch there, and their publicly sold road map is the only map to pinpoint locations of hundreds of places. The Catskills was always a very Jewish place during the twentieth century, and for many less-observant and unobservant Jews it was an important source of Yiddishkeit and knowledge about religion.

Given that so much has been written about the Jewish experience in the Catskills, it is surprising that so little has been written about religion. The importance of religion is dealt with in my *Catskill Culture: A Mountain Rat's Memories of the Great Jewish Resort Area*, Abraham Lavender and Clarence Steinberg's *Jewish Farmers of the Catskills*, and Irwin Richman's *Borscht Belt Bungalows*. Hasidic buyouts of hotels are the subject of Eileen Pollack's *Paradise, New York* and Steve Gomer's film, *Sweet Lorraine*, and the actuality of such buyouts is very evident from any drive in the Catskills. But though the dominant population is ultraorthodox Jews, there are no ethnographies or histories focused specifically on that culture.

Robert Eisenberg's "Bungalow Summer," from his collection *Boychiks in the Hood*, is a brief essay about the Hasidic and ultraorthodox communities that now represent the largest aspect of Jewish life in the Mountains. Among the stops on Eisenberg's tour are the Lubavichers' Ivy League Torah Program and a doctor's office at Fialkoff's Bungalow Colony (he doesn't tell us, but there is a wonderful bakery there). He also reports on his visit to Elat Chayyim, the Jewish Renewal center in Accord that used to be Chait's Hotel, where my mother was chef for a decade. Eisenberg's essay ends with a trip to Monsey, halfway back to New York. Even though they are not about the Catskills, I kept those few pages because they make some interesting summary points.

Allegra Goodman's "The Shul at Kaaterskill Falls," from her novel *Kaaterskill Falls*, tells of an ultraorthodox community that has recently established its summer outpost in the eastern section of the northern Catskills. The location is far from any of the Jewish resort areas, and the book makes no mention of the resort industry. Still, for many readers it is informative about the contemporary orthodox culture in at least one part of the Catskills. Goodman's characters are finely drawn, and she has a talent for portraying their psyches. One element in her setting is common to a number of Catskills communities—even though one sect dominates, there are interactions with other varieties of orthodoxy in the shul they all share.

Bungalow Summer:
The Catskills, New York

Robert Eisenberg

In 1969, I was sent to camp a few miles from the Pennsylvania-New York border. A couple of camp maintenance men, who spent their mornings picking up garbage and heaving it onto a truck while chanting "Ho, Ho, Ho Chi Minh, NLF is gonna win," asked me if they could borrow my sleeping bag to take to a rock concert. When I finally saw them a week later, I asked for it back. "Oh, man, we lost it in the mud," was their terse reply. The mud was Woodstock, and this summer, as every summer in the Catskills north of New York City, the hills are alive with the sound of Yiddish. Only this time the Hasidim are looking for solace amidst the ubiquitous signs of Woodstock II.

"Official Woodstock Guide Pick-up Site" announce placards above the cash registers at food and fuel outlets on the New York State Thruway. The guide itself is instructive. "What is love?" an attached coupon asks. "Do you love your music? Do you love playing in the mud with 250,000 strangers? Do you love pizza? Do you love your life? Woodstock '94 and Pizza Hut."

Are the furrow-browed rapacious businessmen who are putting on this brouhaha merely incarnations of the smooth-browed young men they once were, or have they metamorphosed into something new and more ominous? One thing's for sure: The lanky young Hasid, his index finger absentmindedly scratching the base of his beard while he strolls across the lot of a McDonald's at a roadside oasis, could care less. Nor could the two Hasidim in the back of a taxi ferrying them from South Fallsburg, epicenter of the Catskills summer bungalow colony scene, back to Boro Park—a trip that, the cab driver tells me while filling up his vehicle, runs them a tidy $175 each way.

"They're in the diamond trade, you know," the cab driver confides. "Most of them are, anyway. Diamonds may be a girl's best friend, but they are also a cab driver's."

For those with more limited resources, there are bus services such as Emunah, which generally charges $110 per van load, each way, and provides a curtained aisle to separate men and women during prayer services. This can cause problems, and in recent months a Russian émigré by the name of Sima Rabinowicz refused to relinquish her seat on the men's side of the aisle so that they could commence their supplications. She took her case to the New York Civil Liberties Union, which is representing her in court. In the meantime, men who share the bus with Sima have it stop and wait while they debark and *daven*.

At this time of the year, the permanent Hasidic population north of New York City swells from around 20,000 to well over 50,000, as eager refugees from the urban battlefield take up residence in bungalow colonies and retreats, which are often little more than clusters of shacks centered around threadbare quads sprinkled throughout the several-thousand-square-mile area that constitutes the Catskill region. For a family from Williamsburg or Crown Heights, these meager resorts tucked away in mountain hollows amid thick growths of deciduous trees are often the closest thing they will get to a vacation.

Encroaching on the bungalow colonies are a burgeoning number of camps for children and more conventional hotels. Most are modest, but some resorts approach a level of luxury that would meet the standards of even the most jaded traveler. But whatever the mode of accommodation, a certain cadence of daily activity that cuts across all socioeconomic boundaries unites everyone. Most of the day is taken up with study, preparing and eating meals, a bit of idle socializing, with a minimum of organized physical activity, and none of the planned diversions that would be offered at other resorts.

The Catskills and points south, nearer the city, are not only known for the Hasidic influx, but also for the proliferation of New Age retreats. South Fallsburg alone boasts two ashrams, one of which is run by a Jewish swami, and there is the Foundation for the Course in Miracles, a Christian organization with a former Jew at its helm. There is also a retreat center run by a reconstituted group of Jews that sees itself as the next big leap forward in the evolution of Judaism and proudly wears the label of "neo-Hasidic." It is Elat Chayyim, the Woodstock Center for Healing and Renewal, an outgrowth of Rabbi Zalman Schachter-Shalomi's

Philadelphia-based P'nai Or, and it holds seminars on such subjects as "Jewish Liberation Theology" and "Exploring Jewish Prayer" against a picture-postcard backdrop of farmhouses and mountain trails.

Part of an even larger movement called Jewish Renewal, the Woodstock Center and the ideas from which it is spawned have attracted thousands of adherents in recent years. Rabbi Schachter, its central figure, is the Polish-born son of a Belzer Hasid; he grew up in Vienna, where he attended both a traditional *yeshiva* and a left-wing Zionist high school. This eclectic mix produced a singularly iconoclastic and controversial thinker.

Schachter received his *smicha*, or ordination certificate, from the Lubavitch yeshiva in Brooklyn in 1947, having fled Europe via Morocco some years earlier. Afterward he took on a number of assignments, including a pulpit in Winnipeg, and finally ended up in Philadelphia, where he developed nothing less than his own offshoot of Judaism, a new strand of thought whose central objective revolves around making prayer, rituals, and commandments more meaningful to the contemporary spirit.

The father of ten children, Rabbi Schachter—or Zalman, as he is more commonly referred to—has lectured and studied with native American elders, Buddhist lamas, Catholic theologians, and guru Baba Ram Dass. He has been called everything from a charlatan to a saint. As for his being neo-Hasidic, that is something open to debate. "Neo" as a prefix is pregnant with possibilities, and it may or may not apply to the teachings of Zalman. Just as Herbert Marcuse was a neo-Marxist, Irving Kristol a neo-Conservative, and members of Nirvana were neo-hippies, the philosophy espoused by Schachter may be arguably neo-Hasidic. But as far as any strict resemblance to conventional Hasidism goes, Zalman Schachter is to the Lubavitcher Rebbe what the Beastie Boys are to Steve and Edie.

The charismatic troika that runs the Elat Chayyim retreat consists of Zalman, Arthur Waskow, a rabbi out of the Reconstructionist mold from Philadelphia, and a younger disciple of Zalman's, Rabbi Jeff Roth. This is not to suggest that the set-up is in the least bit patriarchal. Most of the remaining positions of responsibility seem to be occupied by women, and the rabbis often defer to them during services.

Elat Chayyim operates out of a rented lodge, Su Casa, situated in the hilly vicinity of Woodstock. The main dining room serves up three sumptuous vegetarian meals a day, which are accompanied by lively discussion and debate. Upon walking into the unadorned mess hall, one is confronted with the sight of perhaps 150 people, most of them Jews in their forties, at least 80 percent of whom are female. At first glance, I feel like I've stumbled onto the food concessions pavilion at a Holly Near festival. Many of the guests, savoring a typical meal of spanikopita, pesto, eggplant parmigiana, and brown rice, seem to be products of the antiwar movement.

The couple I sit next to have between them made it to Woodstock, the Mobilization Against the War demonstration in Washington, and the militant May Day protests. A man across the table from me, who hails from Berkeley, strenuously attempts to convey the Hasidic nature of the movement. Jewish Renewal is true Hasidism, he asserts. It is the New American Hasidism because it incorporates the concepts of pluralism, egalitarianism, and feminism, as well as respect for Native American culture and sympathy for the Palestinians. The latter have suffered more than the Jews, he argues somewhat incredibly.

Most of the women I talk to were present at the beginnings of the feminist movement, and seem in one way or another to have been connected to Betty Friedan or NOW or Kate Millett. They were the shock troops for the SDS, licking envelopes and boiling water, mimeographing leaflets and serving as intellectual punching bags. Now they've come full circle, poring over kabbalistic texts like dedicated Semitic scholars, taking courses with titles such as "Davenen with Your Life: Exploring Jewish Prayer Forms," and "Devikut and Vipassana: An Exploration of Buddhist and Jewish Methods for Transforming Consciousness."

"Lenny Bruce said, If it's bent, it's okay. If it's broken, it's not," a man in the dessert line tells me. "We bend the tradition, but we don't break it." It has to be bent, he argues, or people won't get it. And if they don't get it, he concludes, "We will disappear."

For many, if not most Jews, prayer seems to be an empty, time-consuming experience that leads to random acts of absurdity like hiding Mickey Spillane novels in High Holiday prayer books, or engaging in prolonged and lovingly detailed mental overviews of one's personal financial statement during a sermon. To a sizable plurality of Jews in this country, the Judaism conveyed to them by mainstream institutions is emotionally sterile if not utterly bankrupt. It is an organizational Arnold Schwartzenegger but a spiritual Don Knotts. People are looking for something with emotional resonance, and for many, Jewish Renewal fits the bill. It links prayer to the heart. Ritualistically, though, it is the virtual antithesis of Hasidism. The image of a woman clad in a tie-dyed *tallis*, holding up the Torah with an adulation reserved for a newborn baby, would be greeted by most Hasidim with the same sort of enthusiasm that would be accorded Carry Nation if she walked into PJ Clark's during happy hour.

But this is but a minor ritualistic faux pas in a long litany of contretemps that would send most Hasidic rebbes into apoplexy. So it is not surprising that Elat Chayyim claims to be only emotionally Hasidic, not halakhically so. "We are not a halakhic [legalistically based] Jewish movement," the blissful executive director of Elat Chayyim, Jeff Roth, tells me. Roth, who also holds a master's degree in social work, has a healthy predilection for giving out spontaneous hugs the way John D. Rockefeller handed out dimes.

Roth and I are walking past an imposing set of slogans written in block letters with a black magic marker on a huge drawing pad. It says, "It Is Perfect. You Are Loved. All Is Clear. I Am Holy." This quartet of maxims is a chant of Zalman's, and each phrase corresponds to a different kabbalistic realm.

With an infinite amount of patience, Roth takes it upon himself to give me a crash introduction to Kabbalah. After a few moments, he stops and invites me to a lecture he's giving in the lodge this afternoon. When I arrive, he is passing around a *Shviti*, a framed diagram spiraling in an arabesque fashion around the Hebrew letters יהוה, or yud-hay-vov-hay. This is the tetragrammaton, the ineffable name of God, a name so holy that only the high priest could pronounce it on Yom Kippur, also referred to as Yahweh, or Yehovah.

The Shviti is hung on the eastern wall of a house in order to designate the direction to face during prayer. The term comes from the phrase "*Shviti Hashem L'negdee Tamid*, I place God before me at all times."

Roth tells us to focus on the name for God in the Shviti's center, which bears an intriguing sort of cross-cultural resemblance to a mandala. Jews today, he says, don't even know how to pronounce the name of God, since we don't know the vowel structure of the four letters. Most Jews refer to God as Adonai, which means Lord or Master, but Jewish Renewal sees this as hierarchical. God, Roth emphasizes, is immanent and inherent rather than transcendent. This is in the tradition of the Ba'al Shem Tov, who saw God everywhere.

At Elat Chayyim, God is referred to in prayers simply as "Ya," intriguingly close to the Rastafarian Ja. So old familiar prayers with the name Adonai are replaced by the term Ya, and most everything referring to God is gender neutralized.

When Roth discusses the pronunciation of God's name, I am reminded of yoga breathing. He intones the letters of God's name, YHWH, without any vowels. The first syllable, yeh, is an inhalation, the second, wah, an exhalation.

"One hay is an inbreath, one hay an outbreath," Roth tells me. "The yud, the initial letter, is the empty lungs at the beginning of the process, the vov, in the middle, the straightest letter in the Hebrew alphabet, is like a full balloon, or the lung when it is full. God is a process. Zalman calls it Empty-In-Full-Out. In-Out is the flow; Empty-Full is the form. Breathing in and out is a reciprocal process. We breathe out carbon dioxide, the trees breathe it in. God breathes out into the dust of the earth. We breathe it in."

He points once more to the Shviti, and quotes once again the passage Shviti Hashem L'negdee Tamid. "Shviti's root, grammatically, means to equate, and l'negdee means to negate. God is me and also the inverse of me.

"Another way to look at it," he explains, "is through the yin-yang." You wouldn't hear Manis Friedman talking this way, I think to myself. "The two hays are like the yin and the yang. The yud represents the dots in the yin-yang, and the vov is the line connecting the two. Vov, which means 'and' in Hebrew, links the lower realm of the hay, the physical world—the world of I-it, as Buber called it—to the higher realm of the yud, the world without form, beyond space and time. 'I Am Holy.' That's the yud, Atziluth, the spiritual world, the first letter. 'All Is Clear.' That's the hay, the intellect, when your mind understands the big picture of how God works. 'You Are Loved.' This is the emotional world. The vov links people to one another. It is the Great And. I-it becomes I-Thou, or I-You. Buber called God 'the Great And.' 'It Is Perfect.' This is the second hay, the physical world. So there are four letters and four realms, one for each."

Roth concludes his lecture by repeating his assertion that God is everywhere, and reminding his listeners that this emphasis on the immanence of God puts Jewish Renewal squarely in the lineage of the Baal Shem Tov, who saw the divine in everything. "And like the Baal Shem Tov, our mission is to serve God with joy."

As I look out the huge picture windows at the majestic scenery, my attention is drawn from the realms of God to the pool below. There, a group of mostly nude women, partly obscured by shrubbery, hold hands and dance 'round and 'round while singing *Hinay Matov Umanayin*, an old Sunday school favorite. This is their ritual immersion in preparation for the Sabbath.

Later on it's the men's turn. This time it's the hot tub, where the group of men strip down to immerse themselves. We are told to close our eyes and breathe rhythmically, and to concentrate in sequential order on our head, our arms, our legs, and our genitals, the latter of which "bring us joy and which bring us trouble, which bring us hope, for a continuation of ourselves into the future." Then once again we immerse ourselves, individually and in unison. Our speaker is

Arthur Waskow, who ends the session with the song *Mayim, Mayim, Mayim,* an invocation for rain from Israel's prestate days, usually accompanied by a dance, and a staple of the Jewish summer camp circuit.

That night and the next morning, Sabbath prayer services become impromptu jam sessions, with congregants breaking out instruments and the resident tennis instructor, a former captain of the Stanford team, tooting on his horn as Rabbi Roth strums his guitar. A woman who donated a Torah her family inherited from a Brooklyn synagogue when it closed passes it around lovingly. Another woman announces to the group that her parents gave her an English name when she was born on a refugee boat leaving Genoa for the United States in 1950, and she wants to change it to Haviva, Hebrew for "precious." After a plethora of hugs and a blessing for good fortune and peace from the Berkeleyite, she sits down and the service resumes.

About three to four of the prayers are familiar, the rest being either improvisational renderings or totally original. Even the familiar ones are performed with a creative flair. The *Shema* is repeated four times, once in each direction. Every time that it is said, the participants make two triangles out of their bodies: one below with legs apart and the other above with arms raised up and stretched out. Then they bring their arms down to the ground to scoop up imaginary water and sprinkle it over themselves and each other. A few lines of the weekly Torah portion are read, some in Hebrew but mostly in English, with a fair amount of liberty taken in the translation.

Late in the evening, after Sabbath has ended, I hop in my car to make a run over to the Nevele, a nearby resort where Mal Z. Lawrence, the last of the great Catskill *tummlers,* or comedians, is performing. The Nevele is one of the few resorts left that still regularly features performers who cater to fans of a certain age, Frankie Valli and Tony Martin being representative of headliners. Tony Martin, who until recently I had thought of as some unsavory hybrid of Dean Martin and Tony Bennett, turns out to have sung with Sinatra in the forties.

The Nevele is a fading complex just outside Ellenville, a few miles from the Jewish Renewal retreat. It could easily serve as the backdrop for an Efferdent commercial. Everyone here looks in some way related to Albert Shanker. Gaggles of Italians who are dressed like extras for the *Goodfellas* nightclub scene and Jews who know every self-deprecating phrase in Yiddish and flaunt it with abandon circulate throughout the lobby.

The building itself is reminiscent of an Intourist hotel somewhere deep in the interior of the Soviet Union. Watermarks discolor the chipped marble foyer, and the furniture is straight out of the fifties, conjuring up images of Meyer Lansky's Havana Riviera congealed in time for eternity by Castro's benign neglect, its doorknobs and towel racks capable of sending any Melrose Avenue retro furniture dealer into an acquisitory frenzy. The carpet is a kaleidoscopic undergrowth of nausea-inducing swirls, and a big brass plaque affixed to the wall reads "President and Mrs. Lyndon B. Johnson slept here, August 19, 1966."

I step into the ballroom and take a seat. A waitress abruptly orders me to move my chair and walks off muttering, "Rude, rude, rude." Soon the curtains open and the MC announces that Alan King will be appearing next week. An old man one table over shakes his head excitedly and says, "Forget it."

Opening for Lawrence is a chanteuse who warms the crowd up with a little Bob Seger sung at a tempo that would put Barry Manilow to sleep. She then segues into a passionate "One Moment in Time" ("Seize that one moment in time/Make it shine"), which must be her anthem.

Then the baldheaded Lawrence comes out, looking like a cross between an aging coke dealer and a real estate syndicator in Newport Beach. He *spritzes*, or lets loose, with the requisite quota of *alter kocker*, old geezer, jokes, including a hilarious send-up of a Yiddish-accented retiree on a CB. Then he launches into a series of Hasidic one-liners. "This is the Hasidic capital here. Right here in the Catskills. Woodbourne, just down the road, has a restaurant called the Glatt Spot and a shop called Mendel the Tzitzis Rebinder. He'll repair them for you, corn row them for you, or make them out of leather so you can flog each other with them. Two T-shirts I bought at the souvenir stand there. One was a Hasid with a revolver. It said 'Make My Day.' The other said 'Lay T'fillin, Not Hookers.'"

After another hour or so it's over, and I follow him backstage. I shake his hand and on my way out overhear him saying that he's been married twice, once to an Italian and the other time to a WASP. Clearly, he's not going to win any awards for promoting Jewish continuity. Even if he is exaggerating, though, Woodbourne sounds intriguing.

The next day I cruise into the town of Woodbourne, which turns out to be a three-block stretch of bustling businesses catering to the summer visitors. There is no Glatt Spot or Mendel the Tzitzis Rebinder, but there is a Glatt Gourmet, a

Netzach Yisrael Take Home Food Store, and a Woodbourne Cholov Yisroel Pizza and Falafel, right down the street from picket fences and colonial houses. There are also two bookstores, one manned by young yeshiva students from New York and the other displaying posters of prominent rebbes for sale in the window like so many baseball stars.

As families push strollers up and down the main strip, I wander into a grocery store and ask an enormous Satmar who could pass as the lead singer for Canned Heat if he could tell me how many bungalow colonies there are in the area. He waves me off and lumbers over to the frozen food section. "You want to know anything, get a Hatzoloh map from the bookstore, it lists everything," he says over his shoulder. Hatzoloh, the nonprofit Hasidic emergency service based in Brooklyn, has ambulances all over the Catskills. It operates with volunteers and does not restrict its services to Jewish clients.

The Jewish bookstore itself, besides having a healthy selection of religious texts, also has on display large numbers of memoirs, including one by an Orthodox former U.S. Army lieutenant who helped liberate Buchenwald. One of his wards was the Klausenberger Rebbe, to whom the lieutenant attributes the most moving sermon he's ever heard.

The rebbe, who lost his wife and all eleven of his children in the war, got up on the pulpit the first Yom Kippur after liberation and listed his sins in the traditional confessional prayer, answering to each of them. We have stolen. But what was there to steal? We have spoken idle words. But we didn't have the energy to speak, only to listen to the orders of our tormentors. We have coveted. Maybe we coveted the slop thrown to pigs when all we had to eat was watery soup. But in the end, we thank God for giving us life and continue to have faith.

I ask the proprietor of the bookstore if he has a Hatzoloh map, and he produces one. Sure enough, it lists over 500 camps, bungalow colonies, resorts, and retreats, ranging from Karnofsky by the Lake to Chai Manor, from Breezy Acres to Zupnick's, spread out comfortably over a twenty-mile radius in and around towns like Hurleyville, Ellenville, Mountaindale, Dairyland, Ulster Heights, and Liberty, to name a few. And as if this cultural dissonance weren't enough, different Hasidic groups that aren't always the best of friends, like the Belzers and the Satmars, are within close proximity to each other, with the modern Orthodox and non-Orthodox European Jews thrown into the mix. Then there are the locals, whose own religious affiliations and ethnic origins span a broad spectrum in their own right. Just outside Woodbourne, for example, is Camp Emunah for

Girls and Camp Shearith Hapletah for boys. Not far away, the Woodbourne Reformed Church, established 1802, stoically surveys the whole scene.

Even though Woodbourne is a small town, the influx of Hasidim has given it a congested urban feel. Windows of the Jewish establishments have inimitably Brooklynesque notices clinging to them: "Lice bugging you? We check hair and clean heads for camps, bungalows, and private parties. We are the experts fully equipped to retrieve these pests from your head. Call Avigail and Yehudis" and "Morah Chanie Kinder Palace. Your child will be loved and cared for the way you'd like in a clean, warm, friendly, and Heimishe atmosphere." There is a leaflet advertising the services of the "Mezuzah Doctor. This doctor makes house calls." And a political poster urges the freeing of jailed Jewish settlers. "Shmuel was arrested," it proclaims above the picture of a fierce-looking Israeli in a knitted *yarmulke*, "under administrative detention orders by the Rabin Government. After the present additional three-month detention order, the Rabin government can renew three- to six-month orders over and over. Write to Yitzhak Rabin. Ask him why he releases thousands of convicted Arab terrorists, while Jews who have never been charged or convicted of any crime languish in Israeli jails."

Until the Jewish stores close up shop every year around Labor Day, the town fathers who occupied the original pews of the Woodbourne Reformed Church are probably doing rotisserie turns in their graves. But maybe not. Without the annual influx of Hasidim, the local economy would fall apart.

In the center of town, one of Woodbourne's few African-Americans, whose parents came here years ago to work at the once glamorous but now fading resort of Grossinger's, collars me near a pay phone and asks me if I'm Jewish.

"Yep," I reply.

"But you're not religious. You're like us."

"Pretty much," I tell him.

"You eat pork, don't you?"

I shake my head back and forth. Then I ask him what he thinks of the Hasidim. They're different, he says. Different from the Jews who used to come up here. "But they're okay. They cheap, though. Always wanting something for nothing. You tell the people they cheap. But they're good people."

The founding families would not be the only ones shocked by the transformation that their town has undergone. Early German Jewish settlers who wanted so much to fit in, with formidable names like Baer, Lowenthal, and Lewinsohn, would strongly disapprove of the Eastern European riffraff. Most of their descendants have probably been absorbed into the general population by now, but a few of them are no doubt students at the Ivy League Torah Program I stumble on while driving out of town on Route 42. Situated on a side road called Synagogue Way, the program, run by the French-born Lubavitcher Rabbi Jacob Goldberg, takes in students from all over the world who are taking their first steps toward full observance of the *mitzvot*. Rabbi Goldberg, in his late forties, leads a class in Chassidus, or Chabad mysticism, in a deep Yiddish accent and with no small amount of humor. When I wander into the classroom he urges me to sit down.

"A mitzvah," he is telling the class, "stays with a person always. An *averah*, or sin, if you do repentance, goes away and can be erased." He touches on the notion of *Mitzvah HaBah BeAverah*, or doing a sin in order to perform a mitzvah, and asks for examples. Stealing an *etrog* to use for Sukkot services, someone volunteers. Stealing money to give to charity, another interjects. The teacher nods approvingly. Stealing to perform a mitzvah is worse than stealing to put it in your own pocket, he inveighs.

I decide to try my hand at this. Fresh from Elat Chayyim, I don't lack for possibilities. What about a woman wearing a tallis on Shabbos so she can pray better, I ask. That's okay, he replies, so long as she is wearing clothes underneath. Everyone laughs. How about playing guitar on the Sabbath to heighten the mood? I persist. Where did you hear about this, he demands. Elat Chayyim, I mumble, like Beaver Cleaver finking on Eddie Haskel. And I suppose they use microphones on Shabbos, too? Sure do, I say. He does a passable imitation of a folk singer strumming his guitar to an imaginary woman in a tallis. Everyone cracks up. *This* is a Mitzvah HaBah BeAverah, he proclaims, somewhat pleased by my example. "Playing a guitar on Shabbos, using a microphone—better you don't go to *shul* at all." He hits the table hard with his hand. "What is this Elat Chayyim?" he demands like an inspector administering an interrogation.

"It's Zalman Schachter-Shalomi's institute."

"*Oy a broch*. What a pity. Schachter was a very smart man," he laments.

"*Meshuggeh off's toit!* Crazier than a loon!" a Hasid in a corner of the room bellows out.

"No, not crazy," says Goldberg, "just confused. A Lubavitcher. Ordained by us. He began on the right path. Then he started making changes. First he wanted blue tzitzis fringes, not white. That's okay, some Hasidim have one or two blue strings on their tzitzis. Then he decided his tallis should be multicolored because in the Kabbalah there is the concept of *Tifereth*, the merging of colors. Each color has a different attribute—red is strength, white is love—and a person should balance and mix these attributes together to make a proper combination of them in the *neshuma*, the soul. Schachter took this concept and materialized it. Also okay, but a little strange. Nowhere in the law, mind you, does it say not to do this.

"Then he started descending," Goldberg continues. "First with the finger cymbals during prayer, then mixing Jewish ideas with those of priests, Indians, Japanese. Eventually, he divorced his wife and married, I think, a Chinese girl. He ruined his family. He was a rabbi in Winnipeg and now he's a . . . a . . ." He momentarily loses his thought.

"And what happened to his children?" someone asks.

"I don't know. One became like a *goy*, I think. Another is totally *hefker*." Hefker is the ultimate put-down. It means wild, unruly, outside the fold. Goldberg obviously means it as a sign of pity.

"*Neboch*," a shame, he finally mutters. The dozen or so students, ranging from a recent Columbia graduate to a senior at State University of New York at Binghamton, with a Brazilian and a couple of Californians thrown in for good measure, listen attentively. "Okay, let's get back to work!" he barks. I take this as my cue to exit.

Ten weeks in the Catskills isn't cheap. A simple bungalow runs $2,000 to $3,000, not including food or transportation. And this is just a run-of-the-mill colony. There are luxury resorts like the much-talked-about Vacation Village in Loch Sheldrake, where the families of accountants and diamond merchants languidly push baby carriages along the lake. The accommodations there consist of modern townhouses. Whatever the colony, though, men usually stay in the city and come up for weekends, unless they are employed by one of the local institutions.

I drive over to Monticello, the main city of the Catskills. Off to one side is a road sign in Yiddish pointing the way to the offices of Dr. Tova Rosen. A woman doctor in a Hasidic community is not unheard of, but it is highly unusual—limited to those who have become religious. Her clinic is situated in a modest house on the periphery of a bungalow colony named Fialkoff's, which caters to a non-Hasidic but Orthodox crowd.

Fialkoff's has 110 bungalows and an Olympic-sized swimming pool, which Mrs. Adler, the owner, invites me to visit. It is the end of the men's daily swimming session, and as I walk through the gate a yeshiva student from Detroit, whose parents became religious twenty years ago, blows on a whistle and orders everyone out. In the main part of the resort, families pass their time lounging at picnic tables, reading, laughing, or nibbling at food, while the younger children play in the sand or on swing sets. Across the street from the colony is a kosher pizza stand and a bakery, the latter owned by a Satmar couple who are in their mid-twenties and already have five children.

Dr. Rosen's house at Fialkoff's is a whitewashed double-decker with a modest gate in front. A downstairs window, adjacent to her examining room, also has a sign with her name in Yiddish. It lights up. I walk into the office and find a *balbatische*—a person of healthy proportions—woman in a navy blue denim dress propped on a swivel chair talking on the phone. She motions to me to sit down. After she hangs up, she begins to talk to me as if she's known me all my life. She's a doctor in Williamsburg most of the year, she tells me, but this summer she's experimenting with an office in the Catskills. In the city, most of her customers are Satmars. She herself is a *ba'alat teshuvah*, having become religious in the distinctively unfashionable period of the early sixties when she was barely in junior high school, well before the phenomenon took off later in the decade. She went to live in Brooklyn with some religious grandparents, leaving her nonobservant parents on the Upper West Side behind. After attending Bais Yaakov girl's high school in Boro Park and getting a B.S. from Long Island University, she went to the University of Tampico in Mexico, where she got her medical degree. It was a pigsty, she tells me. The anatomy lab was a cesspool—you'd rather use a fish hook to retrieve organs than to touch them. Then she came back and opened a clinic in Williamsburg.

She praises the Satmars, even though she isn't one. "They're really into *tzedakah*, charity," she says, and when it comes to taking care of the sick, "to strangers they're better than family." As she goes on and on about the Satmars, a Hasidic woman stands in the doorway shaking her head. The phone rings and Tova answers it. "Don't listen to her," the religious woman, apparently a patient, says. "My sister married a Satmar and they treat women like *lochs*, holes. They walk all over them. Into tzedakah?" she asks rhetorically. "They're into screwing the government!" She relates a food stamp counterfeiting scam for which the perpetrator was sentenced to several years in prison but ran off to Israel instead. "Now he sits, he learns, on his $3 million. He's waiting for the—what do you call it—the statute of limitations to run out so he can return."

While the doctor is busy on the phone, she continues. "I never met one who didn't take advantage. Food stamps, ADC, Section 8 housing, you name it—and that's just the millionaires. They own eight houses but they get welfare. Taxes? They don't know the meaning of the word. They put all their assets in one big kitty—a yeshiva fund—and borrow on it. That way they avoid income and inheritance taxes." I'm glad Dr. Rosen is on the telephone, because if she heard this it would no doubt set off a huge verbal conflagration. "They have black Jews—*Schvartzes*, they call them. They're not really black. They're Satmars. Black sheep is what they are. They smash windows, overturn buses."

"How come?"

"Who knows? Who knows what they fight about? They use the black Jews to collect money from each other."

As she finishes off with the dramatic flourish that there is no law in Williamsburg, that Satmar is the law, a delivery man from UPS walks in with some medical equipment and hands it to Tova. She hangs up the phone and thanks him. "You better get ready for the onslaught," he says. "They're expecting 250,000 kids up here next weekend. They say the parking area alone will be twenty-five square miles." Tova assures him that she intends to spend Woodstock weekend in Boro Park.

As he leaves and the woman in the doorway disappears, a well-dressed matriarch in a queenly turban comes into the office and sits down. "Ah, Mrs. Polakoff," Tova greets her. "I have the IV ready." Mrs. Polakoff is here for a vitamin infusion for her Epstein-Barr. Her husband, now retired, was one of the administrators at a Satmar camp up the road. There are four camps, actually, serving thousands of Satmar children. Her camp alone prepares between 2,000 and 3,000 meals each day, four or five times a day.

The children sit and learn from nine to noon and from three to six. Otherwise, they play. "Baseball?" I ask. "Heavens no, maybe the Vishnitzers, but not us. They sit, they swim, there is a creek for fishing." "They fish?" I am somewhat taken aback. "Not exactly," she replies. "They watch the goyim fish." As she is having her IV hooked up, she tells me that camp tuition is according to income, that there are no TVs or radios present, but there is air-conditioning and telephones. Everyone studies: not just the children, but also the staff and visiting parents.

Dr. Rosen talks about the lice problem at the camps. As Mrs. Polakoff sits there, vitamin solution dripping into her hand, blissfully oblivious to my conversation in English with Dr. Rosen, three boys walk in who don't know a word of English either. They won't begin to learn English until they are eight, Tova tells me. They are the children of the Satmar couple that run the bakery across the street.

The doctor treats only women and children. Occasionally, a man comes in, and she's willing to see him, "but most wouldn't see me for more than a hang-nail. Something like prostates is out of the question." She does a lot of fertility treatment and deals with communicable diseases that arise from the close prox-imity of her patients to one another. Hepatitis is a perennial problem, as is sal-monella. Eighty or 90 percent of the clients are on Medicaid, but she won't ac-cept their cards. It's too much of a hassle. So she deals mostly with insurance companies. Much of her time is taken up with paperwork because she doesn't even have a nurse or assistant. The season starts on June 28 and everyone goes home on Labor Day, with the exception of some yeshivas in South Fallsburg, Mountaindale, and Woodridge, which are open all year round. After the season, she will go back to Williamsburg, where much of her services are performed on credit, and she has an accounts receivable list that would be the envy of most small businesses. But being a woman has its problems. A male physician tried to bully her into sharing office space with him, and the husbands of some of her pa-tients lean on her to alter invoices, ostensibly to inflate their insurance settle-ments, but she steadfastly refuses.

Mrs. Polakoff, her treatment complete, gathers her purse and prepares to board a cab back to her camp. I ask her where it is. Outside Ellenville, she says. Ellenville, isn't that where the Nevele is? Oh yes, she replies, but in the forty years she's been at the camp, she's never been to it. "But I do remember one thing. Years ago, thirty, maybe forty, President Johnson and his wife slept there."

On my way out of the mountains and back to New York, I stop in Monsey, the biggest suburban year-round settlement of Hasidim outside the city, a town with perhaps 20,000 Orthodox of every stripe. It started with a single *kollel* in the early fifties. I decide to pay a visit to Rabbi Moshe Tendler, one of the leading figures of modern American Orthodoxy, much criticized in some Hasidic sectors. He is a professor of biology at Yeshiva University, a well-known bacteriologist, a lead-ing bioethicist, and the head of a congregation in Monsey. Taking the shot-in-the-dark approach, I call him from a few blocks away and he agrees to meet me at his home the next day.

When I arrive, his son, a bearded Yale law school graduate, leads me into the basement study. After about ten minutes, Rabbi Tendler appears. I tell him I'm here to gauge the modern Orthodox response to the explosion, both demographically and qualitatively, of Hasidism in this country, and to ascertain, exactly, what is the difference between the two groups. Amid books on the ethics of medical experimentation, euthanasia, and the Talmud, he tells me there is no such thing as modern Orthodoxy. "There are only the halakhically observant and the nonobservant," he says, "and we are just as observant as Hasidim." But, he concedes, "for survival purposes, you can't top the Hasidim." He relates a little-known phenomenon that the only Orthodox in the Soviet Union who retained their practices were the Lubavitchers. "They kept their coats, their hats, their tzitzis. They drank only Cholov Yisroel milk and baked their own bread. Can you imagine doing that for several generations? And you know why they survived?"

"Why?"

"Because people thought they were crazy. Stalin didn't bother with them. The Talmud says not to pay any special attention to a crazy person. And Stalin, *takeh*, for sure, ignored them. So when *perestroika* dawned it turned out that there were several thousand Lubavitchers, all over the Soviet Union, and they came out of the woodwork."

Tendler admits that there are differences between the two, the modern Orthodox and the Hasidim, but they are rooted in custom rather than law. "In the Midrash, it is said that the Jews managed to survive 210 years in Egypt without losing their identity for two reasons: because they didn't change their language and they didn't change their dress. They had portable ghetto walls. Today it's Yiddish and long cloaks."

To Tendler, this is the crux of the difference between the modern Orthodox and their ultra-Orthodox brethren. But what about the study of secular subjects? The modern Orthodox, after all, are perhaps more disproportionately represented in the professions than any other group in America.

"Satmars come to me with ethical questions—issues of fertility, for example. They need professional advice. And I myself asked Rabbi Aharon Kotler just who will fill these roles if the Orthodox won't? We are the doctors, lawyers, and ethicists for the Hasidim."

Yeshiva University offers degrees in the humanities, but relatively few students major in them. For future lawyers, it's political science, for others, it's the physical or biological sciences, or the rabbinate.

"A Hasidic girl will willingly enter into *shiduch* with a boy from Yeshiva University, but only if the boy wears a hat," he says, referring to the black-rimmed Fedoras of the Hasidim, not the knitted yarmulkes of the modern Orthodox. And apparently, more and more of the modern Orthodox are donning this sartorial symbol of unflappable piety. Moreover, only a distinct minority of Yeshiva University students, according to Tendler, go to movies anymore. A decade or two in the past, movies were much more acceptable, as they still are with older modern Orthodox Jews.

Other outward indicators also point to a shift to the right. The wearing of tzitzis by men outside the pants, once a spotty practice among the modern Orthodox, is more common than ever, and wigs among married women are prevalent.

The move to the right is even reflected in a narrowing of disparate birth rates between the Hasidim and the modern Orthodox. Even though a large number of modern Orthodox find birth control pills acceptable—the rationale being that it doesn't involve a blocking of sperm traveling to the egg because with the pill there is no egg—average modern Orthodox family size is climbing steadily. Whereas a generation ago the modern Orthodox would consider it a novelty for an older couple to have, say, thirty grandchildren, today this is far from uncommon—Tendler himself has forty-six, at the relatively tender age of sixty-eight.

What are some of the other differences between the modern Orthodox and Hasidim, aside from the former's involvement in the professional world? I ask.

The real difference, according to Tendler, is of an ethical nature. "When Hasidim get into trouble, when they do something against the law, they hurt all Jews. If you're going to look like a Jew, if you're going to dress like a Jew, then act ethically," he says, assuring me at length that there are plenty of ethical Hasidic businesspeople, but the few rotten ones make everyone look bad.

The other major criticism of Hasidim by the modern Orthodox involves Israel. "Hasidim don't send their children into the army," he complains. "Halakha demands you defend Eretz Yisroel with your life. Israel feeds and protects the Haredim. The aggressive denigration of a country that does this is wrong. Even Rabin and Peres, who are far from being heroes in our eyes, have helped Torah study to flourish. We owe the Israeli government just like we owe the United States."

Tendler has no doubt about the future of Orthodoxy in America—to him it is onward and upward. But as for the rest of American Jewry, the other 90 percent, he is not nearly so optimistic.

"The Reform thought they'd dance on our graves, but sadly, we'll dance on theirs." I express doubt over this, saying that the majority of Jews in America have not been religious for over seventy-five years, yet they have retained their identity. He reminds me that intermarriage poses new obstacles. "The Reform did one thing wrong. They abolished *gittin*, the Jewish divorce. This makes the offspring of all second marriages into *mamzers*, and mamzers and the descendants of mamzers cannot marry Jews who are not mamzers. Everything will be mixed up, we won't know who is who, and the two groups—the Orthodox and the Reform, will be forever separated. They have cut themselves off from the rest of the Jewish people.

"We are not doing enough to bring them back," he exclaims. "There are Jews in the next town, outside Monsey, who don't identify, who don't give to United Jewish Appeal, but they'd send their kids to our yeshiva—not because it's Jewish, but because of the public schools. But the tuition is $4,000 a year. We need a massive infusion of funds for scholarships, because once we have them as students, we have them for life."

When I tell him that it seems to me that the major differences between the two groups of Orthodox are receding and there appears to be a general shift to the right, he begs to differ. "The modern Orthodox will always be separate because we have a strong aversion to the cult of personality that is focused on the *tzaddik.*"

That part may be true, but overall I am not so sure. With the emergence of tzitzis, of an unwillingness to eat even a salad in a nonkosher restaurant, of an aversion to movies and television, the gulf between the two groups is narrowing. Will we live to see the day when the Hasidic juggernaut swallows up the modern Orthodox like so many minnows, and any differences between the two will be strictly superficial? That day, Rabbi Tendler assures me, will never come.

The Shul in Kaaterskill Falls

Allegra Goodman

The Kaaterskill shul is an old, steep-roofed clapboard building, prim and white. It was built long ago for a Reform congregation, but in the past twenty years the synagogue has filled with Orthodox vacationers. Its arched windows frame men davening in dark suits and black hats.

Elizabeth and the girls walk through the vestibule, where only the racks of wire hangers and an abandoned blue scarf remain of winter. The paneled synagogue is narrow but deep, with rows of long, high-backed benches cushioned in red plush. A mechitza of polished wood and glass separates the men from the women. In front, in the men's section, the seats surround a raised bima fenced with newel posts like a dark porch railing all around.

Sorah and Brocha are still little enough to sit with Isaac in the men's section. It's not sitting they like, though—it's running back and forth. They squirm their way between the dark-suited men to the front wall where the ark stands, its red velvet curtains decorated with gold tassels and lions embroidered in gold thread. Above the ark hangs the ner tamid, the eternal flame encased in red glass. The girls tilt their heads back and dizzy themselves looking all the way up at the embossed tin ceiling, painted robin's-egg blue. Back and forth Sorah and Brocha wriggle between the tall dark rows of men. They like the bima best, because it's in the center and it's crowded. Sorah pushes her little sister in front of her, and the two of them work their way over to the dais, where they grasp the base of the railing and look at the polished shoe tips and trouser cuffs in front of them.

Whenever the reading stops and the Torah rises above them, they look up expectantly. Maybe old Mr. Heiligman will see them; maybe he will give them candy from his blue velvet tallis bag. Small, thin lollipops or sour balls. Either way the choices are orange, red, green, purple, or yellow.

Elizabeth and the three older girls sit in the front row of the women's section. Chani daydreams, siddur open on her lap, while Malki bends over her prayer book, catching up on what she missed by coming late. Ruchel is neither quiet nor industrious. She's leaning forward, blowing the curtain on the mechitza to make it flutter against the glass, rubbing the velvet chairs back and forth with her fingers so the nap stands up rough and then slides down smooth. Elizabeth scans the room for Cecil's wife, but she doesn't see anyone new. She turns to her Tanach and follows the Torah reading. She cannot see the men on the bima, but she knows them all by voice. There is the rich bass of the Hasidic rabbi, Reb Moshe Feurstein, and then Rav Joseph Butler with his strong, slightly acerbic tenor. And then reedy Pesach Lamkin. Although much younger than his colleagues, Pesach Lamkin is the official rabbi of the synagogue. Every summer the shul is full of great rabbis, exacting and learned men who come up to the mountains with their own constituencies. In order to avoid disputes and interrupted vacations, they chose Lamkin to officiate in Kaaterskill. Young, pious, inexperienced, he was likely to offend the fewest people.

Rabbi Lamkin is well liked, but the synagogue hushes as Elizabeth's own rabbi, Rav Elijah Kirshner, reads from the prophets in his precise baritone. Rav Kirshner was the first of all the rabbis to come up to the mountains, and he has hundreds of followers in Kaaterskill. Just after the war, the Rav decided his community should migrate in the summers. In 1938, just before Kristallnacht, they had left Germany en masse from Frankfurt, and resettled in Washington Heights. Then, in the fifties, those with reparation money bought summer houses together in Kaaterskill. The Rav is a grandson of Jeremiah Solomon Hecht, the founder in Germany of neo-orthodoxy, who wrote in his elegant and stylish German, arguing that the generations to come should study science and languages, law, and mathematics—and yet none of these could come before religious law. Rav Elijah Kirshner was born in 1898, only ten years after Hecht's time, and it is said his mother was Hecht's favorite daughter. He earned a doctorate in philosophy at the University of Frankfurt am Main, and then rose to take his grandfather's place. Rav Kirshner brought Hecht's books and his community to America—only a small part of what there once was, but a remnant that he has guided and strengthened. He has founded the Kirshner school and the yeshiva, sustained his people in Washington Heights, even now in the battered parks, the narrow alleyways. The Rav is an extraordinary man. And famous. He knows the mayor of New York, has led prayers in the state legislature. *The New York Times* calls him "the Reverend Doctor."

As usual, at the end of the service, one of the Landauer boys sings the hymn "Anim Zmiros." There is always a Landauer boy to do this, as each succeeds to the position when he turns eight. Isaac watches in the men's section as Avromy Landaur pulls the gold cord and opens the ark curtain for his brother. In their small dark suits they look like miniatures of their father. It is always quite a contrast, the little boy—just a pipsqueak—singing at the front, and the spectacular thirteenth-century poetry, the reedy voice singing the mystic love song to God: *Anim zmiros, vishirim erog, ki elechah nafshi tarog.* . . . I sing hymns and compose songs/Because my soul longs for thee./My soul desires thy shelter,/To know all thy mystery. . . . Landauer's son rattles off the verses. It's like a kazoo performance of Beethoven.

Isaac has always liked Joe Landauer's sons, but his own daughters laugh at them and their nasal voices. The girls pretend they can't tell the Landauer boys apart. After the service, when everyone is talking, crushed together, trying to get out, Isaac says to Elizabeth. "That was a good job Boruch did with '*Anim Zmiros.*'"

And Chani says, "No, that was Yakov-Shloimie."

And Ruchel contradicts, "It was *not* Yakov-Shloimie. It was Avromy. I recognized his voice!" Then they start giggling among themselves.

Near the door, Elizabeth and Isaac catch sight of Cecil Birnbaum with his sister, Regina. Cecil is wearing his old blue suit and wire-rimmed glasses, and he has a vaguely dissatisfied look. His parents, of blessed memory, were pillars of the summer community and the synagogue, but in ways Elizabeth can only marvel at, Cecil has become a gadfly and a malcontent in Kaaterskill.

"Mazel tov," Isaac says.

Elizabeth looks around for Cecil's bride. "Nu, where is she?"

"Oh, Beatrix doesn't come to services," Cecil says grandly.

Elizabeth smiles. Cecil likes to shock people, but she's known him since their first summer in Kaaterskill five years ago and she is used to him. "When did you get back from England?" she asks.

Before Cecil can answer, they are both crushed against the wall as the crowd parts for old Rav Kirshner. Seventy-eight and frail, the Rav is borne forward by two of his nephews, one on each side. His thin hands rest on his nephews' arms—his pale fingers translucent skinned against their dark suits. The Kirshners pull back the children in the Rav's path.

The crowd closes up quickly behind the Rav. There are many Kirshners in

Kaaterskill, but they mill about in shul with Hasids and their little boys with peyyes, modern Orthodox, with wives in hats instead of sheitels. There is even a Conservative rabbi named Sobel, who is revered by no one in the synagogue but Cecil, who shows him the utmost courtesy, partly out of real respect, and partly in order to pique his orthodox neighbors. Rabbi Sobel is struggling to get out in the crush of people, and Cecil holds the door for him. "He walks over here every week," Cecil tells Elizabeth after he passes, "and no one gives *him* the time of day. This is a world-renowned historian—"

Elizabeth doesn't hear him. She is staring after the Rav and his entourage. There, in that mass of black hats and jackets, is a man in a cream suit. It is, unmistakably, Jeremy Kirshner, the Rav's firstborn son. Jeremy Kirshner, Dr. Kirshner, as he is called, is an enigma. He is a rabbi, like his brother Isaiah, but he works as a professor at Queens College. No one speaks about him. If his name comes up, people just say one thing—"He never married, you know"—and they leave it at that.

"Did you see him?" Elizabeth asks Isaac as he joins her.

"I couldn't tell who it was," says Isaac.

"Oh, that was Jeremy Kirshner," Cecil says. "Why?"

"Nothing—just, he never comes up here," says Elizabeth.

"But he came to see me," Cecil says with a flourish.

"I didn't know you were friends," says Elizabeth. It astonishes her.

"Yes, we are friends," says Cecil, "despite the fact that I'm a commoner."

The old Birnbaum house stands alone, set back from the street. Years ago, when Cecil's parents bought the place, they planted the rosebushes on the side of the house, and dogwood trees that now overhang the front walk. Taller than the tall house stands the silver spruce tree, planted when Cecil's sister Regina was born.

"Welcome, come in," calls Regina to Elizabeth and Isaac and their daughters. The girls hang back on the porch, but Elizabeth and Isaac enter the shadowy living room. They see that they are the first to arrive at the party. "This is Beatrix," Regina says, "—from England, like you, Elizabeth."

Beatrix is a thin woman in a sleeveless dress. A mass of coarse black hair falls stiffly around her shoulders. "Hello, very pleased to meet you." Beatrix innocently puts out her hand to Isaac, who draws back. "Don't you shake hands?" she asks.

Quickly Elizabeth shakes her hand instead. She and Isaac sit on the couch, careful not to brush the bunch of wildflowers lying on the coffee table.

"I picked these this morning." Beatrix lifts up the bunch of goldenrod. "I'm going to put them here. What do you think?"

She props the flowers in the twin vases standing on the piano and pours in water from a long-spouted watering can.

"Beatrix," Elizabeth ventures after a moment, "I think it's coming out the bottom."

"What is?" Beatrix lifts one of the vases to check, and a stream of water along with the flowers courses out onto the Steinway.

"They're ornamental vases!" Regina calls, rushing from the kitchen with a dish towel. "Cecil. Could you bring me another rag for the piano?"

"Not on Shabbat," he answers precisely. "I never touch the piano on Shabbat."

"You see, they're ornamental," Regina tells her sister-in-law again as she sponges up the water. "They're from the thirties. They don't have bottoms."

"Oh," Beatrix says. Then she laughs. "How frightfully bourgeois!"

When the other guests arrive and Regina begins to serve, Elizabeth wishes Isaac trusted Cecil's kitchen. "How about some meringues?" Regina offers. "They're just eggs and sugar." Elizabeth hesitates, but then declines.

More than fifty of Cecil's neighbors fill the house. Jeremy Kirshner, however, is absent. Elizabeth looks at the dining-room table set out with Linzer tortes, rugelach, and cheesecakes, an apricot jelly roll, and miniature Danish. There are lattice-crust pies on the sideboard under the freshly dusted painting of a ship tossed in a violent blue-green sea.

"I cleaned this week, of course," Regina tells Elizabeth. Regina has a wry way of talking, although she is much gentler than her brother. She wears glasses as he does, but hers have stylish tortoiseshell frames; her skin is fair and her hair curly and almost red. She doesn't cover it. She is the only person Elizabeth knows who actually lives in California. Regina tells Elizabeth, "I decided the house couldn't wait for Cecil and Beatrix to pass into a domestic stage."

"No, Cecil is more interested in gardening," says Elizabeth. "But you do the house justice." She has never seen it like this—silver polished, Persian carpets vacuumed.

"Well, you didn't know my mother," says Regina. "She really kept at things, and she decorated. She had the eye for it. She had a gardener who paint-ed these flowers up here." She points to the plaster flowers that serve as upper moldings for the walls. "And she picked out the green and gold colors for the dining room."

"That's right," says old Esther Ergman, who knew Regina and Cecil's parents. "And you, Regina. You have to come up and take care of it."

"Not now," Regina says, with a funny little grimace. "They left it to Cecil, not to me. I can't come up and pick up after him. Believe me, it's exhausting. One of these days he'll have to struggle along with his own vacuum cleaner."

Esther asks Elizabeth, "Do you know what Regina said about her brother when she was a child? She said, 'Cecil, you are a monstrosity.' I remember when she said that. She was just a little girl wheeling her doll's carriage in front of my porch, and she wore a little leather purse on her arm—the sweetest thing. And what she said was absolutely true. He was a little imp, Cecil. And if you ask me, he still is."

Elizabeth has noticed this about Cecil and Regina: Though they are in their thirties, both professors at universities, when they return to Kaaterskill, they carry the reputations they had as children. It doesn't matter that Cecil is a learned scholar, expert on modernism and Shaw. Nor does it matter that in his way he is strictly observant. He's still a little mazik to the old people. They haven't forgotten when he lost control of his bicycle and crushed old Friedman's flower bed. And in just the same way Cecil's sister, the research oncologist at UCLA, will always live in the old-timers' memories as the girl with red curly hair and the wicker doll carriage.

"No one since her mother," Esther tells Elizabeth, "—no one else makes rugelach like this."

"I'd like to have the recipe," Elizabeth says.

"Oh, it's very simple," says Regina on her way to the kitchen. "But I've got to go back to L.A. tomorrow. You should watch it being done. And there's a secret," she calls over her shoulder.

"Really?" Elizabeth asks.

Regina disappears behind the swinging kitchen door, and her voice floats out. "Don't overwork the dough."

Elizabeth moves back to the living room, where Cecil and Beatrix stand at the center of a large group of people, Isaac among them. "There is no sign on the synagogue," Beatrix says. "Doesn't it have a name?"

"Of course. But not as good a name as the old one," Cecil says.

"What old one?" asks Joe Landauer, the father of all the Landauer boys in their miniature black suits and hats.

"Ah," says Cecil. "You betray your fleeting residence on the mountain. The original shul, which was Reform, was built by old man Rubin in the 1880s on Bear Mountain, to serve both Bear Mountain and Kaaterskill. And it was called Anshei Sharon."

"Why People of Sharon?" asks Cecil's wife. "How very odd."

She knows Hebrew, Elizabeth thinks. How is that?

"Well, the founders got confused. They thought *sharon* meant 'mountain.' They tried to change it later, but the incorporation papers were filed already, and Judge Taylor refused to bother with them. No, it wasn't our Judge Taylor. It was his great-uncle. But he was a Taylor, so he wouldn't change the papers. Now in due time the shul founder, Rubin, fought with the people in Bear Mountain and moved to Kaaterskill. And he took his shul with him. He put it on rollers and shlepped it down the mountain on a sledge with his team of oxen."

"Cecil, how do you *know* these things?" asks Joe.

"Anyone a resident for over thirty years knows this," Cecil replies airily. "When Rubin deposited the shul in Kaaterskill, naturally he renamed it—and the Bear Mountain shul got a new name too."

"*And?*" asks Beatrix.

"Well, that's the end," Cecil teases.

"But what were their *names?*" his wife demands.

"Oh, that should be obvious," he says. "What are all breakaway synagogues called? Rodef Sholom—because they're seeking peace. And what are all the parent shuls renamed? Sharei Tzedek!"

"Gates of Righteousness," Beatrix cuts in. "Because they were *right!* Of course."

Elizabeth whispers to Isaac, "He's really in love. I've never seen him let someone run away with his punch line before."

The children are feasting on the porch where the grown-ups have left their hostess gifts of Barton's candies. There is a huge selection piled on the green wicker sofa and chairs. Chocolate truffles, cherry creams, bitter mints. The Landauer boys are plastering caramel over their front teeth. The girls move to the other side of the porch in protest.

"Let's go look for snakes," Chani says. She jumps off the porch rail, and her sisters and Esther Ergman's two granddaughters run after her. They run down the little hill at the side of the house and into the acre-deep back garden. Small green apples squeak and mush underfoot as they race over slippery pine needles. They skid around the spruce tree. Hot and out of breath, in their fancy dresses, they run all the way to the unmown grass at the ragged edge of the garden. The girls are wearing scuffed white patent leather shoes, dresses printed with bouquets of flowers, lockets and big sashes, white piqué collars.

Overgrown blackberry bushes separate the Birnbaum and the King lots. White currant bushes and red. Scraggly old raspberry canes. There are no snakes, but the blackberries cluster in the brambles, shining dark and heavy as carpenter bees. Ruchel and Sorah stand in the Birnbaums' blowsy garden with its tall grass and old-fashioned lilac arbor, and they stare at Mr. King's new swimming pool, surrounded by cement and striped lounging chairs. Just yesterday Mr. King yelled at them and Pammy Curtis for eating his blackberries. Admittedly they ate a few. The girls want to go play somewhere else, but they can't stop looking next door. Mr. King's pool is dazzling, an unearthly aqua blue.

Then the girls hear raised voices coming from Mr. King's painted aluminum utility shed. Two men come out arguing onto the terrace. The girls can see them clearly above the bushes. Mr. King, broad and tall, and red in the face. And Mr. Knowlton, a much smaller man, Lark's father from across the street.

"You are never working for me again," says Mr. King.

"Why?" demands Mr. Knowlton, "because I took some extra flagstones?"

"Extras! Knowlton, I hired you to lay down my deck, not your chimney! I'm going to prosecute this."

"You're paranoid," Mr. Knowlton says. "Curtis badmouths me, and you believe it."

"Paranoid? I don't have to listen to Curtis when I can *see* across the street that you've been building your chimney with my flagstones."

"Who said—"

"I don't want to hear it," King snaps. "You can tell Taylor in court." Then he turns and sees the bunch of girls staring at him. He doesn't say a word, because they don't give him a chance. Instinctively, like rabbits, the girls run away, back through the tall grass, past the spruce tree, and up the slippery apple-littered hill.

In the house Elizabeth is asking Beatrix, "How is it you know Hebrew?"

"Oh, I learned it one summer in Israel."

"You must be clever with languages," Elizabeth says. "What sort of mathematics do you practice?"

"Differential topology and things."

"It does sound interesting," Elizabeth says.

"I shouldn't think so," Beatrix demurs. "Not for most people. Who's at the door? Oh, Jeremy!"

The front door opens and Jeremy Kirshner walks in. "Mazel tov, mazel tov," he says to Cecil and Beatrix. "And my apologies for being late." He wears a straw hat with a jaunty air, as if he were going to a garden party in a Renoir painting. He is perhaps forty.

"Good to see you, Jeremy," says Beatrix, "Are you staying all weekend?"

"No, no, I'm leaving tomorrow, early in the morning," he says. "I have to go back for the Summer Institute."

"We should introduce everyone," says Regina, intervening as hostess. "Andras and Nina Melish. Saul and Eva Rubinstein. Philip and Maja Cohen. Esther Ergman, Elizabeth and Isaac Shulman, Joe and Leah Landauer," she goes around the room. "Jeremy was at Columbia with Cecil," she explains.

"But he's my colleague now," Beatrix says lightly. "So you should really say, he is at Queens College with Beatrix." Then she tells Jeremy, "You shouldn't do institutes in the city. You should do them here. It's so much prettier. Much cooler."

"But no one wants to come up here," says Jeremy.

"No, it's just that you don't want to," Beatrix says, and all the satellite conversations in the room dip down a little. They seem to dim. Cecil grins; he loves this kind of thing, creating a frisson, a slight static in the air, a storm warning. Cecil loves watching Beatrix in Kaaterskill, sharp and intellectual, asking questions with all her pointed, worldly innocence.

Jeremy stiffens, surrounded in the living room by his father's followers and their friends. On the couches and on the chairs they sit dressed in their plain clothes, their straightlaced finery. Jeremy Kirshner looks at them with his dark eyes and clever, intent face. He has a young face for his age. He wouldn't look forty, except that his watchfulness gives him away. There is something concentrated and even a little hard about him. He affects a kind of nonchalance in the way he sits and speaks, but he does not carry it off completely. He is self-assured, but he is also studied. He is a specialist in Castiglione and in Renaissance courtly handbooks.

"Well, I'm going to have lots of mathematicians up," Beatrix says, "and we're going to do research under the trees. I'm going to hold a Kaaterskill mathematical institute. Right here."

Jeremy says nothing to this. Regina offers him coffee and a plate of rugelach. He takes one. His father's people are pretending not to look at him, eating food made outside the community, pastry from Regina's alien hands. They are pretending not to watch him taste the crushed nuts and cinnamon, and he is pretending not to notice them watching.

"Dr. Kirshner," Elizabeth says, "if you do come up again, do you think you might be interested in speaking—"

"Speaking?"

"Yes, giving a drash for our ladies' shiur," Elizabeth says.

"Well, if I were here," Jeremy says. He speaks as if from a great distance. "If I had something to say."

Elizabeth blinks. It is as if he were asking her, And who are you? Of course, she is no professor. There is a feeling with Cecil, and even more with Beatrix, of a kind of brisk and academic egalitarianism, as if in their house anyone can say anything. Elizabeth forgot for a moment that it is only they who really can say anything. Cecil is very strange. And his wife, too, with her strange sleeveless tunic of a dress, her loose hair, her Oxford ways. Knowing Hebrew without going to shul. Cecil and Beatrix cast a kind of spell. All the rules are different with them. It strikes Elizabeth that Beatrix and Cecil are so different from the Kirshners she lives with that she doesn't even disapprove of them. Ironic that last summer she was appalled along with all the other Kirshners that a woman from shul was seen in trousers in the park. But if Cecil's wife drove her car down Main Street on Shabbat, Elizabeth wouldn't be shocked at all. It really would be quite natural for Beatrix; it wouldn't be offensive in the same way.

"But what do people do here?" Beatrix asks again. "What is there to do? Besides eat rugelach, of course." She flashes a smile at Regina, who looks stoic.

"Go hiking," Cecil says.

"Play badminton," Elizabeth suggests.

"Oh, badminton, I love it!" Beatrix cries with real enthusiasm. "I'm appalling now, but I used to play at home. It was my only game at school, and I used to practice madly, to show I was proficient in *some*thing physical, because I was hopeless for their ghastly hockey teams. I've found a net, you know, in the cellar, and we could set it up in back. It's still light out. We could chalk the ground. I could do it this afternoon while you're up there praying."

"You could wait till Sunday. Then I'll help you," Elizabeth says, alarmed at the thought of causing Beatrix to transgress.

"Not at all," Beatrix says. "Division of labor. Leave it to me. Leave it to the secular arm." And she stretches out a sinewy bare arm.

When the long day ends and the evening settles over the trees, the men walk back to the synagogue for services. The women sit in their glider rockers and their porch swings and they look into the fading light and talk. They talk about their children and their husbands and the traffic from the city. They talk about berry picking, the blackberries now in season and the blueberries to come. Then they lower their voices so the children will not hear. They speak of Israel and the hijacking of the Air France flight. The hostages in Uganda. The talk of politics mixes with the scent of roses.

Elizabeth sits with Regina on Cecil's porch. "Can't you stay a little longer?" she asks.

"No," Regina says, "I have to get back to the lab."

"Tell me about California," Elizabeth says.

Regina smiles. "Why don't you come out and see for yourself?"

"Oh, I don't think I'll ever have a chance to go to Los Angeles," Elizabeth says. "Tell me what it's like to live there."

"What do you want to know?"

"What's the Jewish community like?" Elizabeth asks. Her question sounds parochial, but it isn't meant that way. She asks out of intense curiosity. She wants to know what it is really like to live there, and so she tries to imagine herself in that place, a part of that community.

"We live in the Pico Robertson area," Regina says. "On a beautiful flat street with palm trees."

"All lined with palm trees?" Elizabeth asks.

"Yes," says Regina, and she looks out at the great trees on Maple, and the tiny jagged pieces of sky cut out between the leaves.

"And where do you daven?" Elizabeth asks.

"In a synagogue that used to be a movie theater."

"No!"

"Really. It's a grand old movie palace with the lights and the curtains and everything. And the women sit in the balcony. The name of the shul is outside on the marquee. And believe me, there isn't any coatroom like there is here."

"No one wears coats?" Elizabeth asks.

"Maybe light jackets in the winter—or a sweater."

Elizabeth laughs in delight. "You must love it there."

"No," Regina says. "I love it here."

Part 7

FOOD

KRAMER'S
On Luzon Lake
HURLEYVILLE, N. Y.
Good Morning!

BREAKFAST

FRUITS

TOMATO JUICE   STEWED FIGS
GRAPE FRUIT   STEWED PRUNES
GRAPE FRUIT JUICE   ORANGE JUICE
BAKED APPLE   PRUNE JUICE
MELON IN SEASON

APPETIZERS (Hot)

BAKED HERRING   FRIED HERRING

APPETIZERS (Cold)

PICKLED HERRING   MATJES HERRING
SMOKED SALMON   PICKLED SALMON

HOT CEREALS

OATMEAL   FARINA   WHEATENA

DRY CEREALS

CORN FLAKES   BRAN FLAKES   ALL BRAN
PUFFED RICE   PUFFED WHEAT   SHREDDED WHEAT
CRACKLES   GRAPE NUTS FLAKES   PEP   KIX
SHREDDED RALSTON   RICE KRISPIES   RICE FLAKES
WHEATIES   RYE KRISP   WHEAT KRUMBLES

EGGS

BOILED ANY STYLE   FRIED   SCRAMBLED
SHIRRED   POACHED ON TOAST
SCRAMBLED with ONIONS or SALMON

OMELETTES

PLAIN   JELLY   CHEESE   ONION

HOT DISHES

GRIDDLE CAKES   FRENCH TOAST

PRESERVES

ASSORTED JAMS and MARMELADES

CHEESE

CREAM CHEESE   AMERICAN CHEESE
and COTTAGE CHEESE

BEVERAGES

COFFEE   POSTUM   COCOA   TEA   MILK

Breakfast menu from Kramer's Hotel, Hurleyville. CATSKILLS INSTITUTE

The SHA-WAN-GAZETTE

GOOD AFTERNOON
ALL YOU LOVELY PEOPLE

COCKTAIL PARTY - at 6:15
IN THE LOWER LOBBY

Canapes, hors d'oeuvres and
liquid refreshments will be
served.

This afternoon at 3: P. M.
there will be a Softball Game
for men. All stout hearted
males report to the ball field
at that time.

Winners of last night's very
entertaining Dance Fiesta were:
   MARILYN FRUITSTONE - Jerk,
   Monkey, Frug - Aw forget it!
   SOL LEDERMAN - Pachanga
Other fine contestants were:
   ROSALYN NEVINS - Cha-Cha
   JEAN SMUCKLER - Cha-Cha
   BETSEY COHEN - Merengue
   MICHELE MASSLER - Jerk, etc.
   ROZZIE GROSSMAN - Frug, etc.
   CHARLES KRUGER - Cha-Cha
   LENNIE GINIGER - Fox Trot
   HARRY RAFTEN - Charleston

There is a Canteen in the lower
lobby. Newspapers and sundry
articles can be obtained there.
Have you tried a pleasant hour
of boating on the lake? We
have a fine fleet of aluminum
boats at your disposal.

   TONIGHT'S SHOW:
   BROADWAY VARIETY REVUE

And don't forget folks, rain or
shine, there'll be something
doing all the time throughout
your stay at Sha-wan-ga.

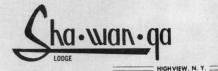

LODGE   ═══ HIGH VIEW, N. Y. ═══

Good Afternoon!

ENPIRE STATE APPLE JUICE
V8 VEGETABLE   APRICOT NECTAR

OLD FASHIONED GREEN SPLIT PEA SOUP, CRISP NOODLES
CHILLED BEET BORSCHT, ROMANOFF
   HOME STYLE SOUR GRASS SCHAV, SLICED HARD BOILED EGG
   CLEAR CONSOMME, WITH CAROLINA RICE

CHOICE OF:
   BROILED EASTERN HALIBUT STEAK, SAUCE CARDINALE
   OPEN HOT PASTRAMI SANDWICH ON RYE, COLE SLAW
   BAKED EGG PLANT STEAK PARMIGIANA, LAKE COMO
   OVEN BROWNED EGG BARLEY, STEWED FRESH MUSHROOMS
   BROAD NOODLE CHARLOTTE, HOT FRUIT SAUCE
   GRILLED DANISH HAM STEAK, GLACED PINEAPPLE RING
   ASSORTED SPRING GARDEN VEGETABLE PLATTER,
                              BAKED POTATO
SNOW-WHIPPED POTATOES   BUTTERED BROCCOLI SPEARS

COLD PLATE SUGGESTIONS:
   FRESH LOUISIANA SHRIMP SALAD PLATTER, GARNI
   SPRING SALAD WITH FRESH VEGETABLES & COTTAGE CHEESE
   HEAVY SOUR CREAM WITH SLICED BANANAS, SLICED PEACHES,
         COTTAGE CHEESE OR FRESH CHOPPED VEGETABLES

PEACH MELBA SHORT CAKE   FRENCH CREAM CHEESE SLICE
            SUNSHINE SPONGE CAKE

         *   *   *

COFFEE   TEA   MILK
   CHOCOLATE MILK   SANKA   POSTUM

Saturday, June 5, 1965

JACQUES P. MORGANSTEIN, MAITRE D'
YOUR MAITRE D', MR. NORMAN ELMONT

Breakfast: 8:30 to 10:00 A.M.   Luncheon: 1 P.M.   Dinner: 7 P.M.
It is the desire of the management to give you the utmost in service.
We would appreciate your cooperation by coming into
the dining room promptly for meals.

Lunch menu from Sha-Wan-Ga Lodge, High View, 1965. Lunch and dinner menus were often full of activities
and entertainment information.   CATSKILLS INSTITUTE

Dining room staff at Kutsher's Country Club, Monticello, 1956. IRA GOLDWASSER

Sylvia Brown, chef at Chaits in Accord, 1970s. PHIL BROWN

F ood dominated life at the hotels. Huge meals of great
variety were the Catskills signature, and the source of
much analysis, humor, and deprecation by guests, dining
room staff, and comedians. Busing and waiting provided the
largest number of jobs for upwardly mobile youngsters.

Sarah Sandberg's "Eating at the Hotel" comes from *Mama
Made Minks*, one of several books she wrote in a very chatty
style, almost like serialized magazine articles. This excerpt gives
an idea of the richness of the meals both in the dining room and
in the napkins that delivered food back to the guest rooms.
Sandberg's furrier family also used the dining room as a place to
parade new minks and recruit customers.

Elizabeth Ehrlich's selection, "Bungalow," is unique in its
focus on eating in bungalow colonies. This is not much of the
lore of the Mountains, since the wives were doing all the cooking and were not likely to provide the massive feasts found in hotels. The piece is a chapter in *Miriam's Kitchen: A Memoir*, a very
tender book that follows Ehrlich's relationship with her mother-
in-law, Miriam, who teaches her how to cook while reliving her
life experiences in the Holocaust and since. In Miriam's bungalow, people eat well, all the classic Jewish dishes. Ehrlich recounts

an interesting Catskills bungalow colony tradition of collective meals of delicatessen or smoked fish on Saturday night in the casino. At the only bungalow colony where my father ran a concession, I remember well this kind of event. We supplied the food—especially rye bread and pastrami, roast beef, and corned beef that my father sliced at the very last minute—and mixers at a per-person price, and the residents brought their own beer or liquor. This is a wonderful example of how food binds people together.

Vivian Gornick included "The Catskills Remembered" in her book *Approaching Eye Level*, and read it at one of the History of the Catskills Conferences. Gornick recounts the difficulties of being a waitress in the Catskills, where waiters predominated. She portrays the competition among the waitstaff, the tension between them and their guests, and the conflicts they had with the maitre d.' This is definitely the harder end of the dining room life, but nevertheless it is true to life. For those in the know, Gornick's fictional names are vividly recognizable—her Stella Mercury employment agency was in really Annie Jupiter's, a New York City agency that supplied many of the hotels.

Eating at the Hotel

Sara Sandberg

Equally unchanging was the summer resort we patronized, Pasternack's Palace (Father had originally been attracted to it by its name) in Fallsburg, Sullivan County. Irving driving, we would join the Fourth of July exodus to the mountains, not to return *en famille* (Irving would drive Father up for weekends) until after Labor Day.

We needed that nine-week vacation to recuperate from our trip.

In those days, motoring to the Catskills required almost as much fortitude as following the old Oregon Trail—and, it often seemed, practically as much time.

The Holland and Lincoln tunnels, the George Washington Bridge, were in some Utopian future. There was, inexorably—aside from swimming with full pack—only one way to get from New York to New Jersey, through which we had to pass. That was by ferry.

The waiting lines would stretch, on holiday weekends, halfway, it would seem, around the world. We often waited two hours to make the twenty-minute crossing. The entire journey, to Fallsburg, took about eight—if you were lucky.

Those were trips that tried the souls of men—especially the souls of the Sandbergs, who were cowards to begin with. We would hold our breaths and pray while Irving negotiated, with our outmoded Cadillac's aging brakes, the sharp, lofty curves, the terrifying ascents and descents, as we alternately climbed and coasted down the mountains, our hearts pounding, our brakes burning.

Only the visions of the rural delights awaiting us at Pasternack's Palace sustained us throughout this ordeal. This was long before the fabulous era of Grossinger's and the Concord, of stage shows, swimming pools, and social directors. Catskill hotels were invariably bedizened with highly euphemistic names—Glick's Mansion, Mandelbaum's Manor, Spitzer's Floral House, Moscowitz's Mayflower Inn—but most of them were actually farms to which a boardinghouse had been appended.

As a result, every rustic joy was ours, the anticipation of which—as the houris awaiting him in Mohammed's Paradise sustain the Arab—enabled us to endure the shattering trials of those trips.

Visions—when we discovered Irving had made a wrong turn and we were hopelessly lost, with less than a gallon of gas, in some primeval wilderness—of swinging languorously in hammocks under the trees until we grew nauseous . . . of taking gay, itchy rides in the hay wagons 'neath a romantic Fallsburg moon . . . of drinking milk, warm and sweet and full of bacteria, straight from the cows; of eating eggs, raw, fresh from the chickens.

Visions—when we got a flat and found that our spare, too, had a flat—of crossing a meadow full of morning glories and daisies and black-eyed Susans, which Goldie and I wove into garlands as we plunged toward our destination, the Nevasink River, in whose crystal-clear depths we would thrash about, wearing black cotton bathing suits and long black stockings and supported by water wings because we weren't completely sold on that Nevasink claim.

Visions—when our motor overheated in the bumper-to-bumper traffic and we broiled under a searing July sun waiting for it to cool off—of doubles and triples of wonderful, indigestible foods. These were my family's visions—not mine. For me they were a nightmare. Mother, always one to prod my meager appetite, would now—since each meal had to be paid for whether it was consumed or not—literally stuff me.

"Sara, you hardly touched the borscht—that you never tasted anything like it in your life!" Mother would use the same hard sell on me that proved so successful in the store.

"Mother," I would plead, "I ate half of it."

"Yeah, but with not a drop of sour cream—and with only one potato!"

She would seize my bowl, fill it to overflowing from the pitcher of sour cream which, like pot cheese, was a staple of every mountain hotel, toss in two more jumbo potatoes.

"Here, *fargrinte*, eat—that you look like you're passing out from consumption!" Any child of that era, to be healthy, had to be fat. If you were skinny, as I was, your life was considered to be hanging by a thread.

"Mother, I can't!" I would protest piteously. "I'll vomit!"

"Force yourself. You'll see how you'll stretch your stomach."

Since Mother did not have the business to attend to and eating three huge meals a day was the chief pastime at the hotel, she was able, to my grief, to give the matter her complete, undivided attention.

My plates seemed bewitched. As quickly as I emptied them they seemed magically to replenish themselves. And how often, when she thought I wasn't looking, did I catch Mother pouring the milk from my glass and replacing it with straight sweet cream!

"Just watch how lovely Goldele eats!" She would beam as my sister consumed, like her parents, an appetizer of chopped liver, stuffed *derma*, or *gefilte* fish; chicken soup or *borscht*; boiled *flanken*, pot roast, or endless variations of chicken; plus side dishes of potato or *lukshen kugel, tsimmes, holishkas, kasha varnishkas*; to say nothing of dill pickles, sauerkraut, and pickled tomatoes—and, naturally, a little fruit, like stewed prunes or figs; followed, of course, by dessert: apple strudel, honeycake—meals that, more than the persecution of two thousand years, have made the survival of the Jews a miracle!

Not only did my family stow away at table banquets that resembled the last meal of a condemned prisoner, but whatever might be left over Mother would wrap in a napkin, stash away in the huge purse she carried for this purpose, and nonchalantly bear off to her room—"in case we should get hungry for a snack in between." You could find almost anything in Mother's room—ranging from Bing cherries to half a chicken.

Visions—when we finally arrived, our clothes sticking to us like Scotch tape, every bone, especially the ones we sat on, individually aching, and discovered that the valise containing all our shoes had been left behind—visions that varied for each one of us in kind. . . .

Visions for Goldie of new boys to be captivated: bellboys, bus boys, guest boys.

Visions for Irving of new girls, ditto: chambermaids, waitresses, single girls who were looking, married girls who were looking.

Visions for me of fresh fodder for my fevered imagination. That elderly man who looked so distressed—mightn't he be suffering, not from gallstones, as he glibly explained, but from some searing secret sorrow?

Visions for Father and Mother of getting a desperately needed sojourn in the sun, of new friends to be made—new customers.

Our summers were not only pleasant but profitable. Mother, who attracted friends the way an empty seat draws mangled straphangers at rush hour, would distribute her business cards to each new acquaintance as she tenderly bade her *adieu*. In due course, practically every one of them would appear at the store, as though by posthypnotic suggestion, for a new coat, a "remodel," a collar and cuffs, storage.

I shall never forget the unvarying sign that our summer idyll was coming to an end.

"Sandberg," Mother would say that last week, with a catch in her voice at the thought of parting with all her friends at Pasternack's Palace, "Sandberg, when you come out for the weekend—don't forget to bring our cards!"

The Catskills Remembered

Vivian Gornick

I have never been able to think of the old Catskill Mountains hotel circuit as the actual setting for all those borscht belt jokes. For me, a college student waitressing in the late fifties, the Catskills was a wild place, dangerous and exciting, where all the beasts were predatory, none pacific. The years I spent working in those hotels were my introduction to the brutishness of function, the murderousness of fantasy, the isolation inflicted on all those living inside a world organized to provide pleasure. It's the isolation I've been thinking about lately—how remarkably present it was, crude and vibrant, there from the first moment of contact.

I walked into Stella Mercury's employment agency one afternoon in the winter of my freshman year at City College. Four men sat playing cards with a greasy deck, chewing gum methodically, never looking up once. The woman at the desk, fat and lumpy with hard eyes and a voiceful of cigarette wheeze, said to me, "Where ya been?" and I rattled off a string of hotels. "Ya worked all those places," she said calmly. "Ain't the human body a mah-h-vellous thing, ya don't look old enough to have worked half of 'em." I stood there, ill with fear that on the one hand she'd throw me out and on the other she'd give me a job, and assured her that I had. She knew I was lying, and I knew that she knew I was lying, but she wrote out a job ticket anyway. Suddenly I felt lonely inside the lie, and I begged her with my eyes to acknowledge the truth between us. She didn't like that at all. Her own eyes grew even harder, and she refused me more than she had when I'd not revealed open need. She drew back with the ticket still in her hand. I snatched at it. She laughed a nasty laugh. And that was it, all of it, right there, two flights above Times Square, I was in the mountains.

That first weekend in a large glittering hotel filled with garment district salesmen and midtown secretaries, weaving clumsily in and out of the vast kitchen all heat and acrimony (food flying, trays crashing, waiters cursing), I gripped the tray so hard all ten knuckles were white for days afterward, and every time I looked at them I recalled the astonishment I'd felt when a busboy at the station next to mine stuck out his fist to a guest who'd eaten three main dishes and said, "Want a knuckle sandwich?" But on Sunday night when I flung fifty single dollar bills on the kitchen table before my open-mouthed mother there was soft exultancy, and I knew I'd go back. Rising up inside this brash, moralistic, working-class girl was the unexpected excitement of the first opportunity for greed.

I was eighteen years old, moving blind through hungers whose force I could not grasp. Unable to grasp what drove me, I walked around feeling stupid. Feeling stupid I became inept. Secretly, I welcomed going to the mountains. I knew I could do this hard but simple thing. I could enter that pig-eyed glitter and snatch from it the soft, gorgeous, fleshy excitement of quick money. This I could master. This, I thought, had only to do with endurance; inexhaustible energy; and that I was burning up with.

The summer of my initiation I'd get a job, work two weeks, get fired. "You're a waitress? I thought you said you were a waitress. What kinda waitress sets a table like that? Who you think you're kidding, girlie?" But by Labor Day I *was* a waitress and a veteran of the first year. I had been inducted into an underclass elite, a world of self-selected Orwellian pariahs for whom survival was the only value.

At the first hotel an experienced waiter, attracted by my innocence, took me under his wing. In the mountains, regardless of age or actual history, your first year you were a virgin and in every hotel there was always someone, sentimental as a gangster, to love a virgin. My patron in this instance was a twenty-nine-year-old man who worked in the post office in winter and at this hotel in summer. He was a handsome vagrant, a cunning hustler, what I would come by the end of the summer to recognize as a "mountain rat."

One night a shot rang out in the sleeping darkness. Waiters and waitresses leaped up in the little barracks building we shared at the edge of the hotel grounds. Across the wide lawn, light filled the open doorway of one of the distant guest cottages. A man stood framed in the light, naked except for a jockstrap.

Inside the barracks people began to laugh. It was my handsome protector. He'd been sleeping with a woman whose gambler husband had appeared unexpectedly on a Thursday night.

The next day he was fired. We took a final walk together. I fumbled for words. Why? I wanted to know. I knew he didn't like the woman, a diet-thin blonde twenty years older than himself. "Ah-h-h," my friend said wearily. "Doncha know nothing, kid? Doncha know what I am? I mean, whaddaya think I am?"

At the second hotel the headwaiter, a tall sweating man, began all his staff meetings with, "Boys and girls, the first thing to understand is, we are dealing here with animals." He stood in the dining-room doorway every morning holding what I took to be a glass of apple juice until I was told it was whiskey neat. "Good morning, Mrs. Levine," he'd nod affably, then turn to a busboy and mutter, "That Holland Tunnel whore." He rubbed my arm between his thumb and his forefinger when he hired me and said, "We'll take care of each other, right, kid?" I nodded, thinking it was his way of asking me to be a responsible worker. My obtuseness derailed him. When he fired me and my friend Marilyn because he caught us eating chocolate tarts behind an alcove in the dining room he thundered at us, his voice hoarse with relief, "You are not now waitresses, you never were waitresses, you'll never *be* waitresses."

At the third hotel I had fifty dollars stolen from me at the end of a holiday weekend. Fifty dollars wasn't fifty dollars in the mountains, it was blood money. My room was crowded with fellow workers, all silent as pallbearers. The door racketed open and Kennie, a busboy who was always late, burst into the room. "I heard you had money stolen!" he cried, his face stricken. I nodded wordlessly. Kennie turned, pulled the door shut, twisted his body about, raised his arm and banged his fist, sobbing, against the door. When I said, "What are *you* getting so excited about?" he shrieked at me, "Because you're a waitress and a human being! And I'm a busboy and a human being!" At the end of the summer, four more robberies having taken place, the thief was caught. It was Kennie.

At the fourth hotel the children's waiter was a dedicated womanizer. A flirtatious guest held out on him longer than usual, and one morning I saw this waiter urinate into a glass of orange juice, then serve it to the woman's child with the crooning injunction to drink it all up because it was so-o-o good.

At the fifth hotel I served a woman who was all bosom from neck to knee, tiny feet daintily shod, smooth plump hands beautifully manicured, childish eyes in a painted face. When I brought her exactly-three-minute eggs to the table she said to me, "Open them for me, dear. The shells burn my hands." I turned away, to the station table against the wall, to perform in appropriate secrecy a task that told me for the first but certainly not the last time that here I was only an extension of my function. It was the Catskills, not early socialist teachings at my father's knee, that made me a Marxist.

One winter I worked weekends and Christmas at a famous hotel. This hotel had an enormous tiered dining room and was run by one of the most feared headwaiters in the mountains. The system here was that all newcomers began at the back of the dining room on the tier farthest from the kitchen. If your work met with favor you were moved steadily toward the center, closer to the kitchen doors and to the largest tips which came not from the singles who were invariably placed in the back of the room but from the middle-aged manufacturers, club owners, and gangsters who occupied the tables in the central tiers, cutting a wide swath as though across a huge belly between the upper and lower ends of the dining room.

As the autumn wore on I advanced down the tiers. By Christmas I was nearly in the center of the room, at one of the best stations in the house. This meant my guests were now middle-aged married couples whose general appearance was characterized by blond bouffants, mink stoles, midnight-blue suits, and half-smoked cigars. These people ate prodigiously and tipped well.

That Christmas the hotel was packed and we worked twelve hours a day. The meals went on forever. By the end of the week we were dead on our feet but still running. On New Year's Eve at midnight we were to serve a full meal, the fourth of the day, but this was to be a banquet dinner—that is, a series of house-chosen dishes simply hauled out, course by course—and we looked forward to it. It signaled the end of the holiday. The next morning the guests checked out and that night we'd all be home in our Bronx or Brooklyn apartments, our hard-earned cash piled on the kitchen table.

But a threatening atmosphere prevailed at that midnight meal from the moment the dining room doors were flung open. I remember sky blue sequined dresses and tight mouths, satin cummerbunds and hard-edged laughter, a lot of drunks on the vomitous verge. People darted everywhere and all at once, pushing to get at the central tables (no assigned seats tonight), as though, driven from one failed part of the evening to another here, at last, they were going to get what *should* come through for them; a good table in the famous dining room during its New Year's Eve meal.

The kitchen was instantly affected: it picked up on atmosphere like an animal whose only survival equipment is hyperalertness. A kind of panicky aggression seemed to overtake the entire staff. The orderly lines that had begun to form for the first appetizer broke almost immediately. People who had grown friendly, working together over these long winter weekends, now climbed over each other's backs to break into the line and grab at the small round dishes piled up on the huge steel tables.

I made my first trip into the kitchen, took in the scene before me, and froze. Then I took a deep breath, inserted myself into a line, held my own against hands and elbows pushing into my back and ribs, and got my tray loaded and myself out the kitchen doors. I served the fruit cup quickly and, depending on my busboy to get the empties off the tables in time, made my anxious way back into the kitchen for the next course which, I'll not forget as long as I live, was chow mein. This time I thought violence was about to break out. All those people, trays, curses being flung about! And now I couldn't seem to take a deep breath: I remained motionless just inside the kitchen doors. Another waitress, a classmate from City College, grabbed my arm and whispered in my ear, "Skip the chow mein, they'll never know the difference. Go on to the next course, there's nobody on the line over there." My heart lifted, the darkness receded. I stared at her. Did we dare? Yes, she nodded grimly, and walked away. It didn't occur to either of us to consider that she, as it happened, had only drunken singles at her tables who of course wouldn't know the difference, but I had married couples who wanted everything that was coming to them.

I made my first mistake. I followed my classmate to the table with no line in front of it, loaded up on the cold fish, and fought my way out the nearest kitchen door. Rapidly, I dealt out the little dishes to the men and women at my tables. When I had finished and was moving back to my station table and its now empty tray, a set of long red fingernails plucked at my upper arm. I looked down at a woman with coarse blond hair, blue eyelids surrounded by lines so deep they seemed carved, and a thin red mouth. "We didn't get the chow mein," she said to me.

My second mistake. "Chow mein?" I said. "What chow mein?" Still holding me, she pointed to the next table where chow mein was being finished and the cold fish just beginning to be served. I looked at her. Words would not come. I broke loose, grabbed my tray, and dived into the kitchen.

I must have known I was in trouble because I let myself be kicked about in the kitchen madness, wasting all sorts of time being climbed over before I got the next dish loaded onto my tray and inched myself, crablike, through the swinging doors. As I approached my station I saw, standing beside the blond woman, the headwaiter, chewing a dead cigar and staring glumly in my direction. He beckoned me with one raised index finger.

I lowered my tray onto the station table and walked over to him. "Where's the chow mein?" he asked quietly, jerking his thumb back at my tables, across the head of the woman whose blue-lidded eyes never left his face. Her mouth was a slash of narrow red. Despair made me simple.

"I couldn't get to it." I said. "The kitchen is a madhouse. The line was impossible."

The headwaiter dropped his lower lip. His black eyes flickered into dangerous life and his hand came up slowly to remove the cigar stub from between his teeth. "You couldn't *get* to it?" he said. "Did I hear you right? You said you couldn't get to it?" A few people at neighboring tables looked up.

"That's right," I said miserably.

And then he was yelling at me, "And you call yourself a waitress?"

A dozen heads swung around. The headwaiter quickly shut his mouth. He stared coldly at me, in his eyes the most extraordinary mixture of anger, excitement, and fear. Yes, fear. Frightened as I was, I saw that he too was afraid. Afraid of the blond woman who sat in her chair like a queen with the power of life and death in her, watching a minister do her awful bidding. His eyes kept darting toward her, as though to ask, All right? Enough? Will this do?

No, the unyielding face answered. Not enough. Not nearly enough.

"You're fired," the headwaiter said to me. "Serve your morning meal and clear out."

The blood seemed to leave my body in a single rush. For a moment I thought I was going to faint. Then I realized that tomorrow morning my regular guests would be back in these seats, most of them leaving after breakfast, and I, of course, would receive my full tips exactly as though none of this had happened. The headwaiter was not really punishing me. He knew it, and now I knew it. Only the blond woman didn't know it. She required my dismissal for the appeasement of her lousy life—her lined face, her hated husband, her disappointed New Year's Eve—and he, the headwaiter, was required to deliver it up to her.

For the first time I understood something about power. I stared into the degraded face of the headwaiter and saw that he was as trapped as I, caught up in a working life that required *someone's* humiliation at all times.

Bungalow

Elizabeth Ehrlich

"Come for the weekend. Come up with the children on Friday, early. Come right in the morning," said Miriam's voice. The line crackled with country static. "You won't have to move a finger, you can just rest with the children."

I said something vague, and said good-bye. I hung up the phone, gripped by useless emotions. It was unfair of me, this I know now, but denial was what I heard in her voice, denial or wistfulness—for a different sort of daughter-in-law, one with perfect nails and a house to match. A daughter-in-law who didn't work, who could spend a whole Friday, indeed a whole summer in Miriam's bungalow, watching the Catskill days drift by with her pretty children and their eager grandmother, while the husband, the *fardiner*, the breadwinner, came up for weekends. A daughter-in-law with time to spend, who was organized and careful with objects and money, who never would have lost a gold necklace, say. An old, long, gold necklace given her by Miriam.

Instead, she got me, a mad circus juggler keeping too many plates aloft, while which ones were crashing I did not know. I went to work; my nails were dull and ragged; money slipped through my hands. I did not even remember the necklace. And to whom could Miriam complain?

Friday would be a regular work day. I would greet the sitter, zip my heart into the closet, kiss the round faces of two small children, and close the apartment door. I would descend eleven flights on the elevator, disappear into the subway under a blazing morning sun, tunnel south under fifty blocks of pavement. Emerging from the depths, I would buy a cup of hot brown coffee, ascend fifty flights on the elevator to my office, and enter a world of printers and telephones, copiers and metal desks, important meetings, artificial light, fluorescent buzz and hum. Nine hours later, if I were lucky, I would reverse the course and meet my children after their day in a parallel universe under the open sky.

This was the frank reality of my life, and I wished it to be acknowledged, perhaps praised, by Miriam. Praised? All day long to leave two *kinderlekh* of that quality? a *meydele*, a *yingele*, a little girl and boy like this?

"Come early, and rest," urged Miriam. There was infinite generosity in this, the door was open. But you need ears to hear.

The next day, Friday, New York was melting: 90 degrees already, reported my clock radio, broadcasting into my uneasy, guilty sleep. The apartment, smelling faintly of kitchen refuse, surely was hotter still. On reflection, everything seemed possible, even a day off work.

So I called, and I packed, and I double-parked the car in front of the building.

Into the elevator I schlepped suitcases and strollers, swimming pool floats, sun hats, sun lotion, insect repellent, extra sweaters, juice cups, portable crib, *Goodnight Moon*, Fluffy Bear, Mr. Turtle, Baby Pillow, Octopus, and Duck. Outside in the brothlike air, I packed the car, I got the children in, I wiped up a juice spill. I set off with a credit card and seven dollars in my pocket. Logistics being as they were, I could not think of a way to stop at the bank. I would have to borrow from Miriam.

Out of town Friday morning! Henry Hudson Parkway, George Washington Bridge, the Palisades—and since the old, borrowed car had no air conditioning, the wind was in our hair. I raised and lowered windows, trying for balance between temperature and noise. I sang! I called attention to birds and trees!

Bear Mountain approached, and the children were asleep. Juice cups fell from their limp, sticky hands. There would be no afternoon nap now, no breather for me at all. . . .

Shah, let them sleep, I imagined Miriam to say. . . .

I found highways and exits; I found myself enjoying the green view, the subdued breathing of two little ones. The office could wait. The best and most important job in the world seemed less important. It blew away. My mind wandered, perhaps too much. In general, I have always been lucky to get where I get in one piece.

The last leg of the trip is a long crooked back road littered with the history of the lower Catskills: nineteenth-century farmhouse close to the road, empty; abandoned chicken coops, trailer homes, economic depression, soap suds spewing into mountain tributaries, a Ukrainian resort, a drug treatment village, rabbits for sale, fishing boats to rent, a summer camp for girls.

And then we are once again at Green Gardens Lodge, parking in crunchy gravel amidst many large Fords, Chryslers, Cadillacs, one Yellow Taxi cab, and also a Mercedes. They have millionaires here, and taxi drivers.

"How can a Jew drive a Mercedes?" Miriam has asked me, more than once. She has not forgotten the German military-industrial complex, and will not forgive.

A ring of forty spruce little cottages, freshly painted, encircling a razored lawn and a few shade trees. There are common rooms and outbuildings, a hotel turned condominium, patches of flowers and shrubs, a tennis court, and a pool with a fence that is locked until after lunch. This is the bungalow colony, my in-laws' summer world.

I turned off the motor, cracked open the car door. It was nearly as hot as New York City. But the hot air was clean, cleansed in the mountain night, and by this time on a Friday, nearly noon, the air was redolent: chicken soup boiling in country kitchens. And Jacob had seen us; he approached over the lawn ready to hoist luggage into his spare, bony, surprisingly strong arms. As far as I can tell, he never changes, never ages.

My little warm ones slid from the car and ran, looking ahead, not back. They belonged here—and still do—among the grannies and uncles and grandpas and aunts, the visiting grandchildren, the Polish and Yiddish conversations, the piped music, the card parties. They ran. The hammock to swing in, the flowers to water, the screen door to bang, lunch all prepared and a huge box of homemade cookies: they ran toward these things.

We ate, I unpacked, the children ran. Ladies in housedresses gathered and greeted, questioned, scolded—barefoot children in an era of deer ticks. I hunted for little shoes and socks in the grass. I took the children to the pool, and Jacob came to watch. I bathed the children after their swim. Miriam fixed ice cream cones. All was in her knowing embrace.

Later, Miriam's Sabbath dinner on the screened porch, and, with the fading sun, the lighting of her Sabbath candles.

My husband found his way there that night. We all slept in the two small rooms of Miriam's bungalow, under fresh line-dried linens warmed by Catskill sun and ironed to silken smoothness under Miriam's practiced hand.

Twenty years ago, Miriam, Jacob, and their circle, acquaintances, family, and friends, bought this place. A few years later I, fresh from the midwest, was feted here with my fiancé. Ten years ago I brought my first baby, to rock in the hammock my husband installed between two shade trees and to feast on the admiration and surreptitious sweets a colony of grandparents could provide in full measure.

Then I brought my two children, escaping a cramped city apartment and frenzied work week to stretch out in Miriam's hospitality amidst the pleasant green. Later we moved to the suburbs, and I left my office job: escape was less urgent. I don't come as often these days. Still, a few times each summer I arrive with my children, three children now, neglecting my own house and garden for two days or three or five. The three children fan out in all directions: this is their place, deeply, completely, and always. They love it. How lucky they are to be here.

Here Miriam cooks her country dishes. If we arrive at lunchtime, lunch is ready. Eggs and onions, perhaps. Before we arrive, Miriam slices five or six onions. She peppers them, softens them over a low flame, adds plenty of oil, and fries the onions to a caramel sweetness. Then she scrambles the onions with five giant eggs, adds a pinch or two of salt, heaps it all on a warm platter, and brings it proudly to the table.

The table is *gemakht*, ready, with barely a centimeter to spare. Here is a plate of sliced melon, blueberries, strawberries, and a bowl of sugar for the berries. There may be ripe tomatoes cut into chunks with raw Spanish onion, oil, and wine vinegar. Perhaps a herring in cream sauce, or a tin of smoked sardines. If there is *mizerya*, finely sliced cucumbers dressed in sour cream beaten with lemon juice, salt, and sugar, there will be little dishes and spoons to nurse the tangy sauce. There are fresh little challah rolls, or heavy slices of corn rye bread festooned with caraway seeds. Cream cheese with scallions.

In my honor, the old coffee percolator spits and taps stovetop. Miriam and Jacob drink instant coffee, a cup each at dawn. I drink high octane coffee all day.

These are jolly grand country lunches on the breezy screened porch crowded around the small porch table.

Neighbors pass by. "Good appetite!" they call, in accented English.

"Send the children over later, I have something for them!" orders *Tante* Sonia at the screen door. Probably chocolate and gum and Polish wafers and lollipops from Aunt Sonia's bottomless supply.

"Sonia! Come in, eat something!" urges Miriam. "Onions! A roll! Why not?"

"I cannot! I ate already, in *mayn bungele!*"

"Grandma, do you have any *plain* cream cheese?"

"*Oy, ye! Ikh hob fargesn!* Yakob, *oytser*, treasure, *nem der* plain cream cheese *fun* Frigidaire. *Un* a seltzer *oykhet*," as well.

"I'll get it," I say. "I'm closer!"

"Why? I am there already!" Jacob rises from his chair with a large gesture.

"He is there already!" explains Miriam. "*Es, mame sheyne!*" Eat, pretty mama, this is your job now. Try to be good at it.

This is a kind of utopia: a glimpse of both idealized future and past. Forty couples, many of them children together in Poland, spared in the war and determined to live with spirit, bought their colony for a future. Each inhabits a neat and perfect summer dwelling where one's own standards, language, and cooking reigns.

There is pride of ownership and independence in *mayn bungele*, and at the same time it could well serve a socialist's dream: A cooperative community of rules and order, where universal committee membership accomplishes maintenance, religious observance, improvements, and entertainment year after year. Hard work done willingly.

Yet no democracy is this. There are officers for life, male only, and each allotted a precious, status-conferring golf cart. Among these, my husband's uncle, the redoubtable Uncle Fred, prime mover and organizer of this place, is mayor, holder of the keys, maintenance supervisor, quality-control man. He books the musicians, handles the taxes, orders the corned beef, buys the Saturday newspaper in town for our Jacob, his loved and respected older brother. Jacob does not drive on *Shabbas*.

Uncle Fred—still Fishl to Jacob—takes his wife, Pearl, shopping, and out to restaurants, and here and there. They like to go and do. Pearl is a perfectly groomed and certain sort of person, whose legs at seventy-something look better in shorts than mine, who once informed me that I was definitely not too young to have children, and again, later, that this was the final correct moment to buy a house, and so we did.

Fred motors about Green Gardens in his golf cart, seeing to a leaky faucet or a fallen tree. He takes in the harness races with a visiting son who calls this place *Greeneh* Gardens, *greeneh* being Yiddish-English slang for "immigrants." Uncle Fred can do anything, and he knows everything. After the war, Pearl had the first winter coat and the first warm boots, of Russian army issue, and the first temporary apartment in Germany and then the first visa to New York: Fred's doing. Later Fred schlepped paint cans on the subway from job to job until he could buy the first car, the first house.

It was Uncle Fred who explained at last this crowd's aversion to the buffet meal. "I was in a concentration camp five years," he said. "I don't stand in line for food." I blanched and cringed: my wedding. No one had told me, and I never understood for ten long years what was the matter quite, what . . .

At Green Gardens, Miriam and Jacob and Fred and Pearl have neighbors, real neighbors. They do informal favors for one another, they share food, they run to town for bread, they offer rides. The support network is there for them now as they age, as the number of widows grows, and the midsummer trips to doctors become more frequent. They meet for *davening* in the synagogue by morning, they have their tennis players and their card players, their golfers, their avid shoppers, their regular walkers. They have their gardeners, like Miriam, whose green thumb has splashed the front of her bungalow with gorgeous color each and every year.

Afternoon, when day's work is done, they gather on the greensward to chat in Yiddish and sometimes in Polish. The women wear loose casual frocks and slippers by day. They dress after dinner. Every evening, there is coffee and cake in the card room, and Saturday night they throw themselves a party—splendid food, dancing, singing, entertainment.

It is a bit like going to Poland for the weekend. In a *shtetl* echo, peddlers pull up to the lawn in their Fords and pop the lids of trunks stuffed with pocketbooks or bath towels. A fish man from the Bronx stops by each week to sell herring and lox.

Down the road, a *frume*—religious—colony runs a kosher store, its moldy shelves stocking pickles, salami, shampoo. Fresh bread is displayed in a cardboard delivery carton, and endless children drip ice cream on the floor. A little store, as Miriam says, "like in Poland."

This is where the walkers go. They have their route, these twenty years. From Green Gardens to the *frume* store is half a mile. Back is one. There and back again is two miles. In the sun, in the rain under an umbrella, after breakfast, before dusk. Never the other way, never up the road past meadow and butterfly, abandoned barn, overgrown graveyard, blackberry bramble, and cattail swamp, to where the running creek empties into pond, full of algae, bobbing beer cans, visiting birds, and a last few frogs. Always the same, reliable two-mile course, punctuated by the comforting sight of the *frume* store.

One woman, her son in the garment center, sells sweaters in her bungalow. Sweaters and dresses and men's polo shirts, stuffed into closets and drawers and boxes. Another woman runs to her neighbor offering a *maykhl*, a savory morsel: stuffed turkey neck or calves' foot jelly, with hard-boiled egg slices suspended in the sturdy aspic, a lemon slice on the side.

Once Miriam made potato latkes in the evening cool, and a dozen people managed to drop by. My children slathered on sour cream, sugar, applesauce. *Tante* Sonia waved her latke as the golf cart zipped her away to a committee meeting, Uncle Fred at the wheel. He likes to help out the ladies. He does whatever he can.

It is secular, our colony, and religious too: live and let live, a virtuous stance. There are ladies in hair-rollers hitchhiking rides on golf carts to the laundry shed on Saturday, and grandchildren whose ritual fringes hang out of their soccer shirts. There are men in skullcaps playing cards on a Friday night. There are women at the beauty parlor on *Shabbas*, while their husbands read Torah with tears in their eyes. There are grandfathers out to Pizza Hut with the children, while their wives make two sets of dishes somehow fit on a bungalow shelf. Two sets of dishes, two sets of spoons, two sets of pots in a tiny little country kitchen.

Comes a knock on the door any day at dawn, and Jacob makes his way to the *shul* to fill out a *minyan*. The little *shul* is lovely, peaceful, filled with colored light. The members built and furnished it. One, a talented artist, crafted the stained glass windows. Another is a rabbi, still another a trained Torah reader. That man bought the prayer books, that one contributed the *bima*, the pulpit. This one donated the Torah scroll.

It is a bit of the fabled Borscht Belt on Saturday night. At 8:15 sharp the whole colony is in the casino, with any friends, children, grandchildren spending the night. The women are coifed, the casino is decorated, everyone is dressed to the nines. The band is playing, perhaps an ensemble of keyboard, percussion, and sax. Start with a *forshpays*, appetizer—chick peas, chunks of pumpernickel-and-rye marble bread, schmaltz herring. Each fine herring bone was tweezed from the velvety fish flesh by this week's ladies' committee on Friday at 7 A.M. in the big kitchen that once served the hotel. I saw them. The ladies in their housedresses worked together, slicing the herrings, dressing them in oil and chopped purple onion. Two men run an open bar for exactly one hour: vodka, whiskey, scotch, orange juice, soda, ginger ale, Coke, ice.

"That's it," say the men as the ice melts down. "The bar is officially closed."

There is a sit-down meal, delicatessen or smoked fish, salads and cookies and cakes. A singer may belt out in Yiddish, French, Italian, Hebrew, or English, and where did these people learn all the words? And is there a language they do not know? for they sing along unapologetically and with feeling. They laugh at a rau-cous comic spiel, and dance waltzes, Israeli circle dances, Russian dances, two-step, disco. I dance with my children, and dance with my father-in-law.

Until one in the morning they dance, long after we, the visiting children, tired out by our frantic middle-aged lives, have rolled into embroidered bunga-low beds.

Miriam's place, Green Gardens, recalls the region's Jewish heyday, already past peak in the 1950s as these folks got back on their shaky but determined feet. It is New York, with its sense of escape from the oppressive heat of immigrant urbana. It conjures the *kokh-aleyns*, the housekeeping cottages of Rockaway Beach, that my father knew as a Brooklyn child. It reverberates with the spirit of the grand resort hotels. It is a last hurrah for all of that, in the Jewish style at least—for the Catskills are still to be discovered by newer groups of immigrant strivers, Korean, Jamaican, Chinese, Dominican. They, the new *greeneh*, will find that the real estate is cheap and plentiful, the air is fresh and the children can run, and that a bungalow colony can be imagined any of a thousand perfect ways.

Miriam's bungalow colony is socialist, private, foreign, American, New York, past, and present. It is work and vacation, reality and idyll. It is the apotheosis of valuable Jewish things in my past as I knew them. It is an oasis out of time. All my roads have led here. But I am only a facilitator after all. This place belongs not to me—who gets cranky sharing two rooms and a bath with six other people and sitting down to eat on schedule—but to the grandparents, and the grand-children too.

By the time she was three, my daughter was staying here for stretches of time on her own. She swung in the hammock and watered the flowers. She went to town with her grandparents to shop, for a frilly dress, a little toy, a book of puzzles. She went to the beauty parlor with her grandmother and had her nails painted red. She went to the card room. She dressed up for the parties. There was no bedtime. Mornings, she slept in, watched cartoons, had chocolate milk for breakfast.

"It's not a wholesome environment," I complained once to my husband. He laughed.

"Give her a bath and wash her hair tonight," I told Miriam by phone during one of these visits. Later I learned my daughter had stormed out of doors, leaving an angry note: "I COME TO BUGLO TO BE FREE." The E's faced backward, as in my own printing at six years of age, when I also longed for freedom.

I close my eyes and I see: that six-year-old girl on the screened front porch, making *kreplekh*, filled dumplings, with her grandmother. Miriam showing her how to place a glass, precisely so, on a rolled-out sheet of noodle dough. Lifting the round with a butter knife, placing on it a bit of sweetened farmer cheese or blueberries. Folding the circle in half, pinching the edges together, effecting a succulent dairy won ton. She, the girl, totally absorbed, eager to be good at it. Learning a small bit of lore. So it shouldn't be lost. Blueberry *kreplekh*.

Once when I was a new bride we sat on the porch of the bungalow talking into Friday night, as the Sabbath candles flickered and fireflies danced outside. Miriam spoke of Poland, and childhood. Her village, hard by the town of Radom, was shadowed by forest. She and her mother used to go to the woods in May to pick mushrooms. There were so many kinds of mushrooms, she told me. One kind for drying, for soups, another for cooking fresh—the best mushrooms in the world came from her forest in Poland.

Especially one kind she remembered, that she had not seen since the old days: a little yellow mushroom, like a chicken's foot, a mushroom called a *kushinushki*, a Polish name. She rhapsodized over those yellow mushrooms.

"My mother used to cook them with sour cream, to eat with potatoes. You never tasted something like this."

Back home that week, I recalled the discussion. At a fancy Manhattan produce boutique I rooted. There, in the tempting fungal array, was a bin of precious chanterelles. They fit the description, yellow, small, shaped like a little chicken's foot, plump and eager. I would bring a bag to the bungalow, I decided, although I could never tell Miriam how much they cost. She had never even seen them in her America: they were not to be had in the Northeast Bronx.

But week after week, rolling into months, there was no intersection between market visits and trips to the Green Gardens colony. As I rushed out of town on a Friday, a billion things to remember pushed any thought of mushroom from my mind. If I went to the market, it meant we were staying in town the weekend. At the market I remembered. Making my country lists, I forgot.

That summer went by, and the next, and the next. In between, Miriam cooked mushrooms from supermarket tins, cooked dried mushrooms from plastic wrappings. Many a fall, winter, and spring went by with mushrooms. Miriam sautéed mushrooms with onions and chopped them finely into hard-cooked eggs and mayonnaise and dill to spread on fresh breads and rolls. With drippings and garlic and a bit of flour, her stewed mushrooms swam in a luxurious gravy over veal meat balls.

Darkly crisped mushrooms and slivered onions festooned her *farfel*, a kind of steamed and fried pasta used as a side dish. In winter, when Sabbath comes early, we sometimes sat down on a Friday eve to Miriam's slow-roasted *dekl*, a cut of beef softer than brisket, that in Miriam's kitchen is baked under a mellifluous crust of sliced mushrooms, oil, garlic, parsley, pepper, paprika. And served on a silver-rimmed meat dish beside a heap of kasha *varnishkes*—buckwheat groats with bowtie noodles.

"These mushrooms are nothing," Miriam would say from time to time, as we swooned, "compared to the little yellow mushrooms we used to get in Poland." She would pause, alone in the memory. "Little yellow mushrooms, like a chicken's foot."

The comment would prick my complacency, reignite my resolve. *Chanterelles*.

One summer Friday at last I remembered. The luggage for the country was already packed, and I was leaving work early with time to spare. I stopped at the market and filled a bag with tender yellow gleanings, a plastic bag, wondering idly if paper wouldn't be better, but they were out of paper bags, then I forgot about it. Forgot, walking home twenty blocks in humid summer heat; forgot, packing the car, forgot while driving, and in a traffic jam, and stopping to change diapers and fill the gas tank, and—I squirm to recall—parking under hot summer heat in an asphalt parking lot while I explored a newly opened factory outlet mall on the way to Green Gardens.

Unpacking, I remembered. There they were in their plastic bag. I set them on the table.

"What is this?" asked Miriam, holding up the warm, damp bag.

"Yellow mushrooms—but I think—"

"These are *kushinushki*!"

"Are they?"

"Where ever did you find them?" Miriam bundled them into the refrigerator, behind something, under something.

"*Ema*, I don't know if they are good."

"They are good!" assured Miriam.

Just then a baby called, a child needed me. I meant to get back to the mushrooms, those perishable fungi, but I always have too much on my mind. We left early on the Sunday . . . and it was the end of the week before we spoke.

"Those mushrooms—" Miriam began.

"Oh, no."

"They aren't the *kushinushki*."

"No?"

"We went and bought all the things for the mushrooms—sour cream, potatoes," recounted Miriam.

"You didn't—eat them?"

"I prepared them for the *Abba*. They looked the same, but they didn't taste good. They were terrible. Nothing like *kushinushki*."

I might have killed my husband's parents. Thank God, thank luck, thank evolution and genetics, that I did not.

Such are the dangers of careless daughters-in-law, and the perils, perhaps? of trying to go home again, as I vicariously was.

Once I suggested barbecue. Some of the bungalows do it, cooking up minute steaks without soiling or heating their always immaculate kitchens, fixed up more in the manner of miniature subdivision homes than 1940s-vintage Catskill bungalows.

"Probably they learned from their children," remarked Miriam, with neither curiosity nor envy in her voice as she watched smoke rise from a charcoal burner a few doors down. Miriam, who could not afford a bungalow makeover, unknowingly made a virtue of preservation. Her bungalow is authentically beautiful. The walls are pine paneled, and she keeps them polished and clean. Accordion folding doors separate the two rooms. The children lay their hot faces on the cool linoleum floor. Mothballs scent the closet, vinyl valises are stowed under the white and gold bedroom furniture, hidden by dust ruffles of eyelet and voile. There is a big white freestanding stove in the pink-and-aqua tiled kitchen, and a plaid sleep-sofa hospitably placed along the far wall, under a sunburst-shaped electric clock ticking summer moments.

We eat our meals on an old metal table on the breezy screened porch, and our meals are the mythical food of vanished Polish summers.

When I said barbecue, my husband looked at his mother with mock interest, his eyebrows up, and mouth turned down, as if to say: "Why not try it, *Ema*?" They exchanged that merry, sour, mutual expression, mother and son.

"It's too dirty," I accused, and Miriam did not deny.

It was also wrong, I see now, the wrong aesthetic, to cook at the last minute over a hot fire, or worse, to see her husband standing on his feet in an apron tending black lumps of meat with a *groyser gopl*, a big fork, breathing carbonized fat.

So at other summer places, such as on my own patio back home, let hot dogs broil for dinner, among the mosquitoes. At Miriam's we snug around the porch table at dusk as a faint breeze rises, flowered plates on our vinyl placemats. Miriam serves a pickled corned beef, simmered all day with pepper, garlic, cloves, bay leaf. She serves Israeli potato salad, made with cucumber pickles and onions and peas. We swallow stewed plums and cherries, chocolate marble cake, and a comforting cup of tea.

In the bungalow I am crowded, and I grow irritable. This is the bungalow: a porch, a front room that includes the kitchen, a bedroom with two double beds, a bathroom. When I come with the children and their belongings and my husband, we have seven people in this space, though it doesn't look it. Miriam knows how to manage. She squirrels away everything, finding places where there are no places, so that the surfaces may appear clean, as they were. Still, rainy days are tough.

I'm on a short fuse here, and this makes me feel guilty. I think about the small cramped spaces occupied with dignity by Miriam early in her life. So she had to live, with others, several families sharing a room or two during the war.

After the war, there were transitional apartments in Germany and Israel, and later the immigrant digs in New York, always kept tidy and gleaming with a sense of worthy pride that no external darkness could extinguish in Miriam. And here I am complaining. I wish to arrive and spread out, be messy and relaxed. I'm an American, spoiled and despoiling. Despite myself I am the product of a frontier heritage and prosperous times.

"You shouldn't know from it," says Miriam, "how much a person can take."

It took me too long with the yellow mushrooms.

I finally got to the country this year with chanterelles in a cool paper bag.

"We will cook them," said Miriam.

She chopped onions and dried them with pepper over a high flame and added oil and fried the onions golden. She cleaned the mushrooms and added them whole to the hot oil and softened the mushrooms and tossed in a pat of butter too—"for the smell." With a fork, she whipped up a whole pint of real sour cream, and she mixed it into the pot with a pinch of salt, a dash of paprika.

Miriam peeled Idaho potatoes, cut them into chunks and boiled them soft and dry. She dressed those steaming potatoes in that sour cream and chanterelle sauce. She had fish too, baked salmon; she had summer squash cooked with peppers and tomatoes; she had buttermilk for drinking. The hot, dry potato flesh absorbed the creamy sauce, and the mushrooms—

I looked out through the porch screen, pleasant and pleasured, removed from the clang and rush of the great world. Something basic and simple and splendidly civilized here. A respite if I want it. A gift. I made resolutions to try to be better.

You never tasted something like this.

"Are these the *kushinushki*?" I asked Miriam.

She paused.

"I think it's the same ones," said Miriam. "I don't remember."

I was stunned, shocked. Three dangerous words for Miriam, who is—suddenly I see—more tired than I have ever seen her. Then I noticed the garden, beneath the porch, for the first year barely abloom. It was always the prettiest.

Every year, clematis vines twined up strings, petunias wagged their bonnets, dahlias pushed forth from bulbs. Every spring, right after Passover, Miriam starts her seeds in egg cartons under the sunny Bronx kitchen window—seeds saved from last year's garden. She plants the seedlings Memorial weekend; by July, the bungalow is dressed in daisies and marigolds and asters and zinnias and mums and impatiens and black-eyed Susans. Nothing fancy, always beautiful, planned and tidy and reliable, the result of invisible effort, always eager to give delight. The kind of flowers she would have.

She barely gardened this year, Miriam. The flowers are sparse. Miriam is growing old.

In my life, I have said things, and done things, that I regret.

Appendices

LINKS TO MORE SOURCES

This annotated bibliography includes books, short stories, and essays about the Catskills. It does not include articles published in magazines and journals, most of which can be located in the bibliographies of the major historical works. The Catskills Institute Web site (http://catskills.brown.edu) contains more material, including unpublished memoirs, interviews, and novels in progress.

FICTION

Novels

Martin Boris, *Woodridge, 1946* (New York: Crown, 1980)

Martin Boris's book centers on "Our Place," a Woodridge restaurant, and its owners, workers, and customers. Boris grew up in Glen Wild, next to Woodridge, and knows the area well; he provides more local lore than most Catskills novels, including an account of daily life on a chicken farm, an important element of the Jewish presence in the Mountains. Restaurant owner Phil points to the ostentatious atmosphere of the resorts, yet knows well that hotel staff make up much of the restaurant's clientele. As in most Catskills novels, there is a lot of sex. Among other things, Boris deals with conflicts between traditional religious traditions and leftist politics. Indeed, this book is one of the few writings we have that addresses communist and socialist activities in the Catskills. Some of the local activists go to Peekskill, on the other side of the Hudson, for the famous rally and concert where Paul Robeson sang and the participants were brutally attacked by the American Legion while police looked on (the actual rally was 1949, but Boris uses fictional license to place it in 1946). Even though the Catskills were just entering their golden age, the 1950s and 1960s, during which the expanded resort area would be larger than ever, Boris's characters—drawing largely on their author's experience—are worried about its decline.

Abraham Cahan, *The Rise of David Levinsky* (New York: Harper, 1917)

Abraham Cahan, founder and editor of the *Jewish Daily Forward*, was one of the most important American Jewish writers in the first half of this century. His classic novel, *The Rise of David Levinsky*, written in 1917, was the first piece of fiction in which the Catskills played an important part. Although the number of chapters is small, their significance is large. Levinsky's rise from poverty to wealth and prestige turns him into a mean person, and our sympathies are usually not with this protagonist. What is significant about the novel is the portrayal of Catskills life. Levinsky vacations in the Tannersville area of the northern Catskills in northern Ulster and southern Greene counties, which became a resort area just before the more familiar Sullivan and southern Ulster counties did. Already, Cahan is telling stories of the large meals and the guests decked out in fancy dress. And romance in the Mountains is in the forefront. He is the first to describe the "husband train" or the "bull train" that brings the men up to their wives each weekend. Cahan also speaks of the pride that Yiddish speakers had in their *mamaloshen* (mother tongue), despite the antagonism of the elite German Jews who had inadvertently opened the region to their coreligionists. Cahan also captures the mutual accommodation to America: the Jewish diners cheer when the band in the dining room plays "The Star Spangled Banner."

Beverly Friend, *Love in the Catskills: The Novel* (inspired by the musical comedy by Stan Turtletaub, Anita Turtletaub, and Tracy Friend) (privately printed, 1998; 106 pages; $12 from Beverly Friend, Oakton Community College, 1600 Golf Rd., Des Plaines, IL, 60016)

After seventy-four years on the job as a busy bellhop at a Catskills resort hotel, Sammy the matchmaking angel has one last chance to prove himself as a *shadchan* (matchmaker). If he fails to make *shidduchs* (matches) he will be consigned to

Mohel Academy, where he will learn the new job of steadying mohels' (ritual circumcisers') hands for circumcisions. Sparks fly and complications arise when he attempts to mix and match secular Jews visiting the resort for a business meeting with orthodox Jews attending a singles' weekend. The business meeting will clinch a big deal with Mr. Yamamoto's microchip firm, but in fact Yamamoto also has an ethereal role. Romantic miscues run throughout the hectic weekend as people try to sort out love, religion, and work.

Allegra Goodman, *Kaaterskill Falls* (New York: Dial, 1998)

Goodman recounts the life of an ultraorthodox community that has recently established its summer outpost in the eastern section of the northern Catskills, near Haines Falls. Unlike the Eastern European Chasidic dynasties most people are familiar with, this Kirschner group (based on a real group of a different name) stems from Germany, and combines neo-orthodoxy with an appreciation of secular knowledge. The location is far from any of the Jewish resort areas, and the novel makes no mention of the resort industry. People live in houses they have bought or rented rather than in bungalow colonies. Still, for many readers the book is informative about the character of contemporary orthodox culture in at least one part of the Catskills. While plot is less important to Goodman than character development, the main action is the effort of Elizabeth Shulman to run a summer store catering to the local orthodox, who otherwise must carry everything up from the specific Washington Heights stores endorsed by their leader, Rav Kirshner. Rav Kirshner gives permission for his people to shop at Elizabeth's store, but he soon dies, and his son withdraws it. Goodman's characters are finely drawn, and she has a talent for portraying their psyches. One element in her setting is common to a number of Catskills communities—even though one sect dominates, there are interactions with other varieties of orthodoxy in the shul they all share.

Harvey Jacobs, *Summer on a Mountain of Spices* (New York: Harper & Row, 1975)

Jacobs's aunts and uncles ran a small hotel that was the model for the Willow Spring of this book. He provides an all-around slice of hotel life in a particularly humorous fashion. The novel is a coming of age piece, and by definition must be full of sex for the lead character, Harry Craft, and many others. A gangster stashes his very attractive girlfriend at the hotel while he is on the run from other mobsters, adding to the sexual excitement. Jacobs deals well with the antipathy between hotel and bungalow colony, including a softball game after which the hotel people defend their lake from the colony dwellers' potential postgame refreshment. This book provides exceptional glimpses into the minds of the hotel owners. Jacobs describes the owner's fascination with building a modern casino (the Catskills casino was a social hall, not a gambling venue), and also a variety of the entertainment that went on there. He treats us to the antics of the emcee and the show he introduces, a song-and-dance team, followed by a magician. It is a very realistic account of small hotel entertainment. Jacobs finishes with a touching return visit, years later, by protagonist Harry Craft.

Terry Kay, *Shadow Song* (New York: Washington Square Books, 1994)

Kay writes beautifully about love, friendship, memory, and returning in this novel that takes place in Pine Hill, in the Fleischmanns area of the northern Catskills. Bobo Murphy, a southern Gentile, works a few summers in a Jewish resort, having found the job through his brother, a local minister. Bobo forms what will become a lifelong relationship with the quirky old Avrum Feldman, and experiences an unrequited love with Amy Lourie, whose parents oppose intermarriage. Many years later, Bobo returns to the Catskills when Avrum dies and arranges Avrum's very untraditional Kaddish, to the consternation of the local rabbi. The trip also brings him back to Amy, and this produces a startling life change. Kay's descriptions of the physical beauty of the Catskills are a delight, and his storytelling is masterful. While the romance element is not autobiographical, Kay got the idea for the book because he indeed was a Georgia youth who worked in the Catskills. *Shadow Song* is a luminous book, full of joy, love, respect, and a warm commemoration of personal history. As in Kay's other writings, there is a strong spirituality as well. As a novel about the Catskills, *Shadow Song* presents a perspective and coloration unlike those of any other novel.

Elinor Lipman, *The Inn at Lake Devine* (New York: Random House, 1998)

Lipman links the culture of two amazingly different resorts—the large Jewish Halseeyon in the Catskills (based on Kutsher's) and the small anti-Semitic Inn at Lake Devine in Vermont. Natalie Marx, incensed at the family's 1962 exclusion from the Inn at Lake Devine, plans revenge. But it is tempered by a later visit when she accompanies Robin, a Gentile summer camp friend, and her family, who just happen to be long-time vacationers at the Inn. Robin is later engaged to one son of the Inn's owners, but dies in a car crash on the way to her wedding at the Inn. Natalie, then a newly graduated chef, stays and helps cook for and tend the mourners, cementing her attachment to the Vermont hotel. By the book's end, Natalie has married the other son, with whom she fell in love when they formed part of a group visiting the Catskills. The two hotels develop other interesting connections as well. Elinor Lipman tackles some thorny issues like anti-Semitism and 1970s intermarriage with complexity, comedy, and tragedy.

Sidney Offit, *He Had It Made* (1959; reprint, Beckham Publications, Box 4066, Silver Spring, MD 20914; 301–384–7995, 1999)

Although set in the fictional Sesame Hotel, *He Had It Made* was based on the real Aladdin in Woodbourne, where author Sidney Offit worked as the steward in addition to renting rooms to guests. He married the owner's daughter, but protagonist Al Brodie's romances, which dominate the book, are not autobiographical. Offit provides a vivid description of the kitchen and dining room staff as well as the tension between bosses and workers, the competition among waiters, and the struggle between the chef and the maitre d.' Al Brodie begins as a conniving and opportunistic person, talking himself into a job even though the dining room has a full staff already. Brodie goes through romances with a counselor and the female maitre d' before getting involved with the owner's daughter, and finally undergoes a major character shift by the end of the book. The dialogue is snappy and funny, and no one has written a better portrayal of the waiter's life.

Eileen Pollack, *Paradise, New York* (Phildelphia: Temple University Press, 1998)

Brought up in a Catskills hotel, Pollack's, Eileen Pollack has captured the myriad experiences of the Mountains in a way that no other novelist has come close to. In the declining years of the Catskills, Pollack writes, "Fifty resorts had once decorated the branches of Paradise [based on Liberty]. Now they clung to the back roads like cracked, fading baubles," and she wants to preserve that old legacy. She takes on difficult themes, such as interracial romance and a guest's death in the hotel. Pollack's characters are richly drawn, and she makes us feel like we are sitting at the pool, hanging out in the kitchen, and setting tables with the waiters. The main character, Lucy, grows from a nine-year-old girl whose parents and grandparents own a small hotel, the Eden, to an adult who prevents a sale to the Hasidim and takes over the hotel, hoping to turn it into a living museum of Catskills life, with anthropologists on hand to interview the guests. Among the clientele during Lucy's childhood are a group of communist guests paying a very low rate guaranteed by Lucy's grandfather, who had once been in charge of a sweatshop where communists led a failed strike. Another low-rate group are Holocaust survivors, eligible for half price. Lucy's friendship and later romance with the educated black handyman, Thomas Jefferson, pervade the book. Pollack describes well the contradiction hotelkeepers' children faced between loyalty to preserving the tradition and the desire to get out of that hard life.

Mel Senator, *Catskill Summers* (Philadelphia: XLibris, 2000)

Mel Senator's fiction is very firmly based on the real events of his fifteen years at a kuchalayn in Ferndale in the 1940s and 1950s, aided by interviews he recently conducted with family and friends. "Summer Farm," with its eight bungalows and twenty-three kuchalayn rooms, continued to operate as a farming enterprise, and Senator gives us a valuable look at how residents' children often helped with farm chores, including a whole chapter on the "garbage run" to the colony's own dump. There is a nice chapter on the significance of softball games played between colonies. Senator's uncle knew local hotel guards, and this permitted the extended family to sneak in. But other people invented all sorts of methods and competed for the most successful trespasses, which Senator describes in fine detail. He explores another aspect of life untouched by most writers—the Chalutzen (Young Pioneer) camps where youth trained for *aliyah* to Israel. The Catskills were an important location for this, and Summer Farm opens its property to such a group with no real estate of its own.

Art Spiegelman, *Maus: A Survivor's Tale—II: And Here My Troubles Began* (New York: Pantheon, 1986)

A significant part of the second book in Art Spiegelman's *Maus* series takes place in the Catskills. It is an appropriate selection for this annotated bibliography for two reasons. One, Spiegelman's father uses the Catskills as a place to recount his concentration camp experiences to his son, Art. Two, the Catskills were indeed a haven for Holocaust survivors right after the war. Art Spiegelman and his wife are vacationing in Vermont when his father Vladek calls from a Catskills bungalow because his girlfriend has left him. Art and Françoise join him at the Cosmopolitan Bungalows, from where Vladek often sneaks into the nearby Pines Hotel to play bingo. It seems fitting that in this area a survivor can talk freely about horrors that are otherwise hard to share.

Reuben Wallenrod, *Dusk in the Catskills* (New York: Reconstructionist Press, 1957)

Reuben Wallenrod was a well-known scholar of Hebrew literature who was also a novelist. Originally written in Hebrew as *Ki Fanah Yom*, and unfortunately not so widely known, this book is a tender portrait of the life at Leo and Lillian Halper's small hotel over the course of the season. Wallenrod captures the feel of a small hotel that started as a little family farm where relatives just came for a while but blossomed into a larger enterprise than the proprietors expected or wanted. Wallenrod offers a valuable glimpse of the largely home-grown entertainment and the Yiddish literary life of hotels of this era. The book ends sadly with the death in a car accident of Leo Halper's dear friend, Morris Toozin. Unlike the way that Catskills hotels typically detached themselves from the occasional death of a guest, Halper brings the body to the hotel, where the funeral is held. Toozin's death parallels what Wallenrod saw as the imminent demise of the Catskills (though it would thrive for two more decades), which indeed is conveyed in the very title. Halper narrowly escapes foreclosure by the bank, but the book is shaped by its epigraph from Jeremiah: "Woe unto us! For the day declineth. For the shadows of the evening are stretched out." Toozin's death also parallels the deaths of the Holocaust, which permeates the book. Leo constantly ruminates over the terrible contradiction of Jews enjoying themselves in the Catskills in 1943 while their fellow Jews are massacred in Europe. Anti-Semitism in the Catskills is also dealt with. Reuben Wallenrod got his inspiration for the book from the six to eight years he spent as guest and writer-in-residence at the intellectually oriented Rosenblatt's Hotel in Glen Wild, where he was good friends with the owner. Wallenrod had deep ties to the land, which enabled him to fictionally portray Rosenblatt's initial efforts at farming and his disappointment at turning his place into a hotel.

Herman Wouk, *Marjorie Morningstar* (New York: Little, Brown, 1955)

Wouk's book, made into a popular film starring Natalie Wood and Gene Kelly, whose theme song "A Very Special Love" was a hit parade song in its day, touches on both romance and the problems of assimilation. Wouk's fictional South Wind Camp shares its name with a real hotel in Woodbourne, still standing. But Wouk himself claims his inspiration was an adult camp in the Adirondacks, though his novel is set in the Catskills. Marjorie Morningstar is the assimilationist name taken by Marjorie Morganstern, whose romance with the highly assimilated Noel Airman (originally Ehrman) frames the book. Working as a counselor at a girls' camp across the lake from the sexually infamous adult camp, South Wind, Marjorie rows to the other side where she meets Noel, the social director who puts on Broadway-type shows reminiscent of those Moss Hart wrote about in his autobiographical *Act One*. Wouk's description of this entertainment is very nicely done. The next year Marjorie returns as a staff member at South Wind itself, despite her mother's fears that she will lose her virginity. Indeed, Marjorie's parents send her uncle along to work as a dishwasher, but he tolerates her affair with Noel. Noel ultimately cannot conceive of Marjorie or any other woman as wanting more than a domestic, suburban life that he finds unimportant.

Short Stories

Hortense Calisher's "Old Stock" is unique in telling the story of a Jewish family at a Gentile-owned boarding house that now has Jewish clientele. As German Jews who have recently had a financial downturn, this family is displeased at staying with Eastern European Jews. That conflict was significant throughout American life, and clearly in the Catskills, where German Jews typically stayed in a different area, around Fleischmanns. Calisher's fifteen-year-old protagonist, Hester Elkin, and her mother visit a nearby woman they have come to know, but are surprised to hear this woman of Dutch heritage make an anti-Semitic remark, apparently unaware of her guests' background. That anti-Semitism casts a shadow on Hester's vacation, as she keeps expecting it to surface in others at the boarding house.

Eileen Pollack's *The Rabbi in the Attic* (New York: Delphinium Books, 1992) features a title piece that is a comic novella about a small orthodox congregation in the Catskills that fires its ultraobservant rabbi, only to find that he refuses to leave the house that came with his job. The congregation has mistreated so many rabbis that the seminary will not send a replacement; the only rabbi the shul's trustees can find is a zealous Reform woman who nearly flunked out of school and can't sing worth beans. If she wants the position, the trustees inform her, she must find a way to evict her predecessor from his house. Another story describes the invasion of Bethel by hordes of hippies during the Woodstock summer of 1969; two other stories involve characters who work at an insurance company that insures various hotels, bungalow colonies, and camps in the Catskills.

In Abraham Raisin's "Two Working-Girls" (in Henry Goodman, ed., *The New Country: Stories from the Yiddish About Life in America* [New York: YUKF Publishers, 1961]), the narrator, only four months in America, sits at a boarding house table across from two twenty-three-year-old assimilated women garment workers. He dislikes their American style of dress, hair, and flirtation, and resents their failure to speak any Yiddish though, as he knows, they come from a Yiddish-speaking home. At the same time, he is attracted to them and their Americanized ways. They dislike him for being a greenhorn. Over the two-week stay, they all soften to each other: the young women begin to speak Yiddish, and he comes to understand their need for a reprieve from their hard labor in the garment industry and the oppressive heat of the city, where people are collapsing. In the end, he is the only one of the guests to see them off at the train.

Thane Rosenbaum's "Bingo by the Bungalow," in *Elijah Visible* (New York: St. Martin's Press, 1996) portrays the intimacy of daily bungalow colony life through Adam Posner's growing up the child of Holocaust survivors. At Cohen's Summer Cottages in Kiamesha Lake, Adam is the only child; his mother is a bingo addict, looking for the small *chotchkies* (knickknacks) from her own and adjoining colonies, and for the mammoth $200 Labor Day jackpot. The omnipresent doom and tragedy of the survivor shows up—Adam suffers a compound fracture learning to play baseball, and his father's heart condition puts him in the hospital at the same time. The communal caretaking by the colony residents reminds us of this important element of bungalow life. As in many of Rosenbaum's stories, the deliverance at the end just doesn't come—we are still waiting for Elijah, for peace. And like others who have written Catskills fiction, Rosenbaum has his protagonist come back as a father, with his own boy, to scour the ruins of Cohen's.

Isaac Bashevis Singer's "The Yearning Heifer" (in his collection, *Passions* [New York: Farrar, Straus & Girous, 1970]) is an autobiographical tale of Singer's foray to a Catskill farm for a quiet place to write. Rather than finding a family that is eager to take in boarders, Singer's character encounters a surly farmer who is angry that his wife has placed an advertisement in the paper. Singer's story gives us a picture of the primitive conditions in which an early twentieth-century farm family lived, the relations between Jewish and Gentile farmers, and a developing friendship between the boarder and his "farmers," as boarding house and kuchalayn renters often referred to their proprietors, even if they were no longer actively engaged in farming.

Singer's five-page "In the Mountains," subtitled "A Fragment" (in Henry Goodman, ed., *The New Country: Stories from the Yiddish About Life in America* [New York: YUKF Publishers, 1961]), is really just a little sketch. Singer shows

Sholem Melnick and his teenage son Ben tending cows and chickens and struggling with plow horses to remove rocks on their Catskills farm. Sholem has become less observant in the New World, but even in the midst of his travails, the beauty of the area strengthens his devoutness as he thinks of God giving Moses the Torah at Mount Sinai.

Steve Stern's *The Wedding Jester* (St. Paul, MN: Graywolf Press, 1999) takes its title from this story, and won the National Jewish Book Award. A bride at the Concord Hotel is taken over by a dybbuk, the spirit of an unsuccessful Mountain comedian, and pandemonium results. An exorcism is required to stop the bride/dybbuk's constant stream of dirty Borscht Belt jokes. Steve Stern's Jewish magical realism style has led some critics to call him a modern-day version of Isaac Bashevis Singer. His writing pulsates with as much mysticism, magic, and *mishegos*. As he captures the many worlds of past, present, and future in one instant, Steve Stern makes us give up our assumptions about what is ordinary life.

NONFICTION

History and Social Science

Phil Brown, *Catskill Culture: A Mountain Rat's Memories of the Great Jewish Resort Area* (Philadelphia: Temple University Press, 1998)

This is the most comprehensive history of the Jewish Catskills, written as a combination of sociology, history, and personal memoirs. Phil Brown grew up in the hotel that his parents owned from 1946 to 1952; after they went broke, they worked their whole lives there, up to 1980. Brown worked as well, from age thirteen all through college. *Catskill Culture* provides background on the farms, hotels, and bungalow colonies, and offers extensive insights into the lives of young workers in the dining room. It also includes material on religion and politics in the area. The book has some 100 graphics, providing a rich accompaniment of menus, rate cards, brochures, postcards, and photos.

John Conway, *Retrospect: An Anecdotal History of Sullivan County, New York* (Fleischmanns, NY: Purple Mountain Press, 1996)

John Conway, the official Sullivan County Historian, adapted this book of short essays from his series in the *Middletown Times Herald Record*. His book covers a broad sweep of Sullivan County history, in a very colloquial, personal tone. It contains a number of essays about the resorts and personalities of the Jewish Catskills. Conway includes much material on local businesses and politicians. There is a chapter on organized crime in the Catskills, a neglected subject.

Alf Evers, *The Catskills: From Wilderness to Woodstock* (Garden City, NY: Doubleday, 1972)

Alf Evers was the leading historian of the Catskills. His book goes back centuries, touching only briefly on the Jewish influx. Nevertheless, this background is important for understanding the milieu into which the Jews were entering. Evers wrote very engaging popular history that is both comprehensive and a pleasure to read.

Alf Evers, *In Catskill Country: Collected Essays on Mountain History, Life, and Lore* (Woodstock, NY: Overlook Press, 1995)

Evers's writings since the classic *The Catskills*; contains more useful material on the early history but less on the Jewish Catskills than his earlier book.

Alf Evers, Elizabeth Cromley, Betsy Blackmar, and Neil Harris, eds., *Resorts of the Catskills* (New York: Architectural League of New York/St. Martin's Press, 1979)

While some of the historical material in this collection is found elsewhere, the real value is the wonderful photographs by John Margolies. The Jewish Catskills are emphasized, but various Gentile resorts are also covered, all the way back to the grand hotels early in the nineteenth century. Elizabeth Cromley's essay provides valuable architectural history, and Betsy Blackmar contributes a useful social history of the resorts.

Myrna Frommer and Harvey Frommer, *It Happened in the Catskills: An Oral History in the Words of Busboys, Bellhops, Guests, Proprietors, Comedians, Agents, and Others Who Lived It* (New York: Harcourt Brace Jovanovich, 1991)

The Frommers interviewed a large number of people who owned hotels, worked in them, and stayed in them. Their book is a treasure trove of photos and other graphics, using excerpts from the interviews to provide a vivid account of the resort life. The book is particularly strong in covering the entertainers and the talent bookers, and also the professional athletes who worked, stayed, and did cameo appearances in the hotels. As well, a number of hotel owners provide inside accounts of their resorts.

David Gold, ed., *The River and the Mountains: Readings in Sullivan County History* (Marielle Press, Attn: David Gold, 337 N. Ardmore Rd, Bexley, OH 43209. $20.00)

For the first time, readers interested in the whole sweep of Sullivan County history have in *The River and the Mountains* a single source to which they can turn. Beginning with the lifestyle of the Delaware Indians and ending with the recent troubles of the resorts, the book sheds light on some lesser-known aspects of Sullivan's past and provides new insight into more familiar subjects as well. Editor David M. Gold has drawn on a wide range of fascinating materials, including letters, memoirs, and interviews, photographs and maps, and historical writing both popular and scholarly, to produce the most comprehensive treatment of Sullivan County's history ever published. Readers interested in the Jewish history of the Catskills will particularly enjoy the chapters on Jewish farms and boarding houses in the early twentieth century, getting to the mountains, organized crime in the Catskills, and the resorts.

Book of Remembrance of the Hebrew Congregation of Loch Sheldrake

The Hebrew Congregation of Loch Sheldrake/Bes Hakeneset Ada Yisroel published this 169-page *Book of Remembrance* to honor the shul's 75 years. Joseph Akselrad has done a wonderful job of putting together this volume. As a companion accomplishment, in June 1997 the shul was added to the National Register of Historic Places. Started by around 40 hotel owners, the shul has been variously dubbed the "Synagogue-on-the-Lake" and a "Jewel of a Shul." The *Book of Remembrance* includes historical, religious, and artistic material. There is a preface by Maurie Sacks, who helped get this shul on the National Register. The volume is available for a minimum contribution of $36 to Hebrew Congregation of Loch Sheldrake, Loch Sheldrake, NY 12759. Only 200 copies of the limited edition of 500 copies are available.

Oscar Israelowitz, *Catskills Guide* (Brooklyn, NY: Israelowitz Publications, 1992 [Box 228, Brooklyn, NY 11229])

Covering the entire Catskills region in an idiosyncratic fashion, this book has information on a whole range of historic subjects, mostly available elsewhere. Its most valuable features are pictures of Catskills synagogues and a list of former synagogues of the region.

Stefan Kanfer, *A Summer World: The Attempt to Build a Jewish Eden in the Catskills, from the Early Days of the Ghetto to the Rise and Decline of the Borscht Belt* (New York: Farrar, Straus & Giroux, 1989)

Kanfer's history starts with early Catskills life before the Jews, and situates the Jews in history by going as far back as the 1830s Sholem colony that failed. Kanfer also spends a good deal of time on Catskills growth, discussing Jewish immigration and living conditions. There is interesting material on gambling, on World War II in the Mountains, and on the interhotel basketball league and game-fixing scandal in the 1950s. Kanfer brings things up to the 1980s when Zen centers and ashrams joined the throngs of Hasidim.

Abraham Lavender and Clarence Steinberg, *Jewish Farmers of the Catskills* (Gainesville: University Press of Florida, 1995)

This is a powerfully researched story of the Jewish farmers of Ulster and Sullivan counties through the whole twentieth century. Lavender is Associate Professor of Sociology and Anthropology at Florida International University; Clarence Steinberg, raised on his parents' Catskills farm, recently retired as a Public Affairs Specialist with the U.S. Department of Agriculture. Based on extensive interviews and lengthy archival research, the authors give us a detailed view of the lives of Catskills farmers, the synagogues they built, and the towns they lived in. This fine book shows the interweaving of people's lives in the farming sector and the resort industry.

Irwin Richman, *Borscht Belt Bungalows: Memories of Catskill Summers* (Philadelphia: Temple University Press, 1998)

Not only did Richman grow up on his family's colony, but he later worked as counselor and camp director in other colonies, and his grandfather provided mortgages to many others. So Richman has a firm background in his subject matter, which he addresses in a wonderful combination of personal memoir and historical research. No one else has provided such a wealth of data on the daily activities of bungalow colony dwellers. This is the only Catskills book to have chapters on religion in the bungalow colonies and on the day camp, a major contribution of Catskills resorts to American life. Richman brings us up to date on the last few decades, during which orthodox and Hasidic Jews have become the predominant bungalow residents. There are lots of wonderful graphics, including probably the only known architectural renderings of bungalows and kuchalayns.

Irwin Richman, *The Catskills in Vintage Postcards* (Charleston, SC: Arcadia Press, 2000 [2 Cumberland St., Charleston, SC, 29401])

This beautiful book has more than 200 black and white illustrations of postcards from all walks of Catskills life. While there is special emphasis on the period from the 1890s to the 1920s, Richman covers the entire history of the area. There are postcards of local life and the grand resorts of the pre-Jewish Catskills. Each has a concise and informative caption.

Irwin Richman, *Sullivan County/Borscht Belt* (Charleston, SC: Arcadia Press, 2001 [2 Cumberland St., Charleston, SC, 29401])

This book has 200 photographs, postcards, and other pieces of memorabilia of the Sullivan County experience, divided into four sections: Sullivan County before the Borscht Belt, Borscht Belt towns, kuchalayns and bungalow colonies, and hotels.

Robert L. Schain, *A Study of the Historical Development of the Resort Industry in the Catskills of New York* Ph.D. diss., New York University, 1969

This is the only dissertation published on the Catskills. Schain worked for years in the Catskills, and at the time of his dissertation research in 1967 and 1968 he was activities director at the Windsor Hotel. Schain interviewed a phenomenal number of staff, guests, owners, and others to provide a valuable history of the Catskills in three periods: 1900–1920, 1920–1945, and 1945–1968. There are detailed descriptions of the organization of hotel staff and their tasks, food and activities, and financing. Schain has many figures on numbers of rooms and guests in various hotels.

Manville Wakefield, *To the Mountains by Rail* (Grahamsville, NY: Wakefair Press, 1970)

This book is important for the early history of the railroads, especially the Ontario and Western (O&W), which people called the "Old and Weary." Up till the early 1950s, the railroad was still an important mode of transportation to the Catskills. Wakefield had been the official Sullivan County historian, and wrote several other books on the region. This book also contains many good photographs and mentions many of the old hotels, which used the O&W's annual "Summer Homes" brochure as a major advertising medium. The foreword by Irwin Richman has several interesting Jewish anecdotes.

Memoirs, Biography, Autobiography

Joey Adams with Henry Tobias, *The Borscht Belt* (New York: Bobbs-Merrill, 1966)

Joey Adams, who died in 1999, was a major comic in the Catskills and a well-known *New York Post* humor columnist. This book remains the classic version of an entertainer's tale of Catskills comedy, music, tummling, and hotel life. The account of kuchalayn life in the 1920s is especially rich. The book contains wonderful photos from the 1930s through the 1950s, offering an insider's story lavishly garnished with jokes and reminiscences.

Esterita Blumberg, *Remember the Catskills: Tales by a Recovering Hotelkeeper* (Fleischmanns, NY: Purple Mountain Press, 1996)

Esterita Blumberg grew up at Green Acres Hotel in Lake Huntington, and eventually operated it. When it burned, her family bought another hotel in Loch Sheldrake to run with the same name. Blumberg wrote a monthly column, "Those Were the Days," for the Catskill/Hudson *Jewish Star*, on which much of this book is based. There is interesting material on leftist politics in the Catskills. The book has many photographs, advertisements, menus, and rate schedules.

H. Charles Bluming, *Jew Boy in Goy Town: A Catskill Mountain Odyssey* (1994; privately printed; $15.00 plus $3.00 mailing from Mildred Bluming, 10375 Wilshire Blvd, Ste. 7B, Los Angeles, CA 90024)

Hy Bluming's engaging memoir is a rare look at the daily life of early Catskills farmers and boarding house operators. This emotionally powerful book gives a great portrayal of Jewish farmers, widespread anti-Semitism, and the early resort experience. Bluming's family arrived in Greenfield Park before World War I, then spent the bulk of their Mountain years in Kerhonkson. Bluming writes about the burning cross and KKK rally near their Kerhonkson hotel, the Sunrise Hill Farm, and the burning out of a nearby Jewish farmer. The struggle against anti-Semitism takes both the brain and the diplomacy of Bluming's father and the brawn of Butch Rosenberg, who stands down an angry mob. With little religious background but a deep solidarity with his Jewish comrades, the rugged carpenter Rosenberg puts all his energy into leading the building of a small shul in Kerhonkson. Butch lovingly carves a Mogen David to crown the shul, and finds it smashed by local anti-Semites. Daring the culprits to meet him in the town center, Butch takes them on successfully, scaring the rest away. Bluming's father uses a different approach. He is the local *shochet* and lay spiritual leader of the small Jewish community, and he exudes deep inner strength in making his way among the difficulties of this area. Harry Bluming marches into the local church to decry the locals who have desecrated the shul. He appeals to everyone's belief in the Constitution and freedom of religion, and asks the church congregation's assistance in protecting the synagogue. His chutzpah works, and the pastor brings his congregation to the dedication of the shul with its second Star of David. Butch, of course, has the honor of carrying the Torah to establish the new shul. Like protagonists in other Catskills books, Hi returns after more than forty years away to find remnants of school, farm, and shul.

Mitzi Crane, *Give Me Liberty or Give Me Monticello* (2000; privately published; $10 from Mitzi Crane, 7705 Dundee Lane, Delray Beach, FL 33446)

This is a charming memoir of a woman who became an entertainer and is still performing in Florida. One of the interesting historical contributions is the life of her parents, whose own parents were temporary partners—one of the variations on the Catskills hotel business—in fifteen hotels. There are interesting stories and lots of reproductions of photos and menus.

Sonia Pressman Fuentes, *Eat First—You Don't Know What They'll Give You: The Adventures of an Immigrant Family and Their Feminist Daughter* (Philadelphia: Xlibris Publishing, 2000)

This is the story of a five-year-old immigrant girl who came to this country with her family from Berlin, Germany to escape the Holocaust and grew up to become a founder of the Second Wave of the women's movement. Through Fuentes's tales and anecdotes we come to know her, her parents, and her brother as the family arrives in the United States in 1934 and two years later settles in Woodridge, where they ran a kuchalayn for five years. Then they built a bungalow colony on the Port Jervis Road in Monticello. Of the book's forty-six chapters, seven take place in the Catskills. (orders@xlibris.com web: http://www.xlibris.com, mail: Xlibris Corp. 123 Chestnut St., Suite 402 Philadelphia, PA 19106)

Tania Grossinger, *Growing Up at Grossinger's* (New York: David MacKay, 1975)

Tania Grossinger's mother was the hostess at the relatives' hotel, so Tania got great inside stories on the staff, guests, and visiting sports figures and entertainers. This is a humorous book that also provides a glimpse of life from an intelligent insider's point of view. She describes such events as occasional drives to New York City with Harry Grossinger on his twice-weekly meat shopping trips, part of the hotel's desire for the best quality food, and the weekly formalized Shabbos sale of the hotel to a Gentile staff member so that entertainment would be considered legitimate. No one else has written about the difficult life of being a "staff kid," a very in-between status in hotel culture. There are great photos of celebrities who frequented the hotel as guests and entertainers.

Moss Hart, *Act One: An Autobiography* (New York: Random House, 1959)

The famous playwright began as a social director in an earlier era when social directors had large staffs that produced full-length variety shows and musicals every week. The adults-only summer camps where Hart worked were places where many people, especially men, sometimes actually slept in tents. Starting in 1929 he worked at the Flagler Hotel, famous for its large casino and elegant shows, where Dory Schary was one of his assistants. Hart describes in detail the weekly schedule of entertainment for which he was responsible, from major theatrical productions to campfires.

Joel Pomerantz, *Jennie and the Story of Grossinger's* (New York: Grosset and Dunlap, 1970)

This is an authorized and "official" biography of the famous Jennie Grossinger and Grossinger's Hotel (indeed, the copyright is in Jennie Grossinger's name), full of stories about the resort from its early founding. Published two decades after Harold Taub's "official" book, it has much more up-to-date information on the golden years of the 1950s and 1960s. There are lots of good descriptions of the food and the many activities, and even of the plane landing on a golf fairway that prompted the hotel to build its own airport.

Arthur Tanney, "Memoirs of Bungalow Life" (http://catskills.brown.edu)

At this point only published on the Catskills Institute Web site, but hopefully soon available in book form, these are very moving reminiscences of Tanney's many years living in colonies, as a child and later as an adult with his own family. Tanney has taken some of the most ordinary activities and experiences of bungalow life and shown how significant they were for people. Romance, day camp, salamander catching, movie night, and sports are among the subjects he eloquently describes. Perhaps the most popular is his piece on Ruby the Knishman, a famous bungalow colony peddler.

Harold Jaediker Taub, *Waldorf in the Catskills: The Grossinger Legend* (New York: Sterling, 1952)

This is an early "official" look at Grossinger's, complete with twenty-four pages of family recipes. Taub walks us through the family history from the earliest days of searching for a place in the country to the many developments that made Grossinger's famous worldwide. The style is chatty, as if we were hearing conversations of generations of Grossingers. There is a particularly interesting chapter on the hotel's support for the U.S. effort in World War II, when Grossinger's sold many war bonds and shipped many packages to the GIs.

Henry Tobias, *Music in My Heart and Borscht in My Blood* (New York: Hippocrene Books, 1987)

Henry Tobias opens this memoir by talking about how the book he wrote with Joey Adams, *The Borscht Belt*, was originally his creation, but Adams's name and involvement finally got it published (Tobias was only a "with" author). Stylistically, this is a similar book (with even a few overlapping stories) by a prolific songwriter who also was a musician and tummler at many Catskills hotels. There are lots of short takes on comics, singers, hotel owners, and booking agents, providing further insight into the entertainment world of the era. There is interesting material on the early use of the term "borscht belt" and on the ways that Catskills entertainment staff used to pirate Broadway shows.

Elizabeth Ehrlich's "Bungalow," from *Miriam's Kitchen* (New York: Penguin, 1998) offers a very tender look at Ehrlich's relationship with her mother-in-law, Miriam, who teaches her how to cook while reliving her life experiences in the Holocaust and since. While we don't usually think of bungalow colony life as full of great food, Miriam's bungalow is a feasting place. Memories are expressed in the food: "The table is *gemakht*, ready, with barely a centimeter to spare. Here is a plate of sliced melon, blueberries, strawberries, and a bowl of sugar for the berries. There may be ripe tomatoes cut into chunks with raw Spanish onion, oil, and wine vinegar. Perhaps a herring in cream sauce, or a tin of smoked sardines. . . . There are fresh little challah rolls, or heavy slices of corn rye bread festooned with caraway seeds. Cream cheese with scallions." Ehrlich recounts an interesting Catskills bungalow colony tradition of collective meals of delicatessen or smoked fish on Saturday night in the casino. This is a wonderful example of how food binds people together.

Robert Eisenberg has a chapter, "Bungalow Summer," in *Boychiks in the Hood: Travels in the Hasidic Underground* (New York: HarperCollins, 1996), giving an account of the Hasidic and ultraorthodox communities that now represent the largest aspect of Jewish life in the Catskills. Among the stops on his tour are the Lubavitchers' Ivy League Torah Program and a doctor's office at Fialkoff's Bungalow Colony. He also reports on his visit to Elat Chayyim, the Jewish Renewal center in Accord.

Vivian Gornick's "The Catskills Remembered," in *Approaching Eye Level* (Boston: Beacon Press, 1996), recounts the difficulties of being a waitress in the Catskills, where waiters predominated. She portrays the competitive edge among the waitstaff, the tension between them and their guests, and the conflicts they had with the maitre d'. This is definitely the harder end of the dining room life. For those in the know, Gornick's fictional names are vividly recognizable—her Stella Mercury employment agency was really Annie Jupiter's, a New York City agency that supplied many of the hotels.

Howard Jacobson, a British Jew, traveled around the world visiting Jewish communities for his book *Roots, Shmoots: Journeys Among Jews* (New York: Penguin, 1995). Chapter 3, "People Who Need People," is a sarcastic look at his Rosh Hashanah stay at the Concord a few years ago. Mostly set in the dining room, it portrays the guests as negatively as possible.

Daniel Pinkwater, known for his humorous commentaries on National Public Radio, wrote a book, *The Afterlife Diet* (Philadelphia: Xlibris, 1999), in which overweight people go to a certain heaven comprised only of their fellow *zaftig* departed—for them, heaven is a Catskills hotel, full of *fressers*. Even there, the guests still complain. This is a very funny book that includes a New York delicatessen where a psychiatrist conducts treatment while people eat; the guests/patients pay a combined bill for therapy and meals at the cash register.

Sarah Sandberg's books *Mama Made Minks* (New York: Doubleday, 1964) and *My Sister Goldie* (New York: Doubleday, 1968) are very chatty memoirs, almost like collections of magazine installments. Both contain segments with titles like "Oh, to Be in Grossinger's Now That April's Here," providing pictures of the dating scene and of the richness of the meals both in the dining room and in the napkins that delivered food back to the guest rooms. Sandberg's furrier family also used the dining room as a place to parade new minks and recruit customers.

The list of hotels maintained by the Catskills Institute is an ongoing project. Each newly found name is another treasure to add to the collective memory of the Catskills hotels. Ben Kaplan, a long-time Catskills resident, was for twelve years the Executive Director of the Sullivan County Resort Association, and for another ten years head of Sullivan County's Office of Public Information. In 1991 he published a list of hotels in the *Sullivan County Democrat* newspaper, in four parts, on July 26, July 30, August 2, and August 6. Many people responded with additional hotel names, adding to the historical record. Ben Kaplan provided me with the original published list and a typescript of the updated list. I am grateful to him and to the *Sullivan County Democrat* for permission to print the whole list, which is based on their initial research. I found many additional names of Ulster County hotels, which have been less well documented and written about, from the 1956 edition of the *Ulster County Resort Association*, kindly located by John A. Umverzagt, and from the undated but clearly World War II–era "Ellenville, Town of Wawarsing on the Shawangunk Trail— A Vacationland Guide," kindly located by Gary Platt. I have discovered other hotel names through my research and interviews.

A very few of the hotels listed may have been small boarding houses, but most appear to have been regular hotels, even if very small. Their number (1,100) vastly exceeds the commonly heard estimate of 500 hotels, making even more significant the extent of hotels in the Catskill Mountains of Sullivan County, Ulster

County, and southern Greene County. I have grouped Fallsburg and South Fallsburg together. For hotels listed in the Ulster County Resort Association and the
Ellenville *Vacationland Guide*, I have grouped Leurenkill hotels in Ellenville, since
Leurenkill was not commonly used as a town name, and have grouped Briggs
Highway hotels in Greenfield Park for the same reason. It is common to find the
same hotel name used in different towns. Sometimes there would be four hotels
with the same name. The word "camp" does not refer to a children's camp but
to an adult resort. Places listed as "cottage" or "cottages" are *not* bungalow
colonies but small hotels with the name "cottage(s)." Most of these are or were
primarily Jewish, but no distinction is made in listing them. People who know of
other hotels not on the list should e-mail catskills@brown.edu so that future listings in the Catskills Institute Archives will include them; updates are placed on
the Web site at once (catskills.brown.edu).

Bungalow Colonies of the Catskills

A bungalow colony list is an ongoing project of the Catskills Institute (catskills.brown.edu). It has been compiled by Phil Brown, Ben Kaplan, Irwin Richman, and Arthur Tanney, with help from others who have contributed names to our Web site and at our conferences. At present it contains 538 bungalow colonies, and we know there are many gaps, so we hope for readers' additions. Most places have only a name, with "bungalow colony" as the understood rest of the name. Places with other names are listed that way, e.g., "cottages." Fallsburg and South Fallsburg are grouped together under Fallsburg. Briggs Highway is included in Greenfield Park.

People who know of bungalow colonies not listed should e-mail catskills@brown.edu or write to Phil Brown, Department of Sociology, Brown University, Box 1916, Providence RI 02912, so that future listings in the Catskills Institute Archives will include them; updates are placed on the Web site at once. Please provide past and present names, owners' names, and number of bungalows, if known. Postcards, photos, and other archival material are always welcome.